ULTIMATE HENDRIX

ULTIMATE HENDRIX

AN ILLUSTRATED ENCYCLOPEDIA OF LIVE CONCERTS AND SESSIONS

JOHN McDERMOTT
with EDDIE KRAMER and BILLY COX

Backbeat Books

An Imprint of Hal Leonard Corporation
New York

PUBLISHED IN 2009 BY BACKBEAT BOOKS
AN IMPRINT OF HAL LEONARD CORPORATION
7777 WEST BLUEMOUND ROAD
MILWAUKEE, WI 53213

TRADE BOOK DIVISION EDITORIAL OFFICES
19 WEST 21ST STREET, NEW YORK, NY 10010

PRINTED IN CHINA

10 9 8 7 6 5 4 3 2 1

COVER PHOTO © JIM MARSHALL

DESIGN: KASEY FREE
EDITORIAL: KJERSTI EGERDAHL
IMAGE RESEARCH: CHRIS CAMPBELL
PRODUCTION COORDINATION: SHIRLEY WOO
PROJECT MANAGEMENT: SHEILA KAMUDA

PRODUCED BY BECKER&MAYER!BOOKS
11010 NORTHUP WAY
BELLEVUE, WASHINGTON 98004
WWW.BECKERMAYER.COM

LIBRARY OF CONGRESS CATALOGING-IN-PUBLICATION
DATA IS AVAILABLE UPON REQUEST.

ISBN: 978-0-87930-938-1

WWW.BACKBEATBOOKS.COM

COVER 1967: MONTEREY POP FESTIVAL. PREVIOUS PAGE MAY 25, 1969: HENDRIX AT THE SANTA CLARA POP FESTIVAL. OPPOSITE MARCH 1967: IN HAMBURG, GERMANY.

INTRODUCTION

I have set out in this book to profile Jimi Hendrix's unique approach to composing and recording by examining his full catalog of live concert and studio recordings, both released and unreleased. To demonstrate just how extraordinary these achievements were within the context of Hendrix's personal and professional life, *Ultimate Hendrix* also provides a diary of the concert, radio, and television appearances made by Hendrix throughout his career. This does not include additional commitments such as press interviews, photo shoots, or even details about his personal life; instead, the focus remains on Hendrix's recording sessions and performances. What these entries make clear is that legendary recordings such as *Electric Ladyland* were created on the fly, as Hendrix shuttled across the globe performing and promoting his career as part of a seemingly ceaseless schedule of public appearances.

The model for this book, and indeed all books of this sort, is Mark Lewisohn's superb, richly detailed 1988 book *The Beatles Recording Sessions*. I cannot claim, as that book did for the Beatles, to document and detail every known Jimi Hendrix recording session, as such a task can unlikely ever be done. Unlike the meticulously detailed information kept by EMI for the Beatles, Jimi Hendrix's recording sessions were never tracked in a consistent and detailed manner—particularly during his early years as an itinerant musician, presented in a loose timeline in Chapter 1. The Beatles recorded the great majority of their sessions at EMI's fabled Abbey Road Studios—a facility owned and operated by their record company—while Hendrix ventured from independent studio to independent studio until May 1970, when he opened his own facility, Electric Lady Studios.

The recording studio, as Billy Cox later described it, was Jimi Hendrix's laboratory. As a result, Hendrix left behind hundreds of reels of multitrack recording tape filled with unfinished sketches, spontaneous moments of inspiration, and countless hours of unrealized ideas—in addition to the handful of albums whose release he authorized. Nothing speaks louder, or more impressively, about his unique talents than the music he created during a remarkable career that lasted fewer than four years.

With 1995's *Jimi Hendrix Sessions*—the predecessor to *Ultimate Hendrix*—I attempted to provide as much information about Hendrix's known studio sessions as was possible at that time. While Hendrix's authorized masterworks have been restored in recent years and remain accessible to consumers throughout the world, far too many Hendrix multitrack masters had been lost or stolen in the years between his untimely death in September 1970 and the publication of my 1995 book. Other essential recordings remained in legal limbo, as bitter arguments over unpaid bills and lost royalties rendered them unavailable for release or even research. Also, when Alan Douglas assumed creative control of the Hendrix archive in 1974 and began the production of *Crash Landing* and *Midnight Lightning*, master tapes were edited without safety copies being made, while other recordings were not properly archived or were never returned to the Hendrix library.

This situation changed dramatically in 1995. Hendrix's father, James "Al" Hendrix, won a lengthy, bitterly contested legal battle to reclaim his ownership of Hendrix's artistic properties, which included Hendrix's master recordings and music publishing. I had supported the Hendrix family during the litigation, and, after their victory, I had the extreme good fortune to be asked by Al Hendrix and his daughter, Janie, to join his newly formed company, Experience Hendrix LLC, and manage the Jimi Hendrix music catalog. Since that time, I have been directly involved in each Jimi Hendrix audio and audiovisual release issued by the company. In addition, Experience Hendrix LLC has cast a wide net since its formation to recover as many "lost" Jimi Hendrix film, video, and sound recordings as possible. Many of these recordings had not yet been discovered when *Jimi Hendrix Sessions* was published in early 1995.

To present a balanced perspective from both the control room and recording studio, Billy Cox and Eddie Kramer have again joined forces with me in this book, sharing their recollections of the sessions that created Hendrix's recorded legacy. Billy Cox, one of Hendrix's closest associates, played bass in Band Of Gypsys and the reunited Jimi Hendrix Experience. Eddie Kramer

had a major role in shaping Hendrix's recorded legacy, engineering all of the guitarist's authorized recordings from *Are You Experienced* to *Band Of Gypsys*.

To detail Hendrix's amazing catalog of recordings, Cox, Kramer, and I drew upon multiple sources. Dates for individual recording sessions listed herein were taken directly from the original tape boxes. However, these dates do not definitively represent all the various mixing and recording sessions or even the final date of completion for any song, as Hendrix—especially from the recording of *Electric Ladyland* forward— regularly returned to masters in an effort to improve

his own performances with new overdubs. To determine set lists at live performances, I have drawn upon existing recordings of concerts, testimony from those present, such as Cox, and news accounts and reviews.

We reviewed original multitrack master tapes whenever possible, supplemented by hours of evaluating unreleased recordings held in private collections. To provide as comprehensive a perspective as possible, we incorporated testimony from musicians who played beside Hendrix, such as Mitch Mitchell, Noel Redding, and Buddy Miles, along with the many engineers who shaped his sound and worked under his direction.

1963–1966

"All this guy did was play his guitar for anybody and everybody—from when he woke up in the morning to the last thing he did before he went to bed."
—JUGGY MURRAY

1963

Immediately after his discharge from the U.S. army in 1962, the nineteen-year-old Jimi Hendrix set his musical career in motion. Teamed up with his former army buddy Billy Cox, he settled in Nashville and struggled to establish his reputation as a guitarist. "In Nashville I played all kinds of stuff, even some rockabilly," Hendrix said later. "In Nashville everybody knows how to play guitar. You walk down the street and people are sitting on the porch playing more guitar. That's where I learned to play, really."

Hendrix and Cox formed a band, which they called the Casuals at first. "We got discharged from Fort Campbell and we continued working in Clarkesville," near the fort, Cox explains. "We got a job back in Clarkesville, and later on some guys who owned a club in Nashville came and told us that we were probably the best band in the area. They wanted us to come and work for them. We gave the club that we were working for about a week's notice. We had entered a contest in Indianapolis and the band we were [up against] knew we were good, but unfortunately we did not win because they were local guys and we were strangers. They won the contest but they knew that we were better than they were. When we came back to Clarkesville, their guitar player and drummer—because we didn't have either anymore—and the [opening] comedian followed us into Nashville. There we found out that there was another band named the Casuals, so we changed our name to King Casuals."

While the King Casuals had secured a steady gig in Nashville, Hendrix refused to limit his opportunities. He actively pursued contacts in the blues and R&B field in an effort to be recognized as a new talent. Hendrix found irregular work as a sideman for contemporary rhythm and blues artists touring the fabled "chitlin' circuit," the network of small supper clubs and nightspots that catered to black audiences throughout the South. "I met a guy named Gorgeous George in Nashville and he got me on some tours," recalled Hendrix. "So I started traveling around, playing around the South."

Hendrix struggled to establish himself and make a living, despite these occasional opportunities to showcase his budding skills as a guitarist. He was determined to find an opportunity and decided to leave Nashville for Harlem, the music center of black America, in late 1963. His fortunes were so low that he had to borrow a coat from friend and fellow guitarist Larry Lee in order to brave the harsh winter of the Northeast. He arrived in Harlem with little money and no immediate prospects for work. "Jimi was looking to just get away and move toward stardom," explains Cox. "I think intuitively he knew he was going to be great. But the object here was to be discovered and he felt his best chance was in New York."

SPRING 1964

With dogged assistance from his girlfriend in New York, Faye Pridgeon, herself a fixture on the Harlem music scene and a friend to many of its leading artists, Hendrix struggled to find a gig. Pridgeon recognized Hendrix's burgeoning ability and knew how determined he was to succeed as a musician. His fortunes turned when Tony Rice, a former associate of soul giant Joe Tex, recommended Hendrix to Ronnie Isley of the Isley Brothers. The group needed a guitarist, so Hendrix auditioned in early 1964 and earned a position with the I.B. Specials, the group's touring band. The Isley Brothers quickly befriended Hendrix and were impressed by his raw talent. Hendrix's first recording session with the group followed shortly after he joined them, resulting in the fiery "Testify (Part One)" and "Testify (Part Two)." The group had recently formed their own label, T-Neck Records, and secured a distribution agreement with Atlantic Records. "Testify" was issued on the T-Neck imprint in June 1964, but it missed the pop charts.

Hendrix took part in another notable session in March 1964, lending guitar to the Don Covay song "Mercy, Mercy." The single was issued by Rosemart Records and distributed by Atlantic in August 1964.

SUMMER 1964

Ronald Isley claims that Hendrix contributed guitar to two additional Isley Brothers recordings in 1964.

According to Isley, the group had signed with Atlantic Records, who organized a session to record their label debut at the company's in-house facility. With some behind-the-scenes assistance from a young Dionne Warwick, the Isleys recorded the aching ballad "The Last Girl," as well as "Looking For A Love." No one has definitively confirmed that these sessions featured Jimi Hendrix because of the date the recordings are said to have taken place: research has shown that this session may have been scheduled on September 23, 1964, at Atlantic Studios in New York. Hendrix could only have participated if work on the two songs began before they were completed in September 1964. Hendrix left the Isley Brothers in Nashville during the summer of 1964, choosing to strike out on his own.

During this period, Hendrix was involved in two separate sessions at the famed Stax Records studio in Memphis. Hendrix's first experience at Stax came as a result of a chance meeting with Booker T. & the MG's guitarist Steve Cropper. During their conversation, Hendrix spoke of his desire to record an original

song he had composed. Intrigued, Cropper invited him to the studio to record a solo demo. Nothing came of the demo, but Hendrix's ability seemed to have struck a chord with Cropper. "It was very strange," Hendrix told *Rolling Stone* in 1968. "We messed around the studio for four or five hours doing different little things. He turned me on to lots of things. He showed me how to play lots of things and I showed him how I played 'Have Mercy' or something like that."

Despite the warm reception Cropper had given him, Hendrix's second visit to Stax led nowhere. Without Cropper present, Hendrix's unique style met with derision from the other studio musicians. "The first time I met Jimi Hendrix was when he was with the Isley Brothers and I was playing with Eddie Floyd," recalls Stax employee and future Buddy Miles Express bassist Roland Robinson. "He was at the Satellite Record Shop outside of the Stax recording studio dressed in a white suit with his hair all processed. He had come over to Stax wanting to play with Steve Cropper and the guys at the studio. Cropper wasn't there, but Jimi hooked up his stuff in the studio. He started playing a bit in his wild style and those guys just kind of laughed and walked out of the studio. Jimi packed up his stuff and left town."

FALL 1964

ON THE ROAD

In September, Hendrix joined a package tour featuring Sam Cooke, Jackie Wilson, and the Valentinos, featuring a young Bobby Womack. "I was playing guitar behind one of the acts on the tour," explained Hendrix in a 1967 interview. "Then I got stranded in Kansas City because I missed the bus. So I was in Kansas City, Missouri, and didn't have any money. This group came up and brought me back to Atlanta, Georgia, where I met Little Richard and started playing with him for a while."

Hendrix became a member of the Upsetters, Little Richard's touring ensemble. Despite Little Richard's shameless claims to the contrary, Hendrix only recorded one single during his brief tenure as Richard's guitarist. The single, "I Don't Know What You Got But It's Got Me (Part One)," backed with "I Don't Know What You Got But It's Got Me (Part Two)," was written by Don Covay and issued by Vee-Jay Records in November 1965. Indicative of Richard's fading pop following, the single reached number 92 on *Billboard*'s Top 100 chart, staying just a single week before dropping off. The song enjoyed far greater success on *Billboard*'s rhythm and blues chart, where it ultimately peaked at number 12.

SPRING 1965

LOS ANGELES

Hendrix's next known recording session took place in Los Angeles, where he befriended Rosa Lee Brooks, a rhythm and blues artist. "Jimi and I had met at the California Club in Los Angeles," says Brooks. "Neither of us were onstage, we were there watching the Ike and Tina Turner Revue. It was love at first sight, and we spent three beautiful months together. We were scouting around looking for work and trying to get gigs at different clubs in Hollywood and L.A."

Shortly after the two met, Hendrix and Brooks co-wrote "My Diary" at the Wilcox Hotel on New Year's Day 1965. "Jimi sang the first verse, 'I know that I will never love again, I know that I will be my only friend' as he started playing what he called a love note," says Brooks. "The rest of the words were written by me. Jimi and I felt that we had an Ike and Tina or Mickey and Sylvia thing happening. We were Jimi and Rose, and this song was our baby."

With their new song completed, Brooks introduced Hendrix to Billy Revis, who ran Revis Records, a local R&B label. "Jimi and I were at the California Club one night and Billy Revis was there," remembers Brooks. "I told Jimi who he was and we both went to him and told him we had a song we would like him to hear. Billy gave us his home address and asked if we would come by the following day, which we did. We played the song for him there and he loved it. He asked if we could get some other musicians together and we said yes. At that time, Major Lance's band was in town performing at Ciro's on the Strip. Jimi was the kind of guy who would walk backstage and introduce himself. We wound up partying with them that night, and Big Francis, the drummer, and Alvin, the bass player, agreed to come and do it."

In addition to sidemen from Major Lance's touring ensemble, another notable Los Angeles–based artist got involved with the recording: Brooks recruited her friend and future Love frontman Arthur Lee to contribute background vocals. "I knew Arthur before I met Jimi," she explains. "He really didn't have that much going for him musically at that time. Arthur and Pat, my singing partner, had a little thing going on back then. I arrived to pick him up at his mother's house on 29th and Arlington Street on the day of the session. When Jimi saw him he became very jealous. Jimi hardly spoke to Arthur, thinking that he and I had something more than a friendship going on. He got into the backseat of my 1959 Chevy Impala and Jimi was up front. All was quiet during the trip except for when Jimi spoke to me."

Produced by Billy Revis, who also organized the horn section, "My Diary" and "Utee" were recorded in a converted garage in March 1965. "Utee," the song's spirited B-side, was a spontaneous effort developed entirely at the session. "Alvin, the bass player, had told us about a dance that was popular in Detroit called the

'U.T.,'" Brooks explains. "He even demonstrated how to do it, and Jimi and I had the steps down pat. Billy Revis said, 'We need a B-side.' So Jimi took off on a rhythm and I just started singing."

While his playing on these two sides highlights Curtis Mayfield's considerable influence on his style, "My Diary" stands as perhaps the finest example of Hendrix's work before forming the Jimi Hendrix Experience, showcasing his emerging sound and identity. "People have tried to claim that Jimi's rock roots didn't start until he got to London and that's just not true," argues Brooks. "If you listen to Jimi's rhythm and lead guitar on 'Utee,' you hear that he was way ahead of his time. He was playing his own style of rock music long before he went to England."

Revis did release the single, but apart from some modest interest in Los Angeles, the song faded from memory, as did his relationship with Rosa Lee Brooks. "Jimi left Los Angeles shortly after we recorded our song," remembers Brooks. "When I turned twenty-one, I started dancing at the Club LaRouge in L.A. At that time, I received a letter from Jimi. He was living in New York and calling himself Maurice James. He had joined the Isley Brothers and asked me to send him sixty dollars to get his guitar out of the pawn shop."

SUMMER 1965

1984: WITH THE ISLEY BROTHERS AT ATLANTIC STUDIOS.

ON THE ROAD AND IN NEW YORK

While touring with Little Richard, an audience member at the Back Bay Theater in Boston made an amateur recording of Hendrix playing with the rock legend. Walter DeVanne, who recorded the performance, recalls the date of the show as April 1965. It remains the only known recording of its kind featuring Hendrix supporting Little Richard. Richard romped through a high-powered set that blended his many hits with recent chart favorites including a version of the Beatles' "I Saw Her Standing There."

Hendrix was back in Nashville in July 1965, when he made an appearance on the Nashville television program *Night Train*. The guitarist can be seen in the backline as part of Little Richard's ensemble, performing behind vocalists Buddy & Stacy (Travis and Stacey Johnson). Their performance of "Shotgun" was broadcast on WLAC in the Nashville area. This black-and-white video recording stands as the earliest known performance footage of Jimi Hendrix in existence.

After Hendrix parted company with Little Richard, Billy Cox steered some session work to his old friend. King/Starday Records had hired Cox as a bassist, and he had a session lined up with a producer who was none other than legendary disc jockey Bill "Hoss" Allen. Allen was producing a single for Frank Howard & The Commanders and asked if Cox knew a guitar player who could also take part. Cox suggested Hendrix, and Hendrix came to the studio eager to impress. Cox composed both songs recorded during the session, "I'm So Glad" and "I'm Sorry For You." Allen had simple requirements and gave Hendrix a modest role in the song's arrangement. Unfortunately, Allen found Hendrix's loud, wild playing so unnerving that he faded the guitar almost completely out of the song's final mix. Allen licensed the single to Barry Records, a small independent label that issued the disc with little fanfare near the close of 1965.

Sometime after his failed session for Hoss Allen and King/Starday Records, Hendrix briefly reprised his position with the Isley Brothers, joining the group in July 1965 for a series of New York dates. Legendary record producer Juggy Murray, whose Sue Records was the home of such R&B greats as Ike and Tina Turner and Baby Washington, witnessed Hendrix performing with the Isley Brothers at Small's Paradise in Harlem. "I thought he was great," remembers Murray. "He came down to my studio [Juggy Sound] a couple of times before he signed a management and recording contract with me." Hendrix signed the contract on July 27, 1965, but not much came of it. While Hendrix's ability as a guitar player was obvious, incorporating that talent into conventional Top 40 R&B proved difficult for Murray. "At that time, Jimi wasn't playing the way that he ended up playing," says Murray. "But I knew this guy was going to be great, so I signed him. Jimi would go up into the studio and rehearse, but how the hell do you record a guy who is a great guitar player without a hit single? I had to find a way to do it."

Despite Murray's impressive stable of artists, Hendrix did not serve as a session guitarist for the label. "He could make more money playing on the road," admits Murray. "Let me tell you, we used to cut four sides in three hours in those days."

With Hendrix forced to return to working as an itinerant sideman, his career at Sue Records stalled without ever starting. "He just wasn't around that often," says Murray. "When he was around, we would rehearse different things with him. We were trying to find a way to get over with him, but we never completed anything. Then he'd get lost and you wouldn't see him for two or three months. But that was Jimi. All this guy did was play his guitar for anybody and everybody—from when he woke up in the morning to the last thing he did before he went to bed. He'd put that guitar down to go to sleep and it would be the first thing he would pick up in the morning. He was a guitar freak, but he was also the nicest human being on earth. He was kind, friendly, and would play for anybody."

Hendrix's final session with the Isley Brothers came on August 5, 1965, yielding the uptempo "Move Over And Let Me Dance" and "Have You Ever Been Disappointed?" Despite their merits, neither of the group's two Atlantic singles enjoyed any notable chart success. After Hendrix left the group, the Isleys moved from Atlantic to Motown's Tamla affiliate. Their debut single there, "This Old Heart Of Mine (Is Weak For You)" provided the group with their most successful crossover single to date, peaking at number 12 on *Billboard*'s Top 100 Chart in February 1966.

Though Hendrix and the group had parted ways, Ronnie Isley insisted that Hendrix and the group maintained a friendship. In 1969, when the group reestablished T-Neck Records, Isley said Hendrix learned that the group was planning to reissue their recordings with him and offered to rerecord his original parts if necessary. "He used to ask us if we had any copies of the records we made together. We didn't because of contracts. But we knew the tapes were coming back to us and when we told him about it he said, 'If there is any stuff I played that isn't right, let me know and I'll come in and do it over.' I told him not to worry about it," said Isley. "Jimi never played anything wrong."

In 1971, the Isley Brothers issued *In The Beginning*, a compilation featuring Hendrix's recordings with the group alongside other early recordings by the group. Hendrix's performances were remixed, placing his guitar more prominently in the mix than in the original releases, usually at the expense of the original saxophone parts. "We remixed it so that Jimi was more upfront," Isley admitted when the album was released. In addition to these remixed versions, an alternate take of "Testify (Part One)" was included.

FALL 1965

NEW YORK AND ON THE ROAD

Looking for new opportunities to further his own career, Hendrix left the Isley Brothers and joined Curtis Knight & the Squires, an R&B group whose enthusiastic live performances of Top 40 pop and soul hits had earned them a modest club following throughout New York and New Jersey. In September 1965, lead singer Curtis Knight introduced Hendrix to producer Ed Chalpin. Chalpin had signed Knight to an exclusive artist contract in February 1965. His company, the New York–based PPX Industries, had created a lucrative business by recording cover versions of top U.S. hits for foreign record companies, who then overdubbed translated lyrics. In addition to creating remakes for foreign markets,

Chalpin tried his hand at breaking into the American singles charts. Chalpin auditioned the Squires at Studio 76 and, after the group recorded a number of finished songs, signed Hendrix to a recording contract. Hendrix signed this one-page agreement at Studio 76 on or about October 15, 1965. Desperate for a chance to realize his music in a recording studio, Hendrix failed to inform Chalpin that he had signed a similar agreement with Sue Records just three months earlier.

Curtis Knight & the Squires recorded a number of original songs with the hope of cracking *Billboard*'s elusive singles charts. These songs, largely composed by Knight, were recorded during sessions staged in October and December 1965. The Squires of this period consisted of Hendrix, Napoleon Anderson, Nathaniel Edmonds, and Marian Booker. While much of their stage repertoire comprised such popular fare as "Sugar Pie, Honey Bunch," and "Hang On Sloopy," under Chalpin's direction, the group experimented with a wide variety of musical genres in an effort to develop an effective formula for chart success. While Knight's brooding "Don't Accuse Me" showcased the group's firm grasp of the blues, the dance-oriented R&B efforts "Simon Says," "Welcome Home," and "Gotta Have A New Dress" took their structure largely from superior Stax and Motown recordings.

Chalpin may also have used one of the Squires recordings with Hendrix as a backing track for "Suey," the flip side of "As The Clouds Drift By," a 1967 single by the noted B-movie actress Jayne Mansfield. Mansfield died in an automobile accident in June 1967, and Hendrix's actual participation in this recording has never been confirmed. Given Chalpin's propensity to repurpose any recording he owned that featured Hendrix via various editing and mixing techniques, it seems odd that this particular recording was not featured among other Curtis Knight & the Squires recordings as part of the myriad of albums that flowed from licenses granted by Chalpin's company PPX.

SPRING 1966

NEW YORK

Despite the modest progress Hendrix had made with Curtis Knight & the Squires, money troubles forced him back out on to the road, first as a member of Joey Dee's Starlighters, and then as a member of King Curtis's Kingpins. On January 21, 1966, Hendrix joined King Curtis at Atlantic Studios and added guitar to Ray Sharpe's "Help Me (Part One)" and "Help Me (Part Two)," which Atlantic's Atco subsidiary issued as a single later that year. Ironically, Atlantic reused this same master recording for three future singles by different artists. In 1966, Atlantic leased the master to Island Records so that its artist Owen Gray could record a vocal atop a sped-up copy of the original backing track. In 1967, producer Jerry Wexler overhauled the same master on behalf of Aretha Franklin, who composed new lyrics and titled the song "Save Me." Wexler mixed out Hendrix's guitar part and dressed up the recording with new overdubs and a vocal by Franklin. One final use of the "Help Me" master came in 1969 when King Curtis returned to the original 1966 recording and supplemented it with additional overdubs. Hendrix's guitar part remained on this "new" recording, titled "Instant Groove," and Atco issued an album and single under that name the same year.

On March 15, 1966, Ed Chalpin secured a licensing deal with Jerry Simon's RSVP Records. Simon released two Curtis Knight singles in 1966, "How Would You Feel" backed with "Welcome Home." "How Would You Feel," which Knight would later call the first black rock protest song, was largely based on Bob Dylan's "Like A Rolling Stone," a massive hit from the previous summer.

On June 10, 1966, PPX entered into a second agreement with RSVP Records for Curtis Knight recordings featuring Hendrix. PPX supplied recordings of "The U.F.O.," "I'm A Fool For You Baby," "Ballad Of Jimmy," "Gotta Have A New Dress," "Knock Yourself Out," and "Your Love." RSVP drew a second single from these titles, issuing "Hornet's Nest" backed with "Knock Yourself Out." Hendrix received credit for arranging both sides of the single. As co-composer of both "Hornet's Nest" and "Welcome Home," Hendrix, named on the disc as "Jimmy Hendrix," received his first publishing credit. Both of these efforts missed the charts entirely. Simon's interest in the group waned, and RSVP did not issue a third single. An additional master tape from the Squires sessions has surfaced

in recent years. The instrumental "Station Break" was among recordings held by Jerry Simon. "Station Break," composed by Hendrix and Simon, has never been commercially issued on any album issued or licensed by PPX, and the recording remains unreleased.

Hendrix's last known session with King Curtis yielded three songs: "Linda Lou," "Baby How About You," and "I Can't Take It," recorded at Atlantic Studios on April 28, 1966. These recordings, however, were not issued at that time and have remained unreleased. Years later, a fire ravaged much of Atlantic's master tape library, destroying these particular masters and many others. Sadly, no safety copies are known to exist.

SUMMER 1966

NEW YORK

Hendrix participated in one or more sessions at Abtone Recording Studios with saxophonist Lonnie Youngblood during 1966. Producer John Brantley, a New York/New Jersey–based record impresario and former associate of Alan Freed, directed these sessions. Hendrix contributed guitar to four lively R&B-styled tracks that Fairmont Records later issued under Youngblood's name. These recordings, "Go Go Shoes" backed with

"Go Go Place" and "Soul Food (That's What I Like)" backed with "Goodbye Bessie Mae," were uptempo dance-oriented numbers not unlike similar efforts marketed by competing labels such as Atlantic and Stax. Neither of these two singles, however, made any kind of chart impact.

Hendrix and Youngblood also contributed to a single by vocalist Jimmy Norman. "You're Only Hurting Yourself," backed with "That Little Old Groove Maker," cited Brantley as producer and was issued on the small SAMAR label in 1966. Brantley also used the underlying instrumental recordings from the 1966 Abtone session with Hendrix as the basis for the 1968 Billy Lamont single "Sweet Thang" backed with "Please Don't Leave." Youngblood received a co-composer credit for "Sweet Thang" alongside Brantley and Lamont. This is most likely because "Sweet Thang" is actually "Wipe The Sweat," a song voiced by Youngblood during the original 1966 session. An alternate version that features Hendrix singing the song's second verse has also been issued on many compilations featuring the Youngblood sessions.

Of all the recordings made for Brantley that feature Hendrix, "(My Girl) She's A Fox" by the Icemen is perhaps the strongest of his pre-Experience career.

Hendrix's Curtis Mayfield–influenced guitar styling is the song's strongest attribute. The Poindexter brothers, Richard and Robert, composed this single, backed with "(I Wonder) What It Takes," which also features Hendrix, and issued it on the SAMAR label in 1966. While this single had little commercial impact, the Poindexters would gain recognition after their brush with Hendrix in 1966. The two brothers later composed the popular R&B hit "Thin Line Between Love And Hate" with Jackie Members for the Persuaders in 1971.

In the years following Hendrix's death, *hundreds* of albums have been fashioned from these Brantley-produced master tapes. Just as other unscrupulous manufacturers misrepresented Hendrix's role and level of participation—if any—with Little Richard, and later Curtis Knight & the Squires, these various compilations routinely use misleading labels to exaggerate Hendrix's contribution. The liner notes, if any are supplied at all, are often incomplete or blatantly inaccurate. Worse still, new overdubs created to *sound* like Hendrix were recorded after his death in an attempt to fill out additional releases. Perhaps the most notorious example was 1971's *Two Great Experiences Together*. In addition to copious amounts of echo added to tracks like "Wipe The Sweat," other tracks were enhanced with new stereo overdubs performed by a pathetic Hendrix sound-alike. The 1966 Jimmy Norman single "You're Only Hurting Yourself" was renamed "Two In One Goes" and laden with new saxophone overdubs so that it, too, could be included. *Two Great Experiences Together* arrived in record shops almost simultaneously with Reprise's *Cry Of Love*. Issued on Maple Records, the album managed to climb to number 127 on the *Billboard* Top 200 Album Chart before it quickly exited and a steady steam of dubious compilations took its place, drawn from the same source material.

No such attention surrounded Hendrix back in 1966, however, as he continued to struggle on the R&B circuit. With his money running out, Hendrix briefly reprised his sideman duties with Curtis Knight, joining the Squires in May 1966 for an extended engagement at the Cheetah, New York's hottest nightspot.

While performing with Knight and the Squires, Hendrix caught the attention of London fashion model Linda Keith, then the girlfriend of Rolling Stones

guitarist Keith Richards. Linda Keith, sitting with friends Roberta Goldstein and Mark Kauffman, was taken with the group's lead guitarist. "I was sitting near the back of the Cheetah when I noticed a guitarist in the backline of Curtis Knight's band whose playing mesmerized me," says Keith. "After the set, I had Mark check him out to see if he wanted to come have a drink with us. Fortunately, he did."

Hendrix was taken with Keith's sincerity and the two quickly became friends. With her encouragement, Hendrix combed Greenwich Village's folk-pop scene for musicians willing to join a group that he would lead, stepping out of his longtime role as a support musician. Billing his ensemble as Jimmy James and the Blue Flames, Hendrix set out to establish himself as a bandleader. While their lineup never really solidified, the Blue Flames featured Randy Wolfe, guitarist Randy California (who later starred as the lead guitarist for the popular group Spirit), and Chas Matthews, a bassist who occasionally handled drum chores. To supplement the meager earnings generated by the Blue Flames, Hendrix sat in with blues guitarist John Hammond Jr. on a number of occasions, most notably at the Cafe Au Go Go. "When we were backing up John Hammond, we used to run back and forth between the Cafe Wha? and the Cafe Au Go Go," says California. "We'd play his two sets *plus* our five sets. Those were tiring nights!"

Shortly after their formation, Jimmy James & the Blue Flames established a residency at the Cafe Wha?, one of the many tiny nightspots that dotted the Village. "We used to play about five sets every night at the Cafe Wha?" remembers guitarist Randy California. "We were mostly doing cover stuff like 'Hey Joe,' 'Wild Thing,' 'Shot Gun,' and 'High Heel Sneakers.' We used to jam a lot and some of the songs would turn out to be pretty long." It was during these extended sets that Hendrix began to incorporate original material he had started to develop, including embryonic versions of songs that would later appear on *Are You Experienced*. "Jimi had fragments of that first album in his set," says guitarist Bob Kulick, whose group Random Blues frequently performed at the Cafe Wha? "He definitely had 'Hey Joe' and he used to play a rough version of 'Third Stone From The Sun.'" Ragamuffins guitarist Ken

Pine echoes Kulick: "He may not have had all of the songs together as they were on *Are You Experienced*, but when I later heard the album, I remembered him playing around with those riffs and melodies."

Performing in the Village served to expand Hendrix's musical horizons, introducing him to many other talented but struggling artists trying to establish themselves. "The scene was pretty liberal at that time, and people could jam and get to know one another easily," recalls musician Paul Caruso.

Before his performances with the Blue Flames at the Cafe Wha? Hendrix often took refuge at the Nite Owl club and joined the club's afternoon jam sessions. Musicians who participated got a free lunch, a policy that, considering the miserable state of Hendrix's finances, proved a tempting draw. His financial condition hampered his development, forcing him to rely on the kindness of friends and girlfriends just to survive. He often resorted to pawning guitars and regarded even seemingly minor expenses like guitar strings as precious commodities. "He broke a guitar string during his show and he threw a fit afterwards," recalls Bob Kulick. "I couldn't understand what the problem was. I figured he just didn't have the particular string he needed, so I opened up my case and gave him one. His eyes lit up and it was only then that I realized how badly off he was."

Though unable to afford even an hour of time in a recording studio, Hendrix was determined to monitor his progress. When he could borrow a tape machine, Hendrix made primitive live recordings of his club performances.

"One night he had set up a Roberts reel-to-reel tape machine which never seemed to run correctly," remembers Ken Pine. "I had seen him try it once before and it didn't work, but on this night, Mark Klingman, who later worked with Buzzy Linhart and Bette Midler, sat in with him. The playing was great, but afterwards, when he tried to play back the tape, the machine had failed him again."

Linda Keith, who was determined to showcase Hendrix's abilities, wanted to document one of the Blue Flames performances to use as a resumé on Hendrix's behalf. "We were trying to record a demonstration tape live from the Cafe Wha? but it was a very amateur effort," remembers Keith. "We couldn't afford to bring Jimi into a studio." Despite the good intentions, the demonstration tape idea—as well as the tape itself—was scrapped.

Keith next decided to trade on her friendship with Andrew Loog Oldham. Oldham, producer and manager of the Rolling Stones, had developed a reputation as one of the brightest young music entrepreneurs and had already launched his own label, Immediate Records. Keith hoped that Oldham would recognize Hendrix's considerable talents, but he did not share her enthusiasm. After witnessing a performance at the Cafe Au Go Go, Oldham passed. Seymour Stein, another record industry entrepreneur, handed down a similar rejection.

Having exhausted Linda Keith's best resources, Keith and Hendrix needed to regroup. One evening, Keith met the Animals bassist Chas Chandler at Ondine's, a popular nightspot. Chandler mentioned his desire to leave the Animals and try his hand at record production. Keith saw her chance and implored Chandler to come see her friend Jimmy James perform at the Cafe Wha? Intrigued, Chandler agreed to go the following day.

In July of 1966, the Animals gathered in New York, preparing for their final tour of North America. "I had gone there about a week ahead of time to see some friends," recalls Chandler. "The night before we were to play in Central Park, someone played me Tim Rose's version of 'Hey Joe,' which had been out for about nine months in America. I was so taken by it that I vowed, 'As soon as I get back to England, I'm going to find an artist to record this song.' Later that evening, we went out to a club called Ondine's. As we walked in, Linda Keith came walking out and we stopped to talk. She told me she was going out with this guy in the Village that I had to see. It hadn't been public, but all of my close friends knew that I was getting into record production after the Animals' impending split and Linda suggested that her friend might be just the guy to start with. So I made arrangements to meet her the next afternoon. I went down to the Village again and saw Jimmy James and the Blue Flames perform at the Cafe Wha? It just so happened the first song Hendrix played that afternoon was 'Hey Joe.'" By chance, Ken

Pine was seated next to Chandler during Hendrix's set. "Chas was so excited that he kept hitting me with his elbow. I thought he was going to crush me," laughs Pine. "I didn't think he was going to survive the set."

After his show, Keith introduced Chandler to Hendrix. "We just sat and talked for about an hour," recalls Chandler. "I told him that I was going off on a tour with the Animals, but I would be back in a week or so. I left then saying, 'I'll come back to New York and if you still feel like it, I'll take you to England and we'll start.' He said, 'Fair enough.'"

While Hendrix's raw potential struck a chord within Chandler, the same could not be said for Hendrix's support group, the Blue Flames. "I wasn't impressed with the Blue Flames at all. They were a pickup band who sounded as if Jimi had met them that day," remembers Chandler. "I didn't bother to make a recording of any of their performances because the drummer was lousy. Randy California, the other guitar player, was a nice young kid, but all he wanted to do was play blues, and I didn't think that just playing blues was the way to make a hit with Jimi Hendrix."

"Jimi asked me to sit in on that first meeting with Chas," remembers California. "Jimi wanted to take me along and be part of it, so I was suggesting that we do more traditional Delta blues. Chas wasn't interested in me at all; he was just interested in Jimi. It was obvious that I was only there because Jimi had asked me to come along. I couldn't have gone along anyway because I was only fifteen at the time. I asked my parents if I could go with Jimi to England but they said no."

In addition to Hendrix's obvious ability, his powerful renditions of "Hey Joe" and "Like A Rolling Stone" convinced Chandler of his future promise. "That afternoon at the Cafe Wha? Jimi was just an explosive kid whose potential struck me," he says. "As much as his version of 'Hey Joe' impressed me, what convinced me of his talent was another song that he did that first day, 'Like A Rolling Stone.' I knew Dylan well and loved his material, but 'Like A Rolling Stone' was the first of his songs that I didn't quite get. It was something about the way Dylan had sung the song. I never felt he expressed it properly. When Jimi sang the song, he did it with tremendous conviction and the lyrics came

right through to me. My initial impression, having heard him play 'Hey Joe' and 'Like A Rolling Stone,' was that I couldn't see his career going in any other way but the place between those two songs. That was where it had to go."

As impressive as Hendrix's abilities seemed, Chandler couldn't help but think that Hendrix had already been spotted and signed to another label. "I was astonished to hear that nobody had ever signed him," says Chandler, "apart from some small labels, where he felt he was actually under contract as a session man. I remember him telling me that he viewed those agreements as a guarantee of session work—not as a recording contract. To that extent, I immediately sat with him and got a list of people he had signed agreements with. I started going around buying them up, including his agreement with Sue Records. Unfortunately, the one he didn't mention was with Ed Chalpin and PPX. Jimi thought it was nothing more than another session-man agreement."

Excited by his discovery, Chandler returned to the Animals to complete the group's remaining tour dates. As he quietly plotted his strategy, Chandler initially kept word of his future plans close to the vest. His new career was about to begin, and he wanted to embark on this new journey with minimal distraction. Immediately following the last scheduled appearance of the Animals on August 6, 1966, his quest began in earnest.

"The last gigs the Animals did were at the Steam Pier in Atlantic City," Chandler remembers. "Michael Jeffery had come to the show, and afterwards, the two of us drove to Philadelphia. I never mentioned anything about Jimi to him; I simply asked him to drop me off at the parents of Bobbi Shore, a girlfriend of mine at that time. I took the train to New York the next morning, checked into the Gorham Hotel, where Hilton Valentine and I shared a suite, and began running around the Village trying to find Jimi."

Chandler's pursuit of Hendrix was complicated by the guitarist's tenuous living arrangements. His protégé-to-be had neither a working phone number nor permanent address. "Jimi was very vague about his living situation," says Chandler. "I knew that he had a room in a place on Broadway, but he never seemed to stay there." Fortunately, the Blue Flames were still performing at the Cafe Wha? and Chandler located Hendrix there. That evening, Chandler reaffirmed his interest in producing and managing Hendrix's career. Hendrix accepted Chandler's offer as genuine and agreed to travel to London with him.

With relatively few contacts in New York, Chandler knew that his experiment would have to be staged in London, so that he could, if necessary, trade on favors to organize a backing group for Hendrix. Eager to begin, Chandler immediately began closing out Hendrix's old contracts and having him fill any final engagements at area clubs. "At the same time that I was buying all of his contracts up, I was thinking to myself that we had to get some musicians together. I was determined, however, to do this in London—not New York," Chandler says. "I told him frankly that there was nothing in the Blue Flames which had interested me. There was an occasional blues solo from Randy, yes, but the rest was utter chaos. The bass player was a jerk and the drummer couldn't play. The way I looked at it was, 'Hey, you've been playing this and nobody's fucking signed you. What's the point in carrying on?'"

While loyal to those who had supported him initially, Hendrix was unwilling to squander his opportunity. He consented to Chandler's requests and fulfilled his remaining gigs with the Blue Flames.

With the help of Animals attorney Lee Dicker, Chandler made his final preparations to take Hendrix to London. "The first thing I did was to get his papers together so that he could get a passport," he says. "He had nothing, as he hadn't been home in so long. Finally, when Hilton Valentine left for London, Jimi and I used the suite we had shared as an office to send letters and telegrams back to his father to get all the details. All Jimi had was an address, but he didn't even know if his father was still living there. Following that, I went down and found Scott English, a songwriter from the Brill Building who was a big mate of mine. To help us get Jimi's passport, Scott agreed to say that he had known Jimi for years."

With his passport in hand, and nothing more to go on than Chandler's reputation and pledge of unwavering support, Hendrix left for London on September 24, 1966.

SEPTEMBER 1966

LONDON

Upon his arrival in London, Chandler immediately set his plan in motion. Despite his inexperience as a producer, Chandler had a firm understanding of the sound and style he wanted his new protégé to showcase. His belief in the commercial prospects of "Hey Joe" was resolute—as long as Hendrix could record a version as forceful and convincing as the performance that had grabbed Chandler's attention at the Cafe Wha?.

In addition to recording "Hey Joe," Chandler understood that Hendrix would need to tour Britain and Europe aggressively to develop a following. His concept was to market Hendrix as a star of the first magnitude, a genuine bluesman imported directly from America. To create a supporting act, Chandler took advantage of auditions that were staged at the Birdland club in London: Eric Burdon was seeking new musicians for the Animals now that Chandler and other original members had left the group. Chandler had his eye out for suitable players to connect with his new protégé. "I was looking for drummers and bass players, even though I didn't know what the band was going to be or what kind of lineup it would have," says Chandler. "We were just looking for musicians." Hendrix's criteria were just as simple. "I was thinking of the smallest pieces possible with the hardest impact," he said.

They selected guitarist Noel Redding first, who had arrived at the audition with the hope of landing a spot in the new Animals. Though the Animals position had been filled, Chandler suggested that he sit in on bass with Jimi Hendrix, a guitarist he was now managing. Armed with Chandler's bass, Redding sat in with Hendrix, pianist Mike O'Neill, and drummer Aynsley Dunbar. "I was handed this bass from Chas and we played three tunes," remembers Redding. "This American gentleman with a funny pair of shoes on and a funny overcoat just sort of told me the chords and we went through them. There were no vocals involved. We played three tunes with this American gentleman and that was it. Then the American bloke said 'Do you want to go down and have a pint or something?' So we went down to this place next door and we both had this discussion. I was asking him all about the American music scene—at that point Sam Cooke, Booker T. and the MG's were my sort of favorites—and he was asking me about the English scene because he'd only been there for about a week, which was like the Move, the Kinks, the Beatles. Then he said, 'Do you want to join my group?' and that was it."

Choosing a drummer proved more difficult, as Hendrix and Chandler had to decide from a pool that included Dunbar, John Banks of the Merseybeats, and Mitch Mitchell, formerly of Georgie Fame & the Blue Flames. "One night Hendrix and I went to a club called Blaises and Jimi got up to jam with Brian Auger," says Chandler. "While he was onstage I started speaking with Johnny Hallyday, the French singer, and his father, Lee. Lee said, 'Johnny's going out for his first French tour in five years. Have you got a band together for this guy? He could be a support act.' I said yes even though I hadn't—I only had the bass player fixed. Lee said that they started their tour in ten days' time and if we joined them in Nice we could do the whole tour. So we sat and did a deal that night. Jimi and I went back to our apartment and tossed a coin to see who was going to be the drummer—we couldn't make up our minds. We had to start rehearsals, the tour started in only ten days. We were lucky: Mitch won the flip. We rang him the next morning and immediately started rehearsals to get an act together for the Johnny Hallyday tour."

Together with Michael Jeffery, the Animals manager who would now team up with Chandler to direct Hendrix's career, the guitarist agreed to change the spelling of his first name to the more exotic Jimi and named his group the Jimi Hendrix Experience.

THURSDAY, OCTOBER 13, 1966

NOVELTY, EVREUX, FRANCE. WITH THE BLACKBIRDS, LONG CHRIS, AND JOHNNY HALLYDAY.

FRIDAY, OCTOBER 14, 1966

UNKNOWN VENUE, NANCY, FRANCE. WITH THE BLACKBIRDS, LONG CHRIS, AND JOHNNY HALLYDAY.

SATURDAY, OCTOBER 15, 1966

SALLE DES FÊTES, VILLERUPT, LORRAINE, FRANCE. WITH THE BLACKBIRDS, LONG CHRIS, AND JOHNNY HALLYDAY.

TUESDAY, OCTOBER 18, 1966

"MUSICORAMA," L'OLYMPIA, PARIS, FRANCE. WITH THE BLACKBIRDS, BRIAN AUGER TRINITY, LONG CHRIS, AND JOHNNY HALLYDAY. **SET LIST:** "KILLING FLOOR" / "HEY JOE" / "WILD THING"

The newly formed Jimi Hendrix Experience were given a fifteen-minute showcase as a support act on this tour. In addition to "Hey Joe," the group featured interpretations of blues and recent R&B chart hits. "We got together with 'Midnight Hour,' 'Land Of 1000 Dances,' 'Everyone Needs Someone To Love,' and 'Respect,'" Hendrix recalled in a 1967 interview.

In Paris, Hendrix thrilled a capacity crowd at the Olympia Theater with his charisma and dramatic stage presence. The national French radio company RTE recorded the group's short performance and the raw, two-track tape represents the first known recording of the group in existence. "Hey Joe" and "Killing Floor" were issued in 2000 as part of the *Jimi Hendrix Experience* box set.

SUNDAY, OCTOBER 23, 1966

DELANE LEA STUDIOS, LONDON, ENGLAND. PRODUCER: CHAS CHANDLER. ENGINEER: DAVE SIDDLE.

Chandler booked time for the Experience's first studio session at London's DeLane Lea Recording Studios. "That was where the Animals had done almost all of their recording," explains Chandler. "I knew the studio well, that's why I took them there."

Limited cash reserves forced Chandler to complete much of the necessary preproduction at his London flat, but still, he considered such an arrangement an improvement on his stint with the Animals. "The Animals had no say on matters like studio time," says Chandler. "When time was available, the studio was booked. Then we went off to a rehearsal room to work our butts off. If we couldn't get time in a rehearsal room, we would come early to a gig and jam for an hour or so. When I started with Jimi, we were sharing the flat and doing all of our work there. That was a luxury the Animals never had. The flat was Jimi's rehearsal room. That was such an advantage. When we took the Experience into rehearsals, Jimi had already developed the song to the point where he could indicate the chord sequences and tempo to Mitch and I would work with Noel about the bass parts. Then everything would come together."

While the comfortable confines of the apartment may have afforded Chandler the privacy to refine Hendrix's sound and style, he rarely extended invitations to either Mitchell or Redding. Chandler didn't care that the other band members might feel excluded. His goals were twofold: establishing himself as a producer and keeping his promise to make Jimi Hendrix as a star. "I wasn't concerned that Mitch or Noel might feel that they weren't having enough—or any—say," he says. "Their say was a bit of nuisance really. I didn't need the confusion. I had been touring and recording in a band for years, and I'd seen everything end as a compromise. Nobody ended up doing what they really wanted to do. I was not going to let that happen with Jimi."

Having presided over a series of rehearsals, Chandler now deemed the group ready for their initial recording session. Hamstrung by his dwindling savings, the focus of the session would be "Hey Joe," the song on which Chandler had based this entire experiment. "I had only enough money to cover the cost for 'Hey Joe,'" remembers Chandler. "I couldn't even think of recording a B-side until I had more cash."

As the session date at DeLane Lea had loomed closer, Hendrix increasingly questioned the range and quality of his singing voice. Unsure of his ability, Hendrix grew edgy in the days before the session, fearing that a poor performance might doom the progress he had made since arriving in London. To Chandler, Hendrix's reservations represented little more than a heightened case of nerves. "Jimi was paranoid about his voice from the very first day I met him," says Chandler. "From my first day in the studio with him to my last, he would always want his voice buried and I would want to place it more forward in the mix."

At the session, Chandler and Hendrix butted heads again. "When Jimi first came to London, his visa had been restricted," says Chandler. "I had received an extension, one that carried us through the date I had scheduled for us to record 'Hey Joe.' The day we were recording 'Hey Joe,' I had gone over to the immigration office in the morning to get some papers completed for a three-month extension of his passport. It took so long that I came straight from immigration to DeLane Lea. Right after we started, Jimi threw a tantrum because I wouldn't let him play his guitar loud enough in the studio. It was a stupid argument over sheer volume. He was playing through a Marshall twin stack and it was so loud in the studio that we were picking up various rattles and noises. He said, 'If I can't play as loud as I want, I might as well go back to New York.' In my pocket I had his passport and immigration papers. I took them out, threw them down on the console, and said, 'Well, here you go. Piss off!' He looked at them, started laughing, and said, 'All right, you called my bluff!' and that was it."

While Chandler had labored to minimize any chance of delays caused by a lack of preparation, capturing the Experience's unique sound required a series of experiments with microphone placements and amplifier settings.

In two hours, all they could afford, the Experience managed to complete an effective backing track. According to Noel Redding, Chandler had the group complete more than thirty different takes before the basic track met his approval. While additional work remained, namely a finished lead vocal from Hendrix and a chorus of female backing vocals, Chandler was pleased with what they had accomplished. Hearing the group's sound on tape made Hendrix's potential seem much more tangible.

With the backing track in hand, it took a considerable investment to capture Hendrix's modest, appealing lead vocal on tape. He recorded a number of attempts at different studios before Chandler felt he had successfully completed the task. Hendrix, however, still harbored some reservations. "It was the first time I had ever sung on a record actually," he said later, but Chandler expressed no such doubts. "Chas was sure it would be a hit," Hendrix explained.

The recording sessions for "Hey Joe" served a dual purpose for Chandler and Hendrix, who used them as a gauge to measure the talents of Mitchell and Redding. "Jimi and I literally used the recording session as a test, to take Mitch and Noel into the studio and see how they worked," explains Chandler. Chandler saw promise in Mitchell and Redding, but his vision for "Hey Joe" was so focused that he felt compelled to replace Redding's bass part with an overdub.

Not wanting to discourage or embarrass Redding, a guitarist by training, Chandler privately replaced the part with his own playing. This was the first and last time that Chandler—whose bass riffs had been an integral part of many chart hits by the Animals—played the instrument on a Jimi Hendrix recording. Chandler revealed this secret overdub to me nearly two decades ago but asked that the information not be revealed until after he and Redding had both passed away.

These quick sessions suited Chandler's budget, but they make it difficult to track the exact schedule of the song's evolution. Chandler labored to secure just the right texture to sit beneath Hendrix's distinctive lead guitar and vocals. "Although we had completed the backing track, we still weren't finished, because we couldn't get the girls' vocals right. I ended up going from one studio to another, trying to get different girls to put the vocals on. Initially, I went to DeLane Lea, but they were booked, so I had to go elsewhere. I nearly screwed it all up because my master tape was one-inch four-track [most London studios used half-inch four-track tape] and it took sessions at three different studios to complete." Chandler finally added backing vocals by the Breakaways, and "Hey Joe" was complete.

TUESDAY, OCTOBER 25, 1966

SCOTCH OF ST. JAMES, LONDON, ENGLAND.
Chandler booked the Experience into this small but popular nightspot in his effort to introduce Hendrix and the Experience to London. A mix of industry personnel and musicians packed in to see Chandler's new protégé. "That was a small place but we were trying to impress booking agents like Harold Davison and Dick Katz," recalls tour manager Gerry Stickells. A contingent of music journalists also squeezed into the tiny venue, eager for a glimpse of this exciting new artist. "Jimi Hendrix seemed to burst on the scene in

London very quickly," remembers *Melody Maker* journalist Chris Welch. "I think that was mainly due to the efforts of Chas Chandler networking and knowing all the journalists like myself, Keith Altham at *New Musical Express*, and Richard Green at *Record Mirror*. The only way that underground music, as we then called it, would get exposure, was through the weekly music newspapers. BBC Radio was very important, as were pirate radio stations such as Radio Caroline and Radio London, but people bought the four or five weekly music papers every week." Welch attributes Hendrix's quick success to Chandler's knowledge of the London scene and his ability to keep things together, which he had developed as a member of the Animals. "In fact, I remember meeting him in the Marquee Club, where everybody went every week to see an amazing array of new groups. Whereas Chas had been sloughing around in all jeans just a few weeks before, he turned up carrying a briefcase and wearing a suit. So, I knew he was a manager now!"

WEDNESDAY, NOVEMBER 2, 1966

DELANE LEA STUDIOS, LONDON, ENGLAND. 6:00 P.M. TO 12:00 A.M. PRODUCER: CHAS CHANDLER. ENGINEER: DAVE SIDDLE.
With "Hey Joe" completed to his satisfaction, Chandler's next task was to produce a B-side. Apart from the handful of cover tunes the group had rehearsed to establish their repertoire, Hendrix had no other original material prepared. "When we discussed what was going to be on the B-side, Jimi said that he could record a version of 'Land Of 1000 Dances,'" remembers Chandler. "I said absolutely no way. If anyone was going to make publishing money, it was going to be him. I told him that he was going to sit down that night and write a new song. That's how 'Stone Free' came about, the first Experience song he ever wrote."

With little money available for experimentation, recording "Stone Free" was decidedly less complicated than "Hey Joe." "'Stone Free' was recorded and mixed in one day," explains Chandler with pride. "I couldn't afford to have the band learn the song in the studio, so I booked a rehearsal at the Averbach House beforehand. Prior to that, we had rehearsed in nightclubs. A

good mate of mine owned a string of clubs in London and the Animals used to be pretty big spenders in them, so he would let me bring the band into them when I needed to."

In addition to governing Hendrix's contributions with a firm hand, Chandler was especially helpful to Redding, providing useful insights about the bass guitar. "Chas would come out into the studio to show me various bass techniques," recalls Redding. "The bass was still new to me, and I was taking in everything I could. Chas told me about little things like different scales and what was classified as a 'walking bass' line, which were simple but very effective."

To create the master, Chandler essentially recorded the group live in the studio, paced by Hendrix's contagious rhythm guitar. "It only took us an hour to cut the track," says Chandler. Overdubs were simple, specifically Mitchell's inventive percussion, harmony vocals from Hendrix, and additional guitar. In addition to "Stone Free," the group also recorded a rough demo of "Can You See Me." Chandler prepared a final mix of "Stone Free" the session concluded, and

Hendrix and Chandler also made a reel-to-reel tape copy of the "Can You See Me" demo recording for further review.

With his master tape in hand, Chandler ventured out to secure a recording contract for Hendrix. "There was no point in me going out marketing myself as an ex-Animal—at least not in my mind," explains Chandler. "That was virtually confirmed when I couldn't even get EMI Records to *listen* to the finished master of 'Hey Joe.' Here I was, an EMI artist still signed to the label as a member of the Animals and I couldn't even get into the A&R Department to play the bloody record. Nobody would even see me. Over at Decca Records, Dick Rowe was just as bad. He looked at me as if I was completely out of my mind."

A chance meeting with Kit Lambert, who co-managed The Who along with Chris Stamp and owned Track Records, resulted in Hendrix joining his label. "I did the deal with Kit Lambert at the Scotch of St. James nightclub," recalls Chandler. "The VIPs were playing that night, and being friends of mine I brought Hendrix down to jam with them. Kit was there and he nearly knocked over the tables trying to get across from me. He was such an outrageous guy. We wrote the deal out on a beer mat at the Scotch."

With a recording contract secured, Hendrix worked closely with Chandler at the flat they shared. Playing his Stratocaster through a small Vox amplifier, Hendrix began to develop the riffs and rhythm patterns for songs such as "Can You See Me" and "Remember." Living with Chandler also began to have a pronounced influence on Hendrix's lyrics and poetry, as Hendrix was soon exposed to Chandler's penchant for science fiction. "I had dozens of science fiction books at home," says Chandler. "The first one Jimi read was *Earth Abides*. It wasn't a Flash Gordon type, it's an end-of-the-world, new-beginning, disaster-type story. He started reading through them all. That's where 'Third Stone From The Sun' and 'Up From The Skies' came from."

TUESDAY, NOVEMBER 8, 1966

BIG APPLE CLUB, MUNICH, GERMANY. TWO SHOWS.

WEDNESDAY, NOVEMBER 9, 1966

BIG APPLE CLUB, MUNICH, GERMANY. TWO SHOWS.

THURSDAY, NOVEMBER 10, 1966

BIG APPLE CLUB, MUNICH, GERMANY. TWO SHOWS.

FRIDAY, NOVEMBER 11, 1966

BIG APPLE CLUB, MUNICH, GERMANY. TWO SHOWS.
Chandler secured an extended engagement for the group in Munich where they could hone their stage repertoire away from the curiosity and excitement that was building for them in the London club scene. Gerry Stickells, a friend of Noel's, was recruited to serve as the fledgling group's road manager. "We rehearsed the band at Saville Row in London," remembers Stickells. "Then we went to the Big Apple Club in Munich to tighten the band up. We went there to play two shows a night to work the band in. The crowd reaction was good but it was kind of like, 'What the hell is this?'"

FRIDAY, NOVEMBER 25, 1966

BAG O' NAILS, LONDON, ENGLAND.

SATURDAY, NOVEMBER 26, 1966

RICKY TICK, HOUNSLOW, MIDDLESEX, ENGLAND. WITH ERIC BURDON AND THE NEW ANIMALS.

SATURDAY, DECEMBER 10, 1966

THE RAM JAM CLUB, LONDON, ENGLAND. WITH JOHN MAYALL'S BLUESBREAKERS.
Intimate club dates such as these continued to spread the word about Jimi Hendrix throughout London. Chandler was keen to expose Hendrix to the music press in the U.K. and welcomed the attention paid to the guitarist by members of the London rock elite. "We did this press reception gig [at the Bag O' Nails]," remembers Noel Redding. "In those days you only played thirty-five or forty minutes. I remember being in the dressing room afterwards and John Lennon walked in. 'Hello there!' he says and I nearly fainted. Then McCartney walked in and then Donovan walked in. I was nearly on the floor then!"

TUESDAY, DECEMBER 13, 1966

CBS STUDIOS, LONDON, ENGLAND. 4:00 P.M. TO 7:00 P.M. PRODUCER: CHAS CHANDLER. ENGINEER: MIKE ROSS.
Unhappy with DeLane Lea and wanting to upgrade their sound quality without squandering their budget, Chandler took Kit Lambert's advice and booked time at CBS Studios on New Bond Street. Lambert had produced some sessions for The Who there, and later recorded "I Can See For Miles" at the facility as well. Located in a former ballroom, CBS Studios had originally housed Oriole Records and Levy Sound Studios. Brothers Jake and Morris Levy owned the studio and produced, recorded, and pressed records by a number of small British pop acts. In 1965, however, CBS Records purchased the entire operation. Not particularly interested in either the studio or the artists under contract to Oriole, CBS instead wanted Oriole's modern, efficient pressing plant to help them establish a

distribution arm in the U.K. After purchasing the studio in 1965, CBS installed a new Studer four-track machine and upgraded the studio's technical capabilities.

Despite the investment made by CBS, the studio's spartan staff consisted of just one technician, recording engineer Mike Ross. Before moving to Levy Sound, Ross had started his career at London's Olympic Studios in 1962. "I was the only engineer at CBS Studios," remembers Ross with a laugh. "I used to open up the studio, take the bookings, and act as my own tape operator. It was just me. I had to do everything."

An injunction won by another tenant within the building limited the studio to mixing during the day, and full recording after four p.m., so that the noise level would not distract the offices below.

"Foxey Lady," one of Hendrix's most provocative songs, was the primary focus of the evening's session. "Mitch arrived well before everyone else and was setting up his drum kit," remembers Ross. "In those days, miking techniques for drums was not that advanced. You would put a microphone on the bass drum and a microphone on top above the kit. As I was setting up, Mitch pulled me aside and informed me that he had done some sessions at Landsdowne Studios recently where he had been able to persuade the engineer to mike all of the tom-toms individually. He said they had achieved a great sound, and asked if I would be interested in trying it here. I had never done it, but I gave it a go. In fact, that session was the first time I had ever used more than two microphones to record drums."

When Hendrix, Redding, and Chandler arrived, Ross was taken aback by the sight of Hendrix's amplifiers. "Jimi came in with four Marshall cabinets, which I couldn't believe," admits Ross. "How was I to mike this? Jimi told me to stick a microphone eight feet away from the cabinets and it would sound great. He actually showed me where to place the microphone, and I put a U-87 valve mike where he had instructed me to." After Ross had set up the microphones and established the desired sounds, Chandler was eager to begin. The group rehearsed each song a number of times before cutting basic tracks. "Jimi didn't record a live vocal," recalls Ross. "I recorded Jimi's lead vocal as an overdub, as well as backing vocals from Mitch, Noel, and Jimi. Jimi also recorded a second guitar as an overdub."

"Chandler was very much in charge," recalls Ross. "Jimi was very shy and quiet and didn't have much to say. He seemed very much in awe of Chandler. What Chas said was law. There was another aspect that was very odd. I was used to the band being a team and having some input. My immediate reaction during the Hendrix session was, 'These two [other] guys are being treated like shit.' It was very much like, 'Play, and do what you are told.' Chandler was very much in command of what was going on. He obviously had a sound in his head and knew what he wanted to hear from Jimi. A lot of producers tend to sit in the control room and produce the engineer. They very rarely go out on to the floor to do anything musical. Chas was a good producer, he would actually go out on the floor and direct. He would work individually with Jimi and Noel and show Mitch what to play and what drums to hit. Most of my communication was directly with Chas."

In addition to securing a basic instrumental track for "Foxey Lady," the group also recorded versions of "Can You See Me," "Love or Confusion," and "Third Stone From The Sun." "We recorded a lot of takes of each song," remembers Ross. "We went through quite a lot of tape. Chas was keen to keep everything because he felt he could always edit the good bits together."

THURSDAY, DECEMBER 15, 1966

CBS STUDIOS, LONDON, ENGLAND. PRODUCER: CHAS CHANDLER. ENGINEER: MIKE ROSS.

According to Redding's diary, Mitchell did not show for this session. In his absence, a rehearsal was staged, with Hendrix and Redding recording two unnamed instrumental demos. The group also completed rough mixes of "Foxey Lady," "Can You See Me" and "Third Stone From The Sun."

Chandler, according to Ross, praised the studio highly, citing its clear advantage in sound quality over DeLane Lea. Despite his enthusiasm for the facility, the Experience never recorded there again after a bitter squabble between Chandler and Jake Levy. "At that time, I don't think Chandler had the money to pay the studio," explains Ross. "When it came to the second day, he still hadn't paid any money. Jake came over to Chas and said, 'Look, if you want to book any more time, you've got to pay for what you have used up to now.' Chas clearly wanted to book more time, but he said, 'I can't, because we are making an album. As soon as the album is finished, you will be paid.' Jake, however, was very mistrustful of people and he told them that while he was sorry, they would not be able to record unless their bill was paid in full. Chandler got quite upset, telling Jake that this was not the way he had done business in the past, this was not how he conducted business with DeLane Lea, and that *he* was sorry, as he would never work in this studio again. It ended on a sour note, which was a shame, as I was enjoying the sessions."

Furious, Chandler left the studio and vowed never to return. One major problem remained, however. "Because Chas had been unable to pay the studio bill, Jake would not release the tapes they had recorded," remembers Ross. "Sometime after, Chas had booked time at DeLane Lea and wanted to record some overdubs on those songs. He fought very hard to get the tapes, but Levy wouldn't release them. In the end, he did finally pay the bill, because he was desperate to get the tapes. . . . When Chas arrived, he told me he was sorry that he would not be able to continue recording at CBS, as he considered Jake's attitude intolerable. I gave him the tapes, we shook hands, and that was the last I ever saw of him."

FRIDAY, DECEMBER 16, 1966

"HEY JOE" / "STONE FREE." POLYDOR 56139. U.K. SINGLE RELEASE.
Track Records was not quite ready to begin full-scale operations—its owners Kit Lambert and Chris Stamp jumped at the chance to land Hendrix even before the startup label was fully on its feet—so Polydor Records, their distributor, issued "Hey Joe" instead. Buoyed by an appearance on the penultimate episode of *Ready Steady Go!*, the single entered the U.K. singles chart on January 5, 1967, and, after a long, steady climb, eventually peaked at number 6.

CHISLEHURST CAVES, BROMLEY, KENT, ENGLAND.
Electronics enthusiast Roger Mayer, who had witnessed Hendrix's recent Bag O' Nails performance,

had befriended the guitarist after the concert. "I was floored," recalls Mayer. "It was like everything I ever imagined. I just went up to him and started talking, telling him what I did. I had been into electronics since 1963 and was totally into avant-garde sounds." Hendrix asked the electronics expert to come down to his performance at Chislehurst Caves. So Mayer went and brought some of his devices, including the Octavia, which boosted a guitar's octaves to various levels. "He tried them out backstage and was thrilled," says Mayer. Mayer continued his friendship with Hendrix and the guitarist utilized creations like the Octavia throughout his career, most notably on "Purple Haze."

WEDNESDAY, DECEMBER 21, 1966

DELANE LEA STUDIOS, LONDON, ENGLAND. PRODUCER: CHAS CHANDLER. ENGINEER: DAVE SIDDLE.
Despite the blowup over finances at CBS Studios, Chandler booked a session at DeLane Lea so that Hendrix could continue recording new material.

One of the more notable recordings from this three-hour session was an alternate version of "Red House," with Hendrix sticking close to the arrangement featured on the December 13, 1966, CBS Studios recording. Each of the takes were cut live in the studio, with Hendrix's lead vocal driving the dark, moody rhythm section. Early takes clearly revealed the song's vast potential, but missed notes plagued both Hendrix and Redding, rendering each of the takes unusable. Before another attempt, Hendrix can be heard on the tape saying, "Oh Lord, see, one little thing throws me off," with a laugh to Chandler in the control room. Someone suggests that more of the studio's lights be turned off, which warrants an immediate response from Hendrix. "Oh yeah, those lights! That's what it was. Oh Lord!" When Hendrix hears that no more lights can be extinguished because of fire laws, he laughs, remarking, "In other words, we're making all this smoke in here. In other words, we're cooking. Is that what you're trying to say?" Chas and Hendrix share a laugh before Redding counts off the intro. This basic track later served as the final master.

Both the CBS Studios version of "Red House" and the DeLane Lea/Olympic version were released later. The earlier recording from CBS Studios was the one released on the May 1967 Track Records album *Are You Experienced*. The group also finished the DeLane Lea rendition of "Red House" at Olympic Studios in early April 1967. It was later added to the popular Reprise Records compilation *Smash Hits*, first released in 1969. "'The [*Smash Hits*] Red House' was definitely done at DeLane Lea, not CBS," says Chandler. "The 'Red House' on the album [*Are You Experienced*] came about during the last fifteen minutes of another session. Noel even played rhythm guitar on the track, playing the bass line. Jimi just winged through one take for reference and we started rolling. Later when we were scrambling to put the album together, we carted that out and gave it a listen. We remixed it at Olympic and added it to the album."

Work on "Remember" also began at DeLane Lea. Like "Red House," it, too, was later revamped at Olympic in April 1967 before it was added to *Are You Experienced*, and later, *Smash Hits*. "'Remember' was an end-of-the-session demo first recorded at DeLane Lea," explains Chandler. "We made a ¼-inch, 7 ½ i.p.s. [inches per second] reel to listen and work on the song at home. This was something we did often. The DeLane Lea recording was much too raggedy. Jimi tightened it up later at Olympic Studios before it became part of the album. In fact, I don't think we kept much of anything on the final record from that original DeLane Lea recording."

WEDNESDAY, DECEMBER 21, 1966

BLAISES, LONDON, ENGLAND.

THURSDAY, DECEMBER 22, 1966

GUILDHALL, SOUTHAMPTON, HAMPSHIRE, ENGLAND. WITH GENO WASHINGTON & THE RAM JAM BAND.

MONDAY, DECEMBER 26, 1966

THE UPPER CUT, LONDON, ENGLAND.

By the close of December, "Hey Joe" had begun to gain traction in the marketplace and the Experience gained confidence and momentum with each performance. "It was a very exciting time to be in London in 1966," remembers *Melody Maker* journalist Chris Welch, "because not only were there lots of venues for bands to play in, there also were what we call the "in clubs," which were nightclubs where people went after hours to drink and chat. The industry sort of met in these clubs and they all featured bands as well. One of the hippest was called Blaises, which I believe was actually an Italian gambling club. . . . We were heading for the back room where the rock-and-roll action was happening. The room was full of people there to see this amazing guitar player. Eric Clapton, Keith Moon, Mick Jagger, the room was filled! Jimi just wandered on, started tuning up, and then went into the act. He stunned everybody by playing the guitar with his teeth. I think that caused quite a sensation. This was just the first number!"

THURSDAY, DECEMBER 29, 1966

TOP OF THE POPS, BBC TV, LIME GROVE STUDIOS, LONDON, ENGLAND. **SET LIST:** "HEY JOE"
Like *Ready Steady Go!*, a *Top of the Pops* appearance represented a significant promotional opportunity for the Experience. In keeping with British music union regulations, Hendrix sang the song live while Mitchell and Redding mimed to a backing track of "Hey Joe." Unfortunately, the BBC has lost this clip, and all that remains is an amateur audio recording made off air.

SATURDAY, DECEMBER 31, 1966

HILLSIDE SOCIAL CLUB, FOLKESTONE, KENT, ENGLAND. WITH THE EXPERIENCE.
Lacking a worthwhile gig for New Year's Eve 1966, bassist Noel Redding arranged for the group to perform at the Hillside Social Club in Folkestone, his hometown. After the gig, the group visited the home of Redding's mother, Margaret. Frigid from the bitter English cold, Hendrix politely asked Margaret to "Let me stand next to your fire . . ."

1967

"Hendrix said rather darkly under his breath, 'Maybe I can smash up an elephant.' I said, 'Well it's a pity you can't set fire to your guitar.'"
—KEITH ALTHAM

WEDNESDAY, JANUARY 4, 1967

BROMEL CLUB, BROMLEY COURT HOTEL, BROMLEY, KENT, ENGLAND.

SATURDAY, JANUARY 7, 1967

NEW CENTURY HALL, MANCHESTER, LANCASHIRE, ENGLAND. WITH THE SILVERTONE SET.

SUNDAY, JANUARY 8, 1967

TOLLBAR, MOJO A GO-GO, SHEFFIELD, YORKSHIRE, ENGLAND.

WEDNESDAY, JANUARY 11, 1967

DELANE LEA STUDIOS, LONDON. PRODUCER: CHAS CHANDLER. ENGINEER: DAVE SIDDLE.

With "Hey Joe" climbing the U.K. singles charts, Jimi Hendrix's early success increasingly justified the grand experiment Chandler had taken on by bringing Hendrix to the U.K.. This became even more apparent when Chandler escorted the group back to DeLane Lea Studios to record the single "Purple Haze," Hendrix's superb sophomore effort.

While Hendrix later spoke of composing pages and pages of lyrics for the song, it was the striking riff that immediately captured Chandler's attention. "'Purple Haze' was written backstage at the Upper Cut Club on Boxing Day [December 26, 1966], the nightclub owned by the British boxer Billy Walker," Chandler explains. "But the riff had come to him about ten days before. I heard him playing it at the flat and was knocked out. I told him to keep working on that, saying, 'That's the next single!' That afternoon at the Upper Cut, he started playing the riff in the dressing room. I said, 'Write the rest of that!' so he did."

In the days before the session, Chandler worked closely with Hendrix to refine his lyrics for the song, as he often did. Chandler had a clear aim: he wanted "Purple Haze" to serve as the follow-up single to "Hey Joe." In order to achieve this goal, Hendrix needed to pare his lyrics down to fit a more conventional pop structure.

"Purple Haze" was the group's most complex studio effort to date. "'Purple Haze' took four hours to record, which, at that time, represented a *long* time in the studio," says Chandler. "Recording 'Hey Joe' had been very conventional, but with 'Purple Haze,' we began experimenting with different sounds and effects. With 'Hey Joe,' I didn't know how to run the place. I was just a dumb bass player trying to become a producer."

Hendrix had also developed the song "51st Anniversary" at the Montagu Square flat he shared with Chandler. "We worked on that over the course of one evening," remembers Chandler. "That song is a good example of Jimi just sitting around the apartment singing and playing his guitar. I would sit across from him and say, 'That's good,' or 'No, change that to something like this.' These were pre-studio edits, if you like. Then we would get together with the band and rehearse the song. We were still rehearsing quite a bit then because we were still trying to refine the act. As it was, we didn't have that many numbers to play, and we were always trying to push new songs in all the time."

Where "Purple Haze" had been the subject of some modest studio experimentation, "51st Anniversary" was the first Experience song to feature overdubbing, rather than retakes, as a recording strategy. "We rehearsed the song with the band, then went into the studio to record," says Chandler. "That was the first song where guitar overdubs played an important role. There was quite a bit of overdubbing on that track, and it was the first time where we consciously thought of approaching the production that way. There were five guitar overdubs all linking in together [picking up where one left off] to sound like one guitar."

"Third Stone From The Sun" was also attempted, with Chandler opting to abandon the December 13, 1966, demo made at CBS Studios in favor of a new version. The group focused on recording the song's basic track, and made multiple attempts to capture a finished master. Though Hendrix had already designed the song's arrangement, the group was unable to complete a master that met their standards.

Compared to the modest experimentation introduced on "Purple Haze" and the multiple overdubs completed for "51st Anniversary," "Fire" was relatively easy for the group to record. The group performed seven takes of the song's basic track live in the studio, experimenting with the tempo early on before settling into the desired groove.

With a basic track for "Fire" in hand, Hendrix turned his attention to "The Wind Cries Mary," a beautiful new ballad. "'The Wind Cries Mary' was written right after Jimi had had a big row with Kathy [Etchingham, his girlfriend]," explains Chandler. "That was recorded at the tail end of the session for 'Fire.' We had about twenty minutes or so left. I suggested that we cut a demo of 'The Wind Cries Mary.' Mitch and Noel hadn't heard it, so they were going at it without a rehearsal. They played it through once and I remember saying that I really liked the feel of the song. Jimi came in and said, 'I have a good idea for an overdub.' So he went back in and played 'between,' as he called it, the notes he had already recorded. He didn't even come back into the control room after he had put the second guitar on. He said, 'I have another idea. Can I put it on?' I said, 'Yeah!' In all he put on four or five more overdubs, but the whole thing was done in twenty minutes. That was our third single."

With his confidence bolstered by the group's recent success, Chandler found himself slowly, but nonetheless increasingly, at odds with Mitchell and Redding, who both began to push for more input on the sound and shape of the recordings. Chandler, however, did not share their view. "By the time of 'The Wind Cries Mary,' Mitchell and Redding were sort of fighting the fact that they had no say during recording sessions," remembers Chandler. "They were starting to come up with suggestions, but Jimi and I had already done as much work as we could *before* we got together with them and went into the studio. Up to that point, the most studio time I had booked had been four hours for 'Purple Haze.' Even then I had to scrape money together to finish it off at Olympic." Finances, reasoned Chandler, dictated not only the length of sessions, but also ultimately determined what role Redding and Mitchell would have in the final shape of the songs. "Sessions were always scheduled one day at a time," explains Chandler. "I can't remember spending two days on one song. We would scrape enough money together and book time in DeLane Lea to record. If DeLane Lea wasn't available, as it hadn't been when I was doing vocal overdubs for 'Hey Joe,'

we just went somewhere else. On those early overdub sessions that we did, we just didn't bring Mitch and Noel in. It wasn't anything against them; it was just pragmatism. There was no point in bringing in anyone else if they weren't going to be doing anything. They would have just been in the way. We didn't say it as such, but we knew that's how it was. Jimi would play me an idea for an overdub and if I thought it worked, it was, 'Let's go get this bloody thing done.' We didn't need to be arguing with Noel for ten minutes and Mitch for five. We *knew* what we wanted to do. We just couldn't afford the time."

WEDNESDAY, JANUARY 11, 1967

BAG O' NAILS, LONDON, ENGLAND.
Intimate club dates such as this immediately spread the word throughout London that Jimi Hendrix was a star of the first magnitude. Chandler was keen to expose Hendrix to the music press in the U.K. and welcomed the attention paid to Hendrix by members of the London rock elite.

THURSDAY, JANUARY 12, 1967

7 $\frac{1}{2}$ CLUB, LONDON, ENGLAND.

FRIDAY, JANUARY 13, 1967

7 $\frac{1}{2}$ CLUB, LONDON, ENGLAND.

SATURDAY, JANUARY 14, 1967

BEACHCOMBER CLUB, NOTTINGHAM, NOTTINGHAMSHIRE, ENGLAND. WITH JIMMY CLIFF AND THE SHAKEDOWN SQUAD.

SUNDAY, JANUARY 15, 1967

THE COUNTRY CLUB, KIRKLEVINGTON, YORKSHIRE, ENGLAND.

MONDAY, JANUARY 16, 1967

7 $\frac{1}{2}$ CLUB, LONDON, ENGLAND.

TUESDAY, JANUARY 17, 1967

7 1/2 CLUB, LONDON, ENGLAND.

WEDNESDAY, JANUARY 18, 1967

TOP OF THE POPS, BBC TV, LIME GROVE STUDIOS, LONDON, ENGLAND.
Chandler secured an appearance on *Top of the Pops* for the Experience to promote their new single "Hey Joe." In keeping with the British Musicians' Union regulations, Jimi sang "Hey Joe" over an instrumental backing track.

7 1/2 CLUB, LONDON, ENGLAND.
Later that evening, the group performed at the 7 1/2 Club for the final night of their three-night engagement.

THURSDAY, JANUARY 19, 1967

SPEAKEASY, LONDON, ENGLAND.

FRIDAY, JANUARY 20, 1967

HAVERSTOCK HILL, COUNTRY CLUB, LONDON, ENGLAND.

SATURDAY, JANUARY 21, 1967

REFECTORY, LONDON, ENGLAND.

SUNDAY, JANUARY 22, 1967

ASTORIA, OLDHAM, LANCASHIRE, ENGLAND.

TUESDAY, JANUARY 24, 1967

MARQUEE CLUB, LONDON, ENGLAND. WITH SYN.

WEDNESDAY, JANUARY 25, 1967

THE ORFORD CELLAR, NORWICH, NORFOLK, ENG-LAND. WITH THE ORFORD DISCOTHEQUE SYSTEM.

FRIDAY, JANUARY 27, 1967

CHISLEHURST CAVES, BROMLEY, KENT, ENGLAND.

Dates beyond London like these in Yorkshire and Lancashire began to materialize for the group as "Hey Joe" gained traction among U.K. music enthusiasts. The Experience, together with their trusted road manager Gerry Stickells, formed a tight-knit team. "They drove themselves in Mitch's car and I drove the van," remembers Stickells. "At the very beginning there was only me, so I would set up the gear, break it down after the show, and we would drive back to London."

SATURDAY, JANUARY 28, 1967

THE UPPER CUT, LONDON, ENGLAND.

SUNDAY, JANUARY 29, 1967

SAVILLE THEATRE, LONDON, ENGLAND. WITH THE WHO, KOOBAS, AND THOUGHTS. **PARTIAL SET LIST:** "ROCK ME BABY" / "LIKE A ROLLING STONE" / "HEY JOE" / "WILD THING"
The Experience joined a powerhouse lineup featuring Track Records labelmates The Who at the Saville Theatre, the Shaftesbury Avenue venue owned by Beatles manager Brian Epstein. Both the afternoon sound check and gig were filmed in part, and excerpts were later edited together with additional footage shot two days later to create a promotional film for "Hey Joe."

TUESDAY, JANUARY 30, 1967

POP NORTH. BBC BROADCASTING HOUSE, LONDON, ENGLAND. **SET LIST:** "HEY JOE" / "ROCK ME BABY" / "FOXEY LADY"
It is believed that the Experience made a live appearance on the BBC radio program *Pop North* on this day. Sadly, none of the performances was archived or rebroadcast by the BBC.

WEDNESDAY, FEBRUARY 1, 1967

NEW CELLAR CLUB, SOUTH SHIELDS, COUNTY DURHAM, ENGLAND. WITH THE BOND.
"This venue had a revolving stage," remembers Stickells. "That was the first time we used a Marshall 200 amplifier and it blew up. We only had one Marshall 100

amplifier for the public address system and Jimi and Noel had to play through that. They were both singing *and* playing all through the same amp!"

THURSDAY, FEBRUARY 2, 1967

IMPERIAL HOTEL, DARLINGTON, COUNTY DURHAM, ENGLAND. WITH WEST COAST PROMOTION.

While Chandler and the group could track their own improvement with each new trip into the recording studio, they received convincing public confirmation of their hard work in late January 1967. "'Hey Joe' suddenly burst on the charts during the first week of January 1967 and continued to climb throughout the month," remembers Chandler. "Jimi and I were staying at my mother's house in Newcastle, as the band had been booked to play at the New Cellar Club in South Shields [February 1, 1967]. As we were sitting there talking, I decided to walk down [the street] to the phone, because my mother had not put one in yet, to ring London and see how things were going. 'Hey Joe' had leapt to number seven in the charts and I knew we were really on our way."

FRIDAY, FEBRUARY 3, 1967

OLYMPIC STUDIOS, LONDON, ENGLAND. 12:00 P.M. TO 5:00 P.M. OVERDUBS RECORDED 5:00 P.M. TO 7:00 P.M. PRODUCER: CHAS CHANDLER. ENGINEER: EDDIE KRAMER.

Unhappy with the sound quality of the recordings made during the group's most recent session at DeLane Lea on January 11, Chandler had also tired of the noise complaints filed by DeLane Lea's neighbors. "There was a bank above the studio," says Chandler, "and it was at the time when computers were just coming in. Every time we went in, we would play so loud that it would foul up the computers upstairs. As a result, we would always have trouble getting in there when we wanted."

The constant complaints and sound quality at De-Lane Lea provoked Chandler to act. Brian Jones and Bill Wyman of the Rolling Stones had lobbied both Hendrix and Chas to move to Olympic Studios, which was recognized as London's leading independent recording facility. With Hendrix cultivating a growing backlog of

new songs to record, Chandler's primary concern was costs. "We had been scratching money together to pay for sessions at DeLane Lea," Chas recalls. "With 'Hey Joe' a hit on the charts, I found myself dealing more with Polydor rather than Track. One day, I finally went storming into Polydor and had a row with them. I said, 'Look, we've got money piling up here. We are trying to put an album together and I want to go to Olympic Studios. They won't fucking accept me because I have no credit history. They wouldn't even let me in without payment in advance!' So Polydor rang them up, opened an account in my name, and guaranteed that the bills would be paid. For the first time, I wasn't worrying about how I was going to pay for sessions. Even though we now had carte blanche, we still recorded the same way, but at least we didn't have to worry about costs."

The move to Olympic, home to such top British acts as Traffic and the Rolling Stones, was a clear sign that the group's standing had measurably improved. At the studio, Chandler and the group were introduced to Eddie Kramer, one of the staff engineers. Studio manager Anna Menzies, who described the Experience as a "raggedy" group Chas Chandler would be bringing in, had assigned Kramer the group. Born in South Africa in 1942, Kramer had come to Olympic in 1966 from Regent Studios. Kramer's career began at London's Advision Studios in 1963. As a "tea boy," Kramer learned the basic principles of sound engineering, disc cutting, and film dubbing. In 1964, he moved to Pye Studios, recording the likes of Sammy Davis Jr. and the Kinks. Kramer's encouraging success at Pye led him to establish KPS Studios, his own two-track demo facility, in 1965. Through his work with such artists as Zoot Money and John Mayall, the reputation of both Kramer and KPS began to spread. Regent Sound bought out KPS in 1966 and enlisted Kramer to supervise the construction of their new four-track studio. Later, Kramer moved to Olympic, where his ability and reputation blossomed under the tutelage of Keith Grant and Glyn Johns.

From the group's very first session with Kramer at Olympic, the engineer changed the way they had previously recorded at other London studios, The pre-Olympic recordings featured Redding's bass and Mitchell's drums recorded in mono on two of the recording tape's four available tracks. Kramer's approach was to record Mitchell's drums in stereo on two tracks, reserving the two remaining tracks for bass and Hendrix's rhythm guitar. As fellow Olympic engineer George Chkiantz explains, such a procedure was uncommon. "Kramer adopted a strategy with Hendrix of getting the original live sound down on four tracks, which, at the time, other engineers, including me, thought was crazy."

Kramer and Chandler then took this tape to another four-track recorder, premixing the four tracks down to two in order to create an opening for two more tracks. These two tracks could then accommodate Hendrix's lead guitar, lead vocal, or any other overdub ideas.

Understanding Chandler's dislike of excessive retakes and Hendrix's penchant for perfection, Kramer's strategy accommodated both men, providing the security that the song's basic track had been recorded and premixed to their mutual satisfaction. With the foundation secured, Hendrix could focus his energies on recording the most effective lead vocal and lead guitar performance. "Hendrix was a lot happier," says Chkiantz. "He felt that the track was never lost, and that his stuff was always down on tape. He and Eddie could just sit there and listen."

The idea to approach Hendrix's music in such a fashion came partly as a result of Kramer's conversations with the guitarist. "Jimi had been exposed to eight-track recording in America," says Kramer. "He liked hearing the basic track across on four tracks. Hearing it this way, four-track recording did not seem like the step backward it really was."

For Chandler, one of his priorities was completing "Purple Haze" so that the group could release the track as their second single. They pulled out the existing January 11 master from DeLane Lea, and overdubbing began. (It is possible, given Chandler's recollections of the sessions for the song, that additional work took place on February fifth and possibly the sixth.) "With 'Purple Haze,' Hendrix and I were striving for a sound and just kept going back in, two hours at a time, trying to achieve it," explains Chandler. "It wasn't like we were in there for days on end. We recorded it and then Hendrix and I would be sitting at home saying, 'Let's try that.' Then we would go in for an hour or two. That's how it was in those days. However long it took to record that one specific idea, that's how long we would book. We kept going in and out."

The Olympic sessions for "Purple Haze" marked the emergence of Chandler, Hendrix, and Olympic engineer Eddie Kramer as a dynamic creative force within the studio control room. Chandler was intent on upgrading Hendrix's performance, so he had the lead guitar and lead vocal parts replaced with new takes. With the Octavia, a device designed by electronics specialist Roger Mayer that boosted the guitar's octaves to various levels, the sound of Hendrix's lead guitar changed dramatically. Kramer suggested an additional guitar effect to enhance the song's ending. "At the end of the song, the high-speed guitar you hear was actually an Octavia guitar overdub we recorded first at a slower speed, then played back on a higher speed," explains Kramer. "The panning at the end was done to accentuate the effect you hear."

RICKY TICK, HOUNSLOW, MIDDLESEX, ENGLAND.
Following the session at Olympic, the group drove to the Ricky Tick club for an evening performance.

TUESDAY, FEBRUARY 7, 1967

OLYMPIC STUDIOS, LONDON, ENGLAND. PRODUCER: CHAS CHANDLER. ENGINEER: EDDIE KRAMER.
Work resumed on "Purple Haze" with a four-to-four mix reduction made by Kramer to free up space on the multitrack master for new rhythm guitar and vocal parts by Hendrix. Other overdubs included the song's distinctive background vocals, supplied by Redding, as well as some exotic background ambience. Chandler explains, "A lot of the background sound on 'Purple Haze' is actually a recording being fed back into the studio through the headphones held around a microphone, moving them in and out to create a weird echo."

WEDNESDAY, FEBRUARY 8, 1967

OLYMPIC STUDIOS, LONDON, ENGLAND. PRODUCER: CHAS CHANDLER. ENGINEER: EDDIE KRAMER.
In "Purple Haze," Chandler was confident he had all

of the necessary ingredients for a timeless single at his disposal: a great song and terrific performances from each member. The song's inventive production supplied the final component. The group made multiple attempts to create the song's exotic atmosphere: the efforts included sound panning suggestions from Kramer for different backing vocal tracks by Hendrix and Redding. With these new overdubs completed, a final mix of "Purple Haze" was prepared for release before the session concluded.

The group also revisited the DeLane Lea four-track master tape of "Fire." Kramer prepared a four-to-four reduction mix in order to add new overdubs. Mitchell contributed a superb drum track, a signature effort that remains among the finest work of his tenure with Hendrix. As only Redding's original bass part now remained from the original DeLane Lea recording, he was instructed to double his bass part in order to give the song a deeper, more strident bottom end. Hendrix recorded two lead guitars double-tracked, with one patched into Roger Mayer's Octavia tone control pedal and playing higher up the fretboard than the other. After the basic track had also been upgraded to Chandler's satisfaction, Kramer prepared a further four-to-four-to-four reduction, blending Redding's original DeLane Lea bass track with Mitchell's drums, while keeping the new Olympic bass part on a separate track for effect. Hendrix put down his lead vocal, and as a finishing touch, Mitchell and Redding contributed the song's background vocals.

Hendrix also retooled "Foxey Lady" during this session. Chandler brought the existing multitrack tape he had begun at CBS Studios on December 13, 1966, to Olympic to do additional work. Redding's bass track was replaced, after which Kramer prepared a four-to-four reduction mix that combined the bass and drums to create an open track for Hendrix to replace one of his two guitar parts. Another four-to-four reduction mix created space for a bass drum overdub by Mitchell that doubled his original part. Lead vocals as well as backing vocals by Redding were completed before a final mix was prepared. A stage favorite throughout the course of Hendrix's career, "Foxey Lady" was set aside as the opening track for the U.K. version of *Are You Experienced,* the group's groundbreaking debut album.

THURSDAY, FEBRUARY 9, 1967

LOCARNO, BRISTOL, GLOUCESTERSHIRE, ENGLAND.

FRIDAY, FEBRUARY 10, 1967

PLAZA NEWBURY, BERKSHIRE, ENGLAND.

SATURDAY, FEBRUARY 11, 1967

BLUE MOON, CHELTENHAM, GLOUCESTERSHIRE, ENGLAND.

SUNDAY, FEBRUARY 12, 1967

SINKING SHIP CLUBLAND, STOCKPORT, CHESHIRE, ENGLAND.

MONDAY, FEBRUARY 13, 1967

SATURDAY CLUB, BBC STUDIOS, BROADCASTING HOUSE, PORTLAND PLACE, LONDON, ENGLAND. PRODUCER: BILL BEBB. **SET LIST:** "FOXEY LADY" (TWO TAKES) / "STONE FREE" / "HEY JOE" / "LOVE OR CONFUSION"

This appearance on the BBC radio program *Saturday Club* came in the middle of a series of U.K. club dates. Hendrix showcased each side of his debut single as well as "Foxey Lady" and "Love or Confusion," two bright new songs the group had recently recorded. Chandler and Hendrix were high on the prospects for "Love or Confusion": they considered the song as a possible single and may have intended its performance here as a preview of sorts.

The session took place in Studio 2, a small facility in Broadcasting House's sub-basement, three floors below street level. The volume the group preferred jolted BBC producer Bill Bebb. "We could hear Jimi through the soundproof glass," Bebb recalled in a 1998 interview. "We could see the glass moving."

The BBC broadcast all the songs but one of the two takes of "Foxey Lady" on February 18 along with a brief interview that DJ Brian Matthew conducted with Hendrix. All of these recordings would later be released as part of the 1998 *BBC Sessions* compilation.

MONDAY, FEBRUARY 20, 1967

DELANE LEA STUDIOS, LONDON, ENGLAND. PRODUCER: CHAS CHANDLER. ENGINEER: DAVE SIDDLE.

The group's crowded schedule, coupled with Olympic's popularity, forced Chandler to return to DeLane Lea so that progress on the Experience's as-yet-untitled debut album could continue. The album received a major boost on this evening, as work on "I Don't Live Today" began.

As in other sessions with Chandler, the group worked on crafting an acceptable basic track first. Once the arrangement and tempo had been settled, Hendrix's focus turned to refining his guitar parts. He used a hand wah-wah unit in this session, a sound device that many fans have come to identify as an important component of the Hendrix sound. While foot-controlled models soon replaced the hand wah-wah, Hendrix manipulated the hand unit with skill, incorporating the distinctive tones on to the master tape.

Before the session concluded, Chandler had a working master in hand. Further improvements, such as a new lead vocal from Hendrix, were later overdubbed at Olympic, where Hendrix, Chandler, and Eddie Kramer prepared a final mix of the track so that the song could become part of their upcoming debut, *Are You Experienced*.

THE PAVILION, BATH, SOMERSET, ENGLAND.
Following their session at De Lane Lea, the group drove out to their gig at the Pavilion.

WEDNESDAY, FEBRUARY 22, 1967

ROUNDHOUSE, LONDON, ENGLAND. WITH SOFT MACHINE, THE FLIES, HILARY & SANDY.
BBC Radio invited the Experience to perform "Hey Joe" on the live program *Parade of the Pops*. Regrettably, no recording is known to exist of this performance. Later that evening, the group performed at the popular London venue the Roundhouse.

THURSDAY, FEBRUARY 23, 1967

THE PAVILION, WORTHING, SUSSEX, ENGLAND.

FRIDAY, FEBRUARY 24, 1967

LEICESTER UNIVERSITY, LEICESTER, LEICESTERSHIRE, ENGLAND.

SATURDAY, FEBRUARY 25, 1967

SATURDAY SCENE, CORN EXCHANGE, CHELMSFORD, ESSEX, ENGLAND. WITH SOUL TRINITY. **PARTIAL SET LIST:** "STONE FREE" / "LIKE A ROLLING STONE"
A Dutch filmmaker helmed the earliest known film and sound recordings of the Experience in concert, filming "Stone Free" and "Like A Rolling Stone" before a packed audience at the Corn Exchange, an unlikely venue for a performance such as this. These two songs were later issued as part of the 2007 *Jimi Hendrix Experience: Live At Monterey* DVD.

SUNDAY, FEBRUARY 26, 1967

CLIFFS PAVILION, SOUTHEND-ON-SEA, ESSEX, ENGLAND. TWO SHOWS. WITH DAVE DEE, DOZY, BEAKY, MICK & TICH, THE NASHVILLE TEENS, KOOBAS, AND FORCE FIVE.

WEDNESDAY, MARCH 1, 1967

DELANE LEA STUDIOS, LONDON, ENGLAND . PRODUCER: CHAS CHANDLER. ENGINEER: DAVE SIDDLE.
While "Like A Rolling Stone" had become part of the Experience's stage repertoire, on this evening the group could not complete an effective studio rendition. According to Noel Redding's comprehensive diary, the group did rehearse on this day, and "Like A Rolling Stone" was likely among the songs they worked on. Despite this preparation, the Experience, much to Chandler's disappointment, were unable to realize a finished master. "I always wanted to do a studio version of 'Like A Rolling Stone,'" explains Chandler. "We did it a few times, but for some reason, Mitch could never keep the time right. It used to drive them nuts because Mitch would either be winding up or slowing down. The thing that bugged me about that one was that the first time I saw Hendrix at the Cafe Wha? in Greenwich Village, the first thing he did was 'Hey Joe'

and the second was 'Like A Rolling Stone,' and for the first time, hearing Jimi sing it, I understood what the lyrics were trying to say. I was a Dylan fan, but I started cooling on him at the time he wrote 'Like A Rolling Stone.' It was the first Dylan song I was struggling with. So we both wanted to record it but we were never successful. I tried over and over to get it."

"PURPLE HAZE" / "51ST ANNIVERSARY." TRACK RECORDS 604 001. SINGLE RELEASE.

With Track Records now in place, "Purple Haze" made an impressive chart showing, building on the success and momentum of "Hey Joe." "Purple Haze" entered the U.K. singles charts on Thursday, March 23, 1967, and rose to number 3, lasting a total of fourteen weeks.

THURSDAY, MARCH 2, 1967

BEAT CLUB. MARQUEE CLUB, LONDON, ENGLAND. **SET LIST:** "HEY JOE" / "PURPLE HAZE"

The Experience were filmed performing "Hey Joe" and "Purple Haze" at the Marquee Club for the German television program *Beat Club*.

TUESDAY, MARCH 7, 1967

TIENERKLANKEN, BELGIUM. **SET LIST:** "HEY JOE" / "STONE FREE"

The Experience made an appearance on the television program *Tienerklanken,* miming both sides of their recent single. Unlike British television performances that required Hendrix to sing live to a backing track, these appearances were poorly pantomimed, with Hendrix falling out of sync almost from the start.

SATURDAY, MARCH 18, 1967

STUDIO 1 NDR, HAMBURG, GERMANY. **SET LIST:** INTERVIEW WITH HENDRIX AND REDDING / "FOXEY LADY" / "HEY JOE" / "STONE FREE" / "FIRE" / "PURPLE HAZE" STAR-CLUB, HAMBURG, GERMANY. TWO SHOWS.

SUNDAY, MARCH 19, 1967

STAR-CLUB, HAMBURG, GERMANY. TWO SHOWS.

A weekend trip to Germany found the group performing March 18 on NDR, the national German radio broadcasting company. A breathless host interviewed Hendrix, as well as Redding, who spoke reasonably fluent German. Redding had picked up the language during previous trips to Germany with his former band the Loving Kind.

After the radio program, the group staged four performances—two each evening—at the Star Club, the notorious German music hall made famous by the residency the Beatles enjoyed there in 1962.

THURSDAY, MARCH 23, 1967

GUILD HALL, SOUTHAMPTON, HAMPSHIRE, ENGLAND.

SATURDAY, MARCH 25, 1967

STARLIGHT ROOM, GLIDERDROME, BOSTON, LINCOLNSHIRE, ENGLAND. WITH THE STEEL BAND, SONS & LOVERS, CHARADES, AND RAY BONES.

SUNDAY, MARCH 26, 1967

TABERNACLE CLUB, STOCKPORT, CHESHIRE, ENGLAND.

MONDAY, MARCH 27, 1967

DEE TIME, BBC STUDIOS, MANCHESTER, ENGLAND. **SET LIST:** "PURPLE HAZE"

The Experience taped a performance of "Purple Haze" on the television program *Dee Time*. The program was later broadcast on April 4. No copies of the broadcast are known to exist.

TUESDAY, MARCH 28, 1967

SATURDAY CLUB, BBC STUDIOS, BROADCASTING HOUSE, PORTLAND PLACE, LONDON, ENGLAND. PRODUCER: BILL BEBB. **SET LIST:** "KILLING FLOOR" / "FIRE" / "PURPLE HAZE"

The Experience made a return appearance on the BBC radio program *Saturday Club*. The group played "Purple Haze" to promote the recently released single and provided radio listeners with their first glimpse of "Fire," a song Hendrix had recorded but not yet released on disc. The group also recorded a version of Howlin' Wolf's recent single "Killing Floor."

This program was broadcast on April 1. Each of these recordings would later be included as part of *BBC Sessions*.

TUESDAY, MARCH 28, 1967

ASSEMBLY HALL, AYLESBURY, BUCKINGHAMSHIRE, ENGLAND.

WEDNESDAY, MARCH 29, 1967

DELANE LEA STUDIOS, LONDON, ENGLAND. PRODUCER: CHAS CHANDLER. ENGINEER: DAVE SIDDLE.
Unable to reserve time at Olympic Studios, Chandler and the Experience returned to DeLane Lea. The focus of this evening's session was "Manic Depression," another superb new Hendrix original. According to Chandler, Hendrix developed the song's distinctive riff quickly. The challenge was to unify the song's intricate rhythm pattern, as Mitch Mitchell's revolving drum part buttressed Hendrix's driving guitar. Mitchell's performance on the song represented his finest studio effort to date, with his fondness for such jazz legends as Elvin Jones clearly apparent.

In between takes of "Manic Depression" the group ran through a loose, instrumental sketch of the 1966 French pop hit by singer/songwriter Michel Ponareff.

While Chandler prepared a rough mix of "Manic Depression" before concluding this session, the effort was later rejected. Chandler, Hendrix, and engineer Eddie Kramer later created a final mix at Olympic Studios during the first week of April 1967.

THURSDAY, MARCH 30, 1967

BBC TV, LIME GROVE STUDIOS, LONDON, ENGLAND.
SET LIST: "PURPLE HAZE" (TWO TAKES)
The Experience continued their promotional efforts on behalf of "Purple Haze" with an appearance on the BBC television program *Top of the Pops*. In keeping with British Musicians' Union regulations, Hendrix sang a live vocal over a prerecorded backing track.

FRIDAY, MARCH 31, 1967

THE ASTORIA, LONDON, ENGLAND. TWO SHOWS.
Chandler had shrewdly agreed to have the Experience be featured as a support act on a package tour across Britain as part of a bill featuring teen idols the Walker Brothers, Cat Stevens, and Engelbert Humperdinck, among others. The tour would feature the group performing two forty- or forty-five-minute sets per engagement and would extend until April 30. Chandler knew that a broader audience was critical to Hendrix's fortunes and felt confident that the Experience would win over the country's teenagers and rock aficionados alike.

The tour opened at London's Astoria Theater and Chandler was determined to try and elevate Hendrix from this grouping of teen idols. "I was sitting backstage in the dressing room with Chas," remembers Keith Altham. "He said, 'Keith, you're a journalist, how can we steal all the headlines this week?' I said, 'You've got to do something dramatic, Chas.' I said, 'You can't smash things up because The Who were doing that.' Hendrix said rather darkly under his breath, 'Maybe I can smash up an elephant.' I said, 'Well, it's a pity you can't set fire to your guitar.' There was a pause sort of about thirty seconds and Chas looked at Gerry Stickells and said, 'Gerry, go out and buy some lighter fuel.'" No one outside the group heard about Hendrix's plan.

At the end of Hendrix's dynamic forty-five minute set, he laid his guitar on the stage floor, doused it with lighter fluid, and set it ablaze. The Astoria crowd completely erupted. "It was a strange situation because it took him a little while to get it alight," recalls Altham. "He was having to dodge behind the amplifiers on the stage with a box of matches and it wasn't going up. Eventually, he did get it going and it sort of took off quite spectacularly. The security guy in the wings was going bananas and trying to rush onstage with a fire extinguisher. Eventually, he did and managed to spray the compere [emcee], who was not too amused. When we came back to the dressing room afterwards all hell broke loose. The security guy said, 'You'll never work in this circuit again! He'll never play again at any of these theaters. How dare he do something like that? He

could have burned the place down. What did he mean by swinging it around his head?' Jimi said, 'Well, I was trying to put it out.'"

London's Fleet Street tabloids had a field day, and the frenzy earned Hendrix such labels as "The Black Elvis" and the "Wild Man of Borneo."

SATURDAY, APRIL 1, 1967

GAUMONT, ST. HELEN STREET, IPSWICH, SUFFOLK, ENGLAND. TWO SHOWS. **PARTIAL SET LIST:** "PURPLE HAZE" / "WILD THING"

SUNDAY, APRIL 2, 1967

GAUMONT, WORCESTER, WORCESTERSHIRE, ENGLAND. TWO SHOWS.

MONDAY, APRIL 3, 1967

OLYMPIC STUDIOS, LONDON, ENGLAND. PRODUCER: CHAS CHANDLER. ENGINEER: EDDIE KRAMER. SECOND ENGINEER: LAURIE (SURNAME UNKNOWN).

Returning to Olympic, the group made significant headway toward completing their debut album. The group recorded a handful of new songs, added overdubs to some unfinished masters, and created final mixes.

Working quickly and confidently, Hendrix began this long and productive session with "Highway Chile," and the group's eighth and final take secured the basic track.

The group did not add overdubs to "Highway Chile" here: instead, Hendrix initiated work on "Waterfall" (as the song was initially marked on the tape box), another of his impressive new compositions. Kramer interrupted the third take and asked the band to restart, requesting a cleaner opening. Mitch objected, citing the ability to fade the track in, but Chandler overruled, and the group's fourth attempt resulted in the master take for this gorgeous ballad. Kramer prepared a four-to-four reduction mix and the song's title became "May This Be Love," as it is now known. Hendrix then recorded two lead vocal overdubs as well as a lead guitar part. "For the solo, Jimi managed to create an effect which sounded backward," recalls Kramer. "This multiple imaging was enhanced during the mixing process by simultaneously panning the rhythm and lead guitar."

As detailed as some of this work was, sometimes mistakes were left in because they added an intangible quality to the overall master. A close listen will reveal the sound of Hendrix turning over his lyric sheet while he records his lead vocal.

Little is known about "Title #3," the next song recorded by the group. A single take was all that the group needed to capture a lively basic track. Pleased with their effort, Hendrix next focused his attention on recording "Title #4," better known as "Are You Experienced?" The complexities involved with the recording of that track seem to have precluded any further work for "Title #3."

The breathtaking "Are You Experienced?" was built start to finish during this session. Eddie Kramer recalls the song's construction. "The structure of the song was recorded first, with Jimi's rhythm guitar, Mitch's drums, and Noel's bass recorded forward." Hendrix's initial take, a loose but often spectacular effort, began with the guitarist strumming the song's distinctive introduction. This part, Kramer says, came from Hendrix's penchant for discovering new sounds. "Jimi had practiced that riff at home, so he knew what it would sound like backward," explains Kramer. "At Olympic, we experimented with the sounds and placements to see what would work best."

A second take barely began before a mistake occurred and Kramer called for a new take. This effort also fell short before a complete fourth take began to showcase the refinements Hendrix had begun to make, trimming parts and tightening the rhythm playing throughout the song. The fifth take was superb, but Hendrix felt he could do better. He called for a playback and cautioned that there were some parts of the take where the group had speeded up. The group returned to the studio and recorded a brief end part for the previous take. Kramer then called for a playback, after which Hendrix kicked off a new take—this classic performance supplied the album's unforgettable title track.

With the basic track having filled all four of the available tracks, Kramer created a four-to-four reduction mix. One of the newly open tracks was dedicated to a backward rhythm track, featuring backward guitar, bass, and percussion. This was first recorded forward, and then Kramer turned the tape around and played it backward on a second machine, while another machine recorded the output to the open track on the four-track master.

Hours of private studying had helped Hendrix master this difficult technique on his personal reel-to-reel tape machine. Fascinated with sounds, Hendrix listened to tapes backward just to study the possibilities of the technique.

Hendrix's fascination with backward tapes caused some mild friction with Mitch Mitchell, who struggled to replicate these unique sounds on demand. "Mitch had started to get uptight because Jimi would want him to play all of the different rhythms we had discovered by playing tapes backward at the flat," says Chandler. "We'd play around with backward tapes to hear the rhythm, which was actually the drums backward. Jimi would want Mitch to play that rhythm."

In addition to the hypnotic effect created by the backward guitar parts, Hendrix further embellished the final master with a piano overdub. "That's Jimi playing the octaves on the wonderful, old, out-of-tune, upright piano at Olympic," says Kramer. "That piano sound, reminiscent of a bell tolling, was an essential part of the basic rhythm track."

Despite all of the experimentation, the group's approach to "Are You Experienced?" was concise, with Chandler encouraging Hendrix's creativity within the boundaries he had established. "This was when Chas's firm hand was on top of the creative process," says Kramer. "The session was very organized."

Final mixes were prepared for "May This Be Love" and "Are You Experienced?" before the session concluded. Mixes were also prepared on this evening for the remaining songs earmarked for the album. These included songs such as "I Don't Live Today" that the group had started at other studios but not finalized until these sessions at Olympic.

TUESDAY, APRIL 4, 1967

OLYMPIC STUDIOS, LONDON, ENGLAND. PRODUCER: CHAS CHANDLER. ENGINEER: EDDIE KRAMER. SECOND ENGINEER: GEORGE CHKIANTZ.

A further four-track-to-four-track reduction mix was made of "Are You Experienced?" to create an open track for Hendrix's lead vocal. The four-track tape had now been filled with the following elements:

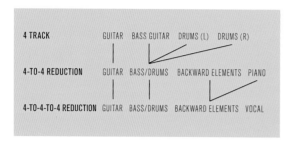

4 TRACK	GUITAR	BASS GUITAR	DRUMS (L)	DRUMS (R)
4-TO-4 REDUCTION	GUITAR	BASS/DRUMS	BACKWARD ELEMENTS	PIANO
4-TO-4-TO-4 REDUCTION	GUITAR	BASS/DRUMS	BACKWARD ELEMENTS	VOCAL

The January 11, 1967, recording of "Third Stone From The Sun" was revisited during this session, and Chandler decided to scrap nearly the entire original recording in favor of new overdubs. "We barely kept anything from the original session," remembers Kramer.

The group also revisited "Highway Chile," and Kramer prepared a four-to-four reduction mix of take 8 from the previous evening. This opened two tracks to accommodate a lead guitar and vocal overdub by Hendrix.

Stereo and mono mixes were made for "Highway Chile" but, as Kramer recalls, Chandler preferred the impact made by the mono mix as opposed to its stereo counterpart. He held back this mono mix from the album project and set it aside in order to pair it with a stereo mix of "The Wind Cries Mary" that he, Hendrix, and Kramer had prepared to serve as the group's third U.K. single.

Hendrix then turned to "Love Or Confusion," a song whose roots reached back to December 1966. Like "Third Stone From The Sun," Chandler elected to overhaul the original recording and take advantage of the superior sound quality Olympic provided. A new four-to-four reduction mix was made, placing this new master three generations away from the original recording. Hendrix added a lead vocal and guitar part before a final mix was prepared and set aside for the album.

"Here He Comes" came in late as a contender for the new album. Inspired by B. B. King's "Rock Me Baby," Hendrix led the group through one clearly enthusiastic take. Near the end of the take, Hendrix can be heard exclaiming, "Yeah!" as the trio swells to a rousing finale.

Unfortunately, they apparently did not attempt any further work, dedicating the remainder of the session to mixing songs earmarked for the new album.

WEDNESDAY, APRIL 5, 1967

RYE MUSE STUDIOS, LONDON, ENGLAND. PRODUCER: CHAS CHANDLER.
Chandler booked a mastering session to cut lacquers for a mono as well as a stereo version for "The Wind Cries Mary" and a mono version of "Highway Chile." He had these delivered to Track Records so that vinyl manufacturing could begin.

WEDNESDAY, APRIL 5, 1967

ODEON, LEEDS, YORKSHIRE, ENGLAND. TWO SHOWS.

THURSDAY, APRIL 6, 1967

ODEON, GLASGOW, LANARKSHIRE, SCOTLAND. TWO SHOWS.

FRIDAY, APRIL 7, 1967

ABC, CARLISLE, CUMBERLAND, ENGLAND. TWO SHOWS.

SATURDAY, APRIL 8, 1967

ABC, CHESTERFIELD, DERBYSHIRE, ENGLAND. TWO SHOWS.

SUNDAY, APRIL 9, 1967

THE EMPIRE, LIVERPOOL, MERSEYSIDE, ENGLAND. TWO SHOWS.
Fresh from their sessions at Olympic, the Experience resumed their place on the Walker Brothers tour, performing five consecutive nights before returning to London to complete the *Are You Experienced* album.

MONDAY, APRIL 10, 1967

MONDAY MONDAY, BBC PLAYHOUSE THEATER, LONDON, ENGLAND.

The Experience reportedly appeared on the BBC radio program *Monday Monday* on this day, performing live versions of "Purple Haze" and "Foxey Lady." No recordings are known to exist of either performance. Later that afternoon, Chandler and Hendrix went to Olympic Studios to continue their work on *Are You Experienced*.

OLYMPIC STUDIOS, LONDON, ENGLAND. PRODUCER: CHAS CHANDLER. ENGINEER: EDDIE KRAMER. SECOND ENGINEER: GEORGE CHKIANTZ.

Chandler returned to the "Third Stone From The Sun" four-track master that the group had upgraded on April 4. Left to add on this session was "Wild Chat," brief dialogue elements spoken by Hendrix and Chandler—both avid science fiction enthusiasts—to integrate into the song's framework. The session appears to have been great fun: Chandler's inability to say his lines correctly left Hendrix in hysterics. Hendrix stammered himself at times, breaking up Chandler and Kramer. In all, they recorded five different takes of various segments. For the final master, select speech excerpts were edited, slowed down, and mixed into the body of the song. Hendrix's bold proclamation, "And you'll never hear surf music again . . ." was actually the front part of a sentence that ended with, "sounds like a lie to me . . ."

Hendrix then recorded what George Chkiantz noted on the tape boxes as "Noises." These sounds included Hendrix voicing various spaceship sounds and others he created by moving his headphones into and away from his vocal microphone.

Kramer devoted specific attention to the song's mixing, where he repositioned Mitchell's percussion and Hendrix's guitar to help intensify the song's exotic atmosphere. "That song was like a watercolor painting," remembers Kramer. "To create a sense of movement within the overall sound, I pushed Mitch's cymbals forward in the mix and panned the four tracks of the finished master. Each track was composed of four, fairly dense, composite images. With four-track recording, you were restricted to panning these multiple layers of sound, whereas now, with twenty-four and forty-eight track recording, what you can pan is unlimited."

TUESDAY, APRIL 11, 1967

GRANADA, BEDFORD, BEDFORDSHIRE, ENGLAND. TWO SHOWS.

WEDNESDAY, APRIL 12, 1967

GAUMONT, SOUTHAMPTON, HAMPSHIRE, ENGLAND. TWO SHOWS.

THURSDAY, APRIL 13, 1967

GAUMONT, WOLVERHAMPTON, STAFFORDSHIRE, ENGLAND. TWO SHOWS.

FRIDAY, APRIL 14, 1967

ODEON, BOLTON, ENGLAND. TWO SHOWS.

SATURDAY, APRIL 15, 1967

ODEON, BLACKPOOL, ENGLAND. TWO SHOWS.

SUNDAY, APRIL 16, 1967

DE MONTFORT HALL, LEICESTER, ENGLAND. TWO SHOWS. The British music press had dubbed Hendrix "The Wild Man of Pop," and his wild stage performances on this package tour upstaged the likes of Cat Stevens and Englebert Humperdinck. "All those sweet people follow us on the bill, so we have to make it hot for them," Hendrix explained in a 1967 interview. "We have to hit 'em and hit 'em good. Although I wasn't scared starting my first big tour, we did wonder how they would accept us, there being so many different acts and us probably the most extreme of all. In Blackpool, the police slipped Mitch and Noel in through side doors and took me around the block five times before helping me in. I lost some hair, but I might have lost the lot if they hadn't been guarding me!"

MONDAY, APRIL 17, 1967

LATE NIGHT LINE UP, BBC TV, LONDON, ENGLAND. **SET LIST:** "PURPLE HAZE" / "MANIC DEPRESSION"

Late Night Line Up was an arts discussion television program and hardly a typical forum for live music—particularly of Hendrix's type. Chandler, however, viewed every television opportunity as an opening to heighten Hendrix's profile. They secured a booking and the group performed live versions of "Purple Haze" and "Manic Depression."

Unfortunately, the original broadcast was not properly archived. A later BBC rebroadcast, which was archived, omitted "Purple Haze," and this remains the sole record of the performance. "Manic Depression" was later issued as part of *BBC Sessions*.

WEDNESDAY, APRIL 19, 1967

ODEON, BIRMINGHAM, WARWICKSHIRE, ENGLAND. TWO SHOWS.

THURSDAY, APRIL 20, 1967

ABC, LINCOLN, LINCOLNSHIRE, ENGLAND. TWO SHOWS.

FRIDAY, APRIL 21, 1967

CITY HALL, NEWCASTLE-UPON-TYNE, NORTHUMBERLAND, ENGLAND. TWO SHOWS.

SATURDAY, APRIL 22, 1967

ODEON, MANCHESTER, LANCASHIRE, ENGLAND. TWO SHOWS.

SUNDAY, APRIL 23, 1967

GAUMONT, HANLEY, STAFFORDSHIRE, ENGLAND. TWO SHOWS.

TUESDAY, APRIL 25, 1967

OLYMPIC STUDIOS, LONDON, ENGLAND. PRODUCER: CHAS CHANDLER. ENGINEER: EDDIE KRAMER.
This session began late on April 24 and continued into the early morning hours of April 25. Chandler, Hendrix, and Kramer made final fixes and mixes (mono and stereo) on eight songs before *Are You Experienced* was

complete: "Foxey Lady," "Manic Depression," "May This Be Love," "I Don't Live Today," "Fire," "Remember," "Third Stone From The Sun," and "Love Or Confusion." "When we finally finished the mixing and sequencing of the album, it was about three a.m.," recalls Chandler. "I'd promised Polydor Records that I would play it for them at eleven that morning. After we finished, I went home and caught a few hours sleep because I had a session booked at the cutting room to make a lacquer in the morning, as Polydor didn't want to hear a reel-to-reel tape copy. I took the lacquer to play for Horst Schmaltze, who was Polydor's head of A&R. As Horst started to put the needle on the record, I broke out in a cold sweat, thinking, 'Christ . . . when he hears this, he's going to order the men in white coats to take me away!' I was suddenly terrified that I had to play these recordings for someone outside the circle. Horst played the first side through and didn't say a word. Then he turned the disc over and played the other side. I started thinking about how I was going to talk my way out of this. At the end of the second side, he just sat there. Finally, he said, 'This is brilliant. This is the greatest thing I've ever heard.' I let out a loud, 'Aaah!' Horst became a great supporter of the band from that point forward. Kit Lambert and Chris Stamp at Track were creative, but from that point on, we had a crusader for us within the Polydor establishment. He and Roland Rennie got behind the marketing and distribution of the album in a big way."

COLSTON HALL, BRISTOL, GLOUCESTERSHIRE, ENGLAND. TWO SHOWS.

WEDNESDAY, APRIL 26, 1967

CAPITOL, CARDIFF, GLAMORGAN, WALES. TWO SHOWS.

THURSDAY, APRIL 27, 1967

ABC, ALDERSHOT, HAMPSHIRE, ENGLAND. TWO SHOWS.

FRIDAY, APRIL 28, 1967

ADELPHI, SLOUGH, BUCKINGHAMSHIRE, ENGLAND. TWO SHOWS.

SATURDAY, APRIL 29, 1967

WINTER, GARDENS, BOURNEMOUTH, HAMPSHIRE, ENGLAND. TWO SHOWS.

SUNDAY, APRIL 30, 1967

GRANADA, LONDON, ENGLAND. TWO SHOWS.

The Walker Brothers tour came to a close with two final performances at the Granada Theater in London. "The tour was a good experience, but our billing position was all wrong," Hendrix explained in a 1967 interview. "But it was a gas, in spite of the hassles. I really learned a lot about British audiences, because every night we had two more to meet and after every show Chas and I would discuss how everything went down and ways to improve."

MONDAY, MAY 1, 1967

"HEY JOE" / "51ST ANNIVERSARY." REPRISE RECORDS 0572. U.S. SINGLE RELEASE.

"Hey Joe" represented Hendrix's debut release for Reprise, his record label for North America. By all accounts, Reprise was an unlikely home for an artist such as Hendrix. The label was best known at that time for albums and singles associated with its founder, Frank Sinatra, and his coterie of friends like Dean Martin, Keely Smith, and Sammy Davis Jr.

Reprise had no standing as an outlet for rock music, but its quiet, tenacious president, Mo Ostin, saw how popular culture and the music business were changing. Ostin had been an accountant for Verve Records and his work there attracted the attention of Sinatra's attorney, Mickey Rudin, when Sinatra was looking for someone to run Reprise. "He came in and showed extraordinary skills and knowledge and love for contemporary music," says Joe Smith, former president of Warner Bros. Records. "It was just the right time for Mo, just the right time for Reprise, just the right time for Warner Bros. We joined forces and he and I became partners and friends for many, many years, and friends to this day."

Ostin and Smith teamed up to confront Sinatra, whose dislike for rock and roll was well established.

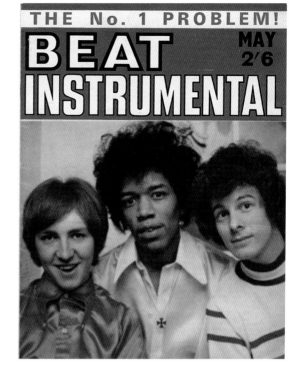

"We had a meeting with Frank," remembers Smith. "We said, 'Frank. We gotta get something else. We're in the business here and we gotta do this.'" Ostin looked carefully at his options. When Ostin learned that famed Atlantic Records chief Ahmet Ertegun had passed on Jimi Hendrix, an unknown American artist who had begun to make waves in London and Europe, Ostin snared the guitarist with a $40,000 advance to distribute his recordings in North America.

Reprise hoped to mirror the success "Hey Joe" had enjoyed in the U.K., but the single missed *Billboard*'s singles chart entirely. AM radio programmers deemed the recording too "hard" for their format, while black stations viewed the song as too rock-oriented for their tight playlists. "'Hey Joe' was played in the predictable places," explains Smith. "The FM stations. Very few AM/ Top 40 stations would take a chance with it, as it was so off the beaten track. But we were satisfied enough that there was recognition and progress that when the album was there, we were going to market the hell out of it. We had an indication that this was something that the public would get into. Enough radio stations were playing 'Hey Joe' to warrant our optimism."

THURSDAY, MAY 4, 1967

BBC TV, LIME GROVE STUDIOS, LONDON, ENGLAND.
SET LIST: "PURPLE HAZE"

The Experience continued their hard work on behalf of "Purple Haze," promoting the song by way of another BBC appearance. Later that evening, they gathered at Olympic Studios for a recording session.

OLYMPIC STUDIOS, LONDON, ENGLAND. PRODUCER: CHAS CHANDLER. ENGINEER: EDDIE KRAMER. SECOND ENGINEER: GEORGE CHKIANTZ.

Noel Redding's "She's So Fine" was created in this session, providing the bassist with his Experience debut as a songwriter. "'She's So Fine' was about hippies," explains Redding. "I had seen some bloke walking about with an alarm clock around his neck attached by a bit of string. He must have figured that it looked very avant-garde to walk around with an alarm clock hanging off of him. I wrote that while we were waiting to do the *Top Of The Pops*. We went to the studio that night and put it down. I showed Hendrix the riff and he liked it because it was in A and there was an open G in it for him to play, which he liked a lot. Hendrix said, 'Let's do it!' The session was great. Hendrix and Mitchell were doing those funny vocals in the background and Chas thought it was wonderful. He also liked it because it was a pop-type record and it had been written by the bass player in his new band, which looked good from a PR point of view. Hendrix thought of the G solo in the middle because I couldn't think of anything. I was overwhelmed that my song was being recorded."

The group struggled through two incomplete takes before a complete third effort. This take, lasting two minutes and twenty-five seconds, was less a working master than a general blueprint. Further recording followed, but after twenty-two unsuccessful takes, Chandler called the group into the control room.

Following a playback of take 22, the group resumed recording. Three quick false starts of "Retake 1" were followed by an enthusiastic fourth take that they designated as the working master. Redding then recorded a lead vocal for the track. This dynamic basic track, sans Redding's vocal, would later be issued as part of *Noel Redding: The Experience Sessions*.

Also recorded was "Taking Care Of No Business," a song of Hendrix's that dated back to his 1965–1966 stint with Curtis Knight & the Squires. "I wasn't stoned," says Chandler with a laugh, "but the lads were a little high and were laughing and joking, wanting to record something. We began talking along the lines of doing a New Orleans walking band type of thing and Jimi said he had something. It was meant to be a New Orleans party-styled thing."

Hendrix began this session by asking Chandler to open his vocal microphone. "I want to say a few words so I can get an idea of the song," Hendrix said. Kramer adjusted to this request by recording the drums in mono to free up a track for Hendrix's live vocal. Hendrix put forward an impromptu, good-humored take that cracked up everyone in the control room.

For the three takes that followed next, Hendrix transformed Olympic Studios into a neighborhood tavern whose bartender (voiced by one of the group's roadies) ousts a down-on-his-luck character (voiced by Hendrix) from the establishment. Hendrix knew exactly the atmosphere he wished to create, instructing his compatriots as to what to say, how to sound, and even how to tinkle the bottles and glasses ("Not too much tinkles . . . OK?" Hendrix instructed) to create the barroom effect he desired.

The group recorded four takes in all before Kramer prepared a four-to-four reduction mix to open space for an overdub of pub chatter by Redding, Mitchell, and an unnamed roadie.

"If 6 Was 9" represented yet another bold creative leap forward for Hendrix. The group recorded "Section A" and "Section B," and these two pieces were edited together to create a single basic track. "Section A" was the opening section, lasting approximately 1:40. "Section B" began where the final vocal (which had not yet been recorded at this stage) begins with the line "White-collar conservative . . . " The alternate version of this song that was later issued as part of the 2000 box set *Jimi Hendrix Experience* reveals the original length of "Section A" before it was later trimmed back.

FRIDAY, MAY 5, 1967

OLYMPIC STUDIOS, LONDON, ENGLAND. PRODUCER:

CHAS CHANDLER. ENGINEER: EDDIE KRAMER. SECOND ENGINEER: GEORGE CHKIANTZ.

The group worked on "Symphony Of Experience" (as it was described on the tape box), better known as the second half of "If 6 Was 9." Hendrix and Mitchell improved the basic rhythm track by inserting new drum and guitar parts throughout, to replace their original efforts.

With an extraordinary band performance in hand from the previous evening, Kramer prepared a four-to-four reduction mix to accommodate more overdubs.

A forceful lead vocal by Hendrix, backing vocals, and additional parts were recorded. Hendrix, Chas Chandler, and guests Graham Nash and Gary Walker joined forces stomping on a drum platform to create the distinctive percussion effect the guitarist desired. Hendrix then added another offbeat touch, playing a battered recorder he had purchased from a London street vendor for two shillings. "Was that too much?" he asked Chandler after recording an overdub of himself playing the instrument. Hendrix had no formal training on the recorder. Nonetheless, he achieved a sound with it that he apparently felt he could not realize on the guitar.

"I adore 'If 6 Was 9,'" admitted Hendrix. "That was a complete jam session, then we put the words on afterwards. That's me on the flute. Gary Leeds and Graham Nash did some foot stomping, and that's (Chas) Chandler's big feet on the fade-out. 'If 6 Was 9' is what you call a great feeling of blues."

Kramer made a further four-to-four reduction of "Taking Care Of No Business" to accommodate a tambourine part by Mitch Mitchell.

Hendrix took another dip into his bag of older songs and next put forward "Mr. Bad Luck," a Hendrix original that dated back to his 1966 performances in Greenwich Village with Jimmy James and the Blue Flames. The group quickly recorded a basic track on to which they recorded overdubs including a lead vocal from Hendrix. Though the song seemed a likely contender for Hendrix's next album, this recording was never released.

"THE WIND CRIES MARY" / "HIGHWAY CHILE." TRACK RECORDS 604 004. SINGLE RELEASE.

"The Wind Cries Mary," the group's third U.K. single, won wide praise from critics who were impressed with Hendrix's gentle touch with a ballad. One of his finest and most enduring works, "The Wind Cries Mary" entered the U.K. singles charts at number 27 and climbed steadily before cresting at number 6.

SATURDAY, MAY 6, 1967

BALLROOM OF THE STARS, THE IMPERIAL NELSON, LANCASHIRE, ENGLAND. WITH THE MOVEMENT AND JO DE BROWN TRUST.

SUNDAY, MAY 7, 1967

SAVILLE THEATRE, LONDON, ENGLAND. WITH GARNET MIMMS. **PARTIAL SET LIST:** "FOXEY LADY" / "CAN YOU SEE ME" / "HEY JOE" / "STONE FREE" / "PURPLE HAZE" / "THE WIND CRIES MARY" / "LIKE A ROLLING STONE" / "WILD THING"

TUESDAY, MAY 9, 1967

OLYMPIC STUDIOS, LONDON, ENGLAND. PRODUCER: CHAS CHANDLER. ENGINEER: EDDIE KRAMER. SECOND ENGINEER: GEORGE CHKIANTZ.

Intrigued by the harpsichord stored in Olympic's vast Studio A, Hendrix climbed behind the instrument and began to develop "Burning Of The Midnight Lamp." This is the first known recording of the song that Hendrix issued as his fourth U.K. single in August 1967.

Chas Chandler later slowed the song's tempo during the July 1967 session at Mayfair Studios in New York, the session that ultimately yielded the finished master. Inspired by the tonal contrast provided by the harpsichord, Hendrix was convinced that he had found the special component he wanted for the new song.

Four takes in all were recorded. Take 1 held a much faster tempo, but Hendrix slowed the pace beginning with the next take. Take 4 was complete, and Hendrix was so eager to hear a playback and measure his progress that the microphone picked up the sound of his boots walking across the studio floor toward the control room before Mitchell and Redding had even finished playing. This recording, lasting just one and a half minutes, later became part of the *Jimi Hendrix Experience* box set.

WEDNESDAY, MAY 10, 1967

RECORDING FOR *TOP OF THE POPS*, BBC TV LIME GROVE STUDIOS, LONDON, ENGLAND. **SET LIST:** "THE WIND CRIES MARY"

The group appeared on the BBC Television program *Top of the Pops* to promote their latest single "The Wind Cries Mary."

THURSDAY, MAY 11, 1967

MUSIC HALL DE PARIS, THEATRE D'ISSY, LES MOULIN-EAUX, PARIS, FRANCE. **PARTIAL SET LIST:** "STONE FREE" / "HEY JOE" / "PURPLE HAZE" / "WILD THING"

FRIDAY, MAY 12, 1967

THE MANOR HOUSE, LONDON, ENGLAND.

The Experience returned from Paris on May 12 as part of "Bluesville '67" at the Manor Club in London. The gig coincided with the U.K. release of *Are You Experienced*.

TRACK RECORDS 612-001. U.K. ALBUM RELEASE. "FOXEY LADY" / "MANIC DEPRESSION" / "RED HOUSE" / "CAN YOU SEE ME" / "LOVE OR CONFUSION" / "I DON'T LIVE TODAY" / "MAY THIS BE LOVE" / "FIRE" / "THIRD STONE FROM THE SUN" / "REMEMBER" / "ARE YOU EXPERIENCED?" Prefaced by the single release of "The Wind Cries Mary," Track Records followed with the group's astonishing debut album. "This is a very personal album, just like all of our singles," explained Hendrix shortly after its release. "I guess you could call it an ad lib album, because we did so much of it on the spot. It's a collection of free-feeling and imagination."

As was the custom in the U.K., a clear distinction existed between albums and singles. Unlike markets such as North America, for example, where Beatles albums issued before 1967's *Sgt. Pepper's Lonely Hearts Club Band* were routinely reconfigured to include both singles and album tracks, "Hey Joe," "Purple Haze," and "The Wind Cries Mary"—as well as their respective B-sides—were withheld from the album in favor of new material. "We never gave it a moment's thought," says Chandler. "The way Jimi and I looked at the situation was that the singles had paved the way for the album.

It wouldn't have said much for him if half of *Are You Experienced* was just those three singles."

Undoubtedly one of the finest debut albums in rock history, *Are You Experienced* overwhelmed critics and fans alike. The album entered the U.K. album charts on May 27, 1967, one week before the Beatles' *Sgt. Pepper's Lonely Hearts Club Band*, and rose to number 2 during an impressive thirty-three-week stay.

SATURDAY, MAY 13, 1967

IMPERIAL COLLEGE, LONDON, ENGLAND.

SUNDAY, MAY 14, 1967

BELLE VUE, NEW ELIZABETHAN, MANCHESTER, LANCASHIRE, ENGLAND.

Chandler booked two further U.K. gigs in London and Manchester before the group departed for Germany to begin a two-week European tour.

MONDAY, MAY 15, 1967

NEUE WELT, BERLIN, BRANDENBURG, GERMANY. TWO SHOWS. WITH THE BEAT CATS, RESTLESS SECT, SHATTERS, AND MANUELA.

TUESDAY, MAY 16, 1967

BIG APPLE, MUNICH, BAYERN, GERMANY. TWO SHOWS.

THURSDAY, MAY 18, 1967

STADTHALLE, OFFENBACH, HESSEN, GERMANY. **SET LIST:** "STONE FREE" / "HEY JOE" / "PURPLE HAZE"

The Experience performed live in front of a studio audience for the German television program *Beat, Beat, Beat*. The program was initially broadcast on May 29.

FRIDAY, MAY 19, 1967

KONSERTHALLEN, LISEBERG NOJESPARK, GOTHENBURG, VASTER, GOTLAND, SWEDEN. WITH CAT STEVENS AND MATS & BRITA. **PARTIAL SET LIST:** "CAN

YOU SEE ME" / "HEY JOE" / "LIKE A ROLLING STONE"
/ "PURPLE HAZE" / "WILD THING"

SATURDAY, MAY 20, 1967

MARIEBERGSSKOGEN, KARLSTAD, VARMLAND, SWE-
DEN. WITH METROSEXTETTEN AND ARNES. **PARTIAL
SET LIST:** "FOXEY LADY" / "HEY JOE" / "THE WIND
CRIES MARY" / "PURPLE HAZE" / "WILD THING"

SUNDAY, MAY 21, 1967

FALKONER CENTRET, COPENHAGEN, ZEALAND,
DENMARK. WITH HARLEM KIDDIES FEATURING KING
GEORGE, DEFENDERS, AND THE BEEFEATERS. **PAR-
TIAL SET LIST:** "FOXEY LADY" / "HEY JOE" / "THE WIND
CRIES MARY" / "PURPLE HAZE" / "WILD THING"

MONDAY, MAY 22, 1967

KULTTUURITALO, HELSINKI, FINLAND. WITH FIRST,
THE WANTONS, AND THE NEW JOYS.

Prior to this performance, the Experience appeared at
Ratakatu Television Studios in Helsinki to mime "Hey Joe"
and "The Wind Cries Mary" over prerecorded tracks.

TUESDAY, MAY 23, 1967

KLUBB BONGO–NEW ORLEANS, MALMO, SKANE, SWE-
DEN. WITH NAMELOSERS.

WEDNESDAY, MAY 24, 1967

POPSIDE, STOCKHOLM TV STUDIO. STOCKHOLM, SWE-
DEN. **SET LIST:** "THE WIND CRIES MARY" / "PURPLE HAZE"
The Experience came into Sweden riding a wave of
momentum. Their busy day began with an appearance
on the Swedish television program *Popside.* The group
performed "Purple Haze" and "The Wind Cries Mary"
live before a small studio audience. This episode was
initially broadcast on June 11, and both songs have since
been issued as part of the *Experience* DVD.

STORA SCENEN, GRÖNA LUND AND DANS IN, TIVOLI
GARDEN, STOCKHOLM, SWEDEN. TWO SHOWS. WITH

PERHAPS AND BREAD. **SET LIST:** "FOXEY LADY" / "ROCK
ME BABY" / "HEY JOE" / "CAN YOU SEE ME" / "PURPLE
HAZE" / "WILD THING"

The group's performances at Stockholm's Tivoli Gardens
smashed attendance records. The venue for their second performance was moved to the larger Dans In to
accommodate the demand for tickets. "I like Sweden,"
Hendrix said in 1967. "The concerts have been much
more successful than we could have expected for a first
visit. When we played the Tivoli Gardens, the PA system
was very bad and the audience didn't really help too
much. But the second job we did later on that night was
very, very good. The kids are great. They sit still and listen to my music and I believe they understand it."

SATURDAY, MAY 27, 1967

STAR PALACE, KIEL, SCHLESWIG-HOLSTEIN, GERMA-
NY. TWO SHOWS.

SUNDAY, MAY 28, 1967

JAGUAR-CLUB, SCALA, HERFORD, NORDRHEIN-WEST-FALEN, GERMANY. WITH THE RIVETS AND THE LIONS.

MONDAY, MAY 29, 1967

"BARBEQUE '67," TULIP BULB AUCTION HALL, SPALD-ING, LINCOLNSHIRE, ENGLAND.

The Experience joined a superb array of talent for this single-day festival, staged on a bank holiday from four p.m. to midnight. The other performers included Cream, the Move, Pink Floyd, Zoot Money and his Big Roll Band, and Geno Washington & the Ram Jam Band—all for the remarkable price of a single British pound.

SUNDAY, JUNE 4, 1967

SAVILLE THEATRE, LONDON, ENGLAND. WITH PRO-COL HARUM, STORMSVILLE SHAKERS, DENNY LAINE & HIS ELECTRIC STRING BAND, AND THE CHIFFONS. **PARTIAL SET LIST:** "SGT. PEPPER'S LONELY HEARTS CLUB BAND" / "LIKE A ROLLING STONE" / "MANIC DE-PRESSION" / "HEY JOE" / "PURPLE HAZE" / "THE WIND CRIES MARY" / "ARE YOU EXPERIENCED?"

The Beatles championed Hendrix during the guitar-ist's early days in London. "Paul McCartney and John Lennon would always be at our gigs," recalls Chandler. "They went out of their way to talk up Jimi to the press and let people know what they thought of him. Jimi and I were very grateful to have their support." The admira-tion was mutual, as Hendrix enjoyed the Beatles and the creative freedom their music embodied.

The Beatles album *Sgt. Pepper's Lonely Hearts Club Band* was released on June 1, 1967, and soon joined *Are You Experienced* at the top of the U.K. al-bum charts. Three days later, the Experience headlined London's Saville Theatre, a venue owned by Beatles manager Brian Epstein. Most of the Saville's audience had only just begun to absorb *Sgt. Pepper's* incred-ible new sounds, so when Hendrix and the Experience opened their set with their own version of the album's title track, it brought the audience—which included Paul McCartney and George Harrison—to their feet. "It's still a shining memory for me," McCartney recalled

in his book *Many Years From Now* (written with Barry Miles). "The curtains flew back and he came walking forward playing 'Sgt. Pepper.' It's a pretty major com-pliment in anyone's book. I put that down as one of the great honors of my career."

TUESDAY, JUNE 5, 1967

OLYMPIC STUDIOS, LONDON, ENGLAND. PRODUCER: CHAS CHANDLER. ENGINEER: EDDIE KRAMER. SEC-OND ENGINEER: LAURIE (SURNAME UNKNOWN).

"Cat Talking To Me," another fine new Hendrix original, took priority on this day. Hendrix recorded seventeen takes of the song, but Chandler had the group return to the second take. Kramer then prepared a four-to-four re-duction mix, and the group added overdubs to this take. Hendrix recorded a second guitar part, while Mitchell added percussion elements such as a cowbell.

"Cat Talking To Me" had considerable promise and would have easily fit as part of *Axis: Bold As Love* had Hendrix been able to complete it. Unfortunately, there is no record of a vocal by Hendrix or any further work on the song.

In 1987, Chandler, Mitchell, and Redding revisited "Cat Talking To Me" for their proposed Jimi Hendrix Experience project. Mitchell composed new lyrics and recorded a lead vocal for this song, but it, too, remains unreleased.

SUNDAY, JUNE 18, 1967

MONTEREY INTERNATIONAL POP FESTIVAL, MONTEREY, CALIFORNIA. PRODUCERS: LOU ADLER AND JOHN PHILLIPS. REMOTE ENGINEER: WALLY HEIDER. **SET LIST:** "KILLING FLOOR" / "FOXEY LADY" / "LIKE A ROLLING STONE" / "ROCK ME BABY" / "HEY JOE" / "CAN YOU SEE ME" / "THE WIND CRIES MARY" / "PURPLE HAZE" / "WILD THING"

The Experience made their U.S. debut with a perfor-mance at the Monterey Pop Festival on the recom-mendation of Paul McCartney, a member of the festi-val's board of directors. "Paul McCartney was the big bad Beatle, the beautiful cat who got us the gig at the Monterey Pop Festival," said Hendrix. "That was our start in America."

The group's dynamic performance at the festival ranks among their finest ever, as the group tore through nine songs. Hendrix was magnificent throughout, building momentum skillfully before concluding the group's performance by setting fire to his hand-painted Fender Stratocaster and smashing it to pieces, an act of sheer destruction that left the Monterey audience stunned.

Hendrix's triumph at Monterey concluded a remarkable journey. Chandler's vision gave the guitarist the opportunity to develop his own sound and style, and in just one year he had catapulted from virtual obscurity in Greenwich Village to a sensational homecoming debut that overwhelmed the audience and his peers alike. "Monterey was predominantly a music festival done up the way it's supposed to be done up. Everything was perfect," explained Hendrix. "When I was in Britain I used to think about America every day. I'm American. I wanted people here to see me. I also wanted to see whether we could make it back here. And we made it, man, because we did our own thing, and it really was our own thing and nobody else's. We had our beautiful rock-blues-country-funky-freaky sound and it was really turning people on. I felt like we were turning the whole world on to this new thing, the best, most lovely new thing. So I decided to destroy my guitar at the end of a song as a sacrifice. You sacrifice things you love. I love my guitar."

None of Hendrix's memorable Monterey performance was commercially issued until August 1970, when Reprise issued *Historic Performances Recorded At The Monterey International Pop Festival*. This single disc, prepared by engineer Eric Weinbang with no involvement by Hendrix, Chandler, or Kramer, featured one side composed of four songs performed by the Experience ("Like A Rolling Stone," "Rock Me Baby," "Can You See Me," and "Wild Thing") backed with selections from Otis Redding's brilliant set the previous night.

Hendrix's Monterey performance has been issued in many forms since that original Reprise release in 1970, but in 2007, Experience Hendrix issued *Jimi Hendrix Experience: Live At Monterey*, a deluxe edition CD and DVD that featured the entire Monterey Pop Festival performance.

TUESDAY, JUNE 20, 1967

FILLMORE AUDITORIUM, SAN FRANCISCO, CALIFORNIA. TWO SHOWS. WITH GABOR SZABO AND JEFFERSON AIRPLANE.

WEDNESDAY, JUNE 21, 1967

FILLMORE AUDITORIUM, SAN FRANCISCO, CALIFORNIA. TWO SHOWS. WITH GABOR SZABO AND BIG BROTHER AND THE HOLDING COMPANY.

THURSDAY, JUNE 22, 1967

FILLMORE AUDITORIUM, SAN FRANCISCO, CALIFORNIA. TWO SHOWS. WITH GABOR SZABO AND BIG BROTHER AND THE HOLDING COMPANY.

FRIDAY, JUNE 23, 1967

FILLMORE AUDITORIUM, SAN FRANCISCO, CALIFORNIA. TWO SHOWS. WITH GABOR SZABO AND BIG BROTHER AND THE HOLDING COMPANY.

SATURDAY, JUNE 24, 1967

FILLMORE AUDITORIUM, SAN FRANCISCO, CALIFOR-
NIA. TWO SHOWS. WITH GABOR SZABO AND BIG
BROTHER AND THE HOLDING COMPANY.

SUNDAY, JUNE 25, 1967

GOLDEN GATE PARK, SAN FRANCISCO, CALIFORNIA.
FILLMORE AUDITORIUM, SAN FRANCISCO, CALIFOR-
NIA. TWO SHOWS. WITH GABOR SZABO AND BIG
BROTHER AND THE HOLDING COMPANY.

San Francisco promoter Bill Graham offered the Experience an extended booking at the Fillmore Auditorium after the Monterey Pop Festival. The gigs were
critical to the group, as they had come to Monterey
with nothing booked in the U.S. apart from their festival appearance. The Experience initially came on
the bill as a support act, along with Gabor Szabo, for
the Jefferson Airplane. That arrangement unraveled
when the Jefferson Airplane backed out of the gigs
and let the Experience take over. "After Monterey we
met Bill Graham who brought us up to San Francisco
to play at the Fillmore," Chandler remembers. "Jimi
murdered the Jefferson Airplane. After one night,
they cried off, giving the top bill to Jimi. From then
on, Graham got Big Brother and the Holding Company
to come on the bill."

On June 25, the group performed a free concert
on Sunday afternoon in the famed Panhandle section
of Golden Gate Park before their final two evening performances at the Fillmore. "We played for nothing and I
really enjoyed it, too," Hendrix said in a 1967 interview.
"Those flower people are really groovy. All the bands
playing for free—that's what I call groovy teamwork. It
was one of the best gigs we've ever played—and it sold
ten thousand albums for us!"

The group's Fillmore performances proved so successful that Graham paid them a $2,000 bonus and pre-
sented each member with an engraved watch as a gift.

WEDNESDAY, JUNE 28, 1967

HOUSTON STUDIOS, LOS ANGELES, CALIFORNIA. PRO-
DUCER: CHAS CHANDLER.

THURSDAY, JUNE 29, 1967

HOUSTON STUDIOS, LOS ANGELES, CALIFORNIA. PRO-
DUCER: CHAS CHANDLER.

FRIDAY, JUNE 30, 1967

HOUSTON STUDIOS, LOS ANGELES, CALIFORNIA. PRO-
DUCER: CHAS CHANDLER.

Eager to continue recording, Chandler booked three
consecutive days at a small facility in Los Angeles that
he recalled as Houston Studios. Despite the studio's
poor sound quality, the group developed two new
songs: "Burning Of The Midnight Lamp" and "The Stars
That Play With Laughing Sam's Dice." Unfortunately,
all of the recordings made here were scrapped, as the
technical quality did not meet Chandler's standards. "I
had never recorded there myself," recalls Chandler. "I
booked three days there because I had been told that it
was a state-of-the-art studio. But it was dire. The place
was like a rehearsal studio compared to Olympic. Los
Angeles was so far behind at that time. I had spoken
to Jimi about ideas for 'Burning Of The Midnight Lamp'
up in San Francisco. One of the ideas we spoke about
was using female vocals again. I even lined [up] three
girls from L.A. who had been groupies of the Animals to
sing." No such overdubs, however, were ever recorded,
as the group simply used the time they had booked to
hone the arrangements for both songs.

"The Stars That Play With Laughing Sam's Dice"
came to life during these Los Angeles sessions, but
the first traces of "Burning Of The Midnight Lamp"
had emerged during the May 1967 sessions at Olympic, when Hendrix toyed with the song's melody on
the studio's harpsichord. In Los Angeles, Redding
took credit for inspiring the song's introduction, as
he remembers being intrigued with the sounds he
had made playing a twelve-string guitar hooked up
to a wah-wah pedal. The balance of the song came
to life under Chandler's watchful eye, as he steered
Hendrix and the group toward completing an acceptable basic track. Despite this work, the group did not
achieve a master. With the group set to return to New
York in early July, Chandler decided to schedule their
next recording sessions there.

SATURDAY, JULY 1, 1967

EARL WARREN SHOWGROUNDS, SANTA BARBARA, CALIFORNIA. WITH COUNTRY JOE & THE FISH, STRAWBERRY ALARM CLOCK, AND CAPTAIN SPEED.

SUNDAY, JULY 2, 1967

WHISKY A GO GO, LOS ANGELES, CALIFORNIA.

MONDAY, JULY 3, 1967

SCENE CLUB, NEW YORK, NEW YORK. WITH TINY TIM AND THE SEEDS.

TUESDAY, JULY 4, 1967

SCENE CLUB, NEW YORK, NEW YORK. WITH TINY TIM AND THE SEEDS.

WEDNESDAY, JULY 5, 1967

RHEINGOLD FESTIVAL, CENTRAL PARK, NEW YORK. WITH THE YOUNG RASCALS AND LEN CHANDLER.
Hendrix and the Experience were the toast of the Los Angeles music scene, enjoying their recent success and befriending the likes of David Crosby, Stephen Stills, and the Electric Flag. New songs continued to flow, and on the flight from Los Angeles to New York, Hendrix composed the lyrics for "Burning Of The Midnight Lamp."

THURSDAY, JULY 6, 1967

MAYFAIR STUDIOS, NEW YORK, NEW YORK. 4:00 P.M. TO 10:00 P.M. PRODUCER: CHAS CHANDLER. ENGINEER: GARY KELLGREN.
Through Chandler's friendship with producer Tom Wilson, with whom he had worked during the final stages of his tenure with the Animals, the Experience booked time over two days at Mayfair Studios in New York. Engineer Gary Kellgren, who came highly recommended by Wilson, ran Mayfair. Though smaller in size than Olympic's impressive Studio A, Mayfair's sound quality offered a distinct improvement over Houston Studios in Los Angeles.

Listed on the tape box as "client: Jim Hendricks," the Experience toiled for six hours. They went through thirty takes and two reels of tape before achieving a complete version of "Burning Of The Midnight Lamp." As Chandler recalls, "'Burning Of The Midnight Lamp' had actually begun as a demo at Olympic. We intended to record it there, but Jimi found the solution to the song in America and we decided to just do it there." In addition to the Baldwin harpsichord played by Hendrix, famed gospel vocalists the Sweet Inspirations provided another distinctive touch. Kellgren's wife, Marta, who also worked at Mayfair, had hired the singers on many occasions for other studio clients. "We were still trying to make commercial singles, but we always tried to feature a shift in our sound," explains Chandler. "We had used female vocals before with 'Hey Joe' and it seemed appropriate that we feature them again. The Sweet Inspirations were a natural fit."

FRIDAY, JULY 7, 1967

MAYFAIR STUDIOS, NEW YORK, NEW YORK. PRODUCER: CHAS CHANDLER. ENGINEER: GARY KELLGREN.
Chandler and the Experience returned to Mayfair, focusing their attention on overdubs and mixing for "Burning Of The Midnight Lamp." Just as Kramer had done for "Purple Haze," Kellgren cleverly recorded a second guitar part from Jimi at 7 1/2 i.p.s. and played it back at 15 i.p.s. to create a distinctive, mandolin-like sound that was particularly effective in tandem with the harpsichord.

SATURDAY, JULY 8, 1967

COLISEUM, JACKSONVILLE, FLORIDA. WITH THE MONKEES, LYNNE RANDALL AND THE SUNDOWNERS.

SUNDAY, JULY 9, 1967

CONVENTION HALL, MIAMI, FLORIDA. WITH THE MONKEES, LYNNE RANDALL AND THE SUNDOWNERS.

TUESDAY, JULY 11, 1967

COLISEUM, CHARLOTTE, NORTH CAROLINA. WITH THE MONKEES, LYNNE RANDALL AND THE SUNDOWNERS.

WEDNESDAY, JULY 12, 1967

COLISEUM, GREENSBORO, NORTH CAROLINA. WITH THE MONKEES, LYNNE RANDALL AND THE SUNDOWNERS.

THURSDAY, JULY 13, 1967

FOREST HILLS STADIUM, NEW YORK, NEW YORK. WITH THE MONKEES, LYNNE RANDALL AND THE SUNDOWNERS.

FRIDAY, JULY 14, 1967

FOREST HILLS STADIUM, NEW YORK, NEW YORK. WITH THE MONKEES, LYNNE RANDALL AND THE SUNDOWNERS.

SATURDAY, JULY 15, 1967

FOREST HILLS STADIUM, NEW YORK, NEW YORK. WITH THE MONKEES, LYNNE RANDALL AND THE SUNDOWNERS.

SUNDAY, JULY 16, 1967

FOREST HILLS STADIUM, NEW YORK, NEW YORK. WITH THE MONKEES, LYNNE RANDALL AND THE SUNDOWNERS.

During the week-long stint in June when the Experience were performing at the Fillmore in San Francisco, co-manager Michael Jeffery had secured a position for the Experience to serve as an opening act for the Monkees on their U.S. tour. "We were sitting in the hotel after the last Fillmore gig [on June 25] when Mike Jeffery phoned from New York," recalls Chandler. "Jimi and I were sitting in my room when Mike got me on the phone and said he had great news. 'I've got them on the biggest tour in America as a support act.' I said, 'That's great. Who is it?' 'The Monkees.' I dropped the fucking phone and had a flaming row with Jeffery. I went berserk."

Chandler was furious that Jeffery had so badly misjudged the American music market. Jeffery, in turn, couldn't understand Chandler's and Hendrix's anger. Jeffery had included the Animals on countless tour packages and viewed the Monkees gambit as similar to what Chandler had done by having the Experience open for the likes of Cat Stevens, Englebert Humperdinck, and the Walker Brothers earlier that same year.

Chandler witnessed the poor reaction the Experience received in Forest Hills, New York, and went to see Dick Clark, the tour's promoter, that evening at the Americana Hotel. The two agreed to pull the Experience out from the tour after only eight dates, remedying Jeffery's gaffe with the claim (fabricated by Chandler and Clark) that the Daughters of the American Revolution considered the group's act obscene. "It was just a device to get off the tour without losing face but it became this massive public relations story overnight," Chandler explains. "We expected to get sued by the DAR. As far as we were concerned, it was just a story for the music business trades so it wouldn't look like he had been jerked off the tour. Dick Clark agreed with me. It was the worst match he had ever seen!"

Hendrix was relieved that the group had been freed from their commitment. "The Monkees were like plastic Beatles," Hendrix remarked. "Don't get me wrong, I liked the Monkees themselves. The personal part was beautiful. I got on with Mickey and Peter and we fooled around a lot together. We pulled out of the tour because there was a hassle. Firstly, we were not getting any billing. All the posters for the show just screamed out Monkees! They didn't even know we were there until we hit the stage. Then they gave us the death spot on the show, right before the Monkees were due on. The audience just screamed and yelled for the Monkees. It was just the wrong audience."

MONDAY, JULY 17, 1967

STUDIO 76, NEW YORK, NEW YORK. PRODUCER: ED CHALPIN. ENGINEER: MICKEY LANE.

Producer Ed Chalpin had learned of Hendrix's international success via reports in industry trade journals. Beginning in May 1967, Chalpin had begun notifying every company he could identify as doing business with Hendrix that his company PPX had previously signed the guitarist to an exclusive three-year contract covering the term between October 1965 and October 1968.

Chandler and Jeffery were frustrated to learn of Chalpin's claim. They felt they had settled the last of

Hendrix's pre-Experience business by purchasing his contracts with Sue and RSVP Records in January 1967. As far as Hendrix knew, his contract with PPX dealt only with the sessions he had completed for Curtis Knight & the Squires—but Ed Chalpin did not agree. Soon the guitarist would be ensnared in litigation in the U.K. as PPX filed suit in Britain's High Court against Hendrix, Track Records, and Polydor Records.

Despite the lawsuit and the negative impact it threatened to have on his career, Hendrix hoped to resolve the issue on a personal basis. He took the highly unusual step of visiting Knight at PPX Studios and offered to sit in on the session as a gesture of friendship. Earlier that same evening, Hendrix had met Roselyn Morris and Toni Gregory, the wife of session musician and current Squires member Ed "Bugs" Gregory, at the Warwick Hotel in New York after he had completed a press conference. When Hendrix inquired about Bugs, he was told that Bugs was recording that evening with Knight. Hendrix agreed to go to the studio to visit his old friends. When they arrived, the session was already in progress. In time, Hendrix joined the proceedings, lending bass and guitar to what he would later describe as a "practice session." Hendrix had brought his wah-wah pedal, and his guitar work can be heard on Knight

recordings including "Happy Birthday," "Love, Love," and "Hush Now."

During the litigation that ensued, Chalpin saw Hendrix's participation in this session as confirmation that he was honoring his PPX contract. Hendrix adamantly took the opposite view. At the conclusion of the session, he told Knight that he had participated as a personal favor, and that while he had no objection to the recording, under no circumstance should his name be used in connection with it. As illogical as Hendrix's actions appeared, he viewed his appearance as a sincere gesture between old friends that would resolve an issue that he felt dealt with Knight's recordings and not those of the Jimi Hendrix Experience. Chalpin was uninterested in such generosity. He viewed the guitarist as a PPX artist and his fight against Hendrix intensified over the months that followed.

With these new recordings in hand, Chalpin moved to accumulate enough material to compose a Hendrix/Knight album release. On July 27, he and Knight met with Jerry Simon to reclaim the seven 1965 Squires master recordings that PPX had previously licensed to RSVP Records. Simon later claimed that Chalpin and Knight had proposed the purchase of the masters to avoid having any competing master recordings by Knight in the marketplace. Simon agreed to the deal, and, for $400, Chalpin and Knight reclaimed seven songs that featured Hendrix as a member of the Squires.

WEDNESDAY, JULY 19, 1967

MAYFAIR STUDIOS, NEW YORK, NEW YORK. 7:00 P.M. TO 1:32 A.M. PRODUCER: CHAS CHANDLER. ENGINEER: GARY KELLGREN.

Chandler called for twenty-one new takes of "The Stars That Play With Laughing Sam's Dice" during this session. The group abandoned the Los Angeles recordings and designated a riotous twenty-first take as the master. The sessions for both "Burning Of The Midnight Lamp" and "The Stars That Play With Laughing Sam's Dice" were among the group's first to utilize eight-track technology. Chandler no longer had to create a four-to-four reduction mix to accommodate overdubbing. Hendrix added some searing lead guitar work to one of the remaining open tracks, invoking sounds he obtained by stomping on customized tone pedals designed by Roger Mayer.

THURSDAY, JULY 20, 1967

SALVATION, NEW YORK, NEW YORK. MAYFAIR STUDIOS, NEW YORK, NEW YORK. PRODUCER: CHAS CHANDLER. ENGINEER: GARY KELLGREN.

After the group's performance at the nightclub Salvation, Hendrix joined Chandler at Mayfair Studios. Additional overdubbing and mixing of "The Stars That Play With Laughing Sam's Dice" was undertaken during this session.

FRIDAY, JULY 21, 1967

CAFE AU GO GO, NEW YORK, NEW YORK. TWO SHOWS.

SATURDAY, JULY 22, 1967

CAFE AU GO GO, NEW YORK, NEW YORK. TWO SHOWS.

SUNDAY, JULY 23, 1967

CAFE AU GO GO, NEW YORK, NEW YORK. TWO SHOWS.

THURSDAY, AUGUST 3, 1967

SALVATION, NEW YORK, NEW YORK.

FRIDAY, AUGUST 4, 1967

SALVATION, NEW YORK, NEW YORK.

SATURDAY, AUGUST 5, 1967

SALVATION, NEW YORK, NEW YORK.

MONDAY, AUGUST 7, 1967

SALVATION, NEW YORK, NEW YORK.

TUESDAY, AUGUST 8, 1967

SALVATION, NEW YORK, NEW YORK.

The group scrambled to fill their itinerary once they had extricated themselves from the Monkees tour, but still enjoyed solid crowds at hastily booked club dates at the Salvation and Hendrix's old Blue Flames haunt the Cafe Au Go Go. "I was completely unknown in America until the word got back that the British dug my kind of music," Hendrix explained in 1967. "Now it's sellout business here. At the clubs in Greenwich Village we were welcomed like gods."

Hendrix cut quite a figure in Greenwich Village during this period. His late-night jam sessions with Eric Clapton at the Gaslight were, by all accounts, extraordinary, as were impromptu sessions with his old friend John Hammond Jr.

STUDIO 76, NEW YORK, NEW YORK. 4:00 A.M. PRODUCER: ED CHALPIN. ENGINEER: MICKEY LANE.

Four days after being served with notice of a U.S. lawsuit against him by PPX, Hendrix inexplicably returned to PPX's Studio 76 to continue recording with Knight. "Gloomy Monday" and other Knight material was recorded during this early-morning session.

Considering the two lawsuits pending against him and his record companies, Hendrix's actions seemed illogical. The guitarist may have hoped his gestures would resolve the matter, but in fact they only complicated an already difficult situation. The stakes were much higher for Chalpin. The producer sought to hold Hendrix to the original 1965 PPX one-page agreement that called for Hendrix to receive a 1 percent artist royalty.

It became clear that Hendrix did not want Chalpin to use his name on any of the material he participated in recording on this evening. This came to light in 1973: While working for Studio 76, recording engineer Mark Linett—who, ironically, later worked for Alan Douglas on several posthumous Jimi Hendrix projects in the late 1980s—discovered a fascinating section of studio chatter that preceded a take of "Gloomy Monday."

Ed Chalpin spoke through the talkback microphone from the control room, while Knight and Hendrix were out in the studio, and the tape starts with Chalpin announcing "Gloomy Monday" over the talkback.

Hendrix (to Chalpin): Okay, look, you can't, you know . . . like, when we do this thing, you can't put my name on the single.
Curtis Knight (agreeing): No, no, hell no.
Hendrix (laughing, indicating to Knight that Chalpin cannot hear him): Okay?
Knight (to Hendrix): You got it.
Chalpin: Rolling!
Hendrix: Edward, can you hear me?
Chalpin: I hear you.
Hendrix: In other words, you can't, you know, you can't use my name for none of this stuff though, right?
Chalpin: I can hear you now that I am rolling.
Knight: You can't use his name for any of this.
Chalpin: Oh, don't worry about it.
Hendrix: No, but... [laughs]
Chalpin: [laughs]
Hendrix: No, serious though, serious though, you know?
Chalpin: Like I said, don't worry about it.
Hendrix: Huh?
Chalpin: I won't use it, don't worry!

Immediately after this exchange, Hendrix launched into the first take of "Gloomy Monday." Though the first take broke down midway through, the second take yielded the master.

WEDNESDAY, AUGUST 9, 1967

AMBASSADOR THEATER, WASHINGTON, D.C. WITH NATTY BUMPO.

THURSDAY, AUGUST 10, 1967

AMBASSADOR THEATER, WASHINGTON, D.C. WITH NATTY BUMPO.

FRIDAY, AUGUST 11, 1967

AMBASSADOR THEATER, WASHINGTON, D.C. WITH NATTY BUMPO. IBC RECORDING STUDIOS, LONDON, ENGLAND. MASTERING ENGINEER: JOHN PANTRY.
The Experience were otherwise engaged, touring in the U.S., but Chandler went back to England to deliver an impressive new single to Track Records in London. He booked a mastering session at IBC Studios for the new single, "Burning Of The Midnight Lamp" / "The Stars That Play With Laughing Sam's Dice." The label released the single one week later.

"HOW WOULD YOU FEEL" / "YOU DON'T WANT ME." LONDON RECORDS 5.260. U.K. SINGLE RELEASE, CURTIS KNIGHT & THE SQUIRES [WITH JIMI HENDRIX].
Ed Chalpin rushed to get a single into the U.K. marketplace, securing a license with London Records for this initial single drawn from his 1965 sessions. The single was credited to Hendrix as opposed to Curtis Knight, signaling a trend by Chalpin that would haunt Hendrix in the months to come.

Ironically, Dick Rowe, the A&R executive who had previously turned down the Beatles and later Chas Chandler when the producer came to him with "Hey Joe," licensed these songs from Chalpin. Rowe came to recognize his error in not signing Hendrix when Chandler had first approached him in 1966. He got word of Chalpin's tapes and came to New York to arrange for a license. By sheer coincidence, Rowe was present on the evening when Hendrix returned to Studio 76.

Rowe's gambit ultimately failed, as the single had little commercial impact despite Hendrix's popularity and the use of his name as the featured artist.

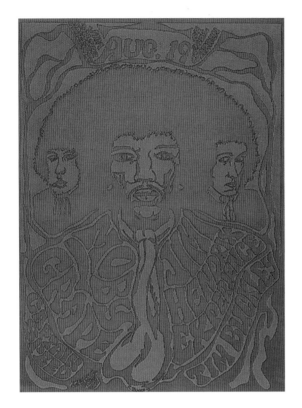

SATURDAY, AUGUST 12, 1967

AMBASSADOR THEATER, WASHINGTON, D.C. TWO SHOWS. WITH NATTY BUMPO.

SUNDAY, AUGUST 13, 1967

"KEEP THE FAITH FOR WASHINGTON YOUTH FUND," AMBASSADOR THEATER, WASHINGTON, D.C. TWO SHOWS. WITH NATTY BUMPO.

TUESDAY, AUGUST 15, 1967

FIFTH DIMENSION CLUB, ANN ARBOR, MICHIGAN. TWO SHOWS.

WEDNESDAY, AUGUST 16, 1967

"PURPLE HAZE" / "THE WIND CRIES MARY." REPRISE 0597. U.S. SINGLE RELEASE.

Prefacing their release of *Are You Experienced* in North America, Reprise tried again to crack *Billboard*'s elu-sive singles chart. "Purple Haze" fared slightly better than "Hey Joe," entering the chart at number 90 and climbing to a high of 65. Reprise later had more success with the *Are You Experienced* album, as steady airplay of "Purple Haze" on underground FM radio stations in major markets like New York and San Francisco fueled sales of the album more dramatically than either of the first two U.S. singles.

FRIDAY, AUGUST 18, 1967

HOLLYWOOD BOWL, HOLLYWOOD, CALIFORNIA. WITH THE MAMAS AND THE PAPAS, SCOTT MCKEN-ZIE. "BURNING OF THE MIDNIGHT LAMP" / "THE STARS THAT PLAY WITH LAUGHING SAM'S DICE." TRACK 604 007. U.K. SINGLE RELEASE.

Hendrix had invested a great deal into the writing and recording of "Burning Of The Midnight Lamp." He was stung by the lukewarm reaction of U.K. music critics, who had been elated by the group's first three singles. Public response also diminished somewhat, and sales of "Burning Of The Midnight Lamp" lacked the chart impact of its predecessors. The single entered the charts on Wednesday, August 30, 1967, and peaked at number 18 during its nine-week stay. Hendrix was unfazed by the song's sales performance; his belief in "Burning Of The Midnight Lamp" never wavered. "I really don't care what our records do as far as chart-wise," Hendrix explained. "Everybody around here hated [that record], but to me that was the best one we ever made. Not as far as recording, because the recording technique was very bad. You couldn't hear the words so good. That's probably what [the problem] was."

SATURDAY, AUGUST 19, 1967

EARL WARREN SHOWGROUNDS, SANTA BARBARA, CALIFORNIA. WITH MOBY GRAPE, TIM BUCKLEY, AND CAPTAIN SPEED.

TUESDAY, AUGUST 22, 1967

DEE TIME, BBC TV, LIME GROVE STUDIOS, LONDON, ENG-LAND. **SET LIST:** "BURNING OF THE MIDNIGHT LAMP"

Back from the U.S., the Experience taped a television appearance miming their new single "Burning Of The Midnight Lamp" over a prerecorded track.

WEDNESDAY, AUGUST 23, 1967

ARE YOU EXPERIENCED. REPRISE RS 6261. U.S. ALBUM RELEASE. "PURPLE HAZE" / "MANIC DEPRESSION" / "HEY JOE" / "LOVE OR CONFUSION" / "MAY THIS BE LOVE" / "I DON'T LIVE TODAY" / "THE WIND CRIES MARY" / "FIRE" / "THIRD STONE FROM THE SUN" / "FOXEY LADY" / "ARE YOU EXPERIENCED?"

While the two singles issued by Reprise had fared poorly on the U.S. charts, label chiefs Mo Ostin and Joe Smith were cautiously optimistic about the commercial prospects for *Are You Experienced*. It was their job to convince their colleagues that Jimi Hendrix could become a major star. "We had about twenty-five or thirty distributors around the country and when we had a new release, Mo or I would go out and sample the records for them and then take their orders right there," says Smith. "The deals were for every seven records they bought, they got one free. So now, I'm playing the Jimi Hendrix album but prefacing it by saying, 'This is the future.' Now this is a crowd of cigar-smoking Sinatra lovers. I said, 'This is the future. This is what we gotta invest our money and our resources in,' and I played the Hendrix album *Are You Experienced* and they were recoiling in shock! One of our biggest distributors was a man named Amos Hielicker from Minneapolis, and his order was seven records and one free. I said, 'What was there about 'this is the future' that you didn't understand?' I took his order sheet and put three zeroes after and said, 'You now have 7,000 Jimi Hendrix records. You figure out how to get rid of them!'"

Are You Experienced found tremendous success, spending a remarkable 106 weeks on *Billboard*'s album chart, including seventy-seven weeks in the Top 40. The album's incredible staying power established Reprise as a rock label to be reckoned with. Hendrix quickly became the jewel of a label that soon included the Grateful Dead, the Kinks, and Van Morrison in its ranks.

The popularity enjoyed by *Are You Experienced* continued throughout Hendrix's career. It was his most popular release at the time of his death in September 1970 and remained so for nearly twenty years, before it was finally surpassed by the Reprise compilation *Smash Hits*. It remains an invaluable introduction to the Hendrix legacy.

THURSDAY, AUGUST 24, 1967

TOP OF THE POPS, BBC TV, LIME GROVE STUDIOS, LONDON, ENGLAND. **SET LIST:** "BURNING OF THE MIDNIGHT LAMP"

Hendrix was scheduled to sing a live vocal over an instrumental recording of "Burning Of The Midnight Lamp" on *Top of the Pops*. The host announced the Experience and a recording of "The House That Jack Built" by the Alan Price Set began to play. After ten seconds, a bemused Hendrix announced, "I'm sorry man, but I don't know the words!" The presenter quickly apologized, and "Burning Of The Midnight Lamp" began to play.

SUNDAY, AUGUST 27, 1967

SAVILLE THEATRE, LONDON, ENGLAND. WITH THE CRAZY WORLD OF ARTHUR BROWN AND TOMORROW. **SET LIST:** "SUMMERTIME BLUES" / "FIRE" / "THE WIND CRIES MARY" / "FOXEY LADY" / "CATFISH BLUES" / "I DON'T LIVE TODAY" / "RED HOUSE" / "HEY JOE" / "PURPLE HAZE"

The Experience performed only one of the two concerts originally scheduled for this date. Word reached the venue during the group's first set that Beatles manager Brian Epstein had been found dead. Out of respect for Epstein's memory, the second performance was canceled.

The Saville had been a pet project for Epstein, and he took pride in booking emerging acts like the Experience. Hendrix's performances at the venue were always memorable. While this performance was not professionally recorded, an image snapped by photographer Karl Ferris later served as the cover for the U.S. edition of *Electric Ladyland*.

TUESDAY, AUGUST 29, 1967

NOTTINGHAM BLUES FESTIVAL, SHERWOOD ROOMS, NOTTINGHAMSHIRE, ENGLAND. **SET LIST:** "SGT. PEPPER'S LONELY HEARTS CLUB BAND" / "KILLING

MOJO

NAVIGATOR ROCK + ROLL NEWS

35 cents

FLOOR" / "FIRE" / "HEY JOE" / "I DON'T LIVE TODAY"
/ "LIKE A ROLLING STONE" / "PURPLE HAZE"

Hendrix headlined this ambitious festival, leading an eclectic lineup—including Jimmy Cliff and Long John Baldry—who were hardly blues artists in the traditional form.

SATURDAY, SEPTEMBER 2, 1967

ZDF TELEVISION, BERLIN, GERMANY.

The Experience performed "Can You See Me" and their new single, "Burning Of The Midnight Lamp," for a German television program at ZDF Studios in Berlin. "That was the opening of German color television," recalls Hendrix tour manager Gerry Stickells. "Traffic [appeared] on that show and everybody was swapping around in the bands because the Germans wouldn't know better." Unfortunately, this video recording, like so many appearances from this era, was not archived, and no copy is known to exist.

SUNDAY, SEPTEMBER 3, 1967

KONSERTHALLEN, LISEBERGS NOJESPARK, GOTHENBURG, VASTER GOTLAND, SWEDEN. TWO SHOWS. WITH THE OUTSIDERS AND LUCAS.

The Swedish tour got off to a rocky start in Gothenburg when equipment problems dogged the Experience throughout their opening night.

MONDAY, SEPTEMBER 4, 1967

STORA SCENEN & DANS IN, GRÖNA LUND, TIVOLI GARDEN, STOCKHOLM, SWEDEN. TWO SHOWS. **SET LIST:** "SGT. PEPPER'S LONELY HEARTS CLUB BAND" / "ROCK ME BABY" / "CATFISH BLUES" / "HEY JOE" / "PURPLE HAZE." **SET LIST:** "KILLIN' FLOOR" / "FOXEY LADY" / "CATFISH BLUES" / "HEY JOE" / "FIRE" / "THE WIND CRIES MARY" / "PURPLE HAZE"

TUESDAY, SEPTEMBER 5, 1967

TONARSKVALL, STUDIO 4, RADIOHUSET, STOCKHOLM, SWEDEN. **SET LIST:** "SGT. PEPPER'S LONELY HEARTS CLUB BAND" / "HEY JOE" / "I DON'T LIVE TODAY" /

"FIRE" / "THE WIND CRIES MARY" / "FOXEY LADY" / "BURNING OF THE MIDNIGHT LAMP" / "PURPLE HAZE"

These Swedish radio recordings captured the group in top form and provided the live debut of "Burning Of The Midnight Lamp." The Experience only performed "Burning Of The Midnight Lamp" a handful of times in concert before pulling it from their stage repertoire. In this performance, Hendrix exchanged the harpsichord utilized on the studio master for the guitar, shading its sound by way of a wah-wah tone control pedal.

Alan Douglas issued these recordings in 1990 as part of the short-lived Reprise box set *Stages. Stages* associate producer Bruce Gary later admitted that both the Stockholm and the 1968 Paris recordings featured in the set had not been sourced from original master tapes but instead from unauthorized bootleg copies he had obtained.

Shortly after Experience Hendrix took over the management of Hendrix's archives in 1995, Eddie Kramer uncovered the original master tape from this performance. "Sgt. Pepper's Lonely Hearts Club Band" and "Burning of the Midnight Lamp" were drawn from this master and included as part of the 2000 box set *Jimi Hendrix Experience.*

WEDNESDAY, SEPTEMBER 6, 1967

VASTERAS IDROTTSHALL, VASTERAS, VASTMANLAND, SWEDEN. TWO SHOWS. WITH MERCY SECT, THE OUTSIDERS, AND AB MUSIK.

FRIDAY, SEPTEMBER 8, 1967

POPLADAN, HOGBO BRUK, GASTRIKLAND, SWEDEN. TWO SHOWS. WITH THE OUTSIDERS, HALIFAX TEAM, AND MIDNIGHTERS.

SATURDAY, SEPTEMBER 9, 1967

MARIEBERGSSKOGEN, KARLSTAD, VARMLAND, SWEDEN. TWO SHOWS. WITH JORGEN REINHOLDS. **PARTIAL SET LIST:** "HEY JOE"

In Karlstad, the Experience played at a fairground and took the stage after an unusual opening act. "I asked who was going on first and they couldn't explain," remembers Stickells. "Then I went out and saw this ramp and the performing seals went out. They weren't even any good. They couldn't bounce the balls on their noses. Jimi thought it was hilarious!"

SUNDAY, SEPTEMBER 10, 1967

STORA SALEN, AKADEMISKA FORENINGEN, LUND, SKANE, SWEDEN. WITH BREAD AND HANSSON & KARLSSON. **SET LIST:** "SGT. PEPPER'S LONELY HEARTS CLUB BAND" / "FOXEY LADY" / "CATFISH BLUES" / "FIRE" / "THE WIND CRIES MARY" / "HAVE MERCY" / "MANIC DEPRESSION" / "PURPLE HAZE"

MONDAY, SEPTEMBER 11, 1967

STORA SCENEN & DANS IN, GRONA LUND, TIVOLI GARDEN, STOCKHOLM, SWEDEN. TWO SHOWS. **SET LIST** [SHOW UNKNOWN]: "FOXEY LADY" / "BURNING OF THE MIDNIGHT LAMP" / "FIRE" / "CATFISH BLUES" / "HEY JOE" / "PURPLE HAZE"

TUESDAY, SEPTEMBER 12, 1967

STJAARNSCENEN, LISEBERGS NOJESPARK, GOTHENBURG, VASTER GOTLAND, SWEDEN. TWO SHOWS.

MONDAY, SEPTEMBER 25, 1967

ROYAL FESTIVAL HALL, LONDON, ENGLAND. WITH BERT JANSCH, PACO PENA, AND SEBASTIAN JORGENSON.
This unique event, dubbed "Guitar-In" by its promoters, presented the Experience atop a diverse bill of guitarists, whose ranks included flamenco stylist Paco Pena, Scottish acoustic folk guitarist Bert Jansch (later known for his work with Pentangle), and the classical guitarist Sebastian Jorgenson. "This was to showcase different guitar styles," remembers Stickells. "They had a lot of 'up-market' and classical guys on the bill. When Jimi came on, this woman, who wasn't expecting to hear him, started to walk out. Jimi stopped right in the middle of the song, stopped dead, and said, 'Good night.' She was so embarrassed." Sadly, this fascinating evening was neither filmed nor professionally recorded.

Hendrix did not jam with any of the other participants, but his inclusion on such a bill made it clear that his reputation as an instrumentalist did not rely on gimmickry or fleeting pop stardom. Instead, he earned recognition for his innovative approach to the guitar and his willingness to push the instrument beyond established commercial or technical barriers.

SUNDAY, OCTOBER 1, 1967

OLYMPIC STUDIOS, LONDON, ENGLAND. PRODUCER: CHAS CHANDLER. ENGINFER: EDDIE KRAMER. SECOND ENGINEER: ANDY JOHNS.
With Hendrix eager to mine a backlog of material he had accumulated over several months, Chandler brought the group back into Olympic Studios. Bursting with confidence, Hendrix seemed eager to assume a more prominent role in the recording process. Chandler accommodated this to a degree, allowing the group increased time to develop material in the studio. "Because the band was well established, Mitch and Noel could hear Jimi's new songs for the first time in the studio, rather than going over them in a separate rehearsal," explains Chandler. "We found that there was less aggravation this way. Jimi would explain the chord sequences to Noel and the tempo he desired to Mitch."

The roles within the control room at Olympic were clearly defined, although Chandler granted Hendrix more latitude than in past sessions. "Eddie Kramer was the engineer on all of *Axis: Bold As Love,*" says Chandler. "I remember George Chkiantz dragging in Keith Grant to help him work some effects out, but it was Eddie who worked directly with us. Eddie and I would be at the desk [console] and George Chkiantz or Andy Johns would be in the corner near where the tape machines were. Roger Mayer built electronic devices for Jimi and he was often in the control room with us as well."

Mayer was well liked by the close-knit team that surrounded Hendrix, and Hendrix generously acknowledged the influence of Mayer's unique electronic adjustments to his guitars and tone control pedals. "The secret of my sound is largely the electronic genius of our tame boffin, who is known to us as Roger The Valve," explained Hendrix. "He is an electronics man working in a government department and he would probably lose his job if it was known that he was working with a pop group. Whatever incredible sounds we think up, he manages to create them. He has rewired my guitars in a special way to produce an individual sound."

This session began with "Little Miss Lover"—announced by Kramer from the control room as "Little Lover, take 1." The group clearly had a firm handle on the arrangement: the strong initial takes demonstrated each musician's confidence and command of their respective parts.

The initial four-track layout was guitar, bass, and stereo drums. A strong first take—always a harbinger of a productive Hendrix session—was sidetracked when Hendrix's guitar fell out of tune. In the interim before work continued, Mitchell devised a drum introduction and worked it into the beginning of the next take. Hendrix and Redding played an identical part on bass and guitar simultaneously, creating the driving force that propels the song atop Mitchell's distinctive rhythm pattern.

Chandler called for the group to come and listen to their efforts after a promising fourth take. Work continued, but a basic track still eluded them. Chandler and Kramer sensed they were close and kept encouraging them from the control room. "Straight in," Chandler called after one take broke down, wanting the group to maintain their focus and momentum. "The tape's still rolling," Kramer offered after another attempt came apart. Take 11 was promising, but the group pressed on and their fourteenth attempt delivered the basic track.

Kramer then "bounced" down this basic track with a four-to-four reduction mix to accommodate a cymbal and percussion overdub from Mitchell.

Next came the gorgeous ballad "One Rainy Wish," a favorite of Chas Chandler's. Once again, the group took command of the song's arrangement from the outset. Hendrix led nine incomplete takes before the session came to a close.

MONDAY, OCTOBER 2, 1967

OLYMPIC STUDIOS, LONDON, ENGLAND. PRODUCER: CHAS CHANDLER. ENGINEER: EDDIE KRAMER. SECOND ENGINEER: ANDY JOHNS.

Work resumed on "One Rainy Wish," and the first take on this evening was slated as take 10, picking up where the nine unsuccessful efforts from the previous evening had left off. The group finally achieved a basic track on take 15. Kramer then bounced down the four-track master to free up two additional tracks for vocal and guitar overdubs by Hendrix including a lead part that featured Mayer's Octavia device. "It comes through a whole octave higher so that when playing high notes it sounds like a whistle or a flute," explained Hendrix.

"I was very keen on that song from the very first moment I heard him play it to me," says Chandler. "Jimi recorded three guitars for that song—not counterplaying—as he had done with 'The Wind Cries Mary.' These guitar parts each picked up where the other one left off. We had some trouble recording it, as there were originally some gaps between the notes, which caused Noel to struggle a bit with the tempo, but it all came together nicely in the end."

The lyrical imagery of "One Rainy Wish" provided an insight to Hendrix's fascination with colors:

> Gold and rose, colors of the dream I had.
> Not too far ago
> Misty blue and lilac too
> Never to grow old

Hendrix had begun to describe his sound in colors, primarily when discussing subtle shadings of his sound. "Jimi would sometimes say, 'Make the guitar sound green or purple, and I would adjust the sound accordingly," recalls Kramer. "He would say, 'Yeah man, that's it!' To me, green suggested reverb, while I always interpreted purple, a more regal color, to mean rich distortion." Hendrix would speak to Kramer of sounds playing in his head or sounds that he had heard in a dream. Colors, as Hendrix described them, could also describe emotions: "Some feelings make you think of different colors. Jealousy is purple; I'm purple with rage or purple with anger, and green is envy. This is how you explain your different emotions in colors toward this certain girl who has all the colors in the world."

Next, Hendrix returned to the "Little Miss Lover" track that they had completed the previous evening. They still had much overdubbing to do, so to make best use of the limited space on the four-track tape Kramer made a four-to-four reduction mix to open up two free tracks for a lead guitar and vocal from Hendrix. It took four takes before Hendrix's wah-wah guitar was completed to his satisfaction.

At this stage, the recording process of this 4-4-4 master encompassed the following work:

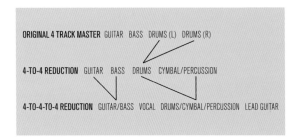

"You Got Me Floatin'," another new Hendrix composition, came next. The group recorded a loose instrumental take, but this served more as a guide track for Mitchell and Redding. Two incomplete takes followed before the session came to a close.

TUESDAY, OCTOBER 3, 1967

OLYMPIC STUDIOS, LONDON, ENGLAND. PRODUCER: CHAS CHANDLER. ENGINEER: EDDIE KRAMER. SECOND ENGINEERS: GEORGE CHKIANTZ, ANDY JOHNS.

"Little Miss Lover" was again the focus and the team toiled with the existing tapes before work began anew; the Experience recorded fifteen new takes of the song. Chandler, pleased, called for overdubbing to begin immediately after the last take. The group successfully added a guitar and vocal from Hendrix, backing vocals from Mitchell and Redding, and cymbal and percussion from Mitchell.

"You Got Me Floatin'" also progressed noticeably over the course of this long evening. Redding employed his Hagstrom eight-string bass to great effect. The group's first take was brimming with potential. A false start scuttled their second effort, while a third attempt broke down near the song's ending. An enthusiastic fourth take yielded the master, and Kramer made a reduction mix to allow for Hendrix's backward guitar and lead vocal. In addition, Hollies guitarist Graham Nash joined Trevor Burton and Roy Wood of the Move on backup vocals.

Despite the session's jovial atmosphere, Chandler never quite warmed to "You Got Me Floatin'." "That was one of the weak songs on the record for me," admits Chandler. "That's why I put it first on the album's second side. I just wanted to get it over with. I never felt that any of us had ever really been into the song. In fact, we added other people's harmonies to the track because we didn't have any other ideas. Trevor Burton and Roy Wood were mates of Noel's and that's how they came in and sang on that. To me, it just wasn't one of his best works."

The remainder of the session went toward mixing, and it took twelve different attempts before Chandler and Hendrix were satisfied with "Little Miss Lover." While stereo phasing would be used with dramatic effect on the "Bold As Love" final master three weeks later, here Chandler, Kramer, and assistant engineer Andy Johns foreshadowed that effort by blending the flanging sound popularized by Abbey Road engineers with a rough attempt at phasing. In addition to creating the *Axis: Bold As Love* master, this session produced an alternate mix that was included as part of the *Jimi Hendrix Experience* box set.

WEDNESDAY, OCTOBER 4, 1967

OLYMPIC STUDIOS, LONDON, ENGLAND. PRODUCER: CHAS CHANDLER. ENGINEER: EDDIE KRAMER. SECOND ENGINEER: ANDY JOHNS.

Hendrix opened this session with a new song that assistant engineer Andy Johns marked on the tape box as "Untitled Jimi Demo #1." This was far more than a simple demo, as all three members worked cohesively to complete a convincing first take. Hendrix pressed onward, recording four additional takes of this new composition. Hendrix had not fully devised an effective ending at this stage, and this remained a hurdle.

Next came an up-tempo instrumental workout somewhat similar in its construction to "Ain't No Telling." While untitled, this was yet another bright new song that Hendrix had in development. Once completed, the group gathered in the control room to review what they had recorded.

When recording resumed, Chandler can be heard on the tape instructing Redding to get close to his bass amplifier. "Get down low," Chandler said over the talkback microphone. "I want to get a ridiculous sound on this one." "This one," as Chandler called it, was "Tune X," later known as "Bold As Love."

The atmosphere in the studio seemed charged with enthusiasm. Hendrix launched the group into the song with the four quiet brushstrokes he prefaced each of the following takes with—although these were removed from the final master created for *Axis: Bold As Love*. They appear to have served as a timing device by Hendrix that indicated to Mitchell and Redding the precise moment for them to land on the song's opening downbeat.

Chandler was determined to achieve a specific bass sound for this recording and, following an enthusiastic initial take, he came on over the talkback and instructed Redding to use the Framus bass guitar as opposed to the Fender. Redding complied, and Hendrix quickly signaled for a new take. Each of the successive takes continued to refine the song's arrangement. Chandler, usually a taskmaster in the studio, sensed how focused

the group was on this song. He and Kramer kept the session moving, offering small points but allowing Hendrix, in particular, to develop the song's rhythmic structure. No finals were achieved before the session concluded, but everyone involved could see that they were on the cusp of realizing something special.

THURSDAY, OCTOBER 5, 1967

OLYMPIC STUDIOS, LONDON, ENGLAND. PRODUCER: CHAS CHANDLER. ENGINEER: EDDIE KRAMER. SECOND ENGINEER: ANDY JOHNS.

Hendrix had dedicated much of the previous evening to "Tune X," the working title for "Bold As Love," but none of those instrumental takes had yielded a satisfactory backing track. Work resumed on this day on "Version II Title X" with all three musicians showcasing a much firmer grasp of the song's arrangement.

The group's enthusiasm seemed to get the better of them during their initial takes. A succession of breakdowns and false starts littered their path before a breakthrough came in the form of a charged, complete take 14. From there, each take seemed to get progressively better, culminating with two superb efforts at takes 19 and 20. Take 21 was equally spirited, with each member deeply focused and locked into the song's rhythmic structure. This alternate take would later be included as part of the *Jimi Hendrix Experience* box set.

Hendrix then tried to focus on the song's ending, recording two short, unsuccessful efforts before attempting the song once more from the top. Take 27, coupled with the second take of an edit piece consisting of the song's ending, served as the working master until further refinements—including the dramatic use of stereo phasing—entered the picture three weeks later.

Next came the gorgeous ballad "Castles Made Of Sand," first marked "Title Z" by assistant engineer Andy Johns. In keeping with Chandler's strategy, the group had the arrangement and their respective parts in hand when recording began. Three false starts caused Chandler to pause the session, and when recording resumed, the group struggled through six unsuccessful takes before Chandler again halted the proceedings.

Under the new heading of "Sand Castles," Hendrix began anew. The previous takes were scrubbed and the guitarist made slow incremental progress before finishing a complete eighth take. The group still did not have the grasp on the song that Hendrix desired, and the guitarist can be heard on the tape between takes describing exactly when and where Mitchell and Redding should come in. The song's tempo was also an issue: Hendrix played the song faster at this stage than the version later issued as part of *Axis: Bold As Love*. Hendrix requested that he and Mitchell record take 16 without Redding on bass. This complete effort sounded considerably sharper. Hendrix and Kramer then spent some time making adjustments to Hendrix's amplifier and guitar tone, recording some short examples for review before recording resumed with the full group. By that time, Redding was back on bass, and take 18 secured the basic track.

FRIDAY, OCTOBER 6, 1967

BBC STUDIOS, PLAYHOUSE THEATRE, LONDON, ENGLAND. PRODUCERS: BEV PHILLIPS, BERNIE ANDREWS. **SET LIST:** "JAMMIN'" / "I WAS MADE TO LOVE HER" / "LITTLE MISS LOVER" / "DRIVIN' SOUTH" / "CATFISH BLUES" / "BURNING OF THE MIDNIGHT LAMP" / "HOUND DOG" / "DRIVIN' SOUTH" / INTERVIEW WITH HENDRIX, MITCHELL, AND REDDING.

This memorable BBC radio session teamed Jimi Hendrix with Stevie Wonder for an engaging jam session. The timing was pure happenstance: Wonder was at the BBC on this afternoon for an interview with DJ Brian Matthew while the Experience had come in to record a session for *Top Gear*. "When Mitch nipped off to the loo, some enterprising person suggested an informal jam between Jimi and myself, with Stevie on drums," explained Redding in his book *Are You Experienced?* The jam that ensued, based on Wonder's Motown hit "I Was Made To Love Her," features a ripping solo that galvanized the groove they were struggling to establish.

Another treat was a rare live version of "Little Miss Lover" and two stinging versions of "Drivin' South," a rare showcase of a song whose roots stretched back to Hendrix's tenure as a sideman for Curtis Knight & the Squires in 1965. "You can tell that it was all completely live," remembered Redding. "We used to just sort of go in there at some unearthly hour, do it, and leave. I always found that the BBC guys were rather good about recording. They used to complain to us about volume, but we said, 'Sorry' and would just play and sing the songs live."

This program was broadcast on October 15, 1967, and the entire session was later issued as part of *BBC Sessions*.

FRIDAY, OCTOBER 6, 1967

THE WELLINGTON CLUB, DEREHAM, NORFOLK, ENGLAND. WITH THE FLOWER PEOPLE AND RUBBER BAND.

SUNDAY, OCTOBER 8, 1967

SAVILLE THEATRE, LONDON, ENGLAND. **PARTIAL SET LIST:** "THE WIND CRIES MARY" / "BURNING OF THE MIDNIGHT LAMP" / "FOXEY LADY" / "WILD THING" / "HOUND DOG" / "CAN YOU PLEASE CRAWL OUT YOUR WINDOW?" / "PURPLE HAZE"

MONDAY, OCTOBER 9, 1967

L'OLYMPIA, PARIS, FRANCE. WITH THE PEBBLES. **SET**

LIST: "STONE FREE" / "HEY JOE" / "FIRE" / "CATFISH BLUES" / "BURNING OF THE MIDNIGHT LAMP" / "FOXEY LADY" / "THE WIND CRIES MARY" / "ROCK ME BABY" / "RED HOUSE" / "PURPLE HAZE" / "WILD THING"
The Experience's triumphant return to Paris came almost exactly one year after their 1966 showcase as a support act for Johnny Hallyday. An exuberant, sold-out crowd roared its approval throughout the evening as the Experience skillfully blended blues favorites with popular songs like "Purple Haze" and "Hey Joe."

The national French radio broadcasters RTE made a two-track recording of this spirited concert, and nearly all of it has since been made commercially available. "The Wind Cries Mary" and "Catfish Blues" were included as part of the 2000 *Jimi Hendrix Experience* box set, while all of the remaining songs—save for "Burning Of The Midnight Lamp" and "Foxey Lady," both the victim of Hendrix's malfunctioning vocal microphone—have been issued on the Dagger Records authorized "bootleg" *Paris '67 / San Francisco '68*.

TUESDAY, OCTOBER 10, 1967

DIM, DAM, DOM, PARIS, FRANCE. "HEY JOE" / "BURNING OF THE MIDNIGHT LAMP"
The Experience appeared on the French television program *Dim, Dam, Dom*, miming, albeit poorly, renditions of "Hey Joe" and their most recent single, "Burning Of The Midnight Lamp."

WEDNESDAY, OCTOBER 11, 1967

PARIS, FRANCE.
The group was filmed by French television miming "The Wind Cries Mary" outside the Montparnasse railway station—a bizarre setting considering the song itself. French film cameras also followed the group through the Paris street marketplace for the program *Au Petit Dimanche Illustre*.

THURSDAY, OCTOBER 12, 1967

DISCORAMA, PARIS, FRANCE. **SET LIST:** "THE WIND CRIES MARY" / "BURNING OF THE MIDNIGHT LAMP"
The group continued their promotional tour, miming

versions of their recent singles "The Wind Cries Mary" and "Burning Of The Midnight Lamp" for the television program *Discorama*.

FRIDAY, OCTOBER 13, 1967

GOOD EVENING. ELSTREE STUDIOS, HERTFORDSHIRE, ENGLAND. **SET LIST:** "LITTLE MISS LOVER"
According to Noel Redding, the Experience made an appearance on the U.K. television program *Good Evening*. The group previewed "Little Miss Lover," a new song not yet released on disc, a practice Hendrix maintained throughout his career—whether on *The Dick Cavett Show*, NBC's *Tonight Show,* or U.K. shows such as this. Hendrix sang a live vocal while the group mimed to an instrumental backing track. Unfortunately, no recording of this appearance is known to exist.

SATURDAY, OCTOBER 14, 1967

OLYMPIC STUDIOS, LONDON, ENGLAND. PRODUCER: CHAS CHANDLER. ENGINEER: EDDIE KRAMER. ASSISTANT ENGINEER: ANDY JOHNS.
After taking a break from recording to accommodate a string of engagements and media appearances in both Britain and France, Hendrix returned to Olympic with Mitch to resume work on the new album.

This evening's session continued the stream of premium original material Hendrix had been recording at the studio. With Mitchell, Hendrix recorded a superb demo of what was titled on this evening as "Little Wing." However, at this early stage of the recording's development, this rendition of "Little Wing" has nearly all of the rhythmic structure of the song Hendrix developed in the coming weeks as "Sweet Angel," which would in turn become his 1970 recording of "Angel."

Hendrix later recast both "Little Wing" and "Angel" as beautiful ballads, but on this evening he used a significantly more aggressive, up-tempo arrangement. He and Mitchell tackled the song with great confidence, charging through an impressive single take. Clearly, the two had run through the song before this demo was recorded: Mitchell navigated his way without any hesitation.

Hendrix does not seem to have recorded a lead vocal for the song, as the session tape indicates that he next created a mix to take away for further review. This fascinating work-in-progress was later issued as part of the 1997 album *South Saturn Delta*.

Additional demo recordings were also made of what would later take form as "South Saturn Delta." Several attempts were made to shape the basic rhythm pattern Hendrix had devised. Hendrix may also have recorded a lead vocal overdub for "One Rainy Wish" on this evening.

SUNDAY, OCTOBER 15, 1967

STARLIGHT BALLROOM, CRAWLEY, SUSSEX, ENGLAND.

TUESDAY, OCTOBER 17, 1967

BBC STUDIOS, THE PLAYHOUSE THEATRE, LONDON, ENGLAND. PRODUCER: JEFF GRIFFIN. **SET LIST:** "HOOCHIE COOCHIE MAN" / "CAN YOU PLEASE CRAWL OUT YOUR WINDOW?" / "DRIVIN' SOUTH"

The Experience turned in an inspired performance for the BBC Radio program *Rhythm and Blues* and host Alexis Korner. The host had earned a reputation as one of the fathers of the British blues movement, and he sat in with the group on "Hoochie Coochie Man," lending slide guitar to Hendrix's interpretation of this Muddy Waters favorite.

This program was initially broadcast on November 13, 1967, and has since been issued in its entirety as part of the *BBC Sessions* album.

WEDNESDAY, OCTOBER 18, 1967

"HUSH NOW" / "FLASHING." U.K. SINGLE RELEASE, CURTIS KNIGHT & THE SQUIRES [WITH JIMI HENDRIX]. LONDON HL 10160.

London Records issued a second U.K. single drawing on the summer 1967 Curtis Knight sessions that Hendrix had participated in at Studio 76. "Hush Now" showcased Hendrix's guitar tone heavily shaded by the use of a wah-wah pedal, while "Flashing" was merely an edited jam session that featured Hendrix playing a Hagstrom eight-string bass guitar that he had recently been given.

Chalpin once more used Hendrix's name as the featured artist on the single. Hendrix was furious over the release. His legal advisors sought a High Court injunction, and, in a deposition filed as part of that case, Hendrix sought to restrain PPX from passing off the single as his recording. "Hush Now," Hendrix explained, had come about as a demonstration of his use of a wah-wah pedal. Hendrix claimed that he was showing the assembled musicians how he had incorporated the device on his own recording "The Stars That Play With Laughing Sam's Dice."

The single was savaged by reviews in British musical journals such as the *New Musical Express*, who took it to task for its inferior quality, particularly as measured against the high standards Hendrix had established in his recordings with the Experience.

SUNDAY, OCTOBER 22, 1967

HASTINGS PIER, HASTINGS, SUSSEX, ENGLAND. WITH THE ORANGE SEAWEED.

MONDAY, OCTOBER 23, 1967

DELANE LEA STUDIOS, LONDON, ENGLAND. PRODUCER: CHAS CHANDLER.

With the lucrative Christmas season coming soon, both Track Records and Reprise put extra pressure on the group to complete the album and capitalize on the dramatic success of *Are You Experienced*. Chandler booked DeLane Lea Studios on this evening so that the group could rehearse in preparation for the upcoming sessions at Olympic.

TUESDAY, OCTOBER 24, 1967

THE MARQUEE, LONDON, ENGLAND. WITH THE NICE. The Experience headlined London's Marquee Club, supported by The Nice. Having heard Hendrix jam with the group's keyboard wizard, Keith Emerson, Chandler briefly considered bringing Emerson to one of the Olympic sessions just to see what might come from such a pairing. "Keith Emerson was a guy Jimi should have done some work with," says Chandler. "Jimi often sat in with The Nice and Keith really played well with him. They could have really put something together, but I was under the gun to finish up the album and we couldn't spare the time."

WEDNESDAY, OCTOBER 25, 1967

OLYMPIC STUDIOS, LONDON, ENGLAND. PRODUCER: CHAS CHANDLER. ENGINEER: EDDIE KRAMER. SECOND ENGINEER: GEORGE CHKIANTZ.

Following a rehearsal at Regent Sound, Chandler and the Experience traveled to Olympic, where they completed work on "Wait Until Tomorrow" and "Little Wing." Hendrix, according to Chandler, kept "Wait Until Tomorrow" under wraps for some time, tinkering with the song over the months prior to these October sessions. "That was originally written as a put-on," explains Chandler. "When he was first experimenting with it, we saw it as a joke, as a comedy song almost." By the time of these October sessions, Hendrix had dropped whatever comedy intentions he may have originally considered.

Of all of the tracks that found their way on to the final album, "Wait Until Tomorrow" proved to be one of the hardest for Hendrix to complete. "For no apparent reason, Jimi could not play the opening notes to his satisfaction," recalls Kramer. Once the group had sufficiently rehearsed the song, formal recording ensued.

An initial false start was followed by a loose but enthusiastic complete instrumental take. "That's a smashing great take there, Jim," Chandler remarked over the talkback microphone. "Do you want to go straight in?" Hendrix instead requested that Mitchell simplify the drum breaks after the guitar solo. Chandler picked up on this and told Mitchell that they could "do 4-4 from now until doomsday" and add any breaks they wanted as overdubs. "Let's keep these basic tracks as simple as we can so that we can do a lot of remixing afterwards," Chandler suggested. Mitchell obliged, reducing the drum breaks for the next two incomplete takes, but their absence threw Hendrix and he instructed Mitchell to put them back in. They made a number of unsuccessful attempts before achieving a satisfactory master with their fourteenth take.

With a basic track in hand, Kramer prepared a four-to-four reduction mix to free up space for new overdubs and to try and finish the song—but Chandler, not wanting the session to bog down, put the track aside for the time being and moved on.

One of Hendrix's finest and most enduring compositions came next. The original idea for "Little Wing," Hendrix told reporter Jules Freemond, had come from an idea he had originally developed while playing in Greenwich Village. "Most of the ballads come across in different ways," he said, explaining his process. "Sometimes you see things in different ways than other people see it. So then you write it in a song. It could represent anything. Some songs I come up with the music first, then I put the words that fit. It all depends. There is no certain pattern that I go by because I don't consider myself a songwriter. Not yet anyway. I just keep music in my head. It doesn't even come out to the other guys until we go into the studio."

"Little Wing" had been in development for some time prior to this session. On October 14, Hendrix and Mitchell had recorded a dynamic instrumental demo of what would later develop as "Angel" and marked it "Little Wing." That rendition bore little resemblance to this recording, yet some confusion about the song and its proper title obviously remained at the outset of this session, as tape operator George Chkiantz first labeled the box "Little Wind" before correcting his notation. Hendrix may well have envisioned "Angel" and "Little Wing" as corrected in some fashion: a lyric draft written in the guitarist's hand and dated "Finished January 14, 1968" sets forth the lyrics of "My Angel Catherina (Return Of Little Wing)."

In the eleven days that separate the October 14 recording and this version, the arrangement of "Little Wing" underwent a dramatic transformation. Hendrix obviously had not fulfilled his creative vision, as he carefully reexamined the muscular intensity of this instrumental version. The song's familiar rhythm structure was evident right from the outset, but Hendrix again took a more aggressive approach than what would develop as the final master.

A second, equally powerful instrumental take went down on tape before Chandler called the group into the control room to review their work. "Chas knew right away what was needed," remembers Eddie Kramer. "He had Jimi slow the tempo down and try it again." Hendrix came close but still could not perfect the song.

An integral part of the song's appeal is Hendrix's exquisite guitar tone, a facet of his recordings that he took great care to perfect. Kramer saw an opportunity to alter his recording technique to better showcase Hendrix's guitar work. "Jimi played through his Marshall amplifier and I recorded his guitar in stereo," says Kramer. "Where we normally recorded Mitch's drums in stereo during this period, we did them in mono so that we could accommodate the stereo guitar as part of the initial four-track we recorded."

THURSDAY, OCTOBER 26, 1967

OLYMPIC STUDIOS, LONDON, ENGLAND. PRODUCER: CHAS CHANDLER. ENGINEER: EDDIE KRAMER. SECOND ENGINEER: ANDY JOHNS.

As he had done the night before, Chandler booked Regent Sound to accommodate another pre-session rehearsal. After running through two songs, the Experience, however, were tossed out of the studio for being too loud. Undaunted, the group moved over to Olympic as planned, where Hendrix completed "Ain't No Telling." This song placed the spotlight squarely on Mitch Mitchell, whose superlative performance on drums ranked among his finest work with the group. Mitchell challenged Hendrix throughout, doubling

Hendrix's rhythm guitar and incessantly pushing his solo. Chandler and Hendrix encouraged such participation from Mitchell, recognizing his emerging skills. Outside of establishing the tempo or providing a particular accent, Hendrix granted Mitchell complete freedom to create different textures to fit each of his songs.

Hendrix led the group through fifteen spirited takes before he felt satisfied. Kramer called for the group to record an end piece to edit on to the basic track. Hendrix complied and the group recorded a few takes of this. Then Chandler called them into the control room while Kramer edited the piece together. Once Kramer finished editing, he created a four-to-four reduction mix to accommodate a lead guitar and vocal from Hendrix. A further reduction was made so that Mitchell and Redding could contribute backing vocals. With editing and overdubbing now complete, Chandler called for mixing to begin. The final mix, lasting just 1:46, was set aside for the album.

FRIDAY, OCTOBER 27, 1967

OLYMPIC STUDIOS, LONDON, ENGLAND. PRODUCER: CHAS CHANDLER. ENGINEER: TERRY BROWN. SECOND ENGINEER: ANDY JOHNS.

With Eddie Kramer unable to attend this session, fellow Olympic engineer Terry Brown was recruited to serve in his place. "I was sort of dropped into the middle of it," remembers Brown. "It was Eddie's gig and he knew everybody." On this evening, the Experience recorded "EXP." "The session was very intense, as the song was so abstract," explains Brown. "There were also quite a few people sitting around listening and watching. While the song was very experimental, Hendrix was on top of what he was doing. We set up to get the sounds Hendrix wanted and then worked for a long time trying to get these bizarre noises he wanted. The speaker system Hendrix was using was pretty abstract. He had a small amplifier stack and this long, six-foot horn mounted on the side of one of his amplifiers. We dimmed the lights very low in the studio and he worked on it until he was satisfied, which took a long period of time."

With the basic track down on tape, Mitchell and Hendrix recorded their "interview" next. Brown manipulated the speed of Hendrix's voice with a hand-cranked VSO (variable speed oscillator). The "Paul Corusoe" character was based on Paul Caruso, a friend of Hendrix's from Greenwich Village. "That was really nice of Jimi," admits Caruso. "I didn't know anything about it until I heard *Axis: Bold As Love* when it came out the following year. I couldn't believe he would do that."

Hendrix then returned to "Castles Made Of Sand." "That track was almost like 'The Wind Cries Mary,' where, after Hendrix had put down his rhythm guitar, there were big gaps to be filled by overdubs," recalls Chandler. "The main problem had been that Hendrix had the guitar parts written out in his head. We had a hard time getting Mitch and Noel to play in time, because they just couldn't get a feel for the tempo. To help them get right smack on time, Hendrix put down a basic guitar line, which we later erased during overdubs and replaced with the parts he wanted." In addition to improving his rhythm guitar, Hendrix also attempted a second and altogether different backward guitar solo for the song that they ultimately rejected in favor of the initial take.

"Personally, I like to write songs like 'Castles Made Of Sand,'" explained Hendrix in a 1968 interview. "I dig writing slow songs because I find it's easier to get more blues and feeling into them."

"Spanish Castle Magic" came next: these early takes feature a slower tempo compared to the song's final version. Hendrix led Mitchell and Redding through four sluggish instrumental takes as the group endeavored to tighten their grip on this promising new song. They all sounded tired by this time, and a basic track seemed unlikely to those in the control room. "That session went on really late," explains Andy Johns. "'EXP' had taken quite a bit of time to do." Chandler also seemed well aware of Hendrix's flagging energy. "Let's try it once more Jim," Chandler said over the talkback microphone before the fourth and final take. "If we don't get it we'll call it a night." That take also missed the mark, and the session came to a close.

SATURDAY, OCTOBER 28, 1967

OLYMPIC STUDIOS, LONDON, ENGLAND. PRODUCER: CHAS CHANDLER. ENGINEER: EDDIE KRAMER. SECOND ENGINEER: ANDY JOHNS. CALIFORNIA BALLROOM, DUNSTABLE, BEDFORDSHIRE, ENGLAND.

This was a busy day for the Experience: they managed to squeeze in a productive session in addition to a performance at the California Ballroom in Dunstable, northwest of London.

The group completed important work on two songs, "Spanish Castle Magic" and "Little Wing." They had tinkered with "Spanish Castle Magic" on a number of occasions during these October sessions before finally perfecting the arrangement on this day. After laboring unsuccessfully on the song just the night before, they came roaring out of the gate with a determined swagger. With Redding using a Hagstrom eight-string bass fed through one of Mayer's Octavia devices, fourteen takes in all were recorded before achieving a basic track. Overdubbing began next: Hendrix recorded his lead vocal and added lead guitar parts. Using his own Hagstrom eight-string bass patched through an Octavia, Hendrix also punched in some bass riffs, replacing portions of Redding's original track.

When Hendrix heard Kramer experimenting with the piano between takes, he immediately recognized another element for the song. "I was fooling around with these jazz chords on the piano," recalls Kramer. "Jimi heard me and said, 'Man, what are those chords? Show

73

me those chords!' I showed him what I had been playing and he said, 'Man, I gotta put those in this song. You play it.' I said no, but I offered to show them to him, and those were the chords he played on the final record."

Hendrix was clearly inspired by the time work on "Little Wing" began. Kramer abruptly stopped Hendrix's first effort due to an undisclosed technical problem in the control room, but Hendrix was undaunted and secured the master immediately thereafter with his second take.

Kramer prepared a four-to-four reduction mix that opened space on the master for new overdubs. Hendrix recorded six takes of lead guitar before tastefully underscoring his vocal and guitar work with the delicate sounds of a glockenspiel. "We used the glockenspiel that was kept in Studio A," recalls George Chkiantz. "That glockenspiel had been used on the previous session before his," explains Kramer. "Jimi always kept an eye out for odd instruments that would be lying about the studio." Prior to the overdub, Hendrix can be heard discussing the instrument with Kramer. After a few test notes he asked, "That doesn't sound too sharp, I hope?" Kramer's response was immediate: "No. It's beautiful." Following the glockenspiel overdub, Hendrix carefully recorded a lead vocal.

During the mixing for the song, Kramer fed Hendrix's guitar through a makeshift Leslie organ speaker constructed by Keith Grant and the Olympic Studios technical staff. The device was held together by bits of a Meccano set, a model construction kit comprising reusable metal strips that came with nuts and bolts to connect the pieces, along with rubber bands and string. "We didn't have any more tracks to work with," explains Kramer. "I had always loved the sound of this little Leslie speaker and had used it when I was recording Traffic. In order to use it effectively, we would perch it on a bar stool in the vocal booth to the left of the control room and feed selected parts of the mix into it. We would then bring the signal into the console to be included."

SUNDAY, OCTOBER 29, 1967

OLYMPIC STUDIOS, LONDON, ENGLAND. PRODUCER: CHAS CHANDLER. ENGINEER: EDDIE KRAMER. SECOND ENGINEER: ANDY JOHNS.

A full evening of work helped the Experience realize two of *Axis: Bold As Love*'s finest songs; "Up From The Skies" and "Bold As Love."

"Up From The Skies" began the evening and was especially noteworthy for Mitchell's superb jazz drumming. Chandler's penchant for preparation came through from the initial take: the producer can be heard on the tape prompting Mitchell before the song's opening. Hendrix weighed in as well, reminding Mitchell of the length of the introduction he wanted. Two superb takes followed, with the second one selected as the working master. Overdubs followed, and Hendrix quickly added another enduring classic to his growing pile of songs for the album.

The group recorded ten takes of "Section II," as the end section of "Bold As Love" was marked, and the best, take 10, was edited to the existing master.

"Bold As Love" introduced stereo phasing as yet another component of Hendrix's sound. When the Beatles came to Olympic to record "Baby You're A Rich Man" (on May 11, 1967) and "All You Need Is Love" (on June 14, 1967), Kramer worked on both recordings. He discussed phasing sound with producer George Martin as well as a new technique that EMI had been using on Beatles recordings: artificial double tracking, or ADT for short. Martin remarked that its secrets could be found in the handbook of the BBC Radiophonic workshop. Phasing sound had actually been discovered by accident, when, in 1959, an American DJ tried to fatten the sound of "The Big Hurt," a recent single by Toni Fisher. To make the song sound bigger, the DJ cued two dubs of the song to play simultaneously, and soon thereafter, the interference known as "phase cancellation" ensued, and a new technique was accidentally born.

Hendrix had been trying to describe an underwater sound that had come to him in a dream, in hopes that Kramer, as he had in the past, could dial up the effect on the recording console. This particular sound proved more of a challenge to create. To fellow Olympic engineer George Chkiantz, whose concentration had focused on the whole concept of tape loops and tape delay, ADT was close, but it was still not exactly what *he* wanted to hear. "I had been bugged for ages by the fact that tape loops and tape echo always gave an even number of beats," explains Chkiantz. "I was always trying to work a system that gave an odd number of beats."

Kramer and Andy Johns both recall Chkiantz's big breakthrough. "One night, while we were working on *Axis: Bold As Love*, George had taken a Small Faces tape ["Green Circles"] and locked himself in Studio B," remembers Johns. He burst into Studio A with a mad expression and said, 'Come and listen to this!' So we all went in, Jimi too, and George had created sound from a stereo mix, depending on the dynamics of the song, coming from behind your head. It wasn't phasing, but it was the first big step."

Further refinements of Chkiantz's discovery proved difficult, because he was using every available machine at Olympic in an effort to capture the sound on tape. Chkiantz appealed separately to Kramer and Glyn Johns for assistance. Johns wanted to use this new sound, a combination of phasing and flanging—yet another of EMI's variations on ADT—as part of "Itchycoo Park," a new recording by the Small Faces. Via this breakthrough, the process made a debut of sorts when it was applied during the mono mixing, but Chkiantz still hadn't made it happen in stereo.

Spurred by Chkiantz's progress, Kramer put more thought into phasing and its possible applications for Hendrix. They decided to try the process on "Bold As Love." Kramer asked Hendrix to listen to a sound he wanted to introduce. Upon hearing phasing, Hendrix exclaimed, "That's it! That's the sound I've been hearing in my dreams!" Kramer, Chkiantz, and Andy Johns then set about organizing what was still a complicated process, and overdubs—complete with phasing—began. A careful listen to the finished master indicates exactly where the process kicked in. At two minutes forty-six seconds into the song, Mitchell's phased drums come through, and just as his roll is rushing from left to right, Kramer pans the drum sound through the speakers, effectively canceling just a split second before Hendrix's guitar dramatically reappears, awash in this new sound. For the first time, phasing had been recorded in stereo.

"The elements of that song were written quickly," recalls Chandler. "Then Eddie and George began experimenting with this sound and that sound until they found what they wanted. I do remember expressing some concern to Eddie that the phasing sound, initially, seemed a bit too pompous or overblown. I just wanted to make sure that the effect didn't overwhelm the entire track. The song, though, was so strong that the phasing only added to its greatness."

As for the nimble bass lines that frame the song's melody, Hendrix overdubbed them. Redding had cut the basic track, but during all of the experimentation, Hendrix had decided to rerecord portions of the bass line, especially during the song's phased outro. As a final touch, dancing amid Hendrix's phased guitar notes are the jangling sounds of Hendrix banging away on the studio's harpsichord.

Kramer and Chkiantz created two phased versions, and the one that was less heavily treated with the effect became the version selected for the master.

The engineers also applied phasing to the October 28 master of "Little Wing." Although the basic track had been completed, Kramer half-phased Hendrix's vocal and fed it through a revolving Leslie organ speaker during the mixing process.

MONDAY, OCTOBER 30, 1967

OLYMPIC STUDIOS, LONDON, ENGLAND. PRODUCER: CHAS CHANDLER. ENGINEER: EDDIE KRAMER. SECOND ENGINEERS: GEORGE CHKIANTZ, ANDY JOHNS.

The group completed "Wait Until Tomorrow" on this evening. Mitchell and Redding added backing vocals on to the October 25 master, and as Hendrix put on his lead vocal, the tape caught him in good humor, laughing as he listened to Mitchell and Redding finish their vocals. Mitchell also added a shaker and tambourine overdub.

Finishing touches were applied to the May 4 master recording of Redding's "She's So Fine" so that the song could go on to the *Axis: Bold As Love* album. Hendrix and Mitchell contributed backing vocals. On September 27, Redding had apparently booked time on his own at Rye Muse Sound Studios to work on "She's So Fine." As neither Chandler nor Hendrix was present, what effect that session had on the overdubbing done that evening is unknown.

The group also revisited the final four-four master for "Spanish Castle Magic," making some small vocal and percussion refinements before this song was designated as complete.

TUESDAY, OCTOBER 31, 1967

OLYMPIC STUDIOS, LONDON, ENGLAND. PRODUCER: CHAS CHANDLER. ENGINEER: EDDIE KRAMER. SECOND ENGINEER: GEORGE CHKIANTZ.

This was a marathon mixing session presided over by Chandler, Hendrix, and Kramer. Thirteen songs, including "EXP," made up the new album. Somehow, after this lengthy session concluded, Hendrix managed to lose the mixes for side one. Apparently, Hendrix had intended to take the masters home. "He went off to a party and took the masters with him," says Chandler. "Coming back, he left one of the boxes in a taxi. It was all scheduled for release! So we rang up Eddie and went into Olympic the next night and mixed the entire A-side of the album again, all in one night."

"It was mixed beautifully," Hendrix lamented afterwards. "But we lost the original mix, so we had to redo it. Chas and I and the engineer, Eddie Kramer, all of us had to remix it the next morning within eleven hours and it's very hard to do that."

WEDNESDAY, NOVEMBER 1, 1967

OLYMPIC STUDIOS, LONDON, ENGLAND. PRODUCER: CHAS CHANDLER. ENGINEER: EDDIE KRAMER. SECOND ENGINEER: GEORGE CHKIANTZ.

Chandler was under a deadline to deliver the finished album to Track Records, and with Hendrix having lost the half of the mixes during the previous evening, the team gathered to try and recreate the work they had done.

"EXP," the album's opening track, proved difficult to reproduce because Terry Brown had engineered the basic track for that recording. Many of his techniques with regard to panning and level changes were done during the pre-mixing process. A remix based on an acetate recording subsequently failed, leaving the three no option but to begin from scratch. Kramer was able to skillfully incorporate panning the sound through the stereo image, to Hendrix's delight. "It had the effect of a motorbike going around and around," remembers Andy Johns.

"The one we had the most trouble with was 'If 6 Was 9,'" remembers Kramer. "I could never get close to what we had already done in terms of quality with the previous rough mix. We were left scratching our heads. Chas asked if anybody had a tape of that rough mix. As it turned out, Noel did. Chas sent someone off to his flat in a cab and they came back with this tiny, three-inch plastic reel that the tape was falling off of. Before we put it on the machine I had to iron out all of the wrinkles. It was recorded at $7\frac{1}{2}$ i.p.s. and the tape was just a nightmare. That tape, though, was transferred to 15 i.p.s. and that's the version that you hear."

THURSDAY, NOVEMBER 2, 1967

OLYMPIC STUDIOS, LONDON, ENGLAND. PRODUCER: CHAS CHANDLER. ENGINEER: EDDIE KRAMER. SECOND ENGINEER: GEORGE CHKIANTZ.

Chandler, Hendrix, and Kramer again returned to Olympic, where they crafted discrete mono mixes of the entire album. The *Axis: Bold As Love* album would mark the final time that Hendrix purposely created mono mixes of his album for release. Other releases in mono would continue to trickle out of Hendrix distributors such as Reprise in the U.S., but these would all be electronically "folded" from stereo to mono by a mastering engineer outside of Hendrix's direction.

TUESDAY, NOVEMBER 7, 1967

CHAS CHANDLER'S APARTMENT, LONDON.

Chandler summoned the group to his London apartment so that they could listen to a test pressing of *Axis: Bold As Love.* "Thankfully," recalled Redding in a diary entry, "when we sat down at Chas's on 7 November to hear the test pressing, it sounded good." Satisfied with the sound quality, Chandler scheduled a mastering session for November 16 so that vinyl lacquers could be prepared for manufacturing.

WEDNESDAY, NOVEMBER 8, 1967

THE UNION, MANCHESTER, LANCASHIRE, ENGLAND. WITH TAMLA EXPRESS.

FRIDAY, NOVEMBER 10, 1967

VITUS STUDIOS, BUSSUM, NOORD-HOLLAND, THE NETHERLANDS. **SET LIST:** "FOXEY LADY" / "CATFISH BLUES" / "PURPLE HAZE" (INCOMPLETE TAKE) / "PURPLE HAZE" (TWO TAKES). HIPPY HAPPY BEURS VOOR TIENERS EN TWENS, AHOY HALLEN, ROTTERDAM, ZUID-HOLLAND, THE NETHERLANDS. WITH THE MOTIONS. **PARTIAL SET LIST:** "STONE FREE" / "MANIC DEPRESSION" / "HEY JOE" / "THE WIND CRIES MARY" / "BURNING OF THE MIDNIGHT LAMP" / "PURPLE HAZE"

The Experience flew from London to Amsterdam to make an appearance on the Dutch television program *Hoepla*. The group's renditions of "Foxey Lady," "Catfish Blues," and "Purple Haze" were transmitted live and later rebroadcast by Dutch VPRO television on November 23, 1967. The *Hoepla* performance of "Catfish Blues" was later issued as part of the 1994 compilation *Jimi Hendrix: Blues*.

After their appearance on *Hoepla*, The Experience followed up by traveling out to Rotterdam for an evening concert.

SATURDAY, NOVEMBER 11, 1967

NEW REFECTORY, UNIVERSITY OF BRIGHTON, SUSSEX, ENGLAND. WITH TEN YEARS AFTER.

MONDAY, NOVEMBER 13, 1967

OLYMPIC STUDIOS, LONDON, ENGLAND. PRODUCER: JIMI HENDRIX. ENGINEER: EDDIE KRAMER.

Just two weeks after achieving the final mixes for *Axis: Bold As Love*, Hendrix returned to Olympic Studios to record "Sweet Angel," a new song he had in the works. In early October 1967, the guitarist had recorded a dynamic instrumental demo of "Sweet Angel" (at that time under the name of "Little Wing") with drummer Mitch Mitchell during sessions for *Axis: Bold As Love*. While he didn't have it developed in time for that album, Hendrix continued to refine the song in the weeks that followed. A significant transformation ensued and, like "Little Wing," Hendrix recast the song as a gentle ballad.

TUESDAY, NOVEMBER 14, 1967

ROYAL ALBERT HALL, LONDON, ENGLAND. TWO SHOWS. WITH THE MOVE, PINK FLOYD, AMEN CORNER, THE NICE, EIRE APPARENT, AND THE OUTER LIMITS. **PARTIAL SET LIST:** "FOXEY LADY" / "FIRE" / "HEY JOE" / "BURNING OF THE MIDNIGHT LAMP" / "SPANISH CASTLE MAGIC" / "THE WIND CRIES MARY" / "PURPLE HAZE"

WEDNESDAY, NOVEMBER 15, 1967

WINTER GARDENS, BOURNEMOUTH, HAMPSHIRE, ENGLAND. TWO SHOWS. WITH THE MOVE, PINK FLOYD, AMEN CORNER, THE NICE, EIRE APPARENT, AND THE OUTER LIMITS.

FRIDAY, NOVEMBER 17, 1967

CITY HALL, SHEFFIELD, YORKSHIRE, ENGLAND. TWO SHOWS. WITH THE MOVE, PINK FLOYD, AMEN CORNER, THE NICE, EIRE APPARENT, AND THE OUTER LIMITS.

SATURDAY, NOVEMBER 18, 1967

THE EMPIRE, LIVERPOOL, ENGLAND. TWO SHOWS.

WITH THE MOVE, PINK FLOYD, AMEN CORNER, THE NICE, EIRE APPARENT, AND THE OUTER LIMITS.

SUNDAY, NOVEMBER 19, 1967

THE COVENTRY THEATRE, COVENTRY, WARWICK-SHIRE, ENGLAND. TWO SHOWS. WITH THE MOVE, PINK FLOYD, AMEN CORNER, THE NICE, EIRE APPARENT, AND THE OUTER LIMITS.

WEDNESDAY, NOVEMBER 22, 1967

GUILD HALL, PORTSMOUTH, HAMPSHIRE, ENGLAND. TWO SHOWS. WITH THE MOVE, PINK FLOYD, AMEN CORNER, THE NICE, EIRE APPARENT, AND THE OUTER LIMITS.

THURSDAY, NOVEMBER 23, 1967

SOPHIA GARDENS PAVILION, CARDIFF, WALES. TWO SHOWS. WITH THE MOVE, PINK FLOYD, AMEN CORNER, THE NICE, EIRE APPARENT, AND THE OUTER LIMITS.

FRIDAY, NOVEMBER 24, 1967

COLSTON HALL, BRISTOL, ENGLAND. TWO SHOWS. WITH THE MOVE, PINK FLOYD, AMEN CORNER, THE NICE, EIRE APPARENT, AND THE OUTER LIMITS.

SATURDAY, NOVEMBER 25, 1967

OPERA HOUSE, BLACKPOOL, LANCASHIRE, ENGLAND. TWO SHOWS. WITH THE MOVE, PINK FLOYD, AMEN CORNER, THE NICE, EIRE APPARENT, AND THE OUTER LIMITS. **SET LIST:** "SGT. PEPPER'S LONELY HEARTS CLUB BAND" / "FIRE" / "HEY JOE" / "THE WIND CRIES MARY" / "PURPLE HAZE" / "WILD THING"

SUNDAY, NOVEMBER 26, 1967

PALACE THEATRE, MANCHESTER, ENGLAND. TWO SHOWS. WITH THE MOVE, PINK FLOYD, AMEN CORNER, THE NICE, EIRE APPARENT, AND THE OUTER LIMITS.

MONDAY, NOVEMBER 27, 1967

"FESTIVAL OF ARTS," WHITLA HALL, QUEEN'S COLLEGE, BELFAST, NORTHERN IRELAND. TWO SHOWS. WITH THE MOVE, PINK FLOYD, AMEN CORNER, THE NICE, EIRE APPARENT, AND THE OUTER LIMITS.

The Experience's second U.K. tour launched in grand fashion at London's famed Royal Albert Hall. They performed two forty-five-minute sets on each of the eleven dates and headed an impressive bill that included the Move, Pink Floyd, Amen Corner, the Outer Limits, Eire Apparent, and the Nice.

In a review of the opening night's performance, Hugh Nolan of *Disc* wrote that Hendrix's "hysterically exciting act provides what must be the most crashing, soulful, thrilling finale any pop bill could hope for—short of perhaps the Beatles, who don't play on pop bills anymore."

The tour continued across the U.K., with the groups performing to packed halls and theaters. Fortunately, some footage exists: John Marshall and Peter

Neal ventured to Blackpool to film both "Purple Haze" and "Wild Thing." These songs were included in the 1968 film *See My Music Talking*, which was later issued as part of the 2001 DVD *Experience*.

FRIDAY, DECEMBER 1, 1967

AXIS: BOLD AS LOVE. U.K. ALBUM RELEASE. TRACK RECORDS 613 003. PRODUCER: CHAS CHANDLER. ENGINEER: EDDIE KRAMER. SECOND ENGINEERS: TERRY BROWN, GEORGE CHKIANTZ, ANDY JOHNS. "EXP" / "UP FROM THE SKIES" / "SPANISH CASTLE MAGIC" / "WAIT UNTIL TOMORROW" / "AIN'T NO TELLING" / "LITTLE WING" / "IF 6 WAS 9" / "YOU GOT ME FLOATIN'" / "CASTLES MADE OF SAND" / "SHE'S SO FINE" / "ONE RAINY WISH" / "LITTLE MISS LOVER" / "BOLD AS LOVE"

Rush-released by Track Records in order to maximize sales during the lucrative Christmas season, *Axis: Bold As Love* enjoyed a warm reception from fans, peaking at the number 5 position during a sixteen-week stay on the U.K. album charts.

Hendrix held himself to extremely high standards and was miffed that Chandler, in spite of the group's present standing, had not set aside the time needed to perfect the album. "The album was made over a period of sixteen days, which I am very sad about," Hendrix said in an interview conducted shortly after the album's release. "But we had to get it out to put in all the kiddies' stockings for Christmas. We were really deep into it and the songs on it are how we felt right then. It could have been so much better. The songs could have been better, too. As soon as you finish you get a hundred completely new ideas."

Hendrix's frustration with the tight schedule for completing the album may have inspired—although no one is certain—his "losing" the mixes for the disc's first side. In any case, the philosophical differences between Chandler and Hendrix over allocating sufficient time for recording and mixing only grew deeper in the months to come. "Jimi needed more time and Chas's discipline was slightly unsympathetic," explains Chkiantz. "There was too much of this background feeling of 'Let's get it on.' We recorded diamonds with little flaws in them. We let stuff get by that should never have gone on the record.

A lot of my grumbles about the sessions were Noel's [backing] vocals. It was the kind of sloppiness that Chas should have stopped before they got on. There were plenty of people around that he could have used."

Despite Hendrix's desire for more time to polish the album, it became an immediate international best-seller, hailed by critics and fans alike.

CENTRAL HALL, CHATHAM, KENT, ENGLAND. TWO SHOWS. WITH THE MOVE, PINK FLOYD, AMEN CORNER, THE NICE, EIRE APPARENT, AND THE OUTER LIMITS. **PARTIAL SET LIST:** "SGT. PEPPER'S LONELY HEARTS CLUB BAND" / "HEY JOE" / "PURPLE HAZE" / "WILD THING"

SATURDAY, DECEMBER 2, 1967

THE DOME, BRIGHTON, SUSSEX, ENGLAND. TWO SHOWS. WITH THE MOVE, PINK FLOYD, AMEN CORNER, THE NICE, EIRE APPARENT, AND THE OUTER LIMITS. **PARTIAL SET LIST:** "SGT. PEPPER'S LONELY HEARTS CLUB BAND" / "PURPLE HAZE"

SUNDAY, DECEMBER 3, 1967

THEATRE ROYAL, NOTTINGHAM, ENGLAND. TWO SHOWS. WITH THE MOVE, PINK FLOYD, AMEN CORNER, THE NICE, EIRE APPARENT, AND THE OUTER LIMITS.

MONDAY, DECEMBER 4, 1967

CITY HALL, NEWCASTLE-UPON-TYNE, NORTHUMBERLAND, ENGLAND. TWO SHOWS. WITH THE MOVE, PINK FLOYD, AMEN CORNER, THE NICE, EIRE APPARENT, AND THE OUTER LIMITS.

TUESDAY, DECEMBER 5, 1967

GREEN'S PLAYHOUSE, GLASGOW, SCOTLAND. TWO SHOWS. WITH THE MOVE, PINK FLOYD, AMEN CORNER, THE NICE, EIRE APPARENT, AND THE OUTER LIMITS. These enthusiastic 1967 tour dates marked the end of the Experience's second U.K. tour and closed out a remarkable year for Jimi Hendrix. He had undergone an extraordinary transformation over the course of this year, from struggling as an unknown guitarist, to appearing on a package tour with the Walker Brothers and Cat Stevens, to headlining sold-out theaters.

Hendrix's skyrocketing popularity was such that he had eclipsed these halls and theaters before the tour even began. As a result, beginning in 1968, the Experience would make the U.S. their base for touring and recording. They never toured the U.K. again, making only a single performance in Woburn in 1968, holding two concerts at the Albert Hall in 1969, and one appearance at the massive Isle of Wight Festival in August 1970.

FRIDAY, DECEMBER 8, 1967

GOOD EVENING, ATV STUDIOS, ELSTREE, ENGLAND. The Experience videotaped a performance for the ATV television program *Good Evening* at the station's facilities in Elstree, playing a version of "Spanish Castle Magic" that was later broadcast on December 10. Sadly, no copies of this appearance are in existence as many video recordings such as these were indiscriminately bulk-erased as a cost-saving measure.

WEDNESDAY, DECEMBER 13, 1967

GET THAT FEELING. U.S. ALBUM RELEASE. CAPITOL RECORDS ST 2856. PRODUCER; ED CHALPIN. ENGINEER: MICKEY LANE. "HOW WOULD YOU FEEL" / "SIMON SAYS" / "GET THAT FEELING" / "HUSH NOW" / "WELCOME HOME" / "GOTTA HAVE A NEW DRESS" / "NO BUSINESS" / "STRANGE THINGS"

Hendrix's sessions with Curtis Knight came back to haunt him when Ed Chalpin approached Capitol Records in November 1967, seeking to license these recordings for U.S. distribution. PPX hoped to create four different albums from its master tapes, and Chalpin offered Capitol thirty-three recordings featuring Hendrix on bass or guitar as a member of Curtis Knight & the Squires. Chalpin's list coupled the 1965 recordings with material from the July 17 and August 8 sessions that Hendrix had participated in.

Nick Venet, Capitol's A&R representative, prepared an eight-song album from the thirty-three tracks Chalpin presented to the label, remixing Chalpin's non-

standard ten-track multitrack master tapes in an effort to upgrade their sound quality. Capitol drew Hendrix's ire when they featured a color photo of the guitarist performing at the recent Monterey Pop Festival for the album's cover art. Nowhere was a picture of Curtis Knight or liner notes detailing the contents. "I didn't trust what Chalpin told me, so I didn't put any liner notes on the cover," Venet later revealed to *Rolling Stone*'s Michael Lydon.

Chalpin's gambit was timed perfectly, as Reprise had not yet issued *Axis: Bold As Love* in the U.S., electing to move that album's release date back into January 1968. *Get That Feeling* confused record buyers anticipating the second Jimi Hendrix Experience album. Many unassuming fans initially responded to the album, impacting Christmas season sales of *Are You Experienced*, before press reports and reviews began to detail the album's content. The *Los Angeles Times* of December 24, 1967, wrote, "Beware when an album shrinks the featured vocalist's name into small type beneath the twice as large name of a backup musician. Hendrix records for Warner Bros. but last July he backed up Knight for what sounds suspiciously like no more than a demonstration record with some after-the-fact engineering tricks." *Rolling Stone* and other publications quickly condemned the album as an inferior quality compilation deceptively packaged to entice fans of the Jimi Hendrix Experience. Hendrix himself spoke forcefully about the album in a January 2, 1968, deposition. He assailed the Capitol album as "malicious" and made clear the distinction between the recordings in question and his work with the Experience. "The [Capitol] label creates the impression that Knight and I recorded as at least equal performers, which is untrue. The Capitol recording is greatly inferior in quality in comparison with recordings today. At PPX, we spent, on the average, about one hour recording a song. Today, I spend at least twelve hours on each song. The difference in time is a measure of the care now being taken to obtain the highest possible technical quality, which is totally lacking in the Capitol record."

Despite the almost universally negative reviews and Hendrix's own condemnation of the release, *Get That Feeling* enjoyed some initial sales, breaking into the *Billboard* album charts and peaking at number 75 before the end of the year.

"FOXEY LADY" / "HEY JOE." REPRISE 0641. U.S. SINGLE RELEASE.

Perhaps as a counter to Capitol Records' release of *Get That Feeling*, a collection of Hendrix's performances as a sideman to Curtis Knight, Reprise issued this single. While both tracks had become staples of underground FM radio outlets, this third Experience single peaked at number 67 during a brief four-week run on the *Billboard* chart.

FRIDAY, DECEMBER 15, 1967

PLAYHOUSE THEATER, BBC STUDIOS, LONDON, ENGLAND. PRODUCERS: BEV PHILLIPS AND BERNIE ANDREWS. **SET LIST:** "WAIT UNTIL TOMORROW" / "DAY TRIPPER" / "RADIO ONE" / "HEAR MY TRAIN A COMIN'" (TAKE ONE) / "SPANISH CASTLE MAGIC" / "HEAR MY TRAIN A COMIN'" (TAKE TWO)

The Experience made their final BBC Radio appearance of 1967 on the popular *Top Gear* program. These recordings, plus an interview with Hendrix by Tony Hall, were recorded at the BBC's Playhouse Theater. Hendrix elected not only to showcase new material from *Axis: Bold As Love* like "Spanish Castle Magic" and "Wait Until Tomorrow," but also to demonstrate the group's fearless creative freedom in the form of an exuberant version of the Beatles' "Day Tripper" and the comical "Radio One," the impromptu theme music Hendrix invented on the spot for the program. "We used to ad lib a lot on those BBC sessions," recalls Redding. "We would ad lib something like 'Hound Dog' because we couldn't think of what to do. Hendrix said, 'Let's do this one,' so we did it and made it up on the spot. Then he also made up a theme for BBC radio that was made up on the spot, because it was all live. We also did that Beatles track 'Day Tripper' and [when it was broadcast] everyone thought it was John Lennon singing the harmony and it wasn't, it was me!"

The program was also noteworthy for the inclusion of "Hear My Train A Comin'," an original blues composition that later became a concert staple for Hendrix. Save for the first take of "Hear My Train A Comin'," these performances were first broadcast on December 24, 1967. All were later issued as part of the 1998 *BBC Sessions* compilation.

TUESDAY, DECEMBER 19, 1967

BRUCE FLEMING PHOTOGRAPHY STUDIO, LONDON, ENGLAND.

The priceless footage of Hendrix performing "Hear My Train A Comin'" on a twelve-string acoustic guitar was filmed when the Experience gathered at Bruce Fleming's photography studio on Great Newport Street in London. Fleming had taken the cover photograph for the Track Records edition of *Are You Experienced*. Coupled with Hendrix's impromptu performance, filmmakers John Marshall and Peter Neal also documented a photo session Fleming conducted for the group as part of their film *See My Music Talking*.

WEDNESDAY, DECEMBER 20, 1967

OLYMPIC STUDIOS, LONDON, ENGLAND. PRODUCER: CHAS CHANDLER. ENGINEER: EDDIE KRAMER. SECOND ENGINEER: GEORGE CHKIANTZ.

This session signaled the beginning of production for what would become *Electric Ladyland*, the group's third album. Hendrix began in fine style, recording the marvelous "Crosstown Traffic." As he had done for "Spanish Castle Magic," Hendrix turned to the piano for inspiration, inverting a series of chords he had successfully incorporated within the final master of *Axis: Bold As Love*'s "Spanish Castle Magic." Kramer again declined Hendrix's invitation to play piano on the track, electing instead to focus his energies behind the mixing console. The chords Hendrix performed were very similar to those he had incorporated into the final master of "Spanish Castle Magic." "The piano sound was very heavily compressed with a Pye limiter and as it was going through that, it was also being EQ'd," explains Kramer. "I also varied the EQ to make it sound like a mini wah-wah. Jimi doubled up the melody line by singing what he's playing on the guitar. Then he put a kazoo on top of that!" Traffic's Dave Mason, observing the session, joined Noel Redding to contribute background vocals.

The group also recorded "Dream" and "Touch You," two of Redding's new songs. "Dream," only Redding's second lead vocal performance with the Experience, provided an unexpected surprise. The track, somewhat reminiscent of Hendrix's own "Love Or Confusion," was particularly strong, powered by Redding's lead guitar work and Hendrix's nimble bass playing. "Hendrix really liked that one," remembers Redding. "I played it to him on the guitar and he picked up the bass. That one was never completed, but it was a good tune with a lot of validity."

Just as Redding had been given a slot on the *Axis: Bold As Love* album, Hendrix renewed his invitation to Mitchell to include a song on the new album. Mitchell had nothing prepared, but Redding offered "Dance," another of his new songs. They recorded a demo version of the song, with Mitchell handling lead vocals. A rough mix was prepared, but Chandler deemed that the track needed more work before it could be included. While "Dance" never materialized in album-ready form, Hendrix lifted Redding's lead guitar line and would later develop the riff as "Ezy Ryder." "The riff to 'Dance' later came out as a tune ["Ezy Ryder"] credited to Hendrix," says Redding. "If I was doing one of my songs in the studio, I'd just pick up a guitar or turn Hendrix's guitar around backward and go through the tune quickly. Hendrix heard me play the riff and he said, 'Yeah, I like that.'"

Neither "Dream" nor "Dance" ever progressed past the demo stage. In addition, the concept of developing a vocal vehicle for Mitchell quickly lost steam and was never reconsidered.

THURSDAY, DECEMBER 21, 1967

OLYMPIC STUDIOS, LONDON, ENGLAND. PRODUCER: CHAS CHANDLER. ENGINEER: EDDIE KRAMER. SECOND ENGINEER: GEORGE CHKIANTZ.

The group completed final touches for "Crosstown Traffic" on this day. Hendrix had also, according to Chandler, already devised an opening for the new album: the sounds of a spaceship landing on earth. "It didn't go by that name at the time, but 'And The Gods Made Love' was an idea that definitely began at Olympic," remembers Chandler. "The spaceship landing was a sound he thought of there."

FRIDAY, DECEMBER 22, 1967

"CHRISTMAS ON EARTH CONTINUED," GRAND AND NATIONAL HALLS, KENSINGTON, LONDON, ENGLAND. SET LIST: "SGT. PEPPER'S LONELY HEARTS CLUB BAND" / "FOXEY LADY" / "WILD THING"

This massive holiday festival also featured Pink Floyd, Eric Burdon and the New Animals, The Move, and a host of top British acts. The concert was filmed for a proposed movie about the event itself, but this never materialized. "I saw the first cut of that," remembers Chandler. "It was lousy. The crew was plastered and the cameras were all jumping around."

THURSDAY, DECEMBER 28, 1967

OLYMPIC STUDIOS, LONDON, ENGLAND. PRODUCER: JIMI HENDRIX. ENGINEER: EDDIE KRAMER. SECOND ENGINEER: GEORGE CHKIANTZ.

This fascinating session with Hendrix and Traffic's Dave Mason presaged Hendrix's future explorations outside the Experience trio concept.

Absent Mitchell and Redding, as well as producer Chas Chandler, "Try Out" began with just Mason on sitar and Hendrix on rhythm guitar. Hendrix seemed to sense right away that he had created something unique, and quickly had the basic track in hand. He was determined not to the let the moment cool off, so he climbed behind the drum kit and overdubbed drums himself. With the aid of a Rhythm Ace, a simple metronome device he had used successfully during a solo session in November for "Sweet Angel," Hendrix recorded twelve different drum takes. These drum parts revealed not only another musical skill Hendrix possessed but also his emerging ability as a producer. Throughout these drum takes, Hendrix can be heard on the tape communicating to Kramer what parts he wanted to serve as pick-ups or edit pieces. He seemed keenly aware of all facets of the song and its individual parts.

Working independently, Hendrix then crafted an elaborate four-track demo of "Sweet Angel," beautifully capturing the essence of his new song. To maintain the song's tempo, Hendrix again used the Rhythm Ace as a guide and successfully recorded bass and guitar parts. One inspired take delivered the master on to which overdubbing began. These further modifications included a lead vocal and bass guitar.

Drums came next, and Hendrix again moved behind the drum kit to create the parts he desired. Kramer recorded five separate attempts, but Hendrix was apparently unsatisfied with his efforts. He switched back to guitar and recorded another complete take of the song at a slower tempo. This new recording brimmed with promise as well. Hendrix attempted once more to overdub the percussion parts himself before the session drew to a close.

Inexplicably, despite its obvious potential, Hendrix did not return to "Sweet Angel" or put it forward for consideration as part of *Electric Ladyland*. Instead, "Sweet Angel" lay dormant for nearly two and a half years until the guitarist revived the song as "Angel" at Electric Lady Studios on July 23, 1970. Working with Mitch Mitchell and Billy Cox, Hendrix altered the song's arrangement to better reflect his cherished R&B roots. First issued as part of 1971's *Cry Of Love*, "Angel" was later featured on *First Rays Of The New Rising Sun*. This engaging demo recording of "Sweet Angel" was also issued after Hendrix's death and has most recently been featured as part of the *Jimi Hendrix Experience* box set.

FRIDAY, DECEMBER 29, 1967

OLYMPIC STUDIOS, LONDON, ENGLAND. PRODUCER: JIMI HENDRIX. ENGINEER: EDDIE KRAMER. SECOND ENGINEER: GEORGE CHKIANTZ.

Hendrix was determined to realize the new song he had recorded the previous day. Joined on this day by Mason and Mitchell, work on the song known as "Little One" resumed.

Kramer retrieved the basic track from the previous day and recorded Mitchell's drum parts as well as a nimble bass overdub by Hendrix, who nailed the part on his second attempt. Kramer then made a four-to-four reduction mix and opened tracks for a slide guitar part by Hendrix as well as additional percussion from Mitch. A further four-to-four to-four reduction was required to accommodate a second rhythm guitar part from Jimi as well as some background shouts from Dave Mason.

This work was followed by a mixing session that provided Hendrix with a 7 1/2 i.p.s. tape copy to take away for further study.

"Little One" was never issued by Hendrix on his own albums, but in 1987, when Noel Redding and Mitch Mitchell were working with Chas Chandler on some of the original Experience masters with an eye toward creating a new album, they chose "Little One" for the proposed project. Redding elected to compose lyrics and sing a vocal over this instrumental recording. His version, titled "There Ain't Nothing Wrong," featured new bass and drums overdubs he and Mitchell recorded under Chandler's supervision in 1987. Legal issues at that time blocked the release of this project, but this song was later featured as part of *Noel Redding: The Experience Sessions*.

1968

"We had jumped from four- to twelve-track and Jimi said, 'Let's fill them all up.' So we filled them all up!"
—EDDIE KRAMER

MONDAY, JANUARY 4, 1968

LORENSBERGS CIRKUS, GOTHENBURG, SWEDEN. TWO SHOWS. WITH BABY GRANDMOTHERS AND MECKI MARK MEN. **PARTIAL SET LIST, FIRST SHOW:** "FOXEY LADY" / "THE WIND CRIES MARY" / "FIRE" / "HEY JOE" / "PURPLE HAZE" **PARTIAL SET LIST, SECOND SHOW:** "SGT. PEPPER'S LONELY HEARTS CLUB BAND" / "FIRE" / "HEY JOE" / "FOXEY LADY" / "THE WIND CRIES MARY" / "CATFISH BLUES" / "PURPLE HAZE"

This turbulent day began with Jimi Hendrix getting into an early-morning hotel brawl that resulted in his arrest for smashing a plate-glass window at the Hotel Opalen. Local police took the guitarist to a nearby hospital, where Hendrix's injured right hand received treatment.

The police eventually released Hendrix and allowed the Experience to play the two concerts they had booked for that evening at Lorensbergs Cirkus but demanded that Hendrix return for his day in court on January 16.

TUESDAY, JANUARY 5, 1968

JERNVALLEN SPORTSHALLEN, SANVIKEN, SWEDEN. WITH BABY GRANDMOTHERS AND MECKI MARK MEN. Hampered by his injured hand and a sore throat, Hendrix and the Experience completed a shorter-than-normal thirty-five-minute set before leaving the stage.

THURSDAY, JANUARY 7, 1968

TIVOLI KONSERTHAL, COPENHAGEN, DENMARK. TWO SHOWS. WITH HANNSON & CARLSSON. **PARTIAL SET LIST:** "SGT. PEPPER'S LONELY HEARTS CLUB BAND" / "FIRE" / "HEY JOE" / "THE WIND CRIES MARY" / "PURPLE HAZE" / "SPANISH CASTLE MAGIC" / "CATFISH BLUES" / "WILD THING"

FRIDAY, JANUARY 8, 1968

STORA SALEN, KONSERTHUSET, STOCKHOLM, SWEDEN. TWO SHOWS. WITH BABY GRANDMOTHERS AND MECKI MARK MEN. **PARTIAL SET LIST:** "SGT. PEPPER'S LONELY HEARTS CLUB BAND" / "EXP" / "UP FROM THE SKIES" / "SPANISH CASTLE MAGIC" / "FOXEY LADY" / "LITTLE WING" / "FIRE" / "CATFISH BLUES" / "THE WIND CRIES MARY" / "PURPLE HAZE"

The Experience rebounded from their rocky start in Gothenburg. The two shows on this night yielded the first known live version of "Little Wing," and Hendrix offered two rare treats in the form of "EXP" and "Up From The Skies" from *Axis: Bold As Love*.

Mitch Mitchell and Noel Redding soon returned to London, but Hendrix and Chas Chandler remained in Gothenburg in anticipation of his scheduled court appearance on January 16. Until that time, Hendrix had been ordered to report briefly to the Gothenburg police headquarters every day. Finally, Hendrix's hearing took place at Gothenburg Municipal Court. Magistrate Gunnel Ohslund found Hendrix guilty and fined the guitarist approximately 9,000 Swedish kronor, although Chandler had already reimbursed the hotel on his behalf. Hendrix and Chandler returned to London the following day.

WEDNESDAY, JANUARY 10, 1968

AXIS: BOLD AS LOVE. REPRISE RECORDS RS 6281. U.S. ALBUM RELEASE. PRODUCER: CHAS CHANDLER. ENGINEER: EDDIE KRAMER. SECOND ENGINEERS: TERRY BROWN, GEORGE CHKIANTZ, ANDY JOHNS. "EXP" / "UP FROM THE SKIES" / "SPANISH CASTLE MAGIC" / "WAIT UNTIL TOMORROW" / "AIN'T NO TELLING" / "LITTLE WING" / "IF 6 WAS 9" / "YOU GOT ME FLOATIN'" / "CASTLES MADE OF SAND" / "SHE'S SO FINE" / "ONE RAINY WISH" / "LITTLE MISS LOVER" / "BOLD AS LOVE"

Track Records, Reprise's London counterpart, issued *Axis: Bold As Love* in December 1967, but Warner Bros. held up the release to avoid conflict with the December release of Capitol Records' *Get That Feeling*, a tepid collection of recordings featuring Hendrix backing Curtis Knight as a member of the Squires. Even with the delayed release, U.S. sales of *Axis: Bold As Love* were hurt by the resulting confusion. Nonetheless, the Experience's skyrocketing popularity, fueled by the phenomenal success of *Are You Experienced*, propelled the album to the number 5 position in *Billboard*'s Top 200 album chart in February 1968.

SUNDAY, JANUARY 21, 1968

LONDON, OLYMPIC STUDIOS. PRODUCER: CHAS CHANDLER. ENGINEER: EDDIE KRAMER. SECOND ENGINEERS: ANDY JOHNS, GEORGE CHKIANTZ.

Recording of *Electric Ladyland* resumed with Hendrix's definitive remake of Bob Dylan's "All Along The Watchtower." Hendrix's admiration for Dylan expressed itself on many occasions, perhaps never more eloquently than in his stirring rendition of "Like A Rolling Stone" at the June 1967 Monterey Pop Festival.

When and how Hendrix was inspired to record "All Along The Watchtower" is not entirely clear. Traffic's Dave Mason has suggested that a small party thrown by Viv Prince provided the impetus, as the place where he, Hendrix, Linda Keith, and Rolling Stones guitarist Brian Jones first heard Dylan's *John Wesley Harding* album. Olympic engineer Andy Johns offers a second perspective. He clearly recalls Hendrix playing recordings of Dylan songs at the studio on more than one occasion. "That was the first time any of us had heard those reels," Johns says. Publicist Michael Goldstein, who also worked for Dylan's manager, Albert Grossman, provided Hendrix with reels of new Dylan songs. This practice, openly encouraged by co-manager Michael Jeffery, was not an unusual one for Grossman. Placing Dylan's songs with artists interested in recording his client's songs was a lucrative practice for Grossman. After the recent U.S. chart failure of "Up From The Skies," Jeffery hoped that a Dylan interpretation could help Hendrix crack what seemed to be impenetrable AM radio playlists.

Brian Jones joined the Experience for the session, along with Dave Mason of Traffic, who Hendrix asked to contribute acoustic guitar. "Dave hung a lot with Jimi and was a regular in the studio," says Kramer. "Jimi was aware of his ability and that he could cover the part adequately." To maximize the effect, however, the group decided that Mason needed a twelve-string guitar instead. With Mason in tow, Andy Johns volunteered to pick up the instrument at his South London flat. "I had my brother Glyn's Harmony twelve-string at this dreadful dive that I was living in," says Johns. "Mason drove me out there in his Jaguar, but as I was in the process of being evicted, I had to climb through the upstairs window to get the guitar."

Upon their return, Hendrix led the group through a series of rehearsals before proper takes ensued. Brian Jones initially began on piano, but after a few unsuccessful attempts, Hendrix elected not to include the instrument. According to Mitch Mitchell, Jones gravitated to percussion next before retreating to the control room for the balance of the session. Hendrix, says Kramer, had a firm understanding of just how the song should be arranged and performed. Mason, playing guitar in the studio's vocal booth, earned his share of Hendrix's reprimands, as he struggled to master the song's chord changes. Hendrix and Redding also clashed, and Redding, angered by Hendrix's seemingly ceaseless quest for perfection, bolted from the studio early in the session. Mason, who regularly assumed bass chores for Traffic's studio recordings, took over in Redding's absence, but Hendrix overdubbed the part himself later that same evening, using a small, custom bass guitar that Bill Wyman had given to Andy Johns.

While no one kept a record of the countless rehearsal takes, the group recorded twenty-four takes of "All Along The Watchtower" before stopping work, and a four-to-four reduction mix was prepared. The group recorded two additional takes on to that new master, and the basic track had been successfully achieved. A rough mix was also prepared.

FRIDAY, JANUARY 26, 1968

LONDON, OLYMPIC STUDIOS. PRODUCER: CHAS CHANDLER. ENGINEER: EDDIE KRAMER. SECOND ENGINEER: PHIL BROWN.

Hendrix again focused on a song that he had not composed, as the Experience recorded their interpretation of Bo Hansson and Janne Karlsson's "Tax Free." Hendrix had discovered the song during an earlier tour of Sweden and appreciated the song's freewheeling arrangement and intricate time changes.

The session began with five rehearsals of the song before any formal attempts to record it. The group went through one version marked "retake" before the actual recording of take 1, which assistant engineer Phil Brown marked as "good." Takes 2 and 3 broke down before the group rebounded with a solid fourth attempt. Hendrix pressed for another opportunity, and this version, take 5, realized the master. Chandler felt that a slight breakdown at the song's close could be improved, so four attempts to record "Edit Section" were made before the fifth proved successful.

After the basic track had been completed, guitar overdubs followed. Mixes were then prepared for both "Tax Free" and "All Along The Watchtower." The best mix that Chandler, Hendrix, and Kramer prepared from this session was later issued as part of 1997's *South Saturn Delta*.

SUNDAY, JANUARY 28, 1968

LONDON, OLYMPIC STUDIOS. PRODUCER: CHAS CHANDLER. ENGINEER: EDDIE KRAMER.
Hendrix returned to the January 26 master recording of "Tax Free" during this productive session. He successfully added the song's distinctive rhythm guitar part to the master, directing the sound through a Leslie organ speaker. "Tax Free," in Chandler's view, was now complete. Hendrix, on the other hand, was not quite as sure. He rerecorded the number at the Record Plant months later, unable even then to decide whether he had recorded the song to his full satisfaction or not.

MONDAY, JANUARY 29, 1968

OLYMPIA, PARIS. TWO SHOWS. WITH ERIC BURDON AND THE NEW ANIMALS. **SET LIST, FIRST SHOW:** "SGT. PEPPER'S LONELY HEARTS CLUB BAND" / "FIRE" / "THE WIND CRIES MARY" / "SPANISH CASTLE MAGIC" / "CATFISH BLUES" / "LITTLE WING" / "PURPLE HAZE." **SET LIST, SECOND SHOW:** "KILLIN' FLOOR" / "CATFISH BLUES" / "FOXEY LADY" / "RED HOUSE" / "DRIVIN' SOUTH" / "THE WIND CRIES MARY" / "FIRE" / "LITTLE WING" / "PURPLE HAZE"
The Experience made a quick trip to Paris to perform two concerts before a wildly enthusiastic audience. The evening's second performance was recorded by RTE, the French national radio broadcasting company, and was issued as part of the short-lived 1990 Reprise box set *Stages*. *Stages* was not reissued by MCA Records when the North American distribution rights to the Hendrix catalog transferred there in 1993.

The group flew to New York the following day

for a press reception organized by publicist Michael Goldstein. Goldstein dubbed the event "The British Are Coming" and made the Experience, as well as the other groups in the Michael Jeffery/Chas Chandler stable, available to journalists and photographers at the Copter Lounge atop the Pan Am Building in Manhattan.

Following the media hoopla in New York, the Experience flew to San Francisco, where their extensive U.S. tour in support of *Axis: Bold As Love* began in earnest at the Fillmore Auditorium.

THURSDAY, FEBRUARY 1, 1968

FILLMORE AUDITORIUM, SAN FRANCISCO. TWO SHOWS. WITH SOFT MACHINE, JOHN MAYALL'S BLUESBREAKERS, AND ALBERT KING. **PARTIAL SET LIST, FIRST SHOW:** "FIRE" / "RED HOUSE" / "PURPLE HAZE" / "FOXEY LADY" / "THE WIND CRIES MARY"

FRIDAY, FEBRUARY 2, 1968

WINTERLAND BALLROOM, SAN FRANCISCO. TWO SHOWS. WITH SOFT MACHINE, JOHN MAYALL'S BLUES-BREAKERS, AND ALBERT KING.

SATURDAY, FEBRUARY 3, 1968

WINTERLAND BALLROOM, SAN FRANCISCO. TWO SHOWS. WITH SOFT MACHINE, JOHN MAYALL'S BLUES-BREAKERS, AND ALBERT KING. **SET LIST, FIRST SHOW:** "SGT. PEPPER'S LONELY HEARTS CLUB BAND" / "FIRE" / "HEY JOE" / "FOXEY LADY" / "THE WIND CRIES MARY" / "KILLING FLOOR" / "LITTLE WING" / "PURPLE HAZE." **PARTIAL SET LIST, SECOND SHOW:** "ROCK ME BABY" / "RED HOUSE" / "FOXEY LADY" / "LIKE A ROLLING STONE" / "PURPLE HAZE"

SUNDAY, FEBRUARY 4, 1968

WINTERLAND BALLROOM, SAN FRANCISCO. TWO SHOWS. WITH ALBERT KING AND BIG BROTHER AND THE HOLDING COMPANY. **SET LIST, SECOND SHOW:** "KILLING FLOOR" / "RED HOUSE" / "CATFISH BLUES" / "DEAR MR. FANTASY" / "PURPLE HAZE"

San Francisco–based impresario Bill Graham booked the Experience to perform eight concerts over four consecutive nights. Tickets were in high demand, thanks in part to the impressive supporting cast, and each of the eight performances sold out.

The Experience were in fine form throughout this remarkable string of performances. Graham shifted the venue on the fourth night from the previously scheduled Fillmore to the larger Winterland Ballroom to accommodate the demand for their final performances. The lineup also changed when Soft Machine drummer Robert Wyatt got into a heated argument with Bill Graham. Graham pulled the group and promptly hired Big Brother and the Holding Company to take their place

Perhaps in homage to blues guitarist Albert King, Hendrix revised the set list for his final Fillmore performance. He began his second set with versions of "Killing Floor," "Red House," and "Catfish Blues" before the proceedings took an unusual turn: Mitch Mitchell invited Buddy Miles onstage to take over his drum kit prior to the start of the next number. "Buddy Miles was with the Electric Flag at Monterey and there came a time when I thought, 'Christ, I'd like to hear what Jimi would sound like with him,'" Mitchell remembers. "So we were playing in San Francisco at one of the Experience gigs and Buddy was there. I said to him, 'Do me a favor, swap seats with me and play.'"

Hendrix launched into a loose, extended instrumental rendition of Traffic's "Dear Mr. Fantasy" with Miles in place of Mitchell. Mitchell then returned to the stage as the Experience closed their performance with "Purple Haze," all to the delight of the sold-out house. An amateur soundboard recording of this performance would later be paired with recordings made at the Paris Olympia Theater on October 9, 1967, and issued as the Dagger Records official "bootleg" *Paris '67/San Francisco '68*.

MONDAY, FEBRUARY 5, 1968

ARIZONA STATE UNIVERSITY, TEMPE, ARIZONA. WITH SOFT MACHINE.

From San Francisco, the Experience ventured across the U.S., performing at a mix of clubs, colleges, and medium-sized auditoriums. Together with their loyal

tour manager Gerry Stickells, the group packed into a rented station wagon. In what can only be described as a remarkable test of their endurance and enthusiasm, the Experience performed sixty concerts in sixty days during the first leg of this tour.

TUESDAY, FEBRUARY 6, 1968

VIP CLUB, TUCSON, ARIZONA. WITH SOFT MACHINE.

THURSDAY, FEBRUARY 8, 1968

SACRAMENTO STATE COLLEGE, SACRAMENTO, CALIFORNIA. WITH SOFT MACHINE AND THE CREATORS.

FRIDAY, FEBRUARY 9, 1968

CONVENTION CENTER, ANAHEIM, CALIFORNIA. TWO SHOWS. WITH THE ANIMALS, EIRE APPARENT, AND

SOFT MACHINE. **PARTIAL SET LIST, SECOND SHOW:** "CATFISH BLUES" / "PURPLE HAZE"

Stage and sound equipment were still primitive during this era, and the group was dogged by various technical snafus at nearly every venue. In Anaheim, Hendrix's second performance at the Anaheim Convention Center was cut short when his amplifier blew.

SATURDAY, FEBRUARY 10, 1968

SHRINE AUDITORIUM, LOS ANGELES, CALIFORNIA. WITH SOFT MACHINE, BLUE CHEER, AND THE ELECTRIC FLAG. **PARTIAL SET LIST:** "ARE YOU EXPERIENCED?" / "THE WIND CRIES MARY" / "UP FROM THE SKIES" / "RED HOUSE" / "WILD THING" / "PURPLE HAZE"

Hendrix enjoyed an afternoon jam session prior to the Shrine Auditorium performance with David Crosby, Electric Flag bassist Harvey Brooks, and Buddy Miles. After the performance, Hendrix was invited to a party at the Laurel Canyon home of Monkees guitarist Peter Tork.

MONDAY, FEBRUARY 11, 1968

ROBERTSON GYM, UCSB, SANTA BARBARA, CALIFORNIA. WITH SOFT MACHINE AND EAST SIDE KIDS.

TUESDAY, FEBRUARY 12, 1968

SEATTLE CENTER ARENA, SEATTLE, WASHINGTON. WITH SOFT MACHINE.

The Experience traveled to Seattle for a concert in Hendrix's hometown, marking his first homecoming in more than five years. Hendrix returned to his father's house afterwards to spend the evening with family and friends, while Mitchell and Redding checked into the Olympic Hotel. Hendrix enjoyed a warm reunion with his father, and his success was a source of tremendous pride for the entire Hendrix family.

WEDNESDAY, FEBRUARY 13, 1968

ACKERMAN BALLROOM, UNIVERSITY OF CALIFORNIA, LOS ANGELES, CALIFORNIA. WITH SOFT MACHINE.

Hendrix began the day at Garfield High School in Seattle, returning to his former school to address a student assembly organized in his honor. Hendrix's equipment wasn't available, so he gave a short speech and nervously answered a few questions from students. Afterwards, Hendrix was given a ceremonial key to the city of Seattle.

Hendrix then flew to Los Angeles for a performance at UCLA that same evening. The ballroom was not equipped for a concert by an act like the Experience. The power supply failed partway through the group's set, and Hendrix was forced to the sidelines until the staff could make repairs.

THURSDAY, FEBRUARY 14, 1968

REGIS COLLEGE, DENVER, COLORADO. WITH SOFT MACHINE.

FRIDAY, FEBRUARY 15, 1968

MUNICIPAL AUDITORIUM, SAN ANTONIO, TEXAS. WITH SOFT MACHINE, THE MOVING SIDEWALKS, AND NEAL FORD & THE FANATICS.

SATURDAY, FEBRUARY 16, 1968

STATE FAIR MUSIC HALL, DALLAS, TEXAS. WITH SOFT MACHINE, THE MOVING SIDEWALKS, AND THE CHESSMEN. **SET LIST:** "ARE YOU EXPERIENCED?" / "FIRE" / "THE WIND CRIES MARY" / "TAX FREE" / "FOXEY LADY" / "HEY JOE" / "SPANISH CASTLE MAGIC" / "RED HOUSE" / "PURPLE HAZE"

SUNDAY, FEBRUARY 17, 1968

WILL ROGERS AUDITORIUM, FORT WORTH, TEXAS. WITH SOFT MACHINE, THE MOVING SIDEWALKS, AND NEAL FORD & THE FANATICS. **SET LIST:** "SGT. PEPPER'S LONELY HEARTS CLUB BAND" / "CAN YOU PLEASE CRAWL OUT YOUR WINDOW?" / "THE WIND CRIES MARY" / "FIRE" / "CATFISH BLUES" / "FOXEY LADY" / "HEY JOE" / "PURPLE HAZE" / "WILD THING"

MONDAY, FEBRUARY 18, 1968

MUSIC HALL, HOUSTON, TEXAS. WITH SOFT MACHINE,

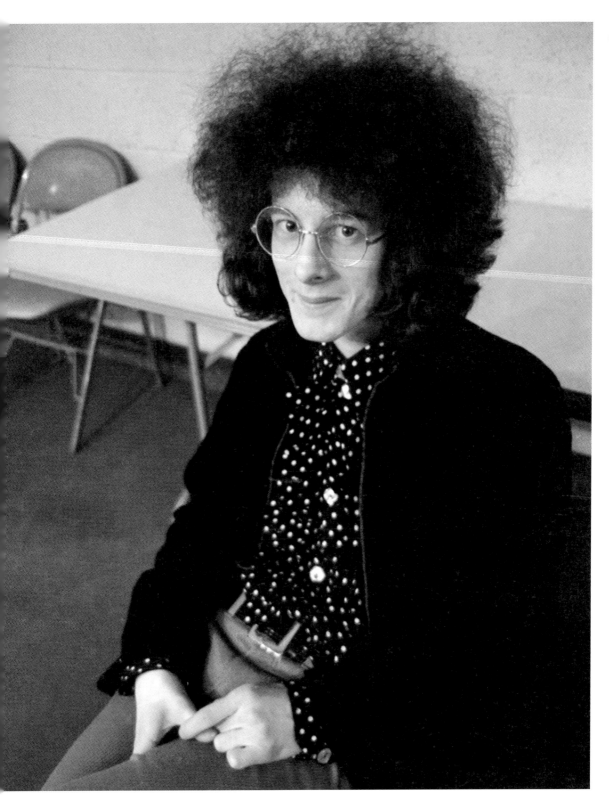

THURSDAY, FEBRUARY 22, 1968

ELECTRIC FACTORY, PHILADELPHIA, PENNSYLVANIA. TWO SHOWS. WITH WOODY'S TRUCK STOP.

FRIDAY, FEBRUARY 23, 1968

MASONIC TEMPLE, DETROIT, MICHIGAN. WITH SOFT MACHINE, MC5, AND THE RATIONALS.

SATURDAY, FEBRUARY 24, 1968

CNE COLISEUM, TORONTO, CANADA. WITH SOFT MACHINE, THE PAUPERS, AND EIRE APPARENT. **SET LIST:** "HEY JOE" / "FOXEY LADY" / "THE WIND CRIES MARY" / "SPANISH CASTLE MAGIC" / "PURPLE HAZE" / "RED HOUSE" / "WILD THING"

After the Experience's performance, Hendrix reportedly engaged in a jam session with Robbie Robertson and members of the Hawks (soon to gain fame as The Band) at a local Toronto club.

NEW YORK, MAYFAIR STUDIOS. PRODUCER: CHAS CHANDLER.

With the Experience in the midst of their extensive U.S. tour, Chas Chandler booked time at Mayfair to transfer a number of half-inch, four-track masters made at Olympic Studios to one-inch, eight-track tape. Unlike the four-track masters, these eight-track tape submasters could be played on a twelve-track machine like the new Scully model at the Record Plant, the New York studio where Chandler and the Experience planned to resume production of the unfinished album *Electric Ladyland*.

Chandler transferred "Dream," "Crosstown Traffic," "Touch You" (formerly called "Dance"), and "Tax Free" so that additional work could be made on these new submasters if necessary. He also transferred the Soft Machine's "Making Sun While The Hay Shines" for fellow producer Tom Wilson.

THE MOVING SIDEWALKS, AND NEAL FORD & THE FANATICS. **SET LIST:** "SGT. PEPPER'S LONELY HEARTS CLUB BAND" / "FIRE" / "HEY JOE" / "FOXEY LADY" / "THE WIND CRIES MARY" / "I DON'T LIVE TODAY" / "CATFISH BLUES" / "PURPLE HAZE"

These Texas performances were enthusiastically received by the audiences who packed all four venues. Hendrix's version of Bob Dylan's "Can You Please Crawl Out Your Window?" made its first known U.S. appearance as part of the group's stage repertoire.

The opening acts for these performances include some notable guitarists in their own right. Hendrix was introduced to future ZZ Top frontman Billy Gibbons, then guitarist for the Moving Sidewalks, and Fabulous Thunderbirds founder Jimmie Vaughan.

WEDNESDAY, FEBRUARY 21, 1968

ELECTRIC FACTORY, PHILADELPHIA, PENNSYLVANIA. TWO SHOWS. WITH WOODY'S TRUCK STOP.

SUNDAY, FEBRUARY 25, 1968

CIVIC OPERA HOUSE, CHICAGO, ILLINOIS. TWO SHOWS. WITH SOFT MACHINE. **PARTIAL SET LIST** [SHOW

UNKNOWN]: "SGT. PEPPER'S LONELY HEARTS CLUB BAND" / "FIRE" / "THE WIND CRIES MARY" / "FOXEY LADY" / "I DON'T LIVE TODAY" / "HEY JOE" / "CAN YOU PLEASE CRAWL OUT YOUR WINDOW?" / "MANIC DEPRESSION" / "LIKE A ROLLING STONE" / "PURPLE HAZE"

MONDAY, FEBRUARY 26, 1968

"UP FROM THE SKIES" / "ONE RAINY WISH" REPRISE 0665. U.S. SINGLE RELEASE.

Overlooking such possible contenders as "Little Wing" and "If 6 Was 9," these two tracks from *Axis: Bold As Love* were coupled for release as the lead single from that album. "Up From The Skies," however, did not improve on the performance of the two previous Experience singles, only reaching number 82 before falling out of the chart after a four-week run.

TUESDAY, FEBRUARY 27, 1968

THE FACTORY, MADISON, WISCONSIN. TWO SHOWS. WITH SOFT MACHINE.

WEDNESDAY, FEBRUARY 28, 1968

THE SCENE CLUB, MILWAUKEE, WISCONSIN. TWO SHOWS. WITH SOFT MACHINE.

THURSDAY, FEBRUARY 29, 1968

THE SCENE CLUB, MILWAUKEE, WISCONSIN. TWO SHOWS. WITH SOFT MACHINE.

SATURDAY, MARCH 2, 1968

HUNTER COLLEGE, NEW YORK, NEW YORK. WITH SOFT MACHINE AND JOHN HAMMOND JR. **PARTIAL SET LIST:** "TAX FREE" / "FOXEY LADY" / "LIKE A ROLLING STONE" / "KILLING FLOOR" / "RED HOUSE" / "FIRE"

SUNDAY, MARCH 3, 1968

VETERANS MEMORIAL AUDITORIUM, COLUMBUS, OHIO. WITH DANTES, 4 O'CLOCK BALLOON AND SOFT MACHINE.

FRIDAY, MARCH 8, 1968

MARVEL GYMNASIUM, BROWN UNIVERSITY, PROVIDENCE, RHODE ISLAND.

SATURDAY, MARCH 9, 1968

NEW YORK UNIVERSITY, LONG ISLAND, NEW YORK. WITH SOFT MACHINE.

MONDAY, MARCH 10, 1968

INTERNATIONAL BALLROOM, HILTON HOTEL, WASHINGTON, D.C. TWO SHOWS. WITH SOFT MACHINE. **SET LIST, FIRST SHOW:** "SGT. PEPPER'S LONELY HEARTS CLUB BAND" / "HEY JOE" / "FOXEY LADY" / "THE WIND CRIES MARY" / "RED HOUSE" / "PURPLE HAZE" / "WILD THING." **SET LIST, SECOND SHOW:** "KILLING FLOOR" / "FOXEY LADY" / "THE WIND CRIES MARY" / "FIRE" / "RED HOUSE" / "I DON'T LIVE TODAY" / "PURPLE HAZE" / "WILD THING"

WEDNESDAY, MARCH 13, 1968

NEW YORK, SOUND CENTER STUDIOS. PRODUCER: JIMI HENDRIX. ENGINEERS: VINCENT J. GAGLIANO, TOM MUCCIO, ANGEL SANDOVAL, LENNY STEA.

The Experience were in New York enjoying a brief respite from their U.S. tour when Hendrix organized this session at Sound Center Studios. This was Hendrix's first session in America where he assumed the dual role of artist and producer away from the watchful eye of Chas Chandler.

Sound Center had earned recognition in New York during this period for having one of the first eight-track recording machines. "We weren't a rich studio," remembers engineer Lenny Stea. "We happened to have this new, very flexible console board that was very quiet but because we didn't have the more expensive equipment that was out there, our engineers made it up. That's where this "sound" came from. A lot of experimental stuff came out of small studios like ours, not the majors."

An interesting group of musicians joined Hendrix on this date, including Stephen Stills, drummer Jimmy Mayes, Paul Caruso on harmonica, and Fugs guitarist

Ken Pine. "He called me at home one afternoon, which really surprised me, as I had not spoken to him for some time," says Ken Pine. "He asked if I would play twelve-string guitar on a session he wanted to do. He was looking to add a bluegrass, country-rock feel. He picked me up and we parked in a parking garage near the studio. He had the wide-brim hat with a feather in the band. The attendant looked at him as if he was from Mars. At the studio, he pulled out some papers and said, 'Check this out.' He had written out the lyrics to Bob Dylan's 'All Along The Watchtower' by hand and told me he had recorded the song in London. He wanted to know what I thought of the song and did I think it was any good!"

Hendrix began this session with "My Friend," a new, Dylan-influenced original he had been developing. "Kenny Pine was on twelve-string guitar," recalls Paul Caruso. "Jimi was on bass, Jimmy Mayes was on drums, and Stephen Stills, who, except for the piano in the introduction, didn't contribute anything else."

They must have spent time rehearsing the arrangement before recording, because the first take made it clear that each musician knew his respective parts. Take 1 was recorded in full without a live vocal from Hendrix. Take 2 broke down, but their next effort yielded the master. Hendrix turned his attention next to recording the bar atmosphere he envisioned. "Jimi had them making believe they were all drunk," says engineer Tom Muccio. "They were just falling all over the floor having fun with the track."

Hendrix then put forward "Angel Catarina," a stark, early rendition of what would later take form as "1983 (A Merman I Should Turn To Be)." Once the basic track was recorded, Hendrix overdubbed a second guitar part. Much work remained before this recording could be considered finished, but the song's promise was clear.

Hendrix remained in the control room as Noel Redding switched to guitar and led Miles on drums and Stephen Stills on bass through a formative instrumental workout of his song "Little Miss Strange." Hendrix had clearly assumed the role of producer, and he can be heard making comments over the talkback microphone as Redding attempted fifteen takes of the song.

Buddy Miles made his recorded debut with Hendrix during these sessions, providing the original drum track for "Somewhere," another promising original song that Hendrix considered for the new album. Miles and Stills struggled to establish the proper tempo Hendrix desired for the song, and a number of early efforts seem more like rehearsals than structured takes. "Jimi would be recording in the studio and he would be creating a stack of tapes like this [measures height with his hand] and I would say "Jim, some of these tapes, you know you can run them again," remembers Angel Sandoval. "He'd say, 'Oh no, just keep putting [new reels of tape] on' . . . and I thought, "Oh my God. . . ."

The initial struggles gave way to a basic track, the brightest aspect of which was a strong performance from Hendrix. "Somewhere" lay fallow until 1971, when Mitch Mitchell overdubbed new drum parts at Electric Lady Studios in an effort to upgrade the existing master. Despite this work, the song was not released as part of the initial posthumous releases that began with *Cry Of Love* in 1971. "Somewhere" was among those unfortunate Hendrix masters on to which producer Alan Douglas posthumously added overdubs from session musicians in 1974 so that the song could be included as part of the controversial compilation *Crash Landing*. In 2000, the 1971 version that featured Mitch Mitchell's overdubbed drum parts was included as part of the *Jimi Hendrix Experience* box set.

THURSDAY, MARCH 14, 1968

NEW YORK, SOUND CENTER STUDIOS. PRODUCER: JIMI HENDRIX. ENGINEERS: VINCENT J. GAGLIANO, TOM MUCCIO, ANGEL SANDOVAL, LENNY STEA.

Work resumed on "My Friend" as Hendrix returned to record a lead vocal and prepare mixes of the song. "Hendrix was infatuated by the recording console because it looked like the inside of a spaceship," recalls Tom Muccio. "It had nice lights on it and offered him a nice big area to work on." He was equally infatuated with the cutting-edge sliding faders, as opposed to the rotary knobs used at Olympic Studios in London.

None of the material recorded during these two March 1968 sessions was released during Hendrix's lifetime. Despite their promise, both "Somewhere" and "My Friend" were passed over for *Electric Ladyland*. "My

Friend" initially appeared on 1971's *Cry Of Love* and, later on, *First Rays Of The New Rising Sun.*

FRIDAY, MARCH 15, 1968

CLARK UNIVERSITY, WORCESTER, MASSACHUSETTS. TWO SHOWS. WITH SOFT MACHINE. **PARTIAL SET LIST, SECOND SHOW:** "FIRE" / "RED HOUSE" / "FOXEY LADY" / "PURPLE HAZE" / "WILD THING"

The impressive sales performance of both *Are You Experienced* and *Axis: Bold As Love* demonstrated the burgeoning popularity the Experience enjoyed in the U.S. General Artists Company (GAC) served the Experience as their American booking agency, and when the company began to organize an extensive U.S. tour, they sorely underestimated the group's drawing power. The agency eschewed bookings at traditional theater venues in lieu of a series of college engagements on campuses such as New York University, Regis, Arizona State, Brown, Hunter, and Xavier, where it hoped young audiences would support the group. Clark University, located one hour west of Boston in Worcester, Massachusetts, was typical of these small college bookings. Filled to capacity, Atwood Hall could accommodate approximately 600 students. Hendrix could easily fill a larger venue, but GAC had set these dates months earlier, and the group had no alternative but to honor them. These engagements provided fans with intimate access to the group, yet nearly all of them were poorly equipped to handle the sound and lighting requirements for the show.

Hendrix's Clark University performance was filmed in part by the BBC for the documentary *All My Loving.* Only "Wild Thing" made the cut, and the remaining footage was subsequently lost or destroyed. Thankfully, a separate source of audio recordings survived, and these, coupled with backstage interviews with Hendrix, Mitchell, and Redding, were issued as the Dagger Records official "bootleg" *Live At Clark University* in 1999.

SATURDAY, MARCH 16, 1968

LEWISTON ARMORY, LEWISTON, MAINE. WITH SOFT MACHINE, THE HANSEATIC LEAGUE, AND TERRY AND THE TELSTARS.

THURSDAY, MARCH 19, 1968

CAPITOL THEATRE, OTTAWA, CANADA. TWO SHOWS. WITH SOFT MACHINE. **PARTIAL SET LIST, FIRST SHOW:** "SGT. PEPPER'S LONELY HEARTS CLUB BAND" / "FIRE" / "PURPLE HAZE" / "LITTLE WING" / "FOXEY LADY" / "RED HOUSE" / "I DON'T LIVE TODAY." **PARTIAL SET LIST, SECOND SHOW:** "KILLING FLOOR" / "TAX FREE" / "RED HOUSE" / "FOXEY LADY" / "HEY JOE" / "SPANISH CASTLE MAGIC" / "PURPLE HAZE" / "WILD THING"

It is likely that Hendrix himself recorded these two spirited Ottawa performances. A two-track mixing console recording made of the evening's second performance was issued as *The Jimi Hendrix Experience: Live In Ottawa*, the fourth release in the Dagger Records series. It showcases the Experience cresting at the peak of their friendship and unity as a group.

TUESDAY, APRIL 2, 1968

PAUL SAUVE ARENA, MONTREAL, CANADA. WITH SOFT MACHINE AND OLIVUS. **SET LIST:** "KILLING FLOOR" / "HEY JOE" / "FIRE" / "THE WIND CRIES MARY" / "FOXEY LADY" / "I DON'T LIVE TODAY" / "MANIC DEPRESSION" / "PURPLE HAZE" / "WILD THING"

THURSDAY, APRIL 4, 1968

CIVIC DOME, VIRGINIA BEACH, VIRGINIA.

FRIDAY, APRIL 5, 1968

SYMPHONY HALL, NEWARK, NEW JERSEY.

SATURDAY, APRIL 6, 1968

WESTCHESTER COUNTY CENTER, WHITE PLAINS, NEW YORK.

THURSDAY, APRIL 18, 1968

RECORD PLANT, NEW YORK, NEW YORK. PRODUCER: CHAS CHANDLER. ENGINEER: GARY KELLGREN.

Rather than return to London and Olympic, Chandler booked time at the Record Plant, the new, twelve-track

studio in Manhattan built by engineer Gary Kellgren, Revlon executive Chris Stone, and producer Tom Wilson.

The Record Plant, which would become Hendrix's creative haven for almost two years, came as the result of an unexpected friendship between Kellgren and Chris Stone. "I was working for the Revlon Corporation in 1967," remembers Stone. "My wife had recently given birth to our first child, and our next-door neighbors knew this young woman about to have her first child [who] was scared to death. Her name was Marta Kellgren. So they arranged for my wife to get together with her. Gary, her husband, came along as well. While the two women talked about what it was like to have children, Gary and I sat in the living room staring at each other. We were forced into a social situation, and Gary, in those days, was extremely shy. He just didn't talk. During our conversation, he invited me down to see

Mayfair Studios, where he worked. At Mayfair, Kellgren was everything. He was the engineer, the janitor, and the equipment technician. I had always had an interest in recording studios, so I asked Gary if I could get into the bookkeeping office. He couldn't see a reason why not and let me have a look at the books. I found out that they were billing $5,000 a week and paying Gary $200. I played this out and told him that what he needed was a manager. I basically didn't want to be his manager, but he was a nice guy and our wives had become friends, so I offered to go see his boss with him. The next afternoon, we sat down with his boss and Gary's salary was raised to $1,000 a week."

Impressed by Stone's tenacity and skill as a negotiator, Kellgren grew closer to him, and their friendship deepened. In confidence, Kellgren told Stone of his desire to open his own recording facility. "He wanted to have his own studio," remembers Stone, "but felt he didn't know how to put things together. He asked if I would be interested in working with him and I was. I put the package together and got us some money to get started."

Still employed by Revlon, Stone's association with the cosmetic giant afforded him with two crucial advantages; credibility and access to venture capital. "Originally, we had asked [engineer] Wes Farrell to be a part of everything, but he didn't want to go along. Tom Wilson became a partner, Kellgren was a partner, I was a partner, and the money was a partner," explains Stone. "The money was Ankie Revson, the former wife of Charles Revson. Everyone thought that Revlon owned the Record Plant, because to get business or credit information they had to call me, and to call me you had to call Revlon. Creditors assumed Revlon owned the studio and I never said they didn't, so we got credit from everybody."

Buttressed by Revson's financial support, work on this daring gambit quickly accelerated. "Ankie Revson financed the entire cost of building and equipping the Record Plant," says Stone. "That meant building and outfitting one studio and doing all the structural work for the second. We purchased a twelve-track, four-track, two-track, and a mono tape machine. That line of machines cost us $35,000. Finished and ready to open, our entire costs were $82,000."

One of the facility's principal attractions was its Scully twelve-track tape machine, marketed to studios as a considerable upgrade over four- and eight-track recording. *Magical Mystery Tour*, the Beatles' most recent release, had only been recorded on four tracks—as had all of Hendrix's previous sessions at Olympic Studios. These new tape machines were extremely rare, so much so that when the Record Plant opened its doors, it owned one of only two units in circulation.

In addition to the technical advantages, Kellgren wanted to upgrade the creative atmosphere within the recording studio. Previously, artists contracted to major labels like Columbia had to record at the facilities owned and staffed by their label. Apart from the producer, the engineering staff was strictly governed by union rules and regulations. Kellgren was sympathetic toward rock and roll and more tolerant of its relaxed rules and open experimentation. He insisted on making subtle changes that would make his clients feel more comfortable. "When we got into the business," Stone says, "recording studios were like hospitals—fluorescent lights, hardwood floors, and white walls. Kellgren initiated the process of changing the recording studio into a living room. The biggest compliment a client could pay us would be to look around and say, 'Wow! I'd like to live here.'"

Kellgren's growing reputation as an engineer, coupled with the respect Tom Wilson enjoyed throughout the industry, helped to soothe any concerns artists and A&R representatives might have voiced about working in a new, independent facility. The owners of the Record Plant took their quest for credibility a step further by hiring engineer Eddie Kramer away from Olympic Studios in London. "We brought Eddie over because he was the star of Olympic," explains Stone. "Having an English engineer was a bit of a coup for them," says Kramer. "The major factor in bringing me over was my relationship with Jimi and the role I played in creating his sound. I had also worked with Traffic and the Rolling Stones, and they wanted to ensure that those clients came to the Record Plant and stayed there." Luring the Experience in as clients established the Record Plant as the leading independent recording studio for rock and roll in New York, if not the entire U.S.

The Record Plant opened for business on Wednesday, March 13, 1968, but because of delays resulting from his immigration status, Kramer did not join the staff until April 18. The studio's first major clients were the Jimi Hendrix Experience, whose lengthy stint provided a tremendous boost to the facility's reputation. As a result, the fledgling studio was booked solid for its first three months in operation. Kellgren and Stone's gamble had become a phenomenal success story. "We had a very profitable business," says Stone. "Look at the ratios. We opened for under $100,000 and charged $85 an hour. Today, it costs you almost two million to open and you charge $175 an hour or $2,000 a day for a lock-out rate. It doesn't compute anymore, but it certainly did in those days."

The Experience's first session at the new studio resulted in basic tracks for "Long Hot Summer Night," another of Hendrix's songs whose development traced back to the October 1967 sessions for *Axis: Bold As Love*. Recording began with a superb demo that featured Mitchell on drums and Al Kooper on piano. A playback followed before the three returned to the studio and resumed recording. A string of inspired but incomplete efforts preceded a robust take 13. Chandler and Hendrix designated this take as the basic track, and bass and guitar parts were then overdubbed.

To thank Kooper for his contribution, Hendrix gave him one of his Stratocasters. "Jimi and I shared the same music publishers," remembers Kooper. "We had also jammed at the Generation Club together. At the session for 'Long Hot Summer Night,' I played piano rather than organ. Jimi saw me fooling around with one of his Stratocasters and he offered the guitar to me as a gift. I refused, but he later had the guitar shipped to my home."

FRIDAY, APRIL 19, 1968

TROY ARMORY, TROY, NEW YORK. WITH SOFT MACHINE. This performance was originally scheduled for April 7, but in the aftermath of the assassination of Martin Luther King Jr., the promoter moved the date out of respect for the fallen civil rights leader—and in hopes that the tensions caused by his murder would not ignite the audience.

SMASH HITS. U.K. ALBUM RELEASE. TRACK RECORDS 613 004. PRODUCER: CHAS CHANDLER. ENGINEERS: EDDIE KRAMER, DAVE SIDDLE. SECOND ENGINEERS: GEORGE CHKIANTZ, ANDY JOHNS. "PURPLE HAZE" / "FIRE" / "THE WIND CRIES MARY" / "CAN YOU SEE ME" / "51ST ANNIVERSARY" / "HEY JOE" / "STONE FREE" / "THE STARS THAT PLAY WITH LAUGHING SAM'S DICE" / "MANIC DEPRESSION" / "HIGHWAY CHILE" / "BURNING OF THE MIDNIGHT LAMP" / "FOXEY LADY"

To satisfy those fans who preferred albums to singles, Track Records compiled this extremely popular release, blending the group's first four singles with such favorites from *Are You Experienced* as "Fire" and "Manic Depression." *Smash Hits* enjoyed strong and steady sales, peaking at number 4 during a healthy twenty-five-week stay on the album chart.

SATURDAY, APRIL 20, 1968

RECORD PLANT, NEW YORK, NEW YORK. 7:00 P.M. PRODUCER: CHAS CHANDLER. ENGINEER: GARY KELLGREN.

Redding's composition "Little Miss Strange Test Session" or "Lilacs For Captain Curry's Coffin Combo," as the tape box was marked, provided the focus of this session. With Hendrix not present, Redding recorded two takes on acoustic guitar with Mitchell on drums before a complete third take yielded the basic track. Redding then added a bass overdub before the session concluded.

SUNDAY, APRIL 21, 1968

RECORD PLANT, NEW YORK, NEW YORK. PRODUCER: CHAS CHANDLER. ENGINEER: EDDIE KRAMER.

More work was completed on the April 20 "Little Miss Strange Test Session" master, known now as "Little Miss Strange." Redding recorded a double-tracked lead vocal and overdubbed an electric guitar part. This early version was issued as part of *Noel Redding: The Experience Sessions*.

Hendrix then recorded a demo of "South Saturn Delta." He overdubbed a second guitar part, but the song was still early in its development, and nothing was

finalized. A rough solo sketch of "Three Little Bears" came next, followed by some untitled demos that Kramer marked on the tape box as "Solo Guitar Ideas."

MONDAY, APRIL 22, 1968

RECORD PLANT, NEW YORK, NEW YORK. 7:00 P.M. TO 5:30 A.M. PRODUCER: CHAS CHANDLER. ENGINEER: EDDIE KRAMER. SECOND ENGINEER: STEVE [SURNAME UNKNOWN].

The fifth take of the body of Hendrix's extended sound painting "1983 (A Merman I Should Turn To Be)" provided the master for the song's first section. A later session on May 8 provided the final components of this extraordinary work.

Traffic was also recording with Kramer and producer Jimmy Miller at the Record Plant during this time, and Hendrix extended an invitation to Chris Wood to contribute. Wood, who played saxophone, flute, and keys in Traffic, added flute to "1983."

TUESDAY, APRIL 23, 1968

RECORD PLANT, NEW YORK, NEW YORK. 7:00 P.M. TO 11:30 P.M. PRODUCER: CHAS CHANDLER. ENGINEER: EDDIE KRAMER.

Via a series of overdubs, Redding added additional acoustic guitars to the "Little Miss Strange" master.

WEDNESDAY, APRIL 24, 1968

RECORD PLANT, NEW YORK, NEW YORK. PRODUCER: CHAS CHANDLER. ENGINEER: EDDIE KRAMER.

The complicated rhythm pattern required for "Gypsy Eyes" demanded a great many takes, fraying nerves and testing Chandler's patience; as a result, the group made little progress.

Additional work on Redding's "Little Miss Strange" was also attempted. Completed overdubs, including Hendrix's lead guitar part, ensured the bassist a spot on the projected double album. "Jimi had a lot of fun putting the lead guitar on," recalls Kramer. "It was a DI [direct injection] with a wah-wah pedal, recorded on top of a ton of acoustic guitars Noel had already put on. Jimi's touch was so sure. He knew just what parts to play to bring that song to life. No matter the song or songwriter, whether it was the Troggs, Bob Dylan, or even Noel, whatever Jimi touched he was able to raise it to a different level."

Nearly all of the existing April 21 master was upgraded as Redding recorded a new lead vocal part. Redding's vocal was skillfully blended with a part from Mitchell, a combination that strengthened the track considerably. The group also completed bass, drum, and guitar overdubs. "I thought it very generous of Jimi to allow Noel to have a spot on the album," says Kramer. "He really had fun with this song. Jimi would not have recorded this if he hadn't liked it or done it just to please Noel. Noel was very serious about his songs, but Jimi was lighthearted about them. I vividly remember him cracking up at Mitch and Noel when they were singing those high harmonies. He had done the same thing when we cut "She So Fine" during the *Axis* sessions. There was always this 'wink, wink' thing with Noel's songs, but Jimi was respectful and wanted to make sure Noel approved of whatever contributions he would make."

While the move from four-track recording at Olympic to twelve-track at the Record Plant seemed like a significant upgrade, the Record Plant's balky Scully twelve-track tape machine frustrated Kramer on more than one occasion and made the task of overdubbing more complicated. "That Scully twelve-track was a nonstandard machine and technical nightmare," says Kramer. "Especially for overdubbing. The punch-ins were full of clicks, bangs, and pops, and they generally sounded like shit."

SUNDAY, APRIL 28, 1968

RECORD PLANT, NEW YORK, NEW YORK. PRODUCER: CHAS CHANDLER. ENGINEER: GARY KELLGREN.
Mixes of "Little Miss Strange" were prepared, but no final master was achieved.

MONDAY, APRIL 29, 1968

RECORD PLANT, NEW YORK, NEW YORK. 5:15 P.M. TO 7:30 P.M. PRODUCER: CHAS CHANDLER. ENGINEER: EDDIE KRAMER.

Hendrix and Mitchell recorded forty-one takes of "Gypsy Eyes" without Redding present, though none was identified as a master. Hendrix and Mitchell struggled in their efforts to hone the song's intricate rhythm track, leading to many incomplete takes. "Jimi's initial rhythm guitar part was recorded using a Fender Bassman top," says Kramer. "We were looking for a specific sound and he got a great tone out of that amplifier." Mitchell's thumping bass drum was an integral part of the song's opening from the very first take. "I remember trying to get as big a bass drum sound as possible," says Kramer.

As the session progressed, Hendrix seemed fully aware of their labor to realize a strong basic track. One of the open microphones captured some chat between the guitarist and Mitchell between takes. "Have you ever done this many takes before?" he asked his exasperated drummer. Mitchell laughed aloud and shouted out another count-off right away.

Tensions deepened between Hendrix and Chandler as Hendrix continued to openly challenge the producer's decisions. The problems were compounded by the hordes of uninvited guests and hangers-on whose presence served only to distract Hendrix from his task. Chandler was concerned with Hendrix's drug use, which had begun to gradually erode the honest, direct communication the two men had previously shared. "It was slow going from the moment we started at the Record Plant," says Chandler. "I was sitting there listening to him play the same song over and over again, thinking to myself, 'What is going on?' Jimi had wanted this to be a double album and I distinctly recall being glad that I had done so much at Olympic, because at this pace, the album would never be finished."

From "Gypsy Eyes" Hendrix turned to "Tax Free." Redding joined the session and the group recorded three takes, with their final effort serving as a new master. This was an entirely different version than the one the group had recorded at Olympic in January. Overdubs were recorded and a mix prepared before the session came to a close.

At a separate session later that evening, Redding, working with Gary Kellgren, prepared a final mix of "Little Miss Strange," and the master was set aside for the album.

TUESDAY, APRIL 30, 1968

RECORD PLANT, NEW YORK, NEW YORK. PRODUCER: CHAS CHANDLER. ENGINEER: EDDIE KRAMER.

Despite his struggle to realize "Gypsy Eyes," Hendrix was determined to make progress. New takes were attempted, but none met Hendrix's standards.

WEDNESDAY, MAY 1, 1968

RECORD PLANT, NEW YORK, NEW YORK. PRODUCER: CHAS CHANDLER. ENGINEER: EDDIE KRAMER.

Hendrix and Mitchell, sans Redding, recorded basic tracks for "House Burning Down." Hendrix's open vocal microphone captured his detailed explanation of the song and its parts—right down to the cymbal part he wanted. The two then recorded a host of instrumental takes in an effort to perfect the song.

Tensions between Hendrix and Redding continued to simmer. Hendrix was determined to realize the sounds he wanted for the album, and if Redding were unable or unwilling to accommodate this, he would simply augment or replace Redding's original contribution or play the entire bass part himself. "Jimi was playing a lot of bass and Noel felt a bit left out," says Kramer. "I think Noel felt the pressure and sensed he was being shoved out. Jimi was a great bass player. If he wanted something that Noel couldn't give him, he would play it himself. Noel felt really put out when this would occur, so there was that tension between the two of them. But Jimi's perspective was to make the track and the album the best it could be. I understood Jimi's thinking on this because, beyond this one issue, I thought that when they played together they were still incredible."

Hendrix and Mitchell revisited "Gypsy Eyes" next, with five instrumental takes recorded. Take 5 was marked complete, but this was still not designated as the master. Hendrix regrouped, and his sixth and final effort resulted in the basic track he desired. Overdubs were then recorded on to this master take.

At this stage, Hendrix was using a slide guitar effect to open the song. He seemed enamored of the slide effect, duplicating it later in the song at a higher octave.

Hendrix then revived "Tax Free," recording two new takes with his guitar fed through a Leslie speaker.

Take 2 held to a slower tempo than either the previous take or the January 1968 recordings from Olympic Studios. Hendrix's third take reverted to the original tempo and provided the master take. Kramer marked this recording "use" and set it aside for mixing.

THURSDAY, MAY 2, 1968

RECORD PLANT, NEW YORK, NEW YORK. ENGINEER: EDDIE KRAMER.

The group focused its attention on "Three Little Bears." At one point during this session, a confrontation flared up between Redding and Hendrix. "I took it out on Jimi, letting him know what I thought of the scene he was building around himself," said Redding in his autobiography, *Are You Experienced?* "There were tons of people in the studio, you couldn't even move. It was a party, not a session. He just said, 'Relax, man. . . . ' I'd been relaxing for months, so I relaxed my way right out of the place, not caring if I ever saw him again."

With Redding gone for the night, Hendrix continued his work on the song. While he and Mitchell were cutting the basic track, they continued past the ending of the song and never stopped playing. "Three Little Bears" by now had evolved into a free-form jam session. Hendrix soon settled into the rhythm pattern that has become known as "South Saturn Delta." While no structured attempt at recording the song was made, the jam session boasted several noteworthy moments, especially a beautiful passage of slow, melancholy notes performed by Hendrix.

He then overdubbed a bass guitar part for "Three Little Bears" as well as a second guitar. The recording of a lead vocal followed next, and Hendrix's irreverent approach revealed his lack of confidence in the song. He can be heard on the tape joking, "This is so silly!" and asking Kramer to stop the playback—but the engineer, sensing the opportunity to wind Hendrix up, continued to feed the song through his headphones. Hendrix completed the take, but further work on "Three Little Bears" ceased.

Though Hendrix never seriously considered "Three Little Bears" for *Electric Ladyland*, the song was mixed and issued in 1972 as part of the posthumous compilation *War Heroes*. In recent years, the song was reintroduced as the B-side of the *Merry Christmas And Happy New Year* EP.

Hendrix and Mitchell also recorded the intriguing instrumental "Cherokee Mist." Hendrix recorded the basic track without a bass, instead using his guitar fed through a wah-wah tone control pedal to frame the song's melodic structure. Taking advantage of the Record Plant's twelve-track recording capability, Hendrix established the basic track with Mitchell and then added two additional overdubs. The first was a dramatic electric sitar part that provided the song with its most distinctive characteristic. It has been rumored that Dave Mason may have performed this sitar part, but close review of the multitrack master reveals it to be Hendrix himself. Hendrix then added a second electric guitar part that alternated between rhythm and lead throughout the song.

Redding's blowout with Hendrix no doubt excluded him from a separate session staged later that morning. After enjoying themselves at the Scene Club just around the corner from the studio, Hendrix, Mitchell, Kramer, Steve Winwood, Jack Casady, and a host of friends traveled back to the Record Plant to jam. Beginning at seven thirty a.m., Kramer frantically set up microphones and made various sound and level adjustments, while Hendrix discussed "Voodoo Chile" with Mitchell, Winwood, and bassist Jack Casady from the Jefferson Airplane. Guitarist Larry Coryell was also among the invited guests, but he declined Hendrix's invitation to contribute. "Jimi asked me to play," remembers Coryell, "but for the first time in my life, I said, 'No. There is nothing I can add to this.'"

Three takes were recorded, although the first take served primarily as an introductory rehearsal. Kramer was ready by the time the musicians were to begin a formal second take. That rendition fell apart when Hendrix broke a guitar string. "Jimi just changed it himself," laughs Winwood. "It may seem hard to believe today but we just waited patiently while he did it." Jimi's extraordinary third take provided the master. This majestic performance became one of the centerpieces of the magnificent album *Electric Ladyland*.

The task of capturing the dramatic session on tape fell to Kramer, who organized his strategy as quickly as possible. "The reason that sound was so open was that Jimi was in the room live, playing guitar at the same time his vocal microphone—one of my favorite M 160s—was open," the engineer says. "The bass tone wasn't exactly the best it could have been, but it doesn't really detract, because the vibe was so strong. Jimi was playing through a Fender Bassman top, and his amp sound was very warm. The track had such great atmosphere and tremendous dynamics; it went from nothing to full-blast. I loved the effect that Winwood created. At one point he created a very English, hornpipe-like dance that was very Traffic-like and just terrific. There was so much excitement when we were cutting that track, I remember being on the edge of my seat hoping that it was all going to work."

Kramer and Hendrix later fine-tuned the basic track, adding several overdubs. "The idea was to make it sound as if it was a live gig. Even though there were some people watching in the studio, the applause was added as an overdub, so that the track would have a party feel. Jimi and I did the tape delay effects in the mix. All of the various background vocals and comments were tracked two or three times, as you can hear Jimi's voice coming from both sides." While Hendrix wanted to feature the ambient crowd noise as part of the song's atmosphere, the noise level generated by those who had observed the session wasn't sufficient. To correct this, Hendrix improvised and overdubbed crowd sounds from 9:00 a.m. to 9:45 a.m.

A strange hybrid of the three takes recorded here was later included as part of 1994's *Jimi Hendrix: Blues*. That track, entitled "Voodoo Chile Blues," is actually a composite track, digitally assembled in 1993 by engineer Mark Linett. He fused portions of takes 1 and 2 and coupled them with a small section of the previously released take 3 to create this new master.

SATURDAY, MAY 3, 1968

RECORD PLANT, NEW YORK, NEW YORK. PRODUCER: CHAS CHANDLER. ENGINEER: EDDIE KRAMER.

The Experience's publicist, Michael Goldstein, had successfully arranged for ABC-TV to produce a short news feature based primarily on the band's triumphant success in the U.S. Filming began on this day, with 16mm cameras capturing the recording of "Voodoo Child (Slight Return)," one of Hendrix's signature songs. The cameras, recalls Kramer, filmed the Experience recording and mixing the track. In addition, ABC filmed interviews with Kramer, Chandler, and co-manager Michael Jeffery. As the group worked in the studio, Nancy Reiner, Jeffery's girlfriend, made sketches of Hendrix as he recorded.

"We learned that song in the studio," remembers Redding. "They had the cameras rolling on us as we played it." "We did that about three times because they wanted to film us in the studio," Hendrix later explained. "'Make it look like you're recording, boys,' one of those scenes, you know? So OK, let's play this in E, now a-one and a-two and a-three and we went into 'Voodoo Child (Slight Return).'"

It is not known whether ABC ever used any of the material they shot this day. All of the footage was lost, discarded, or stolen from ABC's archives sometime after Hendrix's death. This included footage of the group performing at the Fillmore East on May 10 and the Miami Pop Festival on May 18.

SUNDAY, MAY 4, 1968

RECORD PLANT, NEW YORK, NEW YORK. 7:30 P.M. TO 4:30 A.M. ENGINEER: GARY KELLGREN.

One complete take of "Little, Little Girl" was recorded featuring Redding on twelve-string guitar accompanied by an unnamed drummer. Hendrix did not take any part in the recording.

Redding overdubbed an electric guitar part once the basic track had been achieved, and vocal overdubs followed before Gary Kellgren crafted an unusual mix for the song. Kellgren used multiple techniques to create effects throughout the song, including the sound of rushing wind. Kellgren modified the sound of the cymbals, which, when coupled with the drummer using brushes instead of sticks, gave the song a unique percussive backbeat. Kellgren added reverb to Redding's rhythm guitar and treated his vocal to achieve an ethereal quality it did not possess on its own.

Redding did not release this recording during his lifetime, but Kellgren's mix was later issued as part of *Noel Redding: The Experience Sessions*.

Following "Little, Little Girl," Redding also enjoyed what he later described as a fantastic jam with guitarist Larry Coryell. Unfortunately, the whereabouts of these tapes are unknown.

MONDAY, MAY 5, 1968

RECORD PLANT, NEW YORK, NEW YORK. ENGINEER: EDDIE KRAMER.

Beginning at seven a.m., Hendrix completed some work on his own and teamed up with Kramer to finish mixes of "House Burning Down" and "Voodoo Child (Slight Return)."

Later that day, the full group gathered to work on "Walking Through The Garden," another Redding composition drawn from his growing stack of new material. Hendrix moved to bass for this recording, joined by Redding on guitar, Mitchell on drums, an unnamed pianist (possibly Steve Winwood), and Traffic's Chris Wood on flute. The initial take came apart shortly after it began, but a complete second effort secured the basic track.

Mixes were then prepared for a number of songs Hendrix had begun at the Record Plant. A rough mix of "Walking Through The Garden" was completed before Hendrix turned his attention to mixing "Voodoo Chile." These mixes sounded very close to the finished *Electric Ladyland* master, but a later effort created on June 10 outshone them.

The group invested much work on "Voodoo Child (Slight Return)," as Hendrix and Kramer experimented with various panning and phasing techniques. A rough mix of "House Burning Down" was also prepared, but it was later marked "Don't Use" and discarded. While a finished mix of "House Burning Down" still eluded them, they achieved the master version of "Voodoo Child (Slight Return)."

THURSDAY, MAY 8, 1968

RECORD PLANT, NEW YORK, NEW YORK. 12:00 A.M. ENGINEER: EDDIE KRAMER. SECOND ENGINEER: STEVE (SURNAME UNKNOWN).

Fed up with Hendrix's lack of compliance, Chas Chandler stepped down as the album's producer. "Looking back, I walked out very quickly at the Record Plant," admits Chandler. "I would go in there and wait for Jimi and he would show up with eight or nine hangers-on. When he finally did begin recording, Jimi would be playing for the benefit of his guests, not the machines." A further source of frustration for Chandler was Hendrix's inability to judge his own performances or allow Chandler to keep his role as the final arbiter. "We'd be going over a number again and again and I would say over the talkback, 'That was it, we got it.' He would say, 'No, no, no,' and would record another and another and another. Finally, I just threw my hands up and left."

Chandler believed the breakdown could be traced in part to the schedule he and the Experience had maintained over the past eighteen months. "Both the group and I were exhausted," explains Chandler. "I had spent three years with the Animals and the next day I was working with Hendrix. I had put in as much time on the job as Hendrix, Mitchell, and Redding—plus my time with the Animals. The last thing I wanted to be doing was fighting with Jimi in the studio and then Jeffery in the office. I just walked away."

While it wasn't clear until later, Chandler's departure had damaging repercussions. "Chandler had been there from the beginning," says Redding. "He was a guy you could talk to. He kept Hendrix in control—both in and out of the studio. Jeffery didn't care about Mitchell or I. To him, Jimi was *the* star. We couldn't have done it without Jimi, but Jimi couldn't have done it without us. We were working just as hard as he was. Chas understood that."

Rough mixes of "Voodoo Chile," "Three Little Bears," and "Long Hot Summer Night" were completed despite Chandler's departure from the session. Hendrix also returned to "1983... (A Merman I Should Turn To Be)" on this day. The master reel from April 22 was pulled out, and new recordings were added as edit sections to create a single, unified master.

FRIDAY, MAY 10, 1968

FILLMORE EAST, NEW YORK, NEW YORK. WITH SLY AND THE FAMILY STONE. **PARTIAL SET LIST:** "FIRE" / "FOXEY LADY" / "RED HOUSE" / "HEY JOE" / "SUNSHINE OF YOUR LOVE" / "HEAR MY TRAIN A COMIN'"

/ "CAN YOU PLEASE CRAWL OUT YOUR WINDOW?" / "PURPLE HAZE" / "WILD THING"

The Experience were in superb form, performing as part of an amazing double bill with Sly and the Family Stone. Hendrix battled amplifier problems throughout his set but refused to let this disrupt his focus. The group played one of the earliest known concert performances of "Hear My Train A Comin'," and also offered a standout "Red House" lasting more than fifteen minutes. This is one of the rare examples of Hendrix playing a Gibson Les Paul Custom.

FRIDAY, MAY 17, 1968

RECORD PLANT, NEW YORK, NEW YORK. ENGINEER: EDDIE KRAMER.

An overdub and mixdown session dedicated to "Gypsy Eyes" was completed.

SATURDAY, MAY 18, 1968

GULFSTREAM PARK, HALLANDALE, FLORIDA. MIAMI POP FESTIVAL. TWO SHOWS. **SET LIST, FIRST SHOW:** "TAX FREE" / "FOXEY LADY" / "FIRE" / "HEAR MY TRAIN A COMIN'" / "PURPLE HAZE." **SET LIST, SECOND SHOW:** "HEY JOE" / "FIRE" / "I DON'T LIVE TODAY" / "FOXEY LADY" / "RED HOUSE" / "PURPLE HAZE"

The Experience headlined at the Miami Pop Festival, a fledgling, counterculture gathering organized by future Woodstock promoter Michael Lang. They topped a diverse bill whose artists ran the gamut from Chuck Berry to Frank Zappa and The Mothers Of Invention. The festival was staged at Gulf Stream Park, a popular racetrack on the outskirts of Miami. Engineer Eddie Kramer flew down to record Hendrix's two scheduled performances each day on May 18 and 19. The Experience offered inspired renditions of "I Don't Live Today," "Red House," and "Hey Joe" from a makeshift stage constructed atop a flatbed truck. The following day, torrential rains forced the cancellation of the festival and left the promoters bankrupt. Amid the scramble to retrieve their gear and payment, Hendrix dashed for one of the limousines reserved for artists. Kramer spotted Hendrix and jumped in behind him. As they sat in the traffic jam, Hendrix took a pad and pen from his bag

and composed the lyrics to "Rainy Day, Dream Away" as he viewed the scene from the car window.

WEDNESDAY, MAY 22, 1968

RECORD PLANT, NEW YORK, NEW YORK. ENGINEER: EDDIE KRAMER.

This extensive session was dedicated to overdubs and mixing for "1983... (A Merman I Should Turn To Be)." Of all of the songs featured on *Electric Lady land*, "1983" represented the impact that the change in recording technology had on Hendrix. No longer did Kramer have to "bounce" four-track tapes down to free up new tracks for Hendrix as had been done for both *Are You Experienced* and *Axis: Bold As Love*. Hendrix's canvas had expanded, and the guitarist took full advantage. "It was a whole different ball game at the Record Plant," says Kramer. "We had jumped from four- to twelve-track and Jimi said, 'Let's fill them all up.' So we filled them all up! '1983... (A Merman I Should Turn To Be)' and 'Moon, Turn The Tides...Gently Gently Away' provided more opportunities for Jimi to experiment. He could play with the guitars and the percussion and vocals and not lose any sound quality due to additional tape generations when we would have to bounce tracks down. Twelve-track recording was not without its problems, but it was a real step forward for us at that time."

THURSDAY, MAY 23, 1968

PIPER CLUB, MILAN, ITALY.

FRIDAY, MAY 24, 1968

TEATRO BRANCACCIO, ROME, ITALY. TWO SHOWS.

WITH THE TRIAD, DOCTOR K'S BLUES BAND, PIER FRANCO COLONNA, AND BALLETTO ESTILL GROUP.

SATURDAY, MAY 25, 1968

TEATRO BRANCACCIO, ROME, ITALY. TWO SHOWS. WITH THE TRIAD, DOCTOR K'S BLUES BAND, PIER FRANCO COLONNA, AND BALLETTO ESTILL GROUP.

SUNDAY, MAY 26, 1968

TEATRO BRANCACCIO, ROME, ITALY. TWO SHOWS. WITH THE TRIAD, DOCTOR K'S BLUES BAND, PIER FRANCO COLONNA, AND BALLETTO ESTILL GROUP.

THURSDAY, MAY 30, 1968

MONSTERKONZERT, HALLENSTADION, ZURICH, SWITZERLAND.

FRIDAY, MAY 31, 1968

MONSTERKONZERT, HALLENSTADION, ZURICH, SWITZERLAND. **SET LIST:** "VOODOO CHILD (SLIGHT RETURN)" / "STONE FREE" / "I DON'T LIVE TODAY" / "RED HOUSE" / "HEY JOE" / "FOXEY LADY" / "MANIC DEPRESSION" / "FIRE" / "PURPLE HAZE"

Recording for *Electric Ladyland* was put on hold for a brief tour of Italy and Switzerland. In Italy, small but enthusiastic audiences heard the Experience battle through electrical problems in venues not outfitted for their equipment. In Switzerland, the group joined the lineup of Monsterkonzert, two special concerts featuring the Experience, Traffic, John Mayall's Bluesbreakers, Eric Burdon and the New Animals, and the Move. Hendrix premiered the first known live version of "Voodoo Child (Slight Return)" before a rowdy audience who battled with police and pelted the stage with debris.

WEDNESDAY, JUNE 5, 1968

ELSTREE STUDIOS, STUDIO D, BOREHAMWOOD, ENGLAND.

The Experience also scheduled a stop in England so they could tape an appearance with Dusty Springfield on the television special *It Must Be Dusty!* Hendrix performed "Stone Free" and a truncated rendition of "Voodoo Child (Slight Return)." The highlight was an unusual duet that featured Hendrix and Springfield on the pop chestnut "Mockingbird." The program was later broadcast on July 12. Unfortunately, no recording of this program—apart from a 8mm film shot off a television screen by a British fan—has survived.

SATURDAY, JUNE 8, 1968

FILLMORE EAST, NEW YORK, NEW YORK.

Hendrix sat in with the Electric Flag and performed two songs, "South Saturn Delta" and "Hey Joe," recording the performance himself on his consumer-grade reel-to-reel deck. Buddy Miles voiced a slow, moody reading of "Hey Joe" with Hendrix on guitar, but the only known live performance of "South Saturn Delta" was an unusual treat, powered by the lively Electric Flag horn section.

MONDAY, JUNE 10, 1968

RECORD PLANT, NEW YORK, NEW YORK. 4:00 P.M. TO 4:30 A.M. ENGINEER: EDDIE KRAMER.

"Hendrix & Friends," as the tape box described this group, banded together to record "Rainy Day, Dream Away." Joining Jimi were drummer Buddy Miles, percussionist Larry Faucette, Mike Finnigan on organ, and Freddie Smith on saxophone. "Tom Wilson had discovered and produced my little R&B band," says Mike Finnigan. "He introduced us to Hendrix, and Jimi asked me, Larry Faucette, and Freddie Smith to jam on this tune he had in mind. In the early 1960s, Jimmy Smith had made these great, obscure organ quintet albums, which featured organ, congas, guitar, tenor saxophone, and drums. Before we started the session, Hendrix reminded me of this and joked, 'We're going to do a slow shuffle in D. You be Jimmy Smith and I'll be Kenny Burrell.'" The technical setup surprised Finnigan. "Having heard Jimi's first two albums, I thought he'd be using stacks and stacks of amplifiers and electronic toys to get his sound," he says. "To get the right guitar tone for 'Rainy Day, Dream Away/Still Raining, Still Dreaming' he was using this small, blond, thirty-watt Fender Showman amplifier. We couldn't believe it."

The session began with a modest shuffle Kramer noted on the tape box as "Blow." The master take of "Rainy Day, Dream Away/Still Raining, Still Dreaming" followed next. These two tracks were recorded as one, then split by Hendrix and Kramer during a final mixing session on June 28.

In addition to "Rainy Day, Dream Away," the group made a number of attempts at "Have You Ever Been (To Electric Ladyland)." Hendrix's efforts were raw, but the song held considerable promise even at this early stage.

Overdubs and mixes were also prepared for "Voodoo Chile," "1983... (A Merman I Should Turn To Be)," and "House Burning Down." Of these three, "House Burning Down" required the most effort. Hendrix and Kramer filled a tape reel with rejected mix attempts. Velvert Turner, a young African-American guitarist for who Hendrix served as a sort of mentor, was also present and remembers Hendrix explaining his inspiration for "House Burning Down." "Jimi told me how much the riots in Los Angeles [after Martin Luther King Jr.'s death] had affected him, and that this song had been inspired by what he felt there."

TUESDAY, JUNE 11, 1968

RECORD PLANT, NEW YORK, NEW YORK. ENGINEER: EDDIE KRAMER.

Although this tape reel is marked June 11, it was actually started on June 10. The first few minutes reveal the very end of the "Rainy Day, Dream Away" session from the previous day. Mike Finnigan can be heard talking as he left the studio before the recording stopped. No additional recording was made on this reel that day.

On June 11, Kramer resumed recording on this same tape reel. Mitchell joined Hendrix, and the two kicked off what Kramer described as "Tune Up Jam." Hendrix then initiated the first of two takes he titled "Inside Out." His first effort fell apart, but the second take secured the basic track. Hendrix seemed to sense that "Inside Out" had significant potential, and in fact it was based in part on the riff the guitarist later developed as "Ezy Ryder." Hendrix then recorded a second part fed

through a Leslie amplifier. Kramer made a rough mix for Hendrix to take away, but the group did not attempt any further work.

The final recording made during this session was "Drum Solo," a short exploration started by Mitchell. Hendrix joined him partway through, adding free-form distorted guitar to a rather bizarre effort.

THURSDAY, JUNE 13, 1968

RECORD PLANT, NEW YORK, NEW YORK. ENGINEER: EDDIE KRAMER.

A final mix of "House Burning Down" was prepared, with take 2 chosen as the master. This effort served as the master until a new mix created by Hendrix and Kramer on August 27 replaced it.

Hendrix revisited "Gypsy Eyes" again, doubletracking his vocal and spending considerable time on the panning of a slide guitar part and the positioning of two lead guitars within the stereo image.

FRIDAY, JUNE 14, 1968

RECORD PLANT, NEW YORK, NEW YORK. ENGINEER: EDDIE KRAMER.

On this evening, Hendrix engaged in a fascinating attempt to integrate horns into his sound. Mitchell joined Hendrix, and the two focused their attention on his unfinished composition "South Saturn Delta." Their first take broke down, but a second was complete and served as the master.

Noted jazz arranger Larry Fallon was contracted to work with Hendrix on a horn arrangement for the song. For this session, Fallon hired four top New York jazz session players, whose names, unfortunately, were not documented, and sat them in a circle around the guitarist. Hendrix recorded a bass part and, for added effect, recorded his lead guitar overdub live along with the horn section, playing a Les Paul Special guitar fed through a Fender amplifier. A conga overdub from an unnamed percussionist also went down on tape.

Mixes were made at the conclusion of these overdubs, but no final master was achieved. A tape copy of the last mix was made for Hendrix, who took it away

for further review. "South Saturn Delta" stands as one of Hendrix's first fascinating steps toward the blending of rock, R&B, and jazz.

Hendrix then recorded two solo guitar demos of "Have You Ever Been (To Electric Ladyland)." Kramer came over the talkback microphone prior to the third take and asked Hendrix for the song's title. "Electric Ladyland," came Hendrix's reply. This exquisite third take, now a part of the *Jimi Hendrix Experience* box set, has long been a fan favorite.

Immediately following this recording, Mitchell joined Hendrix to record four formal takes of the song. The first three takes were incomplete, while take 4, skillfully embellished with intricate layers of vocal, bass, and guitar overdubs, was later titled "Have You Ever Been (To Electric Ladyland)" and featured as the album's title track. Hendrix and Kramer then prepared a final mix and set the song aside for the album.

Work on ". . . And The Gods Made Love" began next. The group made several attempts to create the appropriate sound effects Hendrix sought. This work stretched well into the early morning hours of June 15. At this stage, they had also decided to join the two separate recordings by way of a cross-fade.

MONDAY, JUNE 17, 1968

RECORD PLANT, NEW YORK, NEW YORK. OVERDUBS, 12:30 P.M. TO 3:15 A.M. REMIXING, 3:15 A.M. TO 10:30 A.M. ENGINEER: EDDIE KRAMER.

This long evening session was dedicated to various bass and guitar overdubs, drum parts, and mixing experiments for "Gypsy Eyes."

"We recorded some different lead guitar parts," says Kramer. "Jimi was playing a straight blues riff—almost sounding like Buddy Guy." At 2:04 and 2:40 into the song, Kramer devised a repeat echo effect for the guitar. This foreshadowed the innovative mixing techniques Hendrix and Kramer utilized to try to create a 3-D phasing/flanging effect. "That was a big thing for us," remembers Kramer. "Jimi really was taken with the concept of sound moving in front and behind you rather than simply *at* you."

TUESDAY, JUNE 18, 1968

RECORD PLANT, NEW YORK, NEW YORK. REMIXING, 9:00 P.M. TO 2:00 A.M. ENGINEER: EDDIE KRAMER.
Hendrix made further progress on "Gypsy Eyes," yet a final master still eluded him.

FRIDAY, JUNE 28, 1968

RECORD PLANT, NEW YORK, NEW YORK. ENGINEER: EDDIE KRAMER.
Final mixing completed for "Rainy Day, Dream Away." The idea to create two separate songs from this one recording—"Rainy Day, Dream Away" and "Still Raining, Still Dreaming"—stems from this mixing session. On the tape box, Kramer wrote specific instructions noting: "2nd $\frac{1}{2}$ edited out onto Side 2."

SATURDAY, JUNE 29, 1968

RECORD PLANT, NEW YORK, NEW YORK. 8:00 P.M. TO 11:00 P.M. ENGINEERS: EDDIE KRAMER, GARY KELLGREN.
This evening began with two lively instrumental recordings featuring Hendrix joined by an unnamed bassist, drummer, and organist.

Once his guests departed, Hendrix began a mixing session for "At Last . . . The Beginning," later known as ". . . And The Gods Made Love." Hendrix would later describe this aural collage as "a ninety-second sound painting of the heavens."

Eddie Kramer remembers that prior to this mixing session, Hendrix had already worked out many of the various sound effects in advance, and he combined these thoughts with the results of some inspired, spontaneous creations designed specifically to replicate the sound of a spacecraft landing. "'. . . And The Gods

Made Love' had loads of tape delay," Kramer explains. "Jimi's voice was slowed way below 3 $\frac{3}{4}$ i.p.s. using a VFO [variable frequency oscillator], then sped up again. We had tape loops running and echo tape feeding back on itself. I was panning one set with my right hand, because there was a limit to how much you could grab with one hand. I rode the main levels on the console, controlling the main feeds with my left hand. Jimi would be using two hands to pan other stuff. It was definitely a four-handed mix that we edited together. In the beginning, you can hear the tape bias whistle changing in the background because it's down so low. Jimi's voice comes in backward and Mitch's tom-toms were slowed down ridiculously. The track is phased and we put a lot of Mitch's cymbals in backward for the effect. The end was the flying saucer effect which Jimi wanted."

MONDAY, JULY 1, 1968

RECORD PLANT, NEW YORK, NEW YORK. ENGINEER, FIRST SESSION: EDDIE KRAMER. ENGINEER, SECOND SESSION: UNKNOWN.
Hendrix and Kramer continued making various experiments with sound effects on ". . . And The Gods Made Love," fine-tuning the volume of each effect and its proper placement within the stereo image, as well as the total length of the track.

Later that evening, Hendrix returned to the Record Plant and sat in on a lively jam session with the Graham Bond Organization. Unfortunately, this recording with Graham Bond, guitarist Ray Russell, and drummer Alan Rushton was marred by technical difficulties. The poor quality of the recording has rendered it useless by commercial standards.

Hendrix played an electric sitar throughout an instrumental jam marked as "Jam With Graham Bond." His contributions can only be heard through the open vocal microphone, as his instrument was not patched through an amplifier. Hendrix had moved from sitar to electric guitar by the time Bond launched into "Dreams Can Come True" but his instrument was still not being properly recorded. The organist then led the ensemble through a charged version of St. Louis Jimmy's "Goin' Down Slow" before recording ceased.

WEDNESDAY, JULY 3, 1968

RECORD PLANT, NEW YORK, NEW YORK. 8:00 P.M. TO 11:00 P.M. ENGINEER: GARY KELLGREN.

Hendrix attempted a series of mixes for "All Along The Watchtower." His last attempt was marked as the master, but he ultimately rejected it in favor of the mix he had previously completed with Eddie Kramer.

SATURDAY, JULY 6, 1968

WOBURN MUSIC FESTIVAL, WOBURN ABBEY, BEDFORDSHIRE, ENGLAND. **SET LIST:** "SGT. PEPPER'S LONELY HEARTS CLUB BAND" / "FIRE" / "TAX FREE" / "RED HOUSE" / "FOXEY LADY" / "VOODOO CHILD (SLIGHT RETURN)" / "PURPLE HAZE"

The group flew to London on July 4 in advance of this outdoor festival performance in the English countryside. Such acts as Geno Washington, Pentangle, and Family opened for the Experience. This concert, remarkably, represented the only U.K. performance by the Experience in all of 1968.

SUNDAY, JULY 7, 1968

RECORD PLANT, NEW YORK, NEW YORK. 6:45 P.M. TO 7:50 P.M. ENGINEER: EDDIE KRAMER.

No member of the Experience was present at this short session. Eddie Kramer experimented with the mixes and cross-fades that eventually linked the first three songs of *Electric Ladyland*'s first side.

WEDNESDAY, JULY 24, 1968

RECORD PLANT, NEW YORK, NEW YORK. ENGINEER: EDDIE KRAMER.

Hendrix again revisited "Gypsy Eyes," but a final master remained out of reach. Progress was being made, however. Hendrix overdubbed two new lead guitar parts and the decision was made during these mixes not to feature a second drum part that Mitchell had recorded in May. The ending still consisted of a long, slow fade, a characteristic that did not change until August 27, when the group created a more dramatic closing.

A series of mix attempts were prepared but apparently, neither Hendrix nor Kramer were convinced that these contained a final mix, as Kramer marked the tape box, "Check with Jimi for usage."

FRIDAY, JULY 26, 1968

RECORD PLANT, NEW YORK, NEW YORK. 2:00 A.M. TO 5:15 A.M. ENGINEER: GARY KELLGREN.

A rough mix of "House Burning Down" was completed. In addition, the group laid down overdubs and created a rough mix for "Long Hot Summer Night."

MONDAY, JULY 29, 1968

RECORD PLANT, NEW YORK, NEW YORK. 1:00 A.M. TO 5:00 A.M. ENGINEER: GARY KELLGREN.

Hendrix returned to "Long Hot Summer Night" and prepared a series of mixes in an effort to achieve the final master. That goal, however, continued to elude him: not one of these efforts was designated as complete.

TUESDAY, JULY 30, 1968

INDEPENDENCE HALL AT THE LAKESHORE AUDITORIUM, BATON ROUGE, LOUISIANA. TWO SHOWS. WITH SOFT MACHINE.

WEDNESDAY, JULY 31, 1968

MUNICIPAL AUDITORIUM, SHREVEPORT, LOUISIANA.

THURSDAY, AUGUST 1, 1968

CITY PARK STADIUM, NEW ORLEANS, LOUISIANA.

FRIDAY, AUGUST 2, 1968

MUNICIPAL AUDITORIUM, SAN ANTONIO, TEXAS. WITH SOFT MACHINE. **PARTIAL SET LIST:** "TAX FREE" / "FIRE" / "FOXEY LADY" / "HEY JOE" / "RED HOUSE" / "PURPLE HAZE"

SATURDAY, AUGUST 3, 1968

MOODY COLISEUM, DALLAS, TEXAS. WITH SOFT

MACHINE. **SET LIST:** "DEAR MR. FANTASY" / "ROCK ME BABY" / "FOXEY LADY" / "I DON'T LIVE TODAY" / "HEY JOE" / "FIRE" / "RED HOUSE" / "PURPLE HAZE" / "WILD THING"

SUNDAY, AUGUST 4, 1968

SAM HOUSTON COLISEUM, HOUSTON, TEXAS. **PARTIAL SET LIST:** "RED HOUSE" / "I DON'T LIVE TODAY" / "SPANISH CASTLE MAGIC" / "FIRE" / "VOODOO CHILD (SLIGHT RETURN)" / "PURPLE HAZE" / "MANIC DEPRESSION"

The Experience once again interrupted progress on *Electric Ladyland*, traveling from New York to Baton Rouge, Louisiana, to begin another large-scale U.S. tour. The increasingly larger venues secured for their concerts confirmed the group's popularity.

In New Orleans, Hendrix, Mitchell, and Redding attended a gathering at Beauregarde Square to listen to music from numerous local groups.

Hendrix closed his San Antonio performance with a dramatic display of destruction, reducing his Stratocaster and smashing several amps on stage to rubble. At Moody Coliseum, the Experience opened their performance with a cover of Traffic's "Dear Mr. Fantasy," extending the string of inspired performances.

WEDNESDAY, AUGUST 7, 1968

RECORD PLANT, NEW YORK, NEW YORK. 11:00 A.M. TO 3:00 P.M. ENGINEER: GARY KELLGREN.
The group revisited "Long Hot Summer Night" and prepared several interesting alternate mixes. Hendrix made multiple attempts at a final mix, focusing his energies on the balance between the piano and guitar, but did not achieve a final version.

The group left the Record Plant and traveled to New York's Central Park, where friend and photographer Linda Eastman photographed the Experience sitting atop the Alice in Wonderland statue, surrounded by small children who had been playing in the park. Hendrix wanted one of these images to serve as the cover for *Electric Ladyland*, a decision that neither of his record companies—Track in the U.K. or Reprise in the U.S.—ultimately honored.

SATURDAY, AUGUST 10, 1968

CHICAGO AUDITORIUM, CHICAGO, ILLINOIS. TWO SHOWS. WITH SOFT MACHINE. **PARTIAL SET LIST:** "RED HOUSE" / "FIRE" / "PURPLE HAZE" / "FOXEY LADY" / "WILD THING"

SUNDAY, AUGUST 11, 1968

COLONIAL BALLROOM, DAVENPORT, IOWA. **PARTIAL SET LIST:** "ARE YOU EXPERIENCED?" / "LOVER MAN" / "TAX FREE" / "FOXEY LADY" / "RED HOUSE" / "I DON'T LIVE TODAY" / "FIRE"

MONDAY, AUGUST 12, 1968

RECORD PLANT, NEW YORK, NEW YORK. ENGINEER: GARY KELLGREN.
This session yielded a fascinating, sparse demo of "Room Full Of Mirrors." Hendrix sang a live vocal while playing guitar, backed only by a harmonica, most likely played by Paul Caruso. With Hendrix sounding somewhat tired, the duo attempted three soulful takes. The first two provided tantalizing sketches but remained incomplete. The third was extremely good, but it, too, came apart without a definitive conclusion.

Take 3 was later mixed and included as part of the *Jimi Hendrix Experience* box set.

FRIDAY, AUGUST 16, 1968

MERRIWEATHER POST PAVILION, COLUMBIA, MARYLAND. WITH SOFT MACHINE. **PARTIAL SET LIST:** "ARE YOU EXPERIENCED?" / "ROCK ME BABY" / "FOXEY LADY" / "HEY JOE" / "FIRE" / "I DON'T LIVE TODAY" / "PURPLE HAZE" / "WILD THING"

SATURDAY, AUGUST 17, 1968

MUNICIPAL AUDITORIUM, ATLANTA. TWO SHOWS. WITH AMBOY DUKES (FOR THE FIRST SHOW ONLY), EIRE APPARENT, VANILLA FUDGE, AND SOFT MACHINE. **PARTIAL SET LIST, SECOND SHOW:** "FIRE" / "RED HOUSE" / "PURPLE HAZE" / "WILD THING"

SUNDAY, AUGUST 18, 1968

CURTIS HIXON HALL, TAMPA, FLORIDA. WITH EIRE APPARENT AND SOFT MACHINE.

MONDAY, AUGUST 20, 1968

THE MOSQUE, RICHMOND, VIRGINIA. TWO SHOWS. WITH EIRE APPARENT AND SOFT MACHINE. **PARTIAL SET LIST, SECOND SHOW:** "FIRE" / "I DON'T LIVE TODAY" / "RED HOUSE" / "PURPLE HAZE"

TUESDAY, AUGUST 21, 1968

CIVIC DOME, VIRGINIA BEACH, VIRGINIA. TWO SHOWS. WITH EIRE APPARENT AND SOFT MACHINE.

FRIDAY, AUGUST 23, 1968

SINGER BOWL, FLUSHING MEADOW, QUEENS, NEW YORK. **SET LIST:** "ARE YOU EXPERIENCED?" / "FIRE" / "RED HOUSE" / "I DON'T LIVE TODAY" / "FOXEY LADY" / "LIKE A ROLLING STONE" / "PURPLE HAZE" / "HEY JOE" / "WILD THING"

The Experience headlined a show billed as the New York Rock Festival, topping a list of performers that included Soft Machine, the Chambers Brothers, and Big Brother and the Holding Company. Immediately after the concert, Hendrix drove back to Manhattan so that he could make further refinements to the *Electric Ladyland* album.

RECORD PLANT, NEW YORK, NEW YORK. ROUGH MIX, 2:00 A.M. TO 7:00 A.M. OVERDUBBING, 7:30 A.M. TO 8 A.M. ENGINEER: EDDIE KRAMER.

Hendrix and Kramer labored with great care to complete "House Burning Down," one of *Electric Ladyland*'s strongest efforts. This lengthy session included a variety of different mixes and overdubs before Hendrix settled on a final mix.

Having devoted hundreds of hours to the making of *Electric Ladyland*, Hendrix was sensitive to suggestions that songs such as "1983... (A Merman I Should Turn To Be)" and "House Burning Down" relied too heavily on gadgets or studio wizardry. "On some records you hear all this clash and bang and fanciness, but all we're doing is laying down the guitar tracks," Hendrix said after the album's release. "We [use] echo here and there, but we're not adding false electronic things. We use the same things everyone else would, but we use it with imagination and common sense. With 'House Burning Down,' we made the guitar sound like it was on fire. It's constantly changing dimensions, and up on top of that the lead guitar is cutting through everything."

SATURDAY, AUGUST 24, 1968

BUSHNELL MEMORIAL ARENA, HARTFORD, CONNECTICUT. WITH EIRE APPARENT.

After working into the early morning at the Record Plant, another gig beckoned that evening in Connecticut.

SUNDAY, AUGUST 25, 1968

CAROUSEL BALLROOM, FRAMINGHAM, MASSACHUSETTS. WITH SOFT MACHINE. **PARTIAL SET LIST:** "JOHNNY B. GOODE" / "HEY JOE" / "FIRE" / "PURPLE HAZE" / "WILD THING"

MONDAY, AUGUST 26, 1968

KENNEDY STADIUM, BRIDGEPORT, CONNECTICUT. WITH EIRE APPARENT AND SOFT MACHINE. **PARTIAL SET LIST:** "ARE YOU EXPERIENCED?" / "FOXEY LADY" / "HEY JOE" / "SPANISH CASTLE MAGIC" / "PURPLE HAZE"

TUESDAY, AUGUST 27, 1968

RECORD PLANT, NEW YORK, NEW YORK. ROUGH MIX, 7:00 P.M. TO 12:00 A.M. TWELVE-TRACK OVERDUB RECORDED, 12.00 A.M. TO 1:00 A.M. ROUGH MIX, 1:00 A.M. TO 3:00 A.M. RECORDING, 4:00 A.M. TO 8:00 A.M. ENGINEERS: GARY KELLGREN, EDDIE KRAMER.

Last-minute work on "Gypsy Eyes" was completed. Kellgren marked this master as the "flange version." Flanging sound, a technique that required an engineer to vary tape speeds manually during a recording, was a technique extensively employed by both Kellgren and Kramer. Hendrix devised a new ending for this recording that featured a distinctive, "watery" lead guitar part heavily flanged by Kellgren as the song drew to a close.

With Hendrix and Kramer busy preparing the master copy of *Electric Ladyland*, Kellgren recorded "How Can I Live," a new Redding original, starting at four a.m. Redding attempted twelve takes, with takes 1, 3, 8, 9, 11, and 12 complete. At one point during the session, Hendrix can be heard playing a snare drum.

Take 12, which featured Mitch Mitchell on drums, Redding on twelve-string guitar, and an unnamed harmonica player (possibly Paul Caruso) was considered a master, but not for *Electric Ladyland*. Redding set this track aside for the debut album of Fat Mattress, his solo outfit. It was not included on that album but was later featured as part of *Noel Redding: The Experience Sessions*.

While Kellgren oversaw the Redding session, Kramer prepared a final mix of "Voodoo Child (Slight Return)."

Needing one more song to complete the double album, the Experience, working on short notice, rallied to record an interpretation of Earl King's "Come On (Let The Good Times Roll)." The group attempted fourteen takes in all, with the last selected as the basic track. To create the master, Kellgren edited the multitrack tape to trim the song down to its bare essentials. "That was done to fill out the album," admits Redding. "I was amazed, because it was just a jam in E. It was boring for the bass player. We just played it live and they took it, thank you. We wouldn't have had a situation like that with Chandler, would we?"

At the end of this marathon session, copies of the album's sequenced, final masters were struck from the originals for Warner Bros. Records. Much to the relief of all parties involved, *Electric Ladyland* was finally complete.

FRIDAY, AUGUST 30, 1968

LAGOON OPERA HOUSE, SALT LAKE CITY, UTAH. WITH SOFT MACHINE.
After only two days off, the Experience flew from New York to Salt Lake City and checked into the Newhouse Hotel prior to their evening performance. Hendrix was still under pressure from the Reprise staff, who

wanted to begin manufacturing *Electric Ladyland*, so he began to compose the liner notes and credits on hotel stationery.

SUNDAY, SEPTEMBER 1, 1968

RED ROCKS PARK, DENVER, COLORADO. WITH VANILLA FUDGE, SOFT MACHINE, AND EIRE APPARENT.
In Denver, Hendrix resumed his efforts to finish the artwork layout and liner notes for *Electric Ladyland*. Hendrix once more made notes on hotel stationery, composing his "Letter To The Room Full Of Mirrors" and carefully detailing how he wanted the album designed. He apologized for the delay in getting information to Reprise, writing that "we have been working very hard indeed doing shows and recording."

Hendrix supplied photos by Linda Eastman, Eddie Kramer, and David Sygall and drew the layout for the inside gatefold sleeve. While Reprise made use of these images, they opted to substitute two images taken by Karl Ferris on the album's front and back cover in place of the Linda Eastman image the group had posed for in Central Park on August 7.

TUESDAY, SEPTEMBER 3, 1968

BALBOA STADIUM, SAN DIEGO, CALIFORNIA. WITH VA-NILLA FUDGE, SOFT MACHINE, AND EIRE APPARENT.

WEDNESDAY, SEPTEMBER 4, 1968

MEMORIAL COLISEUM, PHOENIX, ARIZONA. WITH VA-NILLA FUDGE, SOFT MACHINE, AND EIRE APPARENT. **SET LIST:** "ARE YOU EXPERIENCED?" / "COME ON (LET THE GOOD TIMES ROLL)" / "LITTLE WING" / "VOODOO CHILD (SLIGHT RETURN)" / "FIRE" / "SPANISH CASTLE MAGIC" / "FOXEY LADY" / "LIKE A ROLLING STONE" / "SUNSHINE OF YOUR LOVE" / "HEY JOE" / "STAR SPANGLED BANNER" / "PURPLE HAZE"

The group was in top form on this Western swing, thrilling capacity audiences in Salt Lake City, Denver, San Diego, and here in Phoenix where rare live versions of "Are You Experienced?" "Like A Rolling Stone," and "Little Wing" punctuated an inspired performance.

"ALL ALONG THE WATCHTOWER" / "BURNING OF THE MIDNIGHT LAMP." REPRISE 0767. U.S. SINGLE RELEASE. Hendrix's compelling rendition of this Bob Dylan composition provided the Experience with the crossover single both Jeffery and Chandler, as well as Reprise, had long hoped for in the U.S. market. "All Along The Watchtower" broke quickly: it entered the *Billboard* chart on September 21, 1968, at number 66 and climbed steadily to number 20. Much to Reprise's delight, "All Along The Watchtower" succeeded so dramatically that the single ultimately shifted more units than the combined sales of the group's four previous Reprise singles.

THURSDAY, SEPTEMBER 5, 1968

SWING AUDITORIUM, SAN BERNADINO, CALIFORNIA. WITH VANILLA FUDGE, SOFT MACHINE, AND EIRE APPARENT.

FRIDAY, SEPTEMBER 6, 1968

SEATTLE CENTER COLISEUM, SEATTLE, WASHINGTON. WITH VANILLA FUDGE, SOFT MACHINE, AND EIRE APPARENT. **PARTIAL SET LIST:** "SPANISH CASTLE MAGIC" / "LITTLE WING" / "I DON'T LIVE TODAY" / "RED HOUSE" / "PURPLE HAZE" / "FOXEY LADY" / "FIRE" / "COME ON (LET THE GOOD TIMES ROLL)" / "VOODOO CHILD (SLIGHT RETURN)" / "WILD THING" / "STAR SPANGLED BANNER"

SATURDAY, SEPTEMBER 7, 1968

PACIFIC COLISEUM, VANCOUVER, BRITISH COLUMBIA, CANADA. WITH VANILLA FUDGE, SOFT MACHINE, AND EIRE APPARENT. **PARTIAL SET LIST:** "FOXEY LADY" / "FIRE" / "HEY JOE" / "VOODOO CHILD (SLIGHT RETURN)" / "RED HOUSE" / "PURPLE HAZE"

SUNDAY, SEPTEMBER 8, 1968

SPOKANE COLISEUM, SPOKANE, WASHINGTON. WITH VANILLA FUDGE, SOFT MACHINE, AND EIRE APPARENT. **PARTIAL SET LIST:** "ARE YOU EXPERIENCED?" / "FOXEY LADY" / "LITTLE WING" / "VOODOO CHILD (SLIGHT RETURN)" / "RED HOUSE" / "FIRE" / "PURPLE HAZE"

MONDAY, SEPTEMBER 9, 1968

MEMORIAL COLISEUM, PORTLAND, OREGON. WITH VANILLA FUDGE AND SOFT MACHINE. **SET LIST:** "ARE YOU EXPERIENCED?" / "FIRE" / "HEY JOE" / "FOXEY LADY" / "VOODOO CHILD (SLIGHT RETURN)" / "LITTLE WING" / "SPANISH CASTLE MAGIC" / "RED HOUSE" / "PURPLE HAZE"

FRIDAY, SEPTEMBER 13, 1968

OAKLAND COLISEUM, OAKLAND, CALIFORNIA. WITH VANILLA FUDGE, SOFT MACHINE, AND EIRE APPARENT.

SATURDAY, SEPTEMBER 14, 1968

HOLLYWOOD BOWL, HOLLYWOOD, CALIFORNIA. WITH BIG BROTHER AND THE HOLDING COMPANY AND THE CHAMBERS BROTHERS. **SET LIST:** "ARE YOU EXPERIENCED?" / "VOODOO CHILD (SLIGHT RETURN)" / "RED HOUSE" / "FOXEY LADY" / "FIRE" / "HEY JOE" / "SUNSHINE OF YOUR LOVE" / "I DON'T LIVE TODAY" / "LITTLE WING" / "STAR SPANGLED BANNER" / "PURPLE HAZE"

SUNDAY, SEPTEMBER 15, 1968

MEMORIAL AUDITORIUM, SACRAMENTO, CALIFORNIA. WITH EIRE APPARENT AND VANILLA FUDGE. **PARTIAL SET LIST:** "JOHNNY B. GOODE" / "ARE YOU EXPERIENCED?" / "STONE FREE" / "RED HOUSE" / "FOXEY LADY" / "HEY JOE" / "STAR SPANGLED BANNER" / "PURPLE HAZE"

In the aftermath of the group's Herculean effort to finish *Electric Ladyland*, the Experience were exhausted. The group's incredible pace, coupled with their increasing drug use, afforded them—and Hendrix in particular—virtually no opportunity for creative rejuvenation.

The group's seven-week U.S. tour came to a temporary close following this performance in Sacramento, with the final two weeks of September set aside to provide the group with a much-needed vacation in Los Angeles.

SATURDAY, OCTOBER 5, 1968

INTERNATIONAL CENTER, HONOLULU, HAWAII. WITH TIMES MUSIC COMPANY. **SET LIST:** "SUNSHINE OF YOUR LOVE" / "COME ON (LET THE GOOD TIMES ROLL)" / "HEY JOE" / "I DON'T LIVE TODAY" / "FOXEY LADY" / "STAR SPANGLED BANNER" / "PURPLE HAZE"

The Experience enjoyed a brief Hawaiian respite built around this single performance in Honolulu.

TUESDAY, OCTOBER 8, 1968

FLASHING: JIMI HENDRIX PLAYS, CURTIS KNIGHT SINGS. CAPITOL ST 2894. U.S. ALBUM RELEASE. PRODUCER: ED CHALPIN. ENGINEER: MICKEY LANE. "GLOOMY MONDAY" / "HORNET'S NEST" / "FOOL FOR YOU BABY" / "HAPPY BIRTHDAY" / "FLASHING" / "DAY TRIPPER" / "ODD BALL" / "LOVE LOVE" / "DON'T ACCUSE ME"

After months of contentious litigation, Hendrix and Warner Bros. Records agreed to settle the U.S. claim made by PPX in June of 1968. PPX and Capitol Records were granted certain financial considerations and the distribution rights to one album featuring performances by the Jimi Hendrix Experience. As Reprise was set to issue Hendrix's double LP *Electric Ladyland*, Capitol released *Flashing*, its second compilation of recordings by Curtis Knight & the Squires. Unlike its 1967 predecessor *Get That Feeling*, *Flashing* was somewhat better annotated, actually featuring Knight's image and name on the front cover of the album alongside Hendrix.

Flashing unsuccessfully attempted to blend the R&B-inspired 1965 material with the unstructured 1967

1968 review: "Everything about this record is shoddy; the lack of information about the performers, the repertoire, the brevity, the performances themselves and the sound quality."

THURSDAY, OCTOBER 10, 1968

THE WINTERLAND BALLROOM, SAN FRANCISCO. TWO SHOWS. WITH THE BUDDY MILES EXPRESS. ENGINEERS: WALLY HEIDER, ABE JACOB. **SET LIST, FIRST SHOW:** "ARE YOU EXPERIENCED?" / "VOODOO CHILD (SLIGHT RETURN)" / "RED HOUSE" / "FOXEY LADY" / "LIKE A ROLLING STONE" / "STAR SPANGLED BANNER" / "PURPLE HAZE." **SET LIST, SECOND SHOW:** "TAX FREE" / "LOVER MAN" / "SUNSHINE OF YOUR LOVE" / "HEAR MY TRAIN A COMIN'" / "KILLING FLOOR" / "HEY JOE" / "STAR SPANGLED BANNER" / "PURPLE HAZE"

The Experience kicked off a strident three-night stand at Winterland, promoter Bill Graham's popular San Francisco venue. As these concerts marked the group's two-year anniversary, manager Michael Jeffery enlisted noted remote sound engineer Wally Heider to document all six shows—two each night—over three consecutive days.

Following opening sets by the Buddy Miles Express, the Experience's two performances were loud and raw. Jefferson Airplane bassist Jack Casady joined the group onstage during the evening's second show, lending a second bass guitar to an extended rendition of "Killing Floor" and "Hey Joe."

FRIDAY, OCTOBER 11, 1968

THE WINTERLAND BALLROOM, SAN FRANCISCO. TWO SHOWS. WITH THE BUDDY MILES EXPRESS AND DINO VALENTI. ENGINEERS: WALLY HEIDER, ABE JACOB. **SET LIST, FIRST SHOW:** "ARE YOU EXPERIENCED?" / "VOODOO CHILD (SLIGHT RETURN)" / "RED HOUSE" / "FOXEY LADY" / "LIKE A ROLLING STONE" / "STAR SPANGLED BANNER" / "PURPLE HAZE." **SET LIST, SECOND SHOW:** "TAX FREE" / "SPANISH CASTLE MAGIC" / "LIKE A ROLLING STONE" / "LOVER MAN" / "HEY JOE" / "FIRE" / "FOXEY LADY" / "PURPLE HAZE"

This was perhaps the wildest evening of the three, as the Experience—joined by flautist Virgil Gonsalves—

jams. "Flashing" and "Day Tripper" were actually drawn from the same 1967 jam session that featured Hendrix playing a Hagstrom eight-string bass guitar. Additional edits and overdubs were made after Hendrix departed in order to cut them into two separate "songs." "Love Love" received the same treatment, as Knight later composed lyrics and added a lead vocal to this wah-wah-drenched instrumental jam.

Whereas *Get That Feeling* took many Hendrix fans by surprise, winning initial sales from unsuspecting consumers who thought it was a Jimi Hendrix Experience album, fans and critics alike received *Flashing* poorly. The respected music publication *Down Beat* captured the general sentiment about the album in its December began their performance in an unusual fashion by embarking on an extended, frenetic workout of "Are You Experienced?"

Following his opening set with the Buddy Miles Express, organist Herbie Rich climbed onstage to join the Experience midway through their performance. Rich's tasteful organ fills complemented "Lover Man," "Hey Joe," "Fire," and "Foxey Lady" before the Experience closed the evening with "Purple Haze."

SATURDAY, OCTOBER 12, 1968

THE WINTERLAND BALLROOM, SAN FRANCISCO. TWO SHOWS. WITH THE BUDDY MILES EXPRESS. ENGINEERS: WALLY HEIDER, ABE JACOB. **SET LIST, FIRST SHOW:** "FIRE" / "LOVER MAN" / "LIKE A ROLLING STONE" / "FOXEY LADY" / "TAX FREE" / "HEY JOE" / "PURPLE HAZE" / "WILD THING." **SET LIST, SECOND SHOW:** "FOXEY LADY" / "MANIC DEPRESSION" / "SUNSHINE OF YOUR LOVE" / "LITTLE WING" / "SPANISH CASTLE MAGIC" / "RED HOUSE" / "VOODOO CHILD (SLIGHT RETURN)" / "STAR SPANGLED BANNER" / "PURPLE HAZE"

These final two Winterland shows boasted many raw highlights, especially the versions of "Fire" and "Like A Rolling Stone" from the evening's first performance. Hendrix was plagued by equipment problems—an unfortunate characteristic of the group's entire Winterland residency—that left him frustrated and compromised his sound.

The memory of those technical setbacks may have been the reason that no selections from any of these Winterland performances were ever released during Hendrix's lifetime. While his motives remain unclear, Hendrix may have dismissed them outright, as none of these Winterland master tapes appeared with those presented to Eddie Kramer when the concept of preparing a live Experience disc was briefly considered in June of 1969. Despite their significance, the Winterland tapes were also curiously absent from *Hendrix: In The West*, the first, and arguably best, posthumous collection of his live recordings.

WEDNESDAY, OCTOBER 16, 1968

ELECTRIC LADYLAND, REPRISE 2RS 6307. U.S. ALBUM RELEASE. PRODUCER: JIMI HENDRIX. ENGINEERS: GARY KELLGREN, EDDIE KRAMER. SECOND ENGINEERS: TONY BONGIOVI, GEORGE CHKIANTZ, ANDY JOHNS. ". . . AND THE GODS MADE LOVE" / "HAVE YOU EVER BEEN (TO ELECTRIC LADYLAND)" / "CROSSTOWN TRAFFIC" / "VOODOO CHILE" / "LITTLE MISS STRANGE" / "LONG HOT SUMMER NIGHT" / "COME ON (PART ONE)" / "GYPSY EYES" / "BURNING OF THE MIDNIGHT LAMP" / "RAINY DAY, DREAM AWAY" / "1983... (A MERMAN I SHOULD TURN TO BE)" / "MOON, TURN THE TIDES . . . GENTLY, GENTLY AWAY" / "STILL RAINING, STILL DREAMING" / "HOUSE BURNING DOWN" / "ALL ALONG THE WATCHTOWER" / "VOODOO CHILD (SLIGHT RETURN)"

Completed at a cost of roughly $70,000, *Electric Ladyland* had a significant chart impact, supplying the group with its first number-one album in the U.S.

Despite the album's popularity, Hendrix was disappointed with Reprise's decision to change the album's artwork, compromising his detailed written instructions apparently without notifying him. Moreover, Hendrix revealed that the album's final mix, the result of countless hours of intense preparation, had been thrown off during the mastering and disc-cutting process completed by Warner Bros. "We were recording when we were touring and it's very hard to concentrate on both," Hendrix complained. "Some of the mix came out muddy, with too much bass. We mixed it and produced it, but when it came time for them to press it, quite naturally they screwed it up, because they didn't know what we wanted. There is 3-D sound being used on there that you can't even appreciate because they didn't know how to cut it properly. They thought it was out of phase."

While both Gary Kellgren and Eddie Kramer were acknowledged on the album's inside jacket sleeve for their engineering contributions, the name of one prominent contributor—Chas Chandler—was conspicuously absent. Despite having produced a number of tracks on the double album, such as "Crosstown Traffic" and "Burning Of The Midnight Lamp," Chandler received no credit for his role in the album's production. "When the album came out and I saw that it was 'Produced and Directed by Jimi Hendrix,' I was pissed off," admits Chandler. "I was especially surprised to see how much of what I had done was on there, because I know how

much more time they spent at the Record Plant after I had walked off the project. In all truth, I had expected to see a much different album. While I was pissed that I had received no credit, I put that down to being a maneuver by Michael Jeffery. I saw it as being his way of trying to wipe my name from the history book and nothing more. Quite honestly, I just put the whole thing behind me and moved on."

OCTOBER 14-17, 1968

TTG STUDIOS, LOS ANGELES, CALIFORNIA. PRODUC-ER: JIMI HENDRIX. ENGINEER: JACK HUNT.
Having accepted Michael Jeffery's invitation to produce Eire Apparent's debut disc for Buddah Records nearly six months before, Hendrix struggled to apportion adequate time for the project. Eire Apparent had opened most of the Experience's concerts since mid-August, which accorded Hendrix at least some opportunity to formulate his strategy for the album.

The Experience, now temporarily based in Los Angeles, decided to resume recording at Hollywood's TTG Studios. Located at 1441 N. McCadden Street in Hollywood, TTG Studios was owned and operated by engineer Ami Hadami, a tough, enigmatic veteran of the Israeli military. Opened in 1965, and reputedly named for one of Hadami's military regiments, TTG enjoyed a strong following in the burgeoning Los Angeles market, competing with Bill Putnam's Western United Studios and Wally Heider's renowned Heider Recording. For a mere $55 an hour, clients could use the studio's recently installed Ampex sixteen-track tape machine, one of the first units to be placed in service in Southern California.

Both Chas Chandler and Michael Jeffery had befriended Hadami while recording at TTG with the Animals. In October 1968, after the Experience's three-night stand at San Francisco's Winterland Ballroom—gigs that celebrated the group's two-year anniversary—TTG's Studio B was block-booked to accomodate new recordings by both the Experience and Eire Apparent.

While *Sunrise*, as Eire Apparent's debut album was eventually titled, would not be completed at TTG, Hendrix and the band made significant progress there. In addition to his role as producer, Hendrix stepped out from behind the console to lend guitar to a number of the group's original compositions, including "Captive In The Sun," "Morning Glory," "The Clown," "Let Me Stay," "Mr. Guy Fawkes," "Magic Carpet," "Someone Is Sure To (Want You)," and "Yes I Need Someone." Following the group's last documented session at the studio on October 31, 1968, all of the session tapes were shipped to the Record Plant, where work on the album continued.

The encouraging advances made by Eire Apparent were not achieved without incident, as Hendrix clashed with TTG staff engineer Jack Hunt, who had been assigned by Hadami to engineer the session. The problem, explains fellow TTG engineer Angel Balestier, grew out of Hunt's rigid adherence to structured sessions. "Jack was an excellent engineer, but he ran sessions strictly by the numbers," says Balestier. "If a session was booked until eight p.m., then at eight p.m. you were finished. That wasn't something Jimi was looking for. In those days, you were just waking up at eight!"

Another contentious issue stemmed from Hendrix's and Hunt's inability to compromise on recording techniques. The two were unable to establish a working compromise. "Eire Apparent was just too sterile," recalls Balestier. "Jimi was looking to give their sound the same edge he gave his own. Jack, though, was very structured in the studio. Each instrument was to be baffled and recorded on separate tracks. He also did not want to put that much recording level on the tape because of the possibility of distortion—but that was just the effect Jimi was looking for."

With their differences unresolved, the growing tension between Hendrix and Jack Hunt ultimately resulted in a confrontation. "I had just finished recording the Everly Brothers upstairs in Studio A," recalls Balestier. "Eire Apparent was recording in Studio B and I walked into the control room to grab a long T-plug cord I needed for my next session. Hendrix was just sitting in the [producer's] chair staring up at the ceiling. When he saw me, he said, 'You're going to do my next album, aren't you?' That created a complete scene, because Jack was floored that Jimi hadn't asked him to do it—especially as he had been doing the Eire Apparent sessions. I had never met Jimi prior to that point, but I had seen him perform at Monterey and owned his albums. I told him,

'Sure, I'd love to.' I hadn't gone into the control room to solicit the work, I had only wanted to borrow that particular cable. I explained this to Jack and Ami later, but the issue was never fully resolved. Jack took it pretty hard. He never came in to any of the Hendrix sessions, and, for years, remained pissed off at me."

TTG STUDIOS, LOS ANGELES, CALIFORNIA. PRODUCER: JIMI HENDRIX. ENGINEER: ANGEL BALESTIER.
Though Hendrix's primary responsibility at TTG was the Eire Apparent project, the Experience made an earnest effort to record tracks for their fourth studio album. Having completed *Electric Ladyland* just six weeks before, they immediately shook off any notion of formal preproduction for these sessions. Armed with only a handful of old songs and new ideas, the Experience struggled to focus their energies on the task at hand. Jamming, once Hendrix's principal creative respite, increasingly formed his entire approach to composing and recording new material.

Despite Hendrix's clashes with Jack Hunt during the Eire Apparent sessions, the guitarist placed no restrictions on his new engineer, Angel Balestier, asking only that the tape machine never stop recording. "Jimi told me that once we started recording, I was never to stop the tape or let the tape run out," says Balestier. "As a result, we recorded every tune as it evolved, changing tape only when people stopped to breathe." Also unique to both Balestier and the staff at TTG was the Experience's penchant for performing at maximum volume. "When the Experience first began rehearsing, Ami Hadami came downstairs and wanted the monitors turned down, because the sound was coming right up though the studio upstairs. I pointed out through the control room window to the studio and said, 'Ami, that's not the monitors, that's the *band*.' He couldn't believe it."

While a cauldron of problems simmered between Redding and Hendrix, the Experience enjoyed unprecedented popularity. The Experience's sessions at TTG confirmed their celebrity status in Hollywood, as a bevy of friends, invited guests, and groupies made their way to the studio. Most were content to simply observe, while others sought one of the coveted invitations to join the proceedings and play. In either instance, Hendrix was always obliging, according to Balestier. Though the studio staff tried to maintain a low profile, they could not contain the excitement created by the Experience's sessions. "The visitors that would come by were incredible," remembers Balestier. "With Hendrix, if someone walked into the room, it wasn't like, 'Get him out of here!' Jimi would say, 'Come on in,' or he'd ask us to make room for people. He was extremely polite. He never said no to anybody and never threw anybody out."

With such a policy in effect, a steady stream of well-wishers descended on the studio. "A lot of the guys from the Buffalo Springfield would come by, especially Dewey Martin and Stephen Stills," says Balestier. On one such occasion, Balestier recorded a spirited acoustic jam whose highlight was a furious guitar battle between Hendrix and Stills. "That was a great jam," says Balestier. "Those guys were playing their asses off." Sadly, tapes of this session have either been lost or stolen, as they are not part of the Hendrix tape library.

In addition to the Buffalo Springfield, Buddy Miles came by frequently and joined a number of sessions, as did organist Lee Michaels. "Lee Michaels had been recording upstairs in Studio A when he found out Hendrix was going to be working downstairs," says Balestier. "I admitted that he was, but I told him that I was supposed to keep it quiet. Lee laughed and said he was going to come down anyway, so we moved his B-3 organ into Studio B."

In addition to jams with Stills, Michaels, and Buddy Miles, Mitchell and Hendrix jammed with bassist Carol Kaye. On another occasion Vic Briggs sat in with the Experience. Other notable guests who visited the group included Sonny Bono, Bill Cowsill of the Cowsills, Lou Reed, the Fraternity of Man, the Association, Jim Keltner, Jim Gordon, the Olympics, and even actor Tony Scotti, best known for his role in the film *Valley of the Dolls*.

A number of Hendrix's old acquaintances from the chitlin' circuit also made welcomed appearances, including Leon Heywood, Billy Preston, and other well-known artists. "Ike Turner came by, and while he didn't jam, Jimi was very pleased to see him," Balestier recalls. Another notable visitor was legendary Specialty Records producer Bumps Blackwell. "I ran into Bumps upstairs in the office," says Balestier. "He said, 'I hear you have somebody I worked with downstairs.' Bumps came downstairs and walked into the control room behind Jimi with a plate of food and said, 'Hey, Jimi, you want some chicken?' Jimi turned, and when he saw who it was he started laughing. Bumps sat down and started telling old stories. Out of the blue, Jimi turned to me and said, 'I heard you had a spat with Little Richard.' I told him that *I* didn't have a problem with him, but Ami had wanted me to turn off the equipment because Richard owed the studio money. I went to shut the power off, but Bumps, who was producing, intervened. When I didn't do it, Ami did it himself, which sent Richard into a rage. He started screaming at Ami and told him that he was going to take off his sissy wig and whip his ass right there! By this point, Jimi and Bumps were laughing hysterically, as if they had lived through this one hundred times before. You could see that there was something between Jimi and Bumps. They were genuinely pleased to see each other."

While at the studio, Hendrix, in turn, took a sincere interest in some of Balestier's recent clients. "Ricky Nelson stopped by one of his sessions and he and Jimi got on great," says Balestier. "They talked about all kinds of music. On another night, Jimi asked to hear some of the country and western sessions I had done. I played him some recent things—Everly Brothers recordings I had engineered—and he thought it was real cool. Then he looked at me in a strange way and said, 'How does a Puerto Rican from Brooklyn learn how to do *that* stuff?' I laughed and told him that I was from way, way out in the West Indies and he burst out laughing."

The atmosphere was electric during Experience sessions at TTG. The smell of incense wafted through the studio, and a steady supply of Hendrix's favorite burgers from Stan's Drive-In on Sunset Boulevard fueled the crowd. Drugs, marvels Balestier, were equally plentiful. "Somebody brought a hash cake to one session," he recalls. "We had Kool-Aid that was laced, marijuana cookies, and Thai cigarettes from Vietnam at others. You name it, it was there."

With such behavior on display, it was inevitable that the local police would pay the studio a visit. "One night," says Balestier, "I looked over and saw a cop looking in on the session through the studio door. In a panic, I got Tom Hidley, who was in Studio C, on the phone and told him there was a cop outside the door. He said that he would take a look. Tom escorted the cop into the control room, and he was digging it. He had heard Jimi playing while he was outside walking his beat. He was from the Wilcox Station, in full uniform, badge and all, bopping his head, really into it. I was freaked. I thought we were all going in!"

FRIDAY, OCTOBER 18, 1968

TTG STUDIOS, LOS ANGELES, CALIFORNIA. ENGINEER: ANGEL BALESTIER. SECOND ENGINEER: MARK KAUFFMAN. Similar in name only to the versions of "Izabella" later recorded at the Hit Factory and Record Plant in 1969, this instrumental effort sported an entirely different arrangement reminiscent of "Midnight." Two initial takes marked "tests" went down on tape before proper recording began. Seven new takes followed, with takes 2, 3, and 7 complete. Of these, the seventh take was deemed the best. Following a tape change, however, recording continued. A series of false starts and breakdowns ensued before takes 15, 16, and 18 were each complete and increasingly developed. Take 18, listed as a master and timed at 4:32, clearly stood out, but Hendrix remained unconvinced. The group listened to a playback of take 18 but returned to the studio for more recording. Following false starts on takes 19 and 20, take 21 was complete and warranted a playback. After closely comparing the two, it was decided that take 21 was not as strong as take 18, and Hendrix once again selected take 18 as the master.

With "Izabella" completed, work began on "Messenger," another promising new original. Balestier recorded two takes on this reel, and listed the second as complete. The first, a mid-tempo instrumental effort showed stylings briefly reminiscent of "Castles Made Of Sand." This recording, however, seems more an exploratory jam than a structured attempt to capture a basic track. While a second take of "Messenger" was complete, its tempo and arrangement had completely changed. While Hendrix debuted this spirited number here, he did occasionally invoke familiar passages from "Lover Man." The group also recorded overdubs, with Mitchell adding percussion elements and Hendrix adding additional guitar. Despite this effort, however, "The

Messenger," as Hendrix announced the song to engineer Angel Balestier, remained unfinished at this time.

"ALL ALONG THE WATCHTOWER"/"LONG HOT SUMMER NIGHT." TRACK RECORDS 604 025. U.K. SINGLE RELEASE.

"All Along The Watchtower," the group's fifth U.K. single, enjoyed strong sales, and the Experience triumphantly returned to the top of the charts. The disc peaked at the number 5 position during its eleven-week run.

SUNDAY, OCTOBER 20, 1968

TTG STUDIOS, LOS ANGELES, CALIFORNIA. ENGINEER: ANGEL BALESTIER. SECOND ENGINEER: MARK KAUFFMAN.

Work on "The Messenger" resumed, with the Experience electing to discard all of the takes recorded on October 18 and begin anew. The resulting fifteen takes reveal an intriguing new song for which Hen-

drix planned to record lyrics but never did. The first eight takes were incomplete; the ninth showed promise and warranted a playback, but Hendrix rejected it, too. Take 12 was strong enough for the group to stop and listen to their efforts once more, but they rejected it as well as an incomplete take 13. Obvious progress could be heard on take 14, but it, too, was discarded after a playback. A robust take 14 yielded the master. Overdubs followed, with the highlight a unique piano part performed by Hendrix and recorded at fifty-nine cycles, a slower speed, for effect.

While the Experience were still capable of channeling their tremendous talent in unison, the relationship between Hendrix and Redding had deteriorated even further. Their return to the studio, coming so quickly after the difficult *Electric Ladyland* sessions, did little to resolve their distinctly different approaches to recording. At TTG, Redding's frustration with what he perceived as Hendrix's inability to judge his own performances left him rankled. Redding's own diary notations detail his mounting dismay: "20 October. Recording (nothing done). 24 October. Recording (nothing done). 25 October. Recording (nothing done, again)."

Once a private concern known only to those closest to the group, the growing divide between Hendrix and Redding immediately became apparent to everyone who worked intimately with the group during its stint at TTG. "The distance between Jimi and Noel was *very* apparent," recalls Balestier. "It was sad. You could see it, it was so obvious. They kept two different crowds. They both would say hello to each other, but would keep to their own corners. When people would come for Jimi, Noel would withdraw. The sessions were peaceful, however. I never witnessed any verbal or physical confrontations, but the vibe was always there. Once they got to playing, though, it still worked."

MONDAY, OCTOBER 21, 1968

TTG STUDIOS, LOS ANGELES, CALIFORNIA. ENGINEER: ANGEL BALESTIER. SECOND ENGINEER: MARK KAUFFMAN. This notable session began with the Experience recording "Calling All The Devil's Children." What began as a formative collaboration between Hendrix and Redding soon evolved into a boisterous studio party. Twenty-seven takes of the song's gritty, infectious basic track were recorded before the master was achieved. In the process, Hendrix was duly inspired to create a comedy track—or, as Redding described, a parody of the legendary BBC comedy program *Goon Show*. What followed was, indeed, sheer lunacy, as the Experience, joined by roadie Eric Barrett and a gaggle of visitors, encircled one microphone. Standing on a chair, Hendrix led a hilarious, impromptu comedy sketch, portraying, among other characters, a Bible-thumping preacher. "Bold as *what*?" Hendrix's "preacher" asks on the tape. Amid the screams and ongoing chatter of his "followers," human sirens announce that a bust is about to occur, whereupon Redding bellows, "Flush the toilet! Flush the toilet!" In all, "Calling All The Devil's Children" is a terrific slice of the group's twisted humor, similar in style and pursuit to the Beatles' "You Know My Name (Look Up The Number)."

A request made earlier that evening by Hendrix to Balestier provided the first clue that the evening's plan would be—at the very least—unusual. "Before we started to cut those voices, Jimi asked me if I could get thirteen chicks in the studio. I told him that I would make a few calls and see what I could do. Then so many girls came down to the studio it was unreal. They were girls in the studio, in the vocal booth, and even outside the door to Studio B. When he started to put some guitar overdubs on, Jimi walked over to this beautiful girl and asked what her sign was. When she replied, 'Sagittarius,' Jimi said, 'Does that mean I can ball you?' It was incredible."

The recording of "Calling All The Devil's Children" provided a prime example of the group's spontaneous creativity, and Balestier quickly realized that normal session procedures would not apply to the Experience. "During jams like this, I'd line up a pile of tape reels," recalls Balestier. "We only had one multitrack machine, so as soon as they would stop for conversation, I'd pull the reels off the machine and throw on two new ones without even rewinding the old ones. Terry Betts, one of my tape operators, was real fast at that. He and Bob Porter would each grab a reel and I would grab the middle of the tape and line it up through the guides on the machine. We'd slam it on, hit play/record, and go! Jimi would ask from the studio, 'Did you get that on tape?' and I would say, 'I got every bit of it!' When he played a jam like that, or even just a song idea, Jimi got so charged up knowing that you had recorded the complete take for him. Knowing that he had his ideas down on tape was extremely important to him."

Little could ever hope to follow "Calling All The Devil's Children," save for some inspired jamming, and that was precisely what took place next. The group recorded two separate jam sessions, including four takes of "Jam #1" with Lee Michaels on organ. Take 4, an up-tempo blues-rock effort, featured several spirited moments before it began to unravel shortly after the four-minute mark. An unnamed harmonica player then joined the expanded group for "Jam #2." Lee Michaels again drove the jam, leading one complete take.

Following a playback, the spirited jam "Hear My Freedom Call Me" followed next, minus harmonica but with Michaels again behind the organ. Buddy Miles joined the proceedings with additional percussion. Several exceptional moments shone through in this lengthy jam, including occasional sections led by Hendrix's lead vocal. Sadly, however, like most efforts of this sort, the jam came apart at the close without any resolution.

This ensemble also recorded "Electric Church," a frenetic blues jam that boasted some superb, stinging lead guitar from Hendrix, but little in terms of sustained structure. Miles can be heard playing a second set of drums, providing a unique double-drum tandem with Mitchell. After three short incomplete takes of tune-ups and general instructions between the players, take 4 landed the master. This recording, however, is not the "Electric Church/Red House" later included on *Jimi Hendrix: Blues*. The recording on *Jimi Hendrix: Blues* is actually a skillfully edited combination of the introductions that precede this recording, edited on to a version of "Red House" recorded on October 29. While Miles can certainly be heard on the master recordings of "Electric Church," he did not play any part in the October 29 session. Michaels, however, appears on both, and is joined on the October 29 session by flautist Jim Horn, whose contributions were later mixed out of the recording used to create the "Electric Church/Red House" composite master.

TUESDAY, OCTOBER 22, 1968

TTG STUDIOS, LOS ANGELES, CALIFORNIA. ENGINEER: ANGEL BALESTIER. SECOND ENGINEER: MARK KAUFFMAN. The Experience made a determined effort over the course of this evening to perfect "Mr. Lost Soul," a song originally known as "Mr. Bad Luck." The Experience had completed a version of "Mr. Bad Luck" at Olympic Studios on May 4, 1967, and the recording was an early contender for *Axis: Bold As Love*. However, when the Experience completed production work for that album at the end of October 1967, they did not include the song.

Recording began with twelve takes of "Mr. Lost Soul" recorded on reel one. A spirited first take, timed at 2:53, was complete and worthy of a playback. While the results were encouraging, the group clearly did not have the master take in hand. A series of false starts and incomplete takes followed until a complete take 7 warranted a playback. Still not satisfied, the group returned to the studio and began again. Ensuing takes featured little change to the song's arrangement; instead, Hendrix seemed intent on making refinements to his rhythm guitar part. Take 12 was complete, and also timed at 2:53, but this rendition lacked cohesion, and no playback was required to determine its fate. More recording ensued before the master take was achieved with take 17.

One interesting aspect of these developing takes is that portions of the chord structure demonstrated here would later be incorporated into "Stepping Stone." Balestier prepared a rough mix immediately following the session, and relabeled take 17 "Look Over Yonder," but neither this mix nor the master take was ever issued during Hendrix's lifetime. Eddie Kramer, Mitch Mitchell, and John Jansen later mixed the song so that it could become part of 1971's *Rainbow Bridge*, and later 1997's *South Saturn Delta*.

In addition to getting Hendrix's guitar sound on tape, another crucial task was capturing Hendrix's lead vocal performance—a maneuver that required a particular degree of delicacy. "I tried a number of different techniques to make him feel more comfortable," says Balestier. "I would hang a C12 microphone in the middle of the studio and let him hold on to his guitar. Occasionally, I would hear a little noise on tape from him holding the guitar, but that instrument was his lady. On other occasions, Jimi would sing in the studio and his guitar amp would be in the vocal booth. I'd stick his amp in there and feed him some of the basic track through the speakers out of phase so he wouldn't have to wear headphones. What I would try would depend on Jimi's mood. Sometimes he would get so disgusted, he'd throw his guitar in a corner and walk out. Then he'd come back later and ask to try it again. He was very moody during vocals, and wasn't comfortable having people around. If people were there, he'd never vent his frustration at them. Instead, he would smash his guitar on the floor and walk out. If nothing seemed to work, I would just leave him alone. I kept Studio C unlocked and he would go in there and lock the door. When he came out, he might not want to record again, but I had given him my home number. I told Jimi to call me, no matter what time it was. I lived on Fountain, right by McCadden, and it was a short walk to the studio. There were times when he would call me at three a.m., saying, 'You know, I've got this thing I want to do.' I'd say, sure, I'll be over in a couple of minutes. These sessions could take all night, a couple of hours, or just a half hour. I didn't mind at all."

WEDNESDAY, OCTOBER 23, 1968

TTG STUDIOS, LOS ANGELES, CALIFORNIA. ENGINEER: ANGEL BALESTIER. SECOND ENGINEER: MARK KAUFFMAN. This long, productive evening session featured the recording of three new songs. The session kicked off with two takes of the instrumental "The New Rising Sun," both recorded without Redding's bass guitar. Take 2, vastly different both in sound and scope from the "Hey Baby (Land Of The New Rising Sun)" later featured as part of *Rainbow Bridge*, was deemed the master. Despite the relatively few takes recorded—certainly by the Experience's recent standards—considerable work ensued. Hendrix added a backward guitar part as well as a second lead guitar. A slow- to mid-tempo instrumental, "The New Rising Sun" does feature several high points throughout.

While Hendrix apparently never revived this particular arrangement after leaving TTG, portions of "The New Rising Sun" were briefly considered for use in the film *Rainbow Bridge*. Pulled by Electric Lady Studios engineer John Jansen on February 22, 1971, "The New Rising Sun" was reviewed and rejected for both the film's soundtrack and its accompanying album. Jansen did, however, find a use for the track, varying its speed and using a very brief snippet as part of an experimental composite master he was creating. Later, in 1974, when Allan Douglas assumed control of the Hendrix tape library, Jansen's creation, which also featured pieces from recordings made at the Hit Factory, Record Plant, and Electric Lady, received new overdubs by drummer Allan Schwartzberg and percussionist Jimmy Maeulen. Douglas edited the recording, renamed it "Captain Coconut," and included it as part of 1975's *Crash Landing*. He returned to this recording in 1994 when he reconfigured a version of the song so that it could be issued as part of *Voodoo Soup*.

Three takes of what was titled "Introductions" followed "The New Rising Sun," complete with organ,

harmonica, piano, and Redding now on bass. None bore any obvious connection to the others. The first take was actually a spirited twelve-bar blues jam. This lengthy effort featured some fine playing from Hendrix and Michaels before coming apart shortly before the six-minute mark. The second take began with a beautiful solo guitar part from Hendrix that lasted nearly two minutes before the band joined in behind him. The next recording, announced over the talkback as "'Introductions,' take 3" by Balestier, is actually a melodic solo piano piece performed by Hendrix. At its conclusion, Hendrix can be heard saying, "Let's leave it like that for now."

The group also recorded eight takes of "Peace." However, without Redding's bass to center the song's melody, timing problems hampered their effort, and they did not achieve a basic track.

THURSDAY, OCTOBER 24, 1968

TTG STUDIOS, LOS ANGELES, CALIFORNIA. ENGINEER: ANGEL BALESTIER. SECOND ENGINEER: MARK KAUFFMAN. This session centered on recording the muscular instrumental "Peace." All of the previous day's work was scrapped and the group attempted fifteen new takes. Take 2, timed at 4:41, was listed as "complete" but not chosen as the final master. Twelve more takes followed, with each new take only slightly different from the one before. Take 15, the first take recorded on reel two, was selected as the master.

To realize the searing guitar sound Hendrix desired, Balestier made a concerted effort to try and interpret a particular sound that Hendrix heard clearly in his head but had struggled to verbalize. "Jimi had said that he was looking for a certain sound," says Balestier. "I stood listening in the studio during a rehearsal, then went back into the control room and heard the playback. To my surprise, I wasn't hearing what Hendrix was hearing out in the studio—and that's what his ears were aimed at. So I changed my microphone positions. I put one behind his amplifier and another about six feet away. I instructed Jimi to crank up his amplifier some more, which really disturbed Ami upstairs. What Jimi had been hearing was the sound bouncing off the glass separating the studio from the control room. I put up a microphone to capture that, which now gave me three positions to mix and put on tape. He came inside, listened, and said, 'I'd like to get a little more of *that* here.' That's how Hendrix was. He wasn't like a lot of guys today who would say, 'Give me 3K more and you've got it.' I went back out, put three Manhasset music stands in a corner to bounce more of his sound, changed my microphone positions slightly, and he said, 'Yeah. *That's* what I'm looking for.'"

Precisely when Hendrix composed "Peace" is not known, although the inspiration to change the song's title from "Peace" to "Peace In Mississippi," says Balestier, came as a result of a visit by another of Hendrix's old friends, J. W. Alexander, Sam Cooke's respected manager and music publisher. "Alexander, Bumps Blackwell, and a number of Jimi's old friends from his days on the chitlin' circuit had stopped by. One had carried along a big bag of pumpkin seeds that a relative down south had sent him. This guy bragged that his relative grew the best pumpkins in the county. That started everybody talking about the South. Bumps told us about an album Little Richard had recorded in Clarksdale, Mississippi. Bumps had sent a young black kid out for sandwiches in a red convertible. Shortly after, a local sheriff brought him back, thinking that the kid had stolen the vehicle. When a white employee tried to explain that he had only been sent out for sandwiches, the sheriff looked at him and said, 'Oh, a nigger lover. Well, see that your niggers stay out of my town.' Hearing that changed our mood and there was silence in the control room. Jimi picked up on it and said he was going to call this instrumental song he had been doing 'Peace In Mississippi.' That's how the title came about."

While "Peace In Mississippi" never came out during Hendrix's lifetime, Alan Douglas overhauled it posthumously, inexplicably wiping Mitchell's and Redding's contributions in favor of new overdubs recorded in 1974 by guitarist Jeff Mironov, bassist Bob Babbit, drummer Allan Schwartzberg, and percussionist Jimmy Maeulen. This remake would later be featured as part of 1975's *Crash Landing.*

FRIDAY, OCTOBER 25, 1968

TTG STUDIOS, LOS ANGELES, CALIFORNIA. Hendrix contributed a bass guitar part to a Robert Wyatt demo recording of "Slow Walking Talk." Wyatt, the drummer and leader of the Michael Jeffery–managed combo Soft Machine, would retitle the song "But I'm Clean As A Whistle." Some years later, Wyatt composed his own lyrics and rerecorded the track as "Soup Song." Save for Wyatt's acetate, no multitrack copies of this recording exist in the Hendrix tape library, and the date of this recording cannot be confirmed.

ELECTRIC LADYLAND. TRACK RECORDS 613 008/9. U.K. ALBUM RELEASE. PRODUCER: JIMI HENDRIX. ENGINEERS: GARY KELLGREN, EDDIE KRAMER. SECOND ENGINEERS: TONY BONGIOVI, GEORGE CHKIANTZ, ANDY JOHNS. ". . . AND THE GODS MADE LOVE" / "HAVE YOU

EVER BEEN (TO ELECTRIC LADYLAND)" / "CROSS-TOWN TRAFFIC" / "VOODOO CHILE" / "LITTLE MISS STRANGE" / "LONG HOT SUMMER NIGHT" / "COME ON (PART ONE)" / "GYPSY EYES" / "BURNING OF THE MIDNIGHT LAMP" / "RAINY DAY, DREAM AWAY" / "1983 . . . (A MERMAN I SHOULD TURN TO BE)" / "MOON, TURN THE TIDES . . . GENTLY, GENTLY AWAY" / "STILL RAINING, STILL DREAMING" / "HOUSE BURNING DOWN" / "ALL ALONG THE WATCHTOWER" / "VOODOO CHILD (SLIGHT RETURN)"

Despite keeping the same running order as its Reprise counterpart, the Track Records version of *Electric Ladyland* set off a firestorm of publicity upon its release, as the label had substituted a cover featuring a bevy of naked women. Track's Kit Lambert and Chris Stamp had devised the nude concept largely as a publicity stunt. With the Experience no longer based in London, Track was eager to foster the group's outlaw image among the members of the Fleet Street press. They certainly achieved that goal: reaction to the cover resulted in howls of protests and condemnations. Hendrix, angered that the controversy had cheapened the album's content, moved immediately to distance the group from the issue. "People have been asking me about the English cover and I don't know anything about it," he said after its release. "I didn't know it was going to be used. It's not my fault. I don't even know what the B-side to "All Along The Watchtower' is!"

The resulting furor over the cover may have temporarily enhanced the group's value to London's notorious tabloids, but sales were not significantly impacted: the two-disc set peaked at number 6 on the U.K. album charts before its twelve-week run concluded.

SUNDAY, OCTOBER 27, 1968

TTG STUDIOS, LOS ANGELES, CALIFORNIA. ENGINEER: ANGEL BALESTIER. SECOND ENGINEER: MARK KAUFFMAN. New songs by Hendrix were in short supply, and this lengthy session was largely devoted to jamming. Six takes of "Jam Session" were recorded, with the sixth marked "hold"—although it plainly remains more of a jam than a finished basic track. Take 6 began with solo acoustic piano, soon joined by Hendrix's wah-wah guitar. As Redding and Mitchell come in, the song's slow tempo begins to increase. The jam that follows—lasting in excess of fifteen minutes—provides a splendid early example of Hendrix's firm grasp of the genre later popularized as fusion. Similar in style to *Electric Ladyland*'s extended sound painting "1983 . . . (A Merman I Should Turn To Be)," "Jam Session" created an engaging blend of jazz, blues, and psychedelic rock. Like many similar efforts, however, "Jam Session" begins to fall apart at the close as Hendrix's fellow travelers were left guessing where Hendrix was headed.

Impromptu jam sessions such as these were commonplace at TTG, remembers Angel Balestier. Another such effort, again marked simply "Jam Session," was also recorded on this evening, with the group's sound bolstered by Lee Michaels's distinctive Hammond B-3 organ. The group attempted four takes, with only the first complete.

TUESDAY, OCTOBER 29, 1968

TTG STUDIOS, LOS ANGELES, CALIFORNIA. ENGINEER: ANGEL BALESTIER. SECOND ENGINEER: MARK KAUFFMAN. Perhaps the finest—and certainly the most charged—Experience session at TTG took place on this long evening. Six robust takes of "Here He Comes," later titled "Lover Man," debuted, sounding very much like a vintage Experience stage performance. Hendrix opened the session by creating an extended introduction, marked as take 1. A second take broke down, and the trio regrouped for a complete third take, with Hendrix's and Redding's amplifiers jacked up to maximum volume. This effort was hampered by timing problems, as Mitchell struggled, understandably, to maintain a tempo steered by Hendrix's split-second improvisation. As Hendrix alternated between foot pedals, his concentration shifted, which caused a promising guitar solo to break down. Nevertheless, Hendrix rallied to a close with some vocal scatting and a brief flurry of notes. Take 4 showcased a slight refinement, as Redding's bass now accompanied Hendrix's opening rhythm guitar notes. Though Hendrix muffed the song's opening vocal line, his solo is superb, soaring above the arrangement. Hendrix concluded once more with some scatting and a short burst of guitar notes before bringing the song to a close. Hendrix then asked

Mitchell and Redding to "Go a little faster," before Balestier called for take 5.

While nearly as energetic, takes 5 and 6 lacked the brutish ferocity of the two previous efforts, especially the frenetic fourth take. Nonetheless, Hendrix's playing was especially noteworthy in these takes, particularly during the solo. He cleverly incorporated the melody line of the Beatles' "I Feel Fine" into one solo before shifting seamlessly back into the "Here He Comes" theme.

Although he did not achieve a finished master in this session, Hendrix did attempt to create a basic track by joining the spirited solo section from the first take to the front of the fourth. Eddie Kramer later mixed take 4 and included it as part of 1997's *South Saturn Delta*, where it serves as a pristine example of the post–*Electric Ladyland* Experience.

Next would be the group's primal remake of the band Them's Van Morrison–led anthem "Gloria." Like "Here He Comes," these takes of "Gloria," especially the remarkable take 8, provide another effective example of the sheer intensity which the three-man Experience could generate. And, like "Calling All The Devil's Children," "Gloria" also provided another glimpse of Hendrix's risqué humor.

After "Here He Comes" and "Gloria" set the appropriate mood, the group's lineup expanded to include Lee Michaels on organ and Jim Horn on flute. This ensemble recorded a remake of Hendrix's own "Red House." Takes 1 and 2 were lengthy and enthusiastic, but both incomplete. Takes 3 through 5, however, were all false starts. Reel three contains the version later pared down and coupled with the introductions to the October 21 recording of "Electric Church." This hybrid master later graced *Jimi Hendrix: Blues*.

After the Experience left the studio, Balestier's final task was to transfer selected two-inch, sixteen-track session tapes to one-inch, eight-track tape. While TTG's sixteen-track capability had attracted Hendrix to the studio, the two-inch tapes there were not compatible with the Record Plant's increasingly obsolete one-inch, twelve-track machines. Once completed, these TTG masters and their new submasters were sent on to the Record Plant in New York, where they would remain, largely untouched, until Hendrix's death in September 1970.

WEDNESDAY, OCTOBER 30, 1968

"CROSSTOWN TRAFFIC" / "GYPSY EYES." REPRISE 0792. U.S. SINGLE RELEASE.

Reprise hoped to capitalize on the popularity of "All Along The Watchtower" with this second single from *Electric Ladyland*. Though "Crosstown Traffic" was arguably just as strong an effort as its predecessor, it managed only to reach number 52 before its eight-week chart run concluded.

FRIDAY, NOVEMBER 1, 1968

MUNICIPAL AUDITORIUM, KANSAS CITY, MISSOURI. WITH CAT MOTHER & THE ALL NIGHT NEWSBOYS.

SATURDAY, NOVEMBER 2, 1968

MINNEAPOLIS AUDITORIUM, MINNEAPOLIS, MINNESOTA. WITH CAT MOTHER & THE ALL NIGHT NEWSBOYS. **SET LIST:** "FIRE" / "ARE YOU EXPERIENCED?" / "VOODOO CHILD (SLIGHT RETURN)" / "RED HOUSE" / "FOXEY LADY" / "LITTLE WING" / "SPANISH CASTLE MAGIC" / "SUNSHINE OF YOUR LOVE" / "STAR SPANGLED BANNER" / "PURPLE HAZE"

SUNDAY, NOVEMBER 3, 1968

KIEL AUDITORIUM, ST. LOUIS, MISSOURI. WITH CAT MOTHER & THE ALL NIGHT NEWSBOYS. **PARTIAL SET LIST:** "ROCK ME BABY" / "FOXEY LADY" / "FIRE" / "HEY JOE" / "TAX FREE" / "STAR SPANGLED BANNER" / "PURPLE HAZE"

As October came to a close, the Experience's tumultuous Hollywood stay ended as the group was slated to perform three concerts. They broke the venue's attendance record in Kansas City on November 1.

WEDNESDAY, NOVEMBER 6, 1968

RECORD PLANT, NEW YORK, NEW YORK. PRODUCER: JIMI HENDRIX. ENGINEER, TONY BONGIOVI.

With nearly two weeks available before the Experience's November 15 gig in Cincinatti, Hendrix agreed to produce a group from Michael Jeffery's growing stable

of clients who had opened several shows on their most recent tour: Cat Mother & the All Night Newsboys.

Hendrix approached the Cat Mother project differently from that of Eire Apparent. The group boasted two fine guitarists in Larry Packer and Charlie Chin, so rather than feature his own playing, Hendrix opted for a less prominent role. While Hendrix had a greater influence in the control room than the recording studio, he left the balance of the album's production chores to Record Plant staff engineers Gary Kellgren and Tony Bongiovi.

"I enjoy producing records by other groups," Hendrix said in a 1969 interview. "As long as I like what they are playing. I liked doing the Eire Apparent record, but it was never really finished according to my standards. Then I produced Cat Mother. They are presentable enough, but not as good as I wanted them to be. It was the same as our last LP [Electric Ladyland], it could have been so much better, but we were working all the time and couldn't spend the time we needed in the studio."

Of the many sessions staged for Cat Mother's The Street Giveth . . . and the Street Taketh Away in November, only three reels dating from November 6 are known to exist. A few golden moments shine amid some lackluster jamming by an unknown second guitarist accompanied by Hendrix. As these were Cat Mother sessions and not legendary Experience jams, jam sessions such as this were not pursued further and these tapes were simply put away.

The remaining multitrack tapes recorded for this album have seemingly disappeared, so more actual session dates are not available.

Whereas Eire Apparent's Sunrise missed Billboard's Top 200 album chart entirely, sinking quickly into oblivion despite Hendrix's involvement. Cat Mother proved a pleasant surprise. "Good Old Rock 'N' Roll," the group's high-energy medley of "Sweet Little Sixteen," "Long Tall Sally," "Chantilly Lace," "Whole Lotta Shakin' Goin' On," "Blue Suede Shoes," and "Party Doll," reached number 21 on Billboard's Top 100 chart in July 1969. Fueled by the success of their single, their album debut, The Street Giveth . . . and the Street Taketh Away, peaked at number 55, a highly respectable showing.

FRIDAY, NOVEMBER 15, 1968

CINCINNATI GARDENS, CINCINNATI, OHIO. While photographs exist of this performance, no sound recordings were made to document the songs Hendrix featured.

SATURDAY, NOVEMBER 16, 1968

BOSTON GARDEN, BOSTON, MASSACHUSETTS. WITH THE MCCOYS AND CAT MOTHER & THE ALL NIGHT NEWSBOYS. **PARTIAL SET LIST:** "FIRE" / "SPANISH CASTLE MAGIC" / "VOODOO CHILD (SLIGHT RETURN)" / "RED HOUSE" / "FOXEY LADY" / "PURPLE HAZE" A strong show by the Experience fired the imagination of Jerry Goldstein, whose company, The Visual Thing, held Hendrix's merchandise rights for posters sold at his concerts. Inspired by Hendrix's performance, Goldstein began to formulate a proposal whereby a concert such as this one could be filmed and recorded and shown in theaters throughout the world. Less than a month later, Goldstein secured the approval of Hendrix and his manager, Michael Jeffery, for his concept. They scheduled the filming tentatively for January 1969, when Hendrix was scheduled to tour Europe.

FRIDAY, NOVEMBER 22, 1968

JACKSONVILLE COLISEUM, JACKSONVILLE, FLORIDA. WITH CAT MOTHER & THE ALL NIGHT NEWSBOYS.

SATURDAY, NOVEMBER 23, 1968

CURTIS HIXON HALL, TAMPA, FLORIDA. WITH CAT MOTHER & THE ALL NIGHT NEWSBOYS.

SUNDAY, NOVEMBER 24, 1968

MIAMI BEACH CONVENTION HALL, MIAMI BEACH, FL. WITH CAT MOTHER & THE ALL NIGHT NEWSBOYS.

WEDNESDAY, NOVEMBER 27, 1968

RHODE ISLAND AUDITORIUM, PROVIDENCE, RHODE ISLAND. **SET LIST:** "SGT. PEPPER'S LONELY HEARTS

CLUB BAND" / "FIRE" / "HEY JOE" / "I DON'T LIVE TODAY" / "VOODOO CHILD (SLIGHT RETURN)" / "RED HOUSE" / "SUNSHINE OF YOUR LOVE" / "SPANISH CASTLE MAGIC" / "FOXEY LADY" / "STAR SPANGLED BANNER" / "PURPLE HAZE"

Hendrix celebrated his twenty-sixth birthday with an inspired performance. Following the concert, the Experience drove back to New York for a birthday jam session at the Cafe Au Go Go in Greenwich Village.

THURSDAY, NOVEMBER 28, 1968

PHILHARMONIC HALL, NEW YORK, NEW YORK. TWO SHOWS. WITH FERNANDO VALENTI AND THE NEW YORK BRASS QUINTET. **SET LIST, FIRST SHOW:** "FIRE" / "I DON'T LIVE TODAY" / "HEAR MY TRAIN A COMIN'" / "SPANISH CASTLE MAGIC" / "FOXEY LADY" / "RED HOUSE" / "SUNSHINE OF YOUR LOVE" / "PURPLE HAZE"

The Experience performed two concerts on this night, as part of "An Electronic Thanksgiving," an unusual concert organized by promoter Ron Delsener. The Experience shared the bill with harpsichordist Fernando Valenti and the New York Brass Quintet. Delsener had hoped Hendrix would sit in with the classical group, but only Mitchell agreed to do so once the evening began. Unfortunately, no recordings of Mitchell's participation have surfaced.

A birthday party backstage at the Philharmonic, complete with cake for Hendrix, followed the group's spirited performance.

SATURDAY, NOVEMBER 30, 1968

COBO HALL, DETROIT, MICHIGAN. WITH CAT MOTHER & THE ALL NIGHT NEWSBOYS. **SET LIST:** "FIRE" / "SPANISH CASTLE MAGIC" / "I DON'T LIVE TODAY" / "SUNSHINE OF YOUR LOVE" / "VOODOO CHILD (SLIGHT RETURN)" / "RED HOUSE" / "FOXEY LADY" / "HEY JOE" / "PURPLE HAZE"

Tensions within the group, particularly between Hendrix and Redding, flared up once more. This gig was nearly canceled because Hendrix refused to fly to Detroit with Mitchell and Redding. He was finally persuaded to honor his commitment and took a private

jet from New York to Detroit, arriving just in time for the performance.

SUNDAY, DECEMBER 1, 1968

COLISEUM, CHICAGO, ILLINOIS. WITH CAT MOTHER & THE ALL NIGHT NEWSBOYS. **SET LIST:** "KILLING FLOOR" / "I DON'T LIVE TODAY" / "SPANISH CASTLE MAGIC" / "FOXEY LADY" / "RED HOUSE" / "SUNSHINE OF YOUR LOVE" / "VOODOO CHILD (SLIGHT RETURN)" / "FIRE" / "PURPLE HAZE"

This Chicago performance ended the Experience's recent string of U.S. concerts.

1969

"Jimi was looking for
a sound that was in his
head, and he was doing
all kinds of things to try
and capture that."
—TOM ERDELYI
(TOMMY RAMONE)

SATURDAY, JANUARY 4, 1969

A HAPPENING FOR LULU, STUDIO 4, BBC TELEVISION CENTER, LONDON, ENGLAND. **SET LIST:** "VOODOO CHILD (SLIGHT RETURN)" / "HEY JOE" / "SUNSHINE OF YOUR LOVE"

The Experience gathered in London shortly after the New Year to begin a European tour. They made a memorable appearance on the television program *A Happening For Lulu* on this day. "I had gone to interview Jimi at the BBC in Shepherds Bush," remembers journalist Chris Welch. "There is a roof garden upstairs, so we sat out on the roof. He was always very generous, outgoing, and polite and he said, 'Would you like a drink?' I asked for a pint of lager. He went off to the bar and disappeared for about ten minutes. Eventually he came back and he had bought everybody in the club a drink. It had taken him all this while to buy all that. The soundmen, the cameramen, whoever was working at the BBC that day, he went out and bought them a drink. I think he was trying to say, 'I'm glad to be back in London and it's really nice to meet everybody, all the people that gave me my first break.' He really felt that London was a home to him."

The group performed "Voodoo Child (Slight Return)" and an unforgettable medley of "Hey Joe" and Cream's "Sunshine Of Your Love." Partway through "Hey Joe," Hendrix came to a stop and launched into "Sunshine Of Your Love," dedicating the song to the recently disbanded Cream. This deviation from the script threw the television crew into a panic, and, amid frantic hand signals and waving, Hendrix continued, shouting, "We're being put off the air!"

"It sounded great but it caused panic and confusion with the floor manager," laughs Welch. "Lulu herself looked very worried. I remember this bloke in a brown coat, a union floor manager, shouting 'Pull the plugs on him!' I said, 'You can't do that, it's Jimi Hendrix!' It was very funny to see."

"I remember watching the reaction from the audience because the director's going 'aagh!'" recalls Noel Redding. "But we were live, they couldn't turn us off, and we were going out to millions of people in Britain. The director is going mad. We finished off and they faded out the program. I said, 'God, we're going to be banned from BBC television now.' We went upstairs for a pint and the director, Stanley Dorfman, came over and said, 'That was brilliant!'"

SUNDAY, JANUARY 5, 1969

POLYDOR STUDIOS, LONDON, ENGLAND. 6:00 P.M. TO 9:00 A.M. PRODUCER: JIMI HENDRIX. ENGINEER: CARLOS OLMS.

Hendrix nipped into London's Polydor Studios to add a lead guitar overdub to Eire Apparent's "Rock 'n' Roll Band."

"Eire Apparent had come in around six p.m.," recalled Carlos Olms in a radio interview. "We messed around trying to get the right sound until ten or eleven before Jimi arrived in his very colorful dress. He sat very quietly in a corner. After he heard our work, he started to convert everything to his taste. He started with the drums, setting up each microphone to get the right sound, then the right equalization. The boys had a hard time trying to please him with their sound, but I was impressed with his way of working."

After the microphones and sound adjustments had been made, the group attempted to record the song's basic track. "We did about five or six complete versions," remembered Olms, "but Jimi always found something which he felt was not correct and we would do it again. It was three a.m. before he started to put his [guitar] parts down on tape. He had to play the middle-eight part and the ending."

For the guitar tracks, Hendrix gave Olms specific technical instructions to follow. "He asked me for a very insensitive microphone, because, he said, 'I will play quite loud,'" explains Olms. "We turned the lights down so low in the studio that I could just see the shadow of his guitar and amplifiers. Every time he played his part, we thought it was fantastic. Only Jimi didn't think so. He always raised his hand and said, 'Again.' He was still playing his part at five a.m., but was not satisfied. At the end, he agreed [to stop] only because it was so late. We started mixing and stayed until nine a.m. That was the longest session I had ever been involved with at Polydor. Other employees came into the studio that morning and were surprised to see that we were still there."

TUESDAY, JANUARY 7, 1969

RECORD PLANT, NEW YORK, NEW YORK. ENGINEER: JACK ADAMS.

With Hendrix in London, Hendrix's manager, Michael Jeffery, designated Record Plant engineer Jack Adams to cull the highlights of the October TTG Studios sessions in Los Angeles so that Hendrix could evaluate what had been recorded and how close the Experience had come to finishing an album. Without any direct input from either Hendrix or the group, Adams instead followed the label on each of the tape boxes. He compiled the following: "Messenger" take 15, "Mr. Lost Soul" take 17, "The New Rising Sun" take 2, "Jam Session" take 6, "Peace In Mississippi" take 15, "Izabella" take 18, "Jam #1" with Lee Michaels and Buddy Miles, "Jam #2" with Lee Michaels again, "Electric Church," "Calling All The Devil's Children," and "Jam #4" with extra percussion.

WEDNESDAY, JANUARY 8, 1969

LORENSBERG CIRCUS, GOTHENBURG, SWEDEN. TWO SHOWS. WITH GIN HOUSE BLUES AND BURNING RED IVANHOE. **SET LIST, FIRST SHOW:** "VOODOO CHILD (SLIGHT RETURN)" / "FOXEY LADY" / "SUNSHINE OF YOUR LOVE" / "I DON'T LIVE TODAY" / "HEAR MY TRAIN A COMIN'" / "SPANISH CASTLE MAGIC" / "PURPLE HAZE" / "STAR SPANGLED BANNER"

THURSDAY, JANUARY 9, 1969

KONSERTHUSET, STOCKHOLM, SWEDEN. TWO SHOWS. WITH JETHRO TULL. **SET LIST, FIRST SHOW:** "KILLING FLOOR" / "SPANISH CASTLE MAGIC" / "FIRE" / "HEY JOE" / "VOODOO CHILD (SLIGHT RETURN)" / "RED HOUSE" / "SUNSHINE OF YOUR LOVE." **SET LIST, SECOND SHOW:** "I DON'T LIVE TODAY" / "SPANISH CASTLE MAGIC" / "HEY JOE" / "VOODOO CHILD (SLIGHT RETURN)" / "SUNSHINE OF YOUR LOVE" / "RED HOUSE" / "FIRE" / "PURPLE HAZE" / "STAR SPANGLED BANNER"

FRIDAY, JANUARY 10, 1969

FALKONER CENTRET, COPENHAGEN, DENMARK. TWO SHOWS. WITH JETHRO TULL. **SET LIST, FIRST SHOW:** "FIRE" / "FOXEY LADY" / "TAX FREE" / "SPANISH CASTLE MAGIC" / "RED HOUSE" / "SUNSHINE OF YOUR LOVE" / "I DON'T LIVE TODAY" / "PURPLE HAZE"

SATURDAY, JANUARY 11, 1969

MUSIKHALLE, HAMBURG, GERMANY. TWO SHOWS. WITH EIRE APPARENT. **SET LIST, FIRST SHOW:** "ARE YOU EXPERIENCED?" / "JOHNNY B. GOODE" / "SPANISH CASTLE MAGIC" / "HEAR MY TRAIN A COMIN'" / "FIRE" / "I DON'T LIVE TODAY" / "RED HOUSE" / "SUNSHINE OF YOUR LOVE" / "VOODOO CHILD (SLIGHT RETURN)"

SUNDAY, JANUARY 12, 1969

RHEINHALLE, DUSSELDORF, GERMANY. TWO SHOWS. WITH EIRE APPARENT. **SET LIST, SECOND SHOW:** "SPANISH CASTLE MAGIC" / "FOXEY LADY" / "FIRE" / "RED HOUSE" / "SUNSHINE OF YOUR LOVE" / "COME ON (LET THE GOOD TIMES ROLL)" / "PURPLE HAZE"

MONDAY, JANUARY 13, 1969

SPORTHALLE, KOLN, GERMANY. TWO SHOWS. WITH EIRE APPARENT. **SET LIST:** "COME ON (LET THE GOOD TIMES ROLL)" / "FOXEY LADY" / "RED HOUSE" / "VOODOO CHILD (SLIGHT RETURN)" / "FIRE" / "SPANISH CASTLE MAGIC" / "HEY JOE" / "SUNSHINE OF YOUR LOVE" / "PURPLE HAZE"

TUESDAY, JANUARY 14, 1969

MUNSTERLANDHALLE, MUNSTER, GERMANY. WITH EIRE APPARENT. **SET LIST:** "RED HOUSE" / "FIRE" / "FOXEY LADY" / "ALL ALONG THE WATCHTOWER" / "HEY JOE" / "VOODOO CHILD (SLIGHT RETURN)" / "PURPLE HAZE"

WEDNESDAY, JANUARY 15, 1969

MEISTERSINGERHALLE, NUREMBURG, GERMANY. TWO SHOWS. WITH EIRE APPARENT. **SET LIST, FIRST SHOW:** "COME ON (LET THE GOOD TIMES ROLL)" / "I DON'T LIVE TODAY" / "HEY JOE" / "FIRE" / "RED HOUSE" /

"FOXEY LADY" / "PURPLE HAZE" / "VOODOO CHILD (SLIGHT RETURN)"

FRIDAY, JANUARY 17, 1969

JARHUNDERTHALLE, FRANKFURT, GERMANY. TWO SHOWS WITH EIRE APPARENT. **SET LIST:** "COME ON (LET THE GOOD TIMES ROLL)" / "FIRE" / "RED HOUSE" / "I DON'T LIVE TODAY" / "SPANISH CASTLE MAGIC" / "FOXEY LADY" / "SUNSHINE OF YOUR LOVE" / "HEY JOE" / "PURPLE HAZE" / "VOODOO CHILD (SLIGHT RETURN)"

SUNDAY, JANUARY 19, 1969

LIEDERHALLE, STUTTGART, GERMANY. TWO SHOWS. **SET LIST, FIRST SHOW:** "COME ON (LET THE GOOD TIMES ROLL)" / "FOXEY LADY" / "RED HOUSE" / "SUNSHINE OF YOUR LOVE" / "STAR SPANGLED BANNER" / "PURPLE HAZE." **SET LIST, SECOND SHOW:** "FIRE" / "SPANISH CASTLE MAGIC" / "RED HOUSE" / "FOXEY LADY" / "I DON'T LIVE TODAY" / "HEY JOE" / "STAR SPANGLED BANNER" / "PURPLE HAZE" / "SUNSHINE OF YOUR LOVE" / "VOODOO CHILD (SLIGHT RETURN)"

TUESDAY, JANUARY 21, 1969

WACKEN HALLE, STRASBOURG, FRANCE. TWO SHOWS. WITH EIRE APPARENT. **SET LIST [SHOW UNKNOWN]:** "COME ON (LET THE GOOD TIMES ROLL)" / "HEY JOE" / "SPANISH CASTLE MAGIC" / "RED HOUSE" / "FIRE" / "SUNSHINE OF YOUR LOVE" / "PURPLE HAZE" / "FOXEY LADY" / "VOODOO CHILD (SLIGHT RETURN)"

WEDNESDAY, JANUARY 22, 1969

KONSERTHAUS, WIEN, AUSTRIA. TWO SHOWS WITH EIRE APPARENT. **SET LIST, FIRST SHOW:** "COME ON (LET THE GOOD TIMES ROLL)" / "HEY JOE" / "FIRE" / "HEAR MY TRAIN A COMIN'" / "SPANISH CASTLE MAGIC" / "FOXEY LADY" / "STONE FREE" / "PURPLE HAZE." **SET LIST, SECOND SHOW:** "ARE YOU EXPERIENCED?" / "FIRE" / "LOVER MAN" / "SUNSHINE OF YOUR LOVE" / "SPANISH CASTLE MAGIC" / "VOODOO CHILD (SLIGHT RETURN)"

THURSDAY, JANUARY 23, 1969

SPORT PALAST, BERLIN, GERMANY. TWO SHOWS. WITH EIRE APPARENT. **SET LIST:** "FIRE" / "HEY JOE" / "SPANISH CASTLE MAGIC" / "FOXEY LADY" / "RED HOUSE" / "COME ON (LET THE GOOD TIMES ROLL)" / "SUNSHINE OF YOUR LOVE" / "PURPLE HAZE"

Prior to the European tour, Redding formed his own group, Fat Mattress, as a creative diversion. "We had actually talked about the idea of each member starting a solo project but with the Experience as our main band," explains Redding. "Mitch [Mitchell] would do some jazz type stuff. He had a name called Mind Octopus in mind for that. Hendrix was going to do something like Suns and Rainbows, Band of Gypsys, or whichever title he had. I had actually started Fat Mattress in 1968. The idea in 1969 was to go on tour with Mitch's band, my band, and Hendrix's band, and then, as a finale, we all come on as the Experience. That was the actual plan, but, unfortunately, it didn't happen."

The concept of three Experience-related groups may not have materialized, but interest in the Experience and their new album *Electric Ladyland* helped fill arenas and shift copies of the double album across Europe. Despite the album's wide popularity, the group only performed two songs from *Electric Ladyland* on a regular basis: "Come On (Let the Good Times Roll)" and "Voodoo Child (Slight Return)." "We never had time to rehearse," complains Redding. "That's why we kept playing the same songs." Audience calls for "All Along The Watchtower" were ignored, apart from one known performance in Munster, Germany, on January 14.

In Stockholm, the first of two performances was videotaped for SVT Swedish television. Given the paucity of video footage shot of the band during the entirety of its existence, it is unfortunate that multiple cameras were in place to document this dispirited concert. There were a few bright moments marbled throughout—namely "Sunshine Of Your Love" and "Red House," the latter performed by Hendrix while playing a Gibson SG—but the video recording makes clear Hendrix's dour mood and the tension among the players. The second performance was recorded by Swedish radio and has since been widely bootlegged.

FEBRUARY 1969

In late 1968, Hendrix and his manager, Michael Jeffery, had begun to discuss plans to open a nightclub based on Steve Paul's Scene Club, an artist-friendly nightspot favored by Hendrix and his friends. The concept was to create a facility that would replicate the atmosphere of the Scene Club but also offer an additional advantage: hardwired recording equipment that would allow musicians to record their jam sessions or even a live performance. The idea eventually developed into Hendrix's legendary recording facility, Electric Lady Studios.

Hendrix and Jeffery had admired Cerebrum, a popular new venue in SoHo designed by architect John Storyk. "Cerebrum was a club for the senses," remembers Storyk. "It was a three-dimension, multimedia show that you walked into." Despite an A-list clientele, Cerebrum's run was short-lived. "It had a short life because of the mob," says Storyk. "They couldn't figure out how to get money from us, because we weren't selling liquor or cigarettes, so one day they broke the windows and thoroughly trashed the place. Without adequate insurance, that just did us in."

As the tour progressed, the performances grew stronger and more passionate. This transformation came just ahead of the film crew that had begun to document Hendrix and the Experience for a proposed movie. Hendrix had entered into an agreement in December 1968 with Steve Gold and Jerry Goldstein to create a movie that would document the unique excitement of his stage performance. Gold and Goldstein had no experience as filmmakers (their company, The Visual Thing, licensed merchandise rights from Hendrix to design and manufacture items such as posters sold at his concerts), but what they did have was unprecedented access to the guitarist while on tour.

Gold and Goldstein cobbled together a local crew that included a young German cinematographer, Michael Ballhaus, who later became famous for such films as *Gangs of New York*, and began filming. They documented one of the group's two performances in Strasbourg, France, as well as their stay in Wien, Austria. Gold and Goldstein dispatched additional cameras and crew to film the group's exciting Berlin performance and subsequent return to London.

Jeffery was intrigued by the success the Scene Club enjoyed and befriended its manager, Jim Marron. Jeffery had run nightclubs in Majorca and Newcastle, and he asked Marron to prepare a feasibility study based upon the Generation Club, a bankrupt Greenwich Village nightspot located at 52 West 8th Street whose lease he and Hendrix had recently acquired.

Marron's frank advice was that Hendrix stood no chance of opening a successful nightclub at that location. He explained that 8th Street in the Village was Mafia-run, and four nightspots there were already under their control. Marron instead seized on the studio aspect of the project. He suggested that the balance be shifted to expand the studio component of the project. Storyk was hired to design a nightclub that would incorporate recording capabilities.

On February 23, 1969, the day before Storyk was to present his final drawings, Marron telephoned him with the news that the club concept had been scrapped. The facility would now be designed as a full-fledged recording studio. Storyk was instructed to develop new architectural plans. Marron hired Bob Hansen, a noted acoustical engineer, and Eddie Kramer was assigned to Storyk to help develop the new facility. Over the next two months, Kramer successfully pushed the concept of building a first-class recording facility for Hendrix and eschewing the nightclub component altogether. "Very few people realize it," says Storyk, "but this studio was an accident. Basically I believe it was Kramer catching Hendrix on an off moment."

TUESDAY, FEBRUARY 11, 1969

RECORD PLANT, NEW YORK, NEW YORK. RECORDING: 12:00 A.M. TO 4:00 A.M. ROUGH MIX: 4:00 A.M. TO 5:30 A.M. ENGINEER: TONY BONGIOVI. SECOND ENGINEER: DAVE RAGNO.

Hendrix took advantage of the three-week break between his January 22 Berlin performance and the upcoming February performances at London's Royal Albert Hall to return to the United States.

Without a firm plan in place for recording the fourth Experience album, Hendrix looked for new creative challenges. His friendship with Buddy Miles and the members of the Express had deepened during his extended stay in Los Angeles the previous fall. "Jimi just seemed to be looking for different things to do," recalls Buddy Miles Express bassist Billy Rich. "He and Buddy had grown pretty close. At that time, Buddy was trying to get Jimi to do anything he possibly could with him."

"Jimi was tired of having to do 'Purple Haze' on the road every night," recalls Express guitarist Jim McCarty. "He wanted to make the transition from psychedelia to his own style of funk rock. He was talking to people like Miles Davis and Buddy Miles about doing different projects, but his drug use was wearing him down."

Despite Hendrix's deteriorating relationship with Redding, he still made no overt move to replace him, opting instead to try to develop a stable of players outside the Experience who might be used for recordings. "We did do a bunch of recording," says Rich. "We'd play all night, putting some little things down on tape and just having a ball. Jimi never asked me to join the Experience, but he hinted that he wanted to get together with me at some point. It wouldn't have been with the Experience, because they were a solid thing. He was hoping to also do something else."

In addition to jamming at the Scene or hanging at such local haunts as the Tin Angel, Hendrix enjoyed sharing his impressive record collection. "He and Buddy Miles would listen to Moms Mabley and Pigmeat Markham albums all the time," recalls sometime Hendrix collaborator Velvert Turner. "They had this whole shuck-and-jive routine they would do, which would make them laugh for hours. It was wild, especially when Tootie, Buddy's sister, would make chitlins, sweet potato pie, and all kinds of soul food. Jimi loved that. He used to love to turn us on to the blues records from his collection. He played us Blind Lemon Jefferson, Robert Johnson, and especially Albert King. We would listen to those records for hours."

Having already contributed liner notes to *Expressway To Your Skull*, the Express's debut album, Hendrix agreed to produce *Electric Church*, the forthcoming Buddy Miles Express album. Anne Tansey, a mutual friend and a Mercury Records staff producer, was assigned to work with Hendrix and oversee the project for the label. While Hendrix's schedule would ultimately limit him to producing only four tracks, Tansey, a pioneering female rock producer, was a constant presence in the studio. For those tracks supervised by Hendrix, she would retreat, allowing Hendrix to shape the sound and arrangements as he desired. When Hendrix wasn't present, she took charge of recording the remaining tracks required to deliver the album to Mercury.

While the majority of sessions for *Electric Church* were staged at Mercury Studios, additional dates were held at the Record Plant. Sadly, nearly all of the multitrack master tapes from the sessions at Mercury Studios have been lost, stolen, or destroyed. All that remains is the quarter-inch, 15 i.p.s. album master. With the exception of a couple of notable sessions, no outtakes or alternate tracks are known to exist.

On this evening, Hendrix presided over the production of "I Can See," which would later be retitled "Destructive Love." This recording sported the same arrangement as the released master but was performed in a higher key.

Eager to play, Hendrix stepped out from behind the console to jam, assuming the bass guitar while Miles moved from drums to guitar. Though Miles was a capable guitarist, the long, shambling jam session that ensued was largely uneventful. Following this, Hendrix switched back to guitar as Miles returned to his drum kit and kicked off another jam. With this lineup, Hendrix led the group through two impromptu originals, "World Traveler" and "It's Too Bad." Though they recorded only one take of each, both were quite good. The up-tempo "World Traveler" centered around a guitar-and-organ duel between Hendrix and Duane Hitchings. "It's Too Bad" was even better, a deeply personal original blues composition based largely on Hendrix's relationship with his troubled brother, Leon.

While Hendrix thoroughly enjoyed producing and recording with the Express, his pending commitments to the Experience loomed, beginning with a major concert scheduled February 18 at London's Royal Albert Hall. Of the four tracks Hendrix would ultimately produce for *Electric Church*, his deepest involvement, says Rich, came with the recording of "69 Freedom Special." The song's title was coined by Hendrix and inspired by Tansey's efforts to shorten Rich's recent military commitments. "A lot of energy was put into that session," Rich explains. "It was so much fun that it was like a dream. I'm just sorry that it was edited down before it was put on the album, because there are a few more great solos recorded on that track. I was out of the service and just starting to get a lot of shit off my brain for the first time in two years. The name I had picked out for the song was something like 'The Clap,' which wasn't too cool. In the studio, I was telling Jimi about my whole service thing and he said, 'Well, why don't you call this thing the '69 Freedom Special'?"

"I agreed," says Rich with a laugh, "because some of that shit I'm playing on bass I actually stole from him anyway!"

FRIDAY, FEBRUARY 14, 1969

OLYMPIC STUDIOS, LONDON, ENGLAND. ENGINEER: GEORGE CHKIANTZ. SECOND ENGINEER: RON (SURNAME UNKNOWN).

While in London to prepare for their upcoming engagements at the Royal Albert Hall on February 18 and 24, the Experience returned to Olympic Studios for the first time in more than a year. Unfortunately, the January European tour had further exposed the growing disharmony within the group, especially between Hendrix and Redding, whose relationship had further deteriorated. At Olympic, with their ex-manager Chas Chandler no longer at the helm, the Experience were unable to summon the energy and unity necessary to reverse their sagging spirits.

Redding's scathing diary notations detail his mounting frustration. "On the first day, as I nearly expected, there was nothing doing," Redding noted. "On the second it was no show at all. I went to the pub for three hours, came back, and it was still ages before Jimi ambled in. Then we argued. There seemed no way to get working. Either there was no one there or I'd show up to find the studio so crowded I had trouble squeezing in. Next day, Mitch was late. I suppose it was partly because we didn't want to get it together. The pressure from the public to create something even more brilliant each time, while basically expecting us to stay the same, was crushing. On the last day, I just watched it happen for a while and then went back to my flat."

A scheduling conflict kept Hendrix out of Studio A, the spacious room that had been home to all of his previous work at Olympic. The guitarist was instead booked into the smaller Studio B, and staff engineer George Chkiantz was assigned to engineer the sessions. The two would clash over the volume of Hendrix's amplifiers within the smaller recording space. Hendrix was steadfast in his desire to maintain the tone and volume he preferred. These philosophical differences—compounded with the already strained relations within the band—made the situation even tenser. "We did those sessions in Studio B, and I thought they were terrible," explains Chkiantz. "Hendrix was in a bad mood, but he wanted to come in and do *something*. Studio B was the wrong place for Hendrix to record anyway, because there wasn't room for his sound to properly expand. It was incredibly difficult to record him there. Hendrix's response was to double his amplifiers, which made it nearly impossible to hear anything in the control room. We stuck a couple of layers of screens between the studio window and the control room, but it ended up making zero difference. It was just stupid. He really seemed lost, and the whole thing was very sad."

This evening session began with "Slow Version." Hendrix and the group appeared to have rehearsed the arrangement before recording commenced, as this was not an impromptu jam by any means. Five attempts at recording the song broke down before Hendrix launched into the sixth and final take. This effort, lasting five minutes, would later be issued as part of *Hear My Music*, one of the entries in the Dagger Records official "bootleg" series.

Next, the group played "Midnight Lightning." Even though the song was markedly different from "Slow Version," Chkiantz did not begin his numbering system anew. As a result, "take 7" was actually the first take of this new effort. "Midnight Lightning" was actually an early predecessor of "Ezy Ryder," foreshadowing the many transformations that "Ezy Ryder" later underwent before achieving its final form at Electric Lady Studios eighteen months later.

On this evening, the Experience would record forty-one (thirty-six not counting the five takes of "Slow Version" that began the session) furious takes filled with spectacular moments. The mood may have been sour among the players, but that volatile chemistry impacted these performances in ways that no previous Experience recording session had witnessed. The group struggled to harness "Midnight Lightning" until a complete fourteenth take, and the song suffered a series of false starts and breakdown before a promising nineteenth was completed. Hendrix was still not satisfied and pressed onward. Take 25 provided a rare and unexpected delight: the first known studio recording of "Star Spangled Banner." This impromptu medley stretched beyond ten minutes in length. No other takes of "Midnight Lightning" recorded on this night would revisit "Star Spangled Banner," but another diversion yielded the aptly titled "Blues Jam At Olympic." Hendrix kicked off this boisterous, wah-wah-guitar-drenched jam session, and Mitchell and Redding, two superb musicians who were well used to Hendrix's sudden flashes of inspiration, fell right in behind him. The two alternately challenged and supported the guitarist until the jam drew to a close.

The group invited percussionist Rocki Dzidzornu to take part before the close of reel three. His contributions were part of two solid, complete takes numbered 28 and 33. Take 35 blossomed into a blistering twenty-three-minute effort that, while not a structured take, was the highlight of the evening.

"Slow Version," "Blues Jam At Olympic," and "Ezy Ryder/Star Spangled Banner" would later be included as part of *Hear My Music*.

SUNDAY, FEBRUARY 16, 1969

OLYMPIC STUDIOS, LONDON, ENGLAND. ENGINEER: GEORGE CHKIANTZ.

Hendrix revisited "Slow Version" during this session, and the resulting takes showcase Hendrix adopting a slower tempo and incorporating a wah-wah guitar part. Tension between Chkiantz and Hendrix was evident right from the outset. The engineer pressed Hendrix repeatedly for a song title after the first take broke down. Hendrix seemed to ignore the request before finally saying "Slow Tune." Chkiantz tried again to get Hendrix to turn down his amplifier, but this request was ignored.

Hendrix invited percussionist Rocki Dzidzornu to participate and recorded thirty-three takes of "Slow Version." In various takes, Hendrix experimented with the song's tempo and built upon the foundation of the central riff of "Ezy Ryder." Takes 31 and 33 were the strongest efforts, but no overdubs were attempted as Hendrix seemed content to put the song aside for the time being.

Next, Hendrix kicked off an extended vocal take of "Room Full Of Mirrors," followed by "Shame, Shame, Shame" and "Crying Blue Rain." After these takes, Hendrix and Dzidzornu ran though ideas the guitarist had for "Message To Love," "South Saturn Delta," and other potential songs. Mitchell joined them in progress, and the jam rounded into a version of "Tax Free" that had several strong moments. Redding then joined in on an untitled jam session steered by Hendrix.

With the full group together in the studio now, Hendrix turned his focus to "Lover Man." He had the group adopt a slower tempo than previous stage or recorded versions. The session tape captures Hendrix working out a specific bass pattern with Redding and establishing the tempo before starting. The group, joined once more by Dzidzornu on percussion, was in the midst of a strong take when Hendrix broke a guitar string. Mitchell and Redding kept going, knowing that Hendrix could add the remainder of his part via an overdub if necessary. Hendrix stayed on the floor and can be heard offering instructions to both Mitchell and Redding. Afterwards, he requested a playback so that the musicians could "listen to what each other is playing and come back in and add some accents." Deciding that they could better their efforts, Hendrix called for a new take. His request for accents may have confused Mitchell as this second take came apart almost immediately. "Play it straight," Hendrix instructed Mitchell. An incomplete third take gave way to a strong fourth take brimming with promise.

Sensing a momentum shift, Hendrix stayed on familiar ground, initiating "Sunshine Of Your Love." This Cream song was an Experience favorite, and the group returned to their unique live arrangement for this recording. Their initial effort came apart quickly but a second attempt secured a terrific complete version.

MONDAY, FEBRUARY 17, 1969

OLYMPIC STUDIOS, LONDON, ENGLAND. ENGINEER: GEORGE CHKIANTZ.

The Experience were scheduled to perform two sold-out concerts at London's Royal Albert Hall on February 18 and 24, 1969. Plans were made to film and record both concerts at the famed venue for future release.

Hendrix was determined to have the film crew document the best possible performances for the project. To prepare, he took the unusual step of booking time at Olympic Studios the night prior to the first Royal Albert Hall show. The group recorded many of the numbers they planned to perform to ensure that the concert arrangements had been perfected.

The Experience had been saddled with a heavy slate of public appearances since their formation. Consequently, the group had tired of performing the same material night after night. Increasingly, the stage became a forum to reinvent material such as "Spanish Castle Magic" and "Hear My Train A Comin.'" Both of these vigorous Olympic recordings feature the extended arrangements of those songs that the group had devised that year.

On this night, the group recorded live, without overdubs, charged renditions of "Fire," "Spanish Castle Magic," "Hear My Train A Comin,'" "I Don't Live Today," "Lover Man," and "Red House."

Two songs from this session, take 2 of "Spanish Castle Magic" and take 1 of "Hear My Train A Comin'," were first issued as part of the *Jimi Hendrix Experience* box set.

TUESDAY, FEBRUARY 18, 1969

ROYAL ALBERT HALL, LONDON, ENGLAND. ENGINEER: GLYN JOHNS. ASSISTANT ENGINEER: VIC MAILE. WITH MASON, CAPALDI, WOOD & FROG, AND SOFT MACHINE. SET LIST: "TAX FREE" / "FIRE" / "HEAR MY TRAIN A COMIN'" / "FOXEY LADY" / "RED HOUSE" / "SUNSHINE OF YOUR LOVE" / "SPANISH CASTLE MAGIC" / "STAR SPANGLED BANNER" / "PURPLE HAZE" / "VOODOO CHILD (SLIGHT RETURN)"

This sold-out performance was filmed and professionally recorded, as it was intended to be one of the centerpieces of the proposed theatrical film by Gold and Goldstein. The group's uneven performance, brilliant in spots while ragged in others, coupled with concert lighting that compromised the film crew's ability to cover the entire concert as planned, forced the production to revise their approach and schedule additional filming at the group's second Albert Hall performance on February 24.

SATURDAY, FEBRUARY 22, 1969

LONDON, OLYMPIC STUDIOS. ENGINEER: GEORGE CHKIANTZ. ASSISTANT ENGINEER: ROGER (SURNAME UNKNOWN).

Hendrix began this session by performing alone, showcasing the intricate chord sequences for "Go My Own Way," a new song he had written. He attempted five solo takes before Mitchell and Redding joined him for take 6. Their effort held promise, but Hendrix elected to record the song on his own. Nine takes in all were recorded, but Hendrix was unable to complete a basic track to his satisfaction.

Following a break, the atmosphere in the studio changed considerably. Hendrix turned his attention to what he described as "Hound Dog Blues," the guitarist's unique interpretation of Big Mama Thornton's blues chestnut, "Hound Dog." Traffic's Chris Wood joined this effort on saxophone and flute, with Dzidzornu

on percussion and Jerry Goldstein on piano. The early takes served more as rehearsals as the expanded group struggled to grasp Hendrix's concept for the arrangement. Their efforts eventually resulted in several high-flying takes, each with some inspired guitar work from Hendrix. Following take 16, Wood changed from saxophone to flute. In the end, this portion of the session produced forty-one takes in all, but none improved upon a complete take 19.

Hendrix remained behind in Studio B when "Hound Dog Blues" drew to a close, intent upon committing a series of promising new demos to tape.

Before beginning the first take of "Message To Love," Hendrix honed the distinctive, descending note introduction, making clear, at least in this early incarnation, that such a flourish would serve as the song's opening. Each take began in such a fashion, and that figure later returned again in the song's arrangement.

Hendrix then moved to the piano to experiment with the chords and melody he envisioned for "Valleys Of Neptune." The roots of this song trace back at least as far as the October 1968 sessions at TTG Studios in Hollywood, where Hendrix previewed brief flashes of its melody on both the guitar and piano. He made several attempts during these February sessions to realize the song, but it eluded him. Separate here, "Gypsy Blood" and Valleys Of Neptune" would soon merge during the course of these sessions as Hendrix labored to harness the song's final structure.

After two quiet takes of "Valleys of Neptune," he drew the session to a close. Hendrix revisited the song on different occasions in 1969 and 1970, but he never completed it to his satisfaction.

MONDAY, FEBRUARY 24, 1969

ROYAL ALBERT HALL, LONDON, ENGLAND. ENGINEER: VIC MAILE. WITH FAT MATTRESS, VAN DER GRAAF GENERATOR, AND SOFT MACHINE. **SET LIST:** "LOVER MAN" / "STONE FREE" / "HEAR MY TRAIN A COMIN'" / "I DON'T LIVE TODAY" / "RED HOUSE" / "FOXEY LADY" / "SUNSHINE OF YOUR LOVE" / "BLEEDING HEART" / "FIRE" / "LITTLE WING" / "VOODOO CHILD (SLIGHT RETURN)" / "PURPLE HAZE" / "WILD THING" / "STAR SPANGLED BANNER"

This extraordinary performance stands as one of the finest concerts ever by the Jimi Hendrix Experience.

With the house lights up to accommodate the film crew, Albert Hall took on the appearance of a soundstage. Versions of "Foxey Lady," "Voodoo Child (Slight Return)," and "Little Wing" were first-rate, with Hendrix superbly accompanied by Mitchell and Redding throughout. Coupled with expanded renditions of "Stone Free" and "I Don't Live Today" came a rare treat: a standout rendition of the Elmore James classic "Bleeding Heart."

The film crew extensively documented this day. Camera teams followed each group member throughout the day, tracing Mitchell's arrival from home, Redding's sound check with Fat Mattress, one of the evening's opening acts, and an impromptu jam session at Hendrix's London apartment. The crew even documented the after-show jam and party at the Speakeasy. Unfortunately, the entire footage remains unreleased due to three decades of legal wrangling.

WEDNESDAY, FEBRUARY 26, 1969

OLYMPIC STUDIOS, LONDON, ENGLAND. ENGINEER: GEORGE CHKIANTZ. ASSISTANT ENGINEER: ROGER (SURNAME UNKNOWN).

Hendrix returned to "Valleys Of Neptune," although the tape box notation remained "Gypsy Blood." Redding was not present when the session began but joined Hendrix and Mitchell for the eleventh and final take.

Following a break, recording resumed, and the Experience were joined once again by Wood, Dzidzornu, and an additional, unnamed horn player for the rollicking "12 Bar Blues Jam With Horns." This extended workout was very likely rehearsed prior to recording, as each musician skillfully navigated his way through the song with confidence and verve.

After another break, Redding, Mitchell, and Hendrix returned to record further. Redding put forward one of his new songs, announced by Chkiantz as "Noel's Tune." The group tore through a first take that featured Hendrix on lead guitar, backed by Redding on rhythm guitar and Mitchell on drums. Hendrix then retreated to the control room as Redding and Mitchell continued. Redding slowed the tempo for take 2, concentrating on the song's rhythm guitar part. In all, the group recorded ten instrumental takes before the session concluded.

MARCH 1969

RECORD PLANT, NEW YORK, NEW YORK. PRODUCER: JIMI HENDRIX. ENGINEER: WARREN DEWEY.
Hendrix recorded "Blue Window," a spirited blues workout, together with the Buddy Miles Express. This recording is unique in that it presents Hendrix with a horn section and keyboards as well as a rhythm guitarist. At the close of this enthusiastic session, Hendrix and Dewey created a mix of the recording and put it aside for future consideration.

An edited version of this master lasting 12:51 was later included as part of the *Martin Scorcese Presents The Blues: Jimi Hendrix* album.

TUESDAY, MARCH 18, 1969

RECORD PLANT, NEW YORK, NEW YORK. 4:00 A.M. TO 9:00 A.M. ENGINEER: GARY KELLGREN. SECOND ENGINEER: DAVE RAGNO.
Hendrix took advantage of the Record Plant's recent installation of a new Ampex sixteen-track recording unit. Perhaps inspired by the occasion, he crafted a unique rendition of "Star-Spangled Banner." He attempted three takes in all with the third and final effort serving as the master. Hendrix then performed several guitar overdubs using his tone-control pedals to shade the sound of each. Gary Kellgren also employed a variable speed oscillator to alter the speed of the guitar for dramatic effect. No bass or drum parts were recorded, and there is no evidence to suggest that either Mitchell or Redding was present at the session. The recording represented a unique approach, quite unlike Hendrix's stage versions, including the definitive version performed at Woodstock.

While Hendrix never revisited this particular recording, Kramer remixed the track after Hendrix's death and added it to 1971's *Rainbow Bridge*. "I thought it was a pretty unique rendition of the song," explains Kramer. "I was intrigued by the fact that Jimi was able to make the guitar sound like an early synthesizer, predating the guitar synthesizers which came in later. It just showed

another aspect of his playing. His variety of tone colors was limitless."

After Hendrix and Kellgren completed "Star Spangled Banner," Buddy Miles and an unnamed organist (who may have been John Winfield) joined Hendrix. The group recorded two new songs, "Hey Gypsy Boy" with organ and "Jimi I" with organ and voice. "Hey Gypsy Boy" was actually an embryonic version of what would later evolve as "Hey Baby (Land Of The New Rising Sun)." During early takes, Hendrix can be heard instructing Miles as to the drum pattern he desired. These few takes were nothing more than simple sketches. None represented anything close to a finished master.

After a break, Miles departed and Hendrix's old friend Lonnie Youngblood joined the session. Youngblood had employed Hendrix when the guitarist was a struggling sideman long before his fame. With Youngblood on saxophone and lead vocals, drummer Jimmy Mayes, bassist Hank Anderson, organist John Winfield, and an unnamed percussionist complemented Hendrix. Hendrix toyed with "Come On (Let The Good Times Roll)" before launching into energetic takes of "Let Me Move You" voiced by Youngblood. The group completed a loose, but spirited, second take, and Hendrix moved without hesitation into a third take, which yielded the master. Hendrix's playing throughout both "Let Me Move You" and the twelve-bar "Georgia Blues," also voiced by Youngblood, was first-rate.

The group continued to jam, and the contents of a second reel featured one take of "Jam I," as well as three blues-influenced takes of "Jam II" performed by the same lineup. The third and final take was highlighted for Hendrix's future consideration.

After Hendrix's death, Alan Douglas chose take 8 of "Hey Gypsy Boy" as a candidate for the extensive posthumous overdubbing sessions he supervised for 1975's *Midnight Lightning*. By the time this "new" master was complete, Douglas and co-producer Tony Bongiovi had almost entirely recreated the track as a result of the various edits and looping of Hendrix's lead vocal part.

"Georgia Blues" was issued in 2005 as part of the *Martin Scorcese Blues Series: Jimi Hendrix*.

WEDNESDAY, MARCH 19, 1969

RECORD PLANT, NEW YORK, NEW YORK. ENGINEER: GARY KELLGREN. SECOND ENGINEER: DAVE RAGNO. Working with an unknown group of musicians, Hendrix recorded three demos that sounded more like jam sessions than structured songs. "Untitled Demo #1" got the session off to a promising start. "Untitled Demo #2" was ragged and not as developed as the previous recording. "Jam" followed, and this recording featured Hendrix backed by bass, drums, congas, and cowbell. The drummer struggled to follow Hendrix, and the song came apart. Hendrix then slowed the tempo in an effort to rein everybody in. "Jam #2" improved, but the musicians seemed unable to follow Hendrix as he desired. For "Jam #3" Hendrix switched from guitar to bass. "Jam #4" was actually the same song as "Jam #3," just a different take, and concluded the session.

TUESDAY, MARCH 25, 1969

RECORD PLANT, NEW YORK, NEW YORK. ENGINEER: GARY KELLGREN. SECOND ENGINEER: LLYLLIANNE DAVIS. On this busy evening, Hendrix recorded two separate jam sessions, the first with Mitchell, McCarty of the Buddy Miles Express, and noted jazz bassist Dave Holland, and the second with Miles, Holland, and jazz guitarist John McLaughlin.

Beyond the material committed to tape on this evening, Hendrix enjoyed a lengthy night of musical interaction that stretched well into the following morning, mixing and matching Miles and Mitchell with Dave Holland. "I'd received a phone call in the afternoon," remembers Holland, "asking if I would like to come down and play. I'm not quite sure why I was called, but I was real happy to do it. It was a lot of fun and very informal. Nothing was really planned—Buddy Miles was on drums and Jimi just organized a few jam lines for us to play on. We started and stopped and then started again. It was real loose, and Jimi seemed as if he was putting it together as he went. He put together a couple of riffs and we would play on that for awhile, then Buddy Miles did a few things on the organ and we would play on that."

The first recording made on this evening was listed as "Jimi-Mitch-Dave" on the tape box, though McCarty took part as well. In lieu of slated individual takes, Hendrix began the session by demonstrating the opening chord sequence and tempo of "Villanova Junction Blues" to Holland, McCarty, and Mitchell. A series of false starts ensued as Hendrix continued to adjust the shading of his guitar tone—most notably by the dramatic use of an Octavia tone-pedal device—while instructing the trio as to the arrangement he envisioned. After an initial take broke down, Hendrix moved quickly to maintain the inspiration and directed the group into the nearly seventeen-minute take that followed.

At the outset of this longer take, Hendrix endeavored to incorporate the "Villanova Junction Blues" theme once again. Unfortunately, neither McCarty nor Holland seemed familiar with the melody, so the guitarist soon shifted his direction.

A heavily edited version of the "Jimi-Mitch-Dave" take, ultimately known as "Jimi/Jimmy Jam" was included as part of the 1980 album *Nine to the Universe*. The full, unedited recording was later issued as part of the Dagger Records "bootleg" *Hear My Music*.

McCarty had played well throughout the recording but was unhappy when his impromptu, exploratory effort was released as part of *Nine To The Universe*. "None of that stuff was ever intended to be released," he complains. "To me it was embarrassing. I'm sure that Jimi would have said, 'You're out of your fucking mind!' and never let it happen. It was all about people trying to make a buck off of Jimi Hendrix."

The second recording made on this evening was the famous Hendrix-McLaughlin jam session, with the two guitarists joined by Miles and Holland. While not without its flaws, this recording remains one of the most exciting unreleased performances in the Hendrix library.

John McLaughlin got an invitation to play that night from Alan Douglas, the producer who had signed McLaughlin to his Douglas Records label. "[He] came down to the Village Vanguard to see me," John McLaughlin said in a 1982 interview. "He said that he was going to be recording tonight and why don't I come down. Jimi was there, but I didn't see it in the terms people see it. I wasn't even interested in that side of things. I walked into the studio and the thing that knocked me out was Buddy Miles. I didn't know who this guy was, but he was playing some fatback boogaloo on the drums, which just made me want to play. Basically, it was Jimi's session and Jimi's music. There was a lot of partying going on and we had a loosely organized jam. We played from two to eight in the morning. I was playing acoustic guitar with a pick-up and Jimi was playing electric."

While a faulty connection intermittently caused McLaughlin's signal to distort or drop out entirely, he still managed to fire off a series of his trademark runs and bends on top of Hendrix's roaring rhythm support. Hendrix was more than equal to the task, with his ferocious blues playing challenging McLaughlin at every turn. Though the jamming among the assembled players reportedly lasted for hours, all that remains of this special summit is one thirty-minute reel of recording tape.

Despite the many scintillating moments contained within this recording, McLaughlin remains unconvinced. "The music wasn't all that great, I'm sorry to say. I love Jimi, but the music wasn't that great. We played some good things. Just because it was my name and Jimi Hendrix's name is no excuse. Only since Mahavishnu came out and I began to receive some recognition was this event transformed into something other."

TUESDAY, APRIL 1, 1969

OLMSTEAD RECORDING STUDIOS, NEW YORK, NEW YORK. ENGINEER: EDDIE KRAMER.

Though all of their efforts to complete a fourth studio album had previously fallen apart, the Experience staged another rally to try to rescue the group from its creative doldrums. In an effort to improve the creative atmosphere and limit the number of distractions from friends and hangers-on that Hendrix might have faced at the Record Plant, the Experience moved to Olmstead Recording Studios, a small facility new to the group and located at the top of a midtown Manhattan building.

Despite their new surroundings, the band's old problems immediately rose to the surface. Hendrix was now handling the dual responsibility of artist and producer. Lacking the firm hand of Chandler, the group desperately needed a strong voice to moderate their disputes and channel Hendrix's energies into productive recording. "I went over to Olmstead only to help Jimi out," remembers Kramer. "I wasn't being paid, but I hadn't worked with Jimi for some time and wanted to hear what he was doing. Olmstead was located at the top of a building on 54th Street in Manhattan. It was like a penthouse, all painted in white. Though it was a small studio, a lot of jazz sessions had been done there. I remember that the sessions didn't go very well, as things were pretty crazy. There was a *lot* of partying going on."

The group's initial session at Olmstead was largely dedicated to the recording of "Midnight Lightning" (later known as "Midnight") and "Peoples, Peoples," an early, up-tempo rendition of "Bleeding Heart." While the general mood was encouragingly upbeat, these instrumental efforts revealed the group's inability to focus their effort on the task at hand.

"Midnight," like "Tax Free," was a structured song as opposed to an impromptu jam session. The Experience devoted considerable time to establishing the song's intricate rhythm pattern. With that properly established, Hendrix carefully labored over a series of inspired lead guitar lines. Despite its promise, "Midnight" would not be completed during Hendrix's lifetime. Take 8 was later edited and posthumously issued, initially as part of 1972's *War Heroes*, and later as part of 1997's *South Saturn Delta*.

The Experience initially modeled its version of "Bleeding Heart" on the original recording by one of Hendrix's favorite artists, the legendary slide guitarist Elmore James. The band had performed an exceptional stage interpretation of the blues classic in its original twelve-bar arrangement at its February 24 Albert Hall concert. But, beginning with these April 1969 Olmstead Studios sessions, Hendrix began to tinker with the song's structure, modifying its elements until he had reinvented it as his own, maintaining the song's blues heritage but altering the arrangement to accommodate a faster tempo.

WEDNESDAY, APRIL 2, 1969

OLMSTEAD RECORDING STUDIOS, NEW YORK, NEW YORK. ENGINEER: EDDIE KRAMER.

Hendrix dedicated this evening to the blues, focusing on "The Train" better known as "Hear My Train A Comin'," and "Midnight Lightning" ("Midnight"). Though the group attempted structured takes for both numbers, the recordings made here were largely jams.

THURSDAY, APRIL 3, 1969

OLMSTEAD RECORDING STUDIOS, NEW YORK, NEW YORK. ENGINEER: EDDIE KRAMER.

This proved to be another difficult session, with the Experience again struggling to complete a suitable basic track for "Midnight Lightning." The group's best effort was take 5, which rambled for nearly eight minutes and was listed on the tape box as "Crying Blue Rain." Some of the passages from the jam sessions in between takes recalled "Peace In Mississippi." Hendrix would vary the "Midnight" theme for his next take, creating the song that would become "Trash Man." A malfunctioning microphone gave Mitchell's snare drums a distorted, thrashing character and provided a perfect complement to Redding's eight-string bass and Hendrix's strident guitar tone.

"Trash Man" was among scores of promising Hendrix studio recordings left unfinished by the guitarist at the time of his death in 1970. Unfortunately, this recording was later edited with overdubs by session musicians so that it could be included as part of the controversial 1975 album *Midnight Lightning*. That album and its counterpart, *Crash Landing*, have long been deleted from Hendrix's catalog. The original Olmstead "Trash Man" recording has since been issued as part of the Dagger Records official "bootleg" *Hear My Music*.

FRIDAY, APRIL 4, 1969

OLMSTEAD RECORDING STUDIOS, NEW YORK, NEW YORK. ENGINEER: EDDIE KRAMER.

This session produced two reels filled mostly with jams based largely on the "Trash Man" theme. A third reel was dedicated to early takes of what would become "Crash Landing." At this stage, Hendrix was focused on developing the song's central guitar line.

"CROSSTOWN TRAFFIC" / "GYPSY EYES." TRACK RECORDS 604 029. U.K. SINGLE RELEASE.

With no other product scheduled for delivery, Track Records delved into *Electric Ladyland* to try to generate some sales. This release simply wilted, as the Experience, busy recording in New York, were unable to generate any momentum behind the release. Lacking this effort, the disc managed to reach the number 37 position during its brief, three-week chart stay.

SATURDAY, APRIL 5, 1969

RECORD PLANT, NEW YORK, NEW YORK. 4:00 A.M. TO 7:25 A.M. ENGINEER: BOB HUGHES.

The Experience gave up recording at Olmstead and returned to the Record Plant, hoping to make progress. Here, they concentrated on two takes of a new song titled "Ships Passing Through The Night," producing rough mixes but no finished master.

SUNDAY, APRIL 6, 1969

RECORD PLANT, NEW YORK, NEW YORK. 9:30 P.M. TO 8:30 A.M. ENGINEERS: SANDY (SURNAME UNKNOWN), LEE BROWN.

The tape box for this session was appropriately marked "Tape of False Takes." The session began with a ragged jam session featuring Hendrix on a Coral electric sitar and joined by an unknown bassist and drummer. Hendrix may have been given the instrument by noted session guitarist Vinnie Bell, who had popularized use of that instrument. Bell was in a separate studio at the Record Plant doing session work.

Hendrix completed further work on "Ships Passing Through The Night," the early working title for what would later evolve as "Night Bird Flying." He also made an early stab at "Ezy Ryder," but all Hendrix possessed at this stage was a firm handle on the song's distinctive guitar riff. No formal takes were attempted.

MONDAY, APRIL 7, 1969

RECORD PLANT, NEW YORK, NEW YORK. ENGINEER: SANDY (SURNAME UNKNOWN).

Another attempt was made to complete a finished master of "Hear My Train A Comin'." A number of terrific takes held promise, but none seemed to satisfy Hendrix's design for the song.

Inexplicably, Hendrix also attempted a remake of "Stone Free." Perhaps because Reprise, his U.S. record company, had held the song back from their original version of *Are You Experienced*, Hendrix elected to record a new rendition of this first-ever Experience composition, rather than concentrate on new material—a decision that spoke volumes about the creative deterioration the Experience had suffered in recent months.

The version recorded on this evening showcased a more sophisticated arrangement than that of the November 1966 recording that had originally served as the B-side for "Hey Joe." The Experience managed to complete a strong basic track. Hendrix then called for a rough mix, which he took away for further study.

Before concluding the session, Hendrix put forward "Lullaby For The Summer," another song effort built upon the theme that would later evolve as "Ezy Ryder." No takes were slated here, as Hendrix seemed to be searching for the patterns he desired to cohesively knit the song together.

WEDNESDAY, APRIL 9, 1969

RECORD PLANT, NEW YORK, NEW YORK. "STONE FREE":

1:00 A.M. TO 1:30 A.M. "GET MY ARSE BACK TOGETHER": 1:30 A.M. TO 4:00 A.M. PLAYBACKS: 4:00 A.M. TO 4:30 A.M. OVERDUBS: 4:30 A.M. TO 6:00 A.M. ENGINEERS: SANDY (SURNAME UNKNOWN), LEE BROWN.

This session began with Hendrix adding a guitar overdub to the April 7 "Stone Free" master. The group recorded new takes of "Hear My Train A Comin'," marked on the tape box as "Get My Arse Back Together," with Hendrix also adding a lead guitar overdub. The engineers did not attempt to mix either track, as Hendrix no doubt decided that more work was still required.

FRIDAY, APRIL 11, 1969

DORTON ARENA, RALEIGH, NORTH CAROLINA WITH FAT MATTRESS. **PARTIAL SET LIST:** "STONE FREE" / "HEAR MY TRAIN A COMIN'" / "RED HOUSE" / "PURPLE HAZE"

SATURDAY, APRIL 12, 1969

SPECTRUM, PHILADELPHIA, PENNSYLVANIA. WITH FAT MATTRESS. **SET LIST:** "FIRE" / "RED HOUSE" / "FOXEY LADY" / "I DON'T LIVE TODAY" / "HEAR MY TRAIN A COMIN'" / "STONE FREE" / "STAR SPANGLED BANNER" / "PURPLE HAZE" / "VOODOO CHILD (SLIGHT RETURN)"

The Experience's 1969 U.S. tour began in Raleigh, North Carolina, and would be their largest to date. Hendrix's surging popularity required his two promoters, Concerts East and Concerts West, to rent sports arenas as opposed to accepting bookings at smaller-capacity theaters. Hendrix played at the Spectrum, the home of Philadelphia's major league hockey and basketball franchises, in front of 14,500 people—a typical arena-size crowd. "The Experience were one of the few arena acts at that time," explains Experience tour manager Gerry Stickells. "Apart from the festivals, where they obviously played a major part, they could tour arenas, and there weren't that many acts selling out arenas at that time."

MONDAY, APRIL 14, 1969

RECORD PLANT, NEW YORK, NEW YORK. 3:00 A.M. TO 7:00 A.M. ENGINEER: GARY KELLGREN. SECOND ENGINEER: LEE BROWN.

Hendrix returned to "Stone Free" and successfully completed lead guitar and vocal overdubs for the April 7 master. "Insert #1," which required nine takes and "Insert #2," which required seven, were superimposed on to take 11 of that earlier session.

Though Hendrix had now completed a new version of "Stone Free," he did not submit it to Reprise for release. The label instead issued the original 1966 recording as part of the popular July 1969 U.S. album *Smash Hits*. Relegated to the Hendrix tape library, "Stone Free" became yet another pearl in the growing collection of material the guitarist was developing for his fourth album.

After Hendrix's death, Alan Douglas pulled a take of "Stone Free" from this session on August 7, 1974, saddled it with new overdubs, and issued it as "Stone Free Again" on the controversial—and long out of print—*Crash Landing*. The original recording has since been restored and added to the *Jimi Hendrix Experience* box set.

Following his work on "Stone Free," Hendrix recorded a number of takes of "Ships Passing Through The Night." These takes differ from the recordings made on April 6. Here, Hendrix's approach is darker and steeped in the Delta blues tradition of John Lee Hooker. He was backed by an unknown group of musicians, including a trumpet player, a bassist, and a drummer. These takes resembled little more than engaging demos, as Hendrix had only begun to develop the song's arrangement. He did not manage to create a finished master.

Hendrix followed this effort with "Solo Guitar," a demo of a new idea he wanted committed to tape. A jam session with an unknown bassist and drummer was followed by a similarly styled effort with Mitchell and Redding. After two short jams, Hendrix, Mitchell, and Redding took a group stab at "Sunshine Of Your Love."

Following a break, Hendrix returned to the studio with Buddy Miles, organist Larry Young, and several guests. The three musicians moved into a jam session that featured Young leading an up-tempo jazz-styled workout with Hendrix and Miles. Next, Hendrix, an unnamed bassist (not Dave Holland, who was also present), and Miles jammed. Hendrix, Miles, Young, and Holland then kicked off a splendid, extended musical exploration. This recording provides yet another compelling example of Hendrix's ability to meet any musical challenge head-on. His fellow musicians responded in kind, insistently pushing Hendrix and Young throughout this memorable recording.

An edited version of this jam session later enjoyed notoriety when it was issued as part of the 1980 *Nine To The Universe* album.

THURSDAY, APRIL 17, 1969

RECORD PLANT, NEW YORK, NEW YORK. ENGINEERS: SANDY (SURNAME UNKNOWN), LEE BROWN.

Prior to this session, Hendrix took a meeting at Jeffery's 37th Street offices. The primary topic was Electric Lady Studios, still nameless at the time. Architect John Storyk was set to deliver his plans in the coming days, and construction would be set in motion to transform the space into a first-class recording facility. Hendrix and Jeffery had agreed to fund the construction costs equally, pegged at this stage at $500,000. Hendrix also began to put forward ideas as to the name of the new project. Early contenders included "Sky Stepping Research," "Rhythm Cake, Inc.," and "Electric Temple," but no final determination was made.

Later that evening, Hendrix had time reserved at the Record Plant, where he returned to "Lullaby For The Summer" and made multiple attempts at developing the song. In this particular exercise, he can be heard playing the distinctive riff of "Ezy Ryder." None of the takes were slated, and Hendrix offered no vocals, concentrating instead on transforming that single riff into a complete song.

A third reel recorded on this night was labeled "Jam With Harmonica. Chorus left/Chorus right." Leading a group of friends whose ranks included Hendrix's girlfriend, Devon Wilson, on backing vocals, Paul Caruso on harmonica, and an unnamed percussionist, Hendrix recorded a particularly raw and raucous rendition of "Keep On Groovin'," which was clearly the highlight of this wild, undisciplined session. Incredibly, Hendrix went to the trouble of adding overdubs to this master. A rough mix was prepared, but no finished master was achieved.

FRIDAY, APRIL 18, 1969

ELLIS AUDITORIUM, MEMPHIS, TENNESSEE. TWO SHOWS.

WITH FAT MATTRESS. **SET LIST, SECOND SHOW:** "FIRE" / "I DON'T LIVE TODAY" / "HEAR MY TRAIN A COMIN'" / "SUNSHINE OF YOUR LOVE" / "STONE FREE" / " FOXEY LADY" / "STAR SPANGLED BANNER" / "PURPLE HAZE" / "VOODOO CHILD (SLIGHT RETURN)"

Burdened with an exhaustive schedule of recording sessions and personal appearances, Hendrix and Redding saw their relationship deteriorate further. "Noel was getting irritated because he wanted to play guitar," remembers Stickells. "Since there was only a handful of us out the road, he could only talk to so many people. It isn't like today where you have thirty guys around you that you vent to." Frustrated, Hendrix reached out to Billy Cox in Nashville, hoping his old friend might assist him through a difficult time in his life and career. "I went to the concert in Memphis and it was great to see him," said Cox. "He looked good, but he had changed since I had last seen him. He wasn't the tall, chubby guy I knew. It looked as if he had dropped about twenty-five pounds. We sat down in his dressing room and talked and talked. He asked for my help and that was all he had to say. I told him I would do whatever I could to help him. I went back to Nashville, closed my publishing company, and dropped everything else and left for New York."

SATURDAY, APRIL 19, 1969

SAM HOUSTON COLISEUM, HOUSTON, TEXAS. WITH FAT MATTRESS AND CHICAGO TRANSIT AUTHORITY. **PARTIAL SET LIST:** "FIRE" / "FOXEY LADY" / "PURPLE HAZE" / "SUNSHINE OF YOUR LOVE" / "VOODOO CHILD (SLIGHT RETURN)"

SUNDAY, APRIL 20, 1969

MEMORIAL AUDITORIUM, DALLAS, TEXAS. WITH FAT MATTRESS AND CAT MOTHER & THE ALL NIGHT NEWSBOYS. **SET LIST:** "STONE FREE" / "HEAR MY TRAIN A COMIN'" / "FOXEY LADY" / "I DON'T LIVE TODAY" / "FIRE" / "RED HOUSE" / "STAR SPANGLED BANNER" / "PURPLE HAZE" / "VOODOO CHILD (SLIGHT RETURN)"

The Experience always seemed to rise to the occasion for their shows in Texas, and this superb Dallas performance proved no exception. Hendrix's expanded

arrangement for "Stone Free" made this song one of the highlights of the 1969 U.S. tour and this performance in particular.

MONDAY, APRIL 21, 1969

RECORD PLANT, NEW YORK, NEW YORK. ENGINEER: GARY KELLGREN.

When Cox arrived in New York to meet Hendrix, he realized that Hendrix's problems were not entirely musical. "Jimi had told me all of these fabulous stories about how a limousine would pick me up at the airport, and I believed all this of course," Cox explains. "Nobody from the office, however, was there to pick me up. That's when I started to realize that Jimi wanted me here, but the office didn't seem so sure. At that point, I knew it was going to be a battle from there on."

Following Cox's arrival, Hendrix revealed some troubling news to his friend. "When I arrived in New York, Jimi sat me down and admitted that his creativity had drawn dry," Cox recalls. "He just felt that he couldn't think of anything new."

By reaching out to Cox, Hendrix may have been trying to find his musical compass, someone who might allow him—privately—to examine just where and how he had veered off the track. "With me, Jimi knew that I had a direct link to him musically," says Cox. "He knew that I was familiar with his style, sound, and creativity. I hadn't played with him in a long while, but when I first heard 'Foxey Lady,' I knew that to be an old song of his we used to call 'Stomp Driver' in Nashville. Jimi's creativity had been stifled, and I guess he thought of me because even in the early days we had always been able to make up stuff. We enjoyed doing that, but we could never use any of it because our living depended upon playing cover tunes or behind an artist who had already recorded his own songs. Jimi must have felt that I could help him pull all of the pieces of ideas that he had together into something as good as those three albums he had released."

Three days after the backstage meeting in Memphis, Cox joined Hendrix at the Record Plant recording studio in New York. "The first session I did was at the Record Plant," says Cox. "Jimi was basically trying to see how well we played together. After we started, I looked up and saw the smile on his face and I was smiling, too. We had just fell right into it, and we jammed for two or three hours. His playing was just as I remembered, but now there was much more freedom. Finally, we went into the patterns for "Hello My Friend" (which would later be developed as "Straight Ahead") and "Earth Blues." Even today, all these years later, I still cannot hear 'Straight Ahead' without it taking me back to that moment."

After their jam session, Hendrix escorted the bassist to the nearby Scene Club, one of the guitarist's favorite local haunts. While there, Hendrix encountered Al Marks, the manager for the Maryland-based rock group the Cherry People. "We heard that there was going to be a jam for guitar players at Steve Paul's Scene Club that night," remembered Marks. "All of a sudden Jimi Hendrix walked in with two people. He sat down in the corner and no one was bothering him. Everybody at my table was going, 'Wow! That's Jimi Hendrix!'" Marks approached Hendrix to see if he remembered their meeting backstage at the Monterey Pop Festival. "He did not, but told me it was cool to sit and talk with him," says Marks. "He asked what I was doing in New York, and I told him that our band was trying to get out of its contract with the record company. He laughed and said, 'Yeah, record companies . . .' Then he said, 'So you got a band here? Do you have a drummer?' I said, 'Yes. He is sitting right over there.' He then asked if we were doing anything at three or four o'clock that morning. I said no and asked him why. He was going to cut some things in the studio and wondered whether our drummer would like to sit in. I immediately said he would. Jimi then said, 'Well, you didn't ask him.' I didn't have to ask him. He's *gonna* do it. He wanted to know if the guy was any good and I told him that Rocky [Isaac] was a great drummer. He introduced me to Billy Cox, who was sitting with him. Billy mentioned that he was a bass player. I asked about Noel Redding, but Jimi told me that Noel would not be sitting in. He described Billy as his buddy and said that the session would be with him. We agreed to meet later at the Record Plant. I walked to my table and told the band, 'You are not going to believe this, but Jimi Hendrix just asked Rocky to sit in.' Everybody at the table told me I was full of shit. I asked the guys to trust me and waved over to Jimi's table. Jimi waved back and gave us the peace sign. [Cherry People guitarist] Chris Grimes,

Rocky Isaac, and I made plans to go while the other guys went back to this hostel we were staying at.

"We were alone in the studio for about forty-five minutes before Gary Kellgren showed up with an assistant engineer and a tall, beautiful black woman [Devon Wilson] whom we were told was Jimi's girlfriend. Gary reassured us that while Jimi was always late, he had phoned about the session and was on his way over. Twenty minutes later, Jimi and Billy Cox walked in with a friend who was a photographer [Willis Hogans Jr.]. Jimi was really cool and wanted to know if we were OK. Rocky saw him and said, 'You're Jimi Hendrix.' Jimi laughed and said, 'Man, I know who I am. Don't you think I know who I am?' We all just about fell on the floor laughing. Rocky admitted to him that he was really nervous. Jimi laughed and said, 'Just relax. It will all be cool.'

"Jimi was playing through an old acoustic amplifier and not a Marshall. It had one big cabinet with a small head. Billy was playing through an Ampeg rig, and a set of drums had been set up for Rocky. Jimi then started to move his amp and I told him that I would do that for him. He said that if I really wanted to move something for him, his car was out front and if he didn't move it across the street it was going to be towed. I asked for the keys and told him I would do it. He owned a silver Corvette, and by the time I was outside I thought, 'Shit, I don't know how to drive a stick shift. I am going to ruin Jimi's Corvette.' I opened the door and it was automatic. I thought, 'My God everything is working for me tonight!' I got in the car and there were all of these tapes on the passenger seat. His car had a cassette player built into the dashboard, and I had never seen anything like that before. Sitting on the seat were these tapes that were marked, 'Me, Steve Winwood' and 'Me, Buddy Miles.' I parked the car, came back in, and he told me that he wanted a percussion section. Jimi asked me to play maracas—which I had never played before in my life—and Chris Grimes to play tambourine.

"We recorded 'Room Full Of Mirrors' and it took forever because Rocky couldn't keep the beat on drums. Midway through the session, Jimi turned to him and said something to the effect of, 'Man, do you know how to play drums? What's going on?' I had been banging one of the maracas against my leg for three and a half hours, and my leg was black and blue. I told Rocky quietly that he'd better get things right because I couldn't walk! I had a knot on my leg that seemed four inches big. I was afraid that we were going to screw up the chance of a lifetime."

Hendrix directed Cox, Isaac, Grimes, and Marks through thirty-one takes of the song. The first take featured a blistering solo from Hendrix, but this effort came apart when technical problems with his head-phones mix broke his concentration. "The guitar disap-peared all of sudden," remarked Hendrix to Kellgren. "We were getting into something nice." Hendrix then asked Kellgren if they could come and listen to a play-back of the take. Kellgren agreed, and the group re-treated to the control room to listen to their work.

When recording resumed, Isaac struggled to estab-lish the drum pattern Hendrix was seeking. The group struggled to grasp Hendrix's vision, and none of the twenty-one takes that filled this first reel was complete. Hendrix's patience began to grow thin as he tried to in-struct Isaac between takes as to what he was seeking.

Kellgren loaded a second reel of tape, and the group attempted ten more takes. It wasn't until the thirty-first and final take of the evening that they were able to complete a basic track. "By eight that morning, Jimi said that we were going to give it one last try and if we didn't get it we would have to come back the next morning," Marks explains. "Jimi then just started wailing on the guitar and singing live on top of it. Rocky finally delivered what he believed was a good take and Gary Kellgren yelled 'Yeah' over the talkback microphone when we had finished. Jimi let us know that we were done for the night. Before we left, he told us that he had a couple more tracks that he wanted to cut on Thursday at the same time. We thought he meant after midnight Wednesday evening. As he was walking out, he gave each of us $100 cash and said to Rocky, 'Man, I would practice a bit if I was you.' Billy laughed and shook his head, and they walked out together. Gary Kellgren then came over and asked us our names and if we were in the Musicians' Union. We were, but Gary told us not to declare the work because Jimi had paid us more than union scale for the session. Union scale at that time for a session was $35. We were strutting. Jimi Hendrix had paid us $100 to play with *him*.

"We told the guys back at the hostel about the ses-sion and they didn't believe us until we showed them the $100 bill Jimi had given each of us. We then drove back to Washington and made a plan to bring Mike Burke and Richard Harrington, a critic for the *Washing-ton Post* who also wrote for a paper called the *Unicorn Times,* to prove that we actually were going to record again with Jimi Hendrix."

Never issued during Hendrix's lifetime, take 31 of "Room Full Of Mirrors" was issued posthumously as part of the *Jimi Hendrix Experience* box set.

After this eventful first session, Cox and Hendrix continued playing together, in and out of the studio. They enjoyed their private time together, getting re-acquainted, defining Hendrix's future direction, and simply having some fun. "He and I would get a little amp, wherever he was or I was, and we would prac-tice," Cox recalls. "We enjoyed this. We didn't bowl or play golf. Music was our life. We loved every note we made.

"We played better with each other," says Cox, "not necessarily note for note, but pattern for pattern. We remembered patterns, not notes. A lot of times we would come up with a pattern that was four bars long, eight bars, or sixteen bars—all even. Other times, Jimi would come up with patterns that were seven bars, nine bars, or thirteen bars, which was weird. On top of that,

we did not tune to standard tuning. In order for him to sing, we tuned down a half step, which made playing and singing easier."

Hendrix warned Cox not to spend time down at Michael Jeffery's East 37th Street office. "Jimi told me not to hang down there," remembers Cox. "Honestly, I didn't want to get into any of the politics. I had enough pressure on my mind just trying to play and remember all of this new music. I wasn't doing any gigs. We would do some jamming at the Scene and a few other clubs, but that was it. I owned a Panasonic cassette player and would take tapes home from the studio. I would listen and practice to those tapes all day so that I would be ready for the recording sessions."

As Hendrix and Redding saw increasingly less of each other, Cox and Redding avoided the potential embarrassment of bumping into each other at the studio. "The Experience were just finishing up their last committed [concert] dates," recalls Cox. "That's all they were doing." Still, the two could not avoid each other entirely. "I did meet Noel once, in the lobby of the Penn-Garden hotel, and it was very cordial."

Working either in Hendrix's apartment or Cox's hotel room at the Penn-Garden, Hendrix began mining Cox's extensive R&B and blues background in an effort to create new music. Even simple bass lines from Cox could spark new ideas for Hendrix. "Jimi needed the bass to work off of. He would take something I played and improve on it. We were always trying to top each other and by the time I gave up—because he was just too good—he had created a song. It was nothing more than good-natured competition. He would play through his little practice amp, and I had created a way with my General Electric tape recorder whereby I could plug my bass guitar in and get a helluva bass tone with just one or two watts. Jimi would oftentimes play on his acoustic because it gave him a bit more presence than the electric. We made tape after tape of these informal sessions and would listen to them for ideas. Jimi would pull these patterns; we would play and create songs from them."

TUESDAY, APRIL 22, 1969

RECORD PLANT, NEW YORK, NEW YORK. ENGINEER: GARY KELLGREN.

Shifting gears once more, Hendrix teamed up with Cox and Miles to recorded four reels of "Mannish Boy," an up-tempo blues original inspired by Muddy Waters and worthy of considerable promise. This marked the first session by the trio that would become known as the Band Of Gypsys and whose work with Hendrix would have a significant impact on his great legacy.

Much of the early takes were devoted to developing the song's infectious groove. Hendrix offered direction throughout, suggesting changes to both Miles and Cox whenever he felt them necessary. Despite the multiple number of individual takes recorded, Hendrix was again unable to complete a basic track to his satisfaction. As a result, "Mannish Boy" joined his growing pile of unrealized multitrack masters stored in the Record Plant's tape vault.

"Mannish Boy" was considered for both *War Heroes* and *Loose Ends* but it remained unreleased. For 1994's *Jimi Hendrix: Blues*, engineer Mark Linett revived the song by digitally editing different takes to create a single master.

THURSDAY, APRIL 24, 1969

RECORD PLANT, NEW YORK, NEW YORK. 8:00 P.M. TO 9:00 A.M. ENGINEER GARY KELLGREN. SECOND ENGINEER: BOB HUGHES.

Hendrix again teamed up with Cox, Isaac, Grimes, and Al Marks on percussion. So enthused were the three members of the Cherry People to work again with Hendrix that they mistakenly arrived a day early for the session, with their friend Mike Burke and *Washington Post* critic Richard Harrington in tow. When the receptionist at the Record Plant told them Hendrix had not scheduled a session, Harrington turned around and went home. The others could not be deterred. "We had no place to stay," says Marks, "so we asked if we could hang out at the studio. They let us in and we crashed on the floor of the studio. In the morning, Vinnie Bell and Tony Mottola from the *Tonight Show* band woke us up. They were arriving to do session work for a movie soundtrack. These guys were in suits and we were a bunch of scraggly hippies in buckskin jackets."

Hendrix eventually called the studio, discovered that the Cherry People were already there, and asked them to come back at nine p.m. "Somehow we then lost Rocky," says Marks. "We couldn't locate him, so we ended up spending the day walking around the city. He showed up back at the studio around seven p.m. looking refreshed. He asked us where we had been because Jimi had reserved a hotel room for us. We were stunned. Rocky had left a note for us but the guy at the Record Plant had forgotten to tell us. We all ran over to the hotel room Jimi had reserved for us and took quick showers. When we returned to the studio, Jimi and Rocky were going over the new songs he wanted to play. The first number we did was 'Bleeding Heart.' We did about fifteen or sixteen takes and it seemed to work out fairly well. It was the same lineup as the previous session."

The group committed a number of promising "Bleeding Heart" takes to tape, including one strong take, confidently sung by Hendrix and punctuated by a blistering lead guitar solo. "Let's listen to that!" laughed Hendrix after the take concluded.

When recording resumed, Hendrix premiered a new song: "Hey Country Boy." "Jimi wanted to try another song, so Chris and I took the opportunity to switch instruments," remembers Marks. "My leg was so damn sore that I couldn't keep doing it anymore, so I took over tambourine and Chris picked up the maracas." Before Hendrix began, he reminded Kellgren to save the previous "Bleeding Heart" take, and the engineer affirmed this quickly over the talkback microphone.

"Hey Country Boy" was a medium-tempo effort whose most striking trait was Hendrix's use of his wah-wah tone-control pedal throughout the song. The lyrics bore close similarity to what would later develop as "Hey Baby (Land Of The New Rising Sun)." After one incomplete take, Hendrix stopped and asked Cox to retune his E-string. "What's wrong with those strings?" he chided Cox playfully.

Prior to starting up again, Hendrix asked Cox to add some nice accents, but the take came apart quickly when Isaac struggled to maintain proper time on drums. "Come in on time," Hendrix instructed Isaac. When they started again, Isaac faltered once more, causing Hendrix to remark, "That's not on time. If you don't start on time then you wait for the second time to come in." Hendrix was trying to keep the atmosphere light, joking about the problem with Isaac, but when the next take began he leaned into the microphone and said "Drums!" making it clear as to the starting point for the drummer. More tuning problems for Cox sidelined the next attempt, but Hendrix was determined to stay on task. A strong effort followed and lasted for several minutes before the song came apart. As no ending had yet been devised, none of the musicians, including Hendrix, knew how to bring the song to an effective close.

As "Hey Country Boy" broke down, Hendrix began to play the figure that would evolve as "Message To Love." Cox picked it right up and tried to follow. Hendrix then stopped and sang the notes so Cox would understand the pattern. While Cox took hold immediately, Isaac again struggled, causing Hendrix to scrap the take. The guitarist turned to Isaac and sang the drum part to him, specifically instructing him to avoid the snare ("That sounds too bright," he said) and instead feature the tom-tom. Hendrix then kicked off "Hey Country Boy," and the group managed to complete an effective backing track. Near the close of the song, Hendrix worked in the "Message Of Love" figure, and the group managed to stay with him effectively. Enthused, Hendrix then veered back into "Hey Country Boy" and the group stayed with him, causing him to exclaim "Yeah!" From this point, Hendrix kept switching between the melody lines of "Hey Country Boy" and "Message To Love" every eight bars. When the song came to a close, he spoke to the band. "That's nothing but a change over from different patterns," he explained. When the next take broke down, Hendrix led the group to the control room to listen to a playback.

Once recording resumed, an unnamed organ player joined the group. Hendrix slowed the song's tempo and opted not to sing a live guide vocal. While the group made progress, they were still unable to complete a basic track to Hendrix's satisfaction. Sounding somewhat discouraged, Hendrix called for a playback.

Next came "Crash Landing Jam," an up-tempo song whose theme would largely evolve into "Freedom" over the course of the next year. The lyrics, even at this early stage, were openly inspired by Hendrix's relationship with his girlfriend Devon Wilson. A new song, however promising, offered no relief as Hendrix was still frustrated by problems with Isaac's time-keeping. After an incomplete first take, Hendrix instructed Isaac to "Listen to the patterns. Don't make it too nervous-sounding." In his dual role as artist and producer, Hendrix did his best to try to explain what he was looking for to each musician. He stopped one take to specifically instruct the organ player, singing and demonstrating where and what to play. His frustration grew when Isaac questioned him. "Listen to everything and *then* I'll show you," he admonished. "Listen to everything. Don't play this time. Just listen to what is going on."

In between takes for "Crash Landing," Hendrix launched directly into "Drone Blues," a spirited workout in D. Less a song than an inspired example of Hendrix's quicksilver imagination, "Drone Blues" nonetheless seemed to galvanize the group as they rallied and realized three solid, complete takes of "Crash Landing" before pausing to change tape reels.

After recording resumed, the group struggled through a string of false starts and incomplete takes

before they realized an acceptable basic track. "Jimi asked everybody to leave the studio," recalls Marks. "I asked him if we were being thrown out and he explained that he would not allow anybody to be in the studio while he recorded vocals on a track. In the control room, Gary Kellgren told us that it was just an idiosyncrasy that Jimi had. Gary went out and constructed a booth around him. Jimi had a sheet with lyrics and he stood behind there and sang beautifully. We were bug-eyed in the control room. Then, all of sudden, [Cherry People lead guitarist] Punky Meadows, who had been sleeping in the back of the studio, woke up and started walking across the room. Jimi saw him and literally flipped out. He threw down the papers in his hand and yelled, 'What the fuck are you doing in the studio when I am doing vocals?' In the control room, Gary Kellgren put his hands to his head. Apparently, that was the worst thing anyone could do on a Hendrix session. He yelled to us, 'Get him out of there!' We hustled Punky out to the bathroom and Jimi regained his composure and started doing vocals again. When he finished, he walked in to the control room and said, 'Man, no one walks through that studio when I am doing vocals. Didn't Gary tell you that?' We explained that Punky had been asleep and we didn't know where he was. Jimi laughed. 'Punky? What kind of name is Punky?' Punky came out from hiding and they met. All Jimi kept asking him was what kind of name was Punky? It was funny."

Hendrix completed lead guitar and vocal overdubs quickly, free of the burden of having to teach his musicians the song. With this work completed, he escorted the group back out to the studio and began with "Bleeding Heart." The group's first efforts again failed but Hendrix tried to rally them. "We got it now, though," he laughed. "We got it by the balls! Now listen, all I can say about this tune is that I want the breaks uneven sometimes to give it more excitement. I'll nod to you when I really want you to come down." A charged lead guitar solo by Hendrix highlighted the following take but the group was unable to complete the track. Hendrix stayed with the song for another thirty minutes before setting it aside.

"Night Messenger," the final track attempted during this lengthy session, showcased the continuing development of the demo "Ships Passing Through The Night" (later titled "Night Bird Flying"). Hendrix spent a short amount of time on this number before drawing to a close.

SATURDAY, APRIL 26, 1969

LOS ANGELES FORUM, LOS ANGELES, CALIFORNIA. ENGINEERS: WALLY HEIDER, ABE JACOB. **SET LIST:** "TAX FREE" / "FOXEY LADY" / "RED HOUSE" / "SPANISH CASTLE MAGIC" / "STAR SPANGLED BANNER" / "PURPLE HAZE" / "I DON'T LIVE TODAY" / "VOODOO CHILD (SLIGHT RETURN)" / "SUNSHINE OF YOUR LOVE"

Wally Heider recorded the Experience's raucous performance on this evening and set it aside for possible use on a proposed live album.

While none of these performances were issued during Hendrix's lifetime, the Forum concert was later mixed and included as an enticement to buy 1991's *Lifelines*, a bizarre and long since out of print multidisc set made up from a previously aired radio program.

SUNDAY, APRIL 27, 1969

OAKLAND COLISEUM, OAKLAND, CALIFORNIA. WITH CAT MOTHER & THE ALL NIGHT NEWSBOYS. **SET LIST:** "FIRE" / "HEY JOE" / "SPANISH CASTLE MAGIC" / "HEAR MY TRAIN A COMIN'" / "SUNSHINE OF YOUR LOVE" / "RED HOUSE" / "FOXEY LADY" / "STAR SPANGLED BANNER" / "PURPLE HAZE" / "VOODOO CHILD (SLIGHT RETURN)"

The band capped off this inspired evening with an eighteen-minute extended jam of "Voodoo Child (Slight Return)." Jefferson Airplane bassist Jack Casady joined the group onstage for this final number. In 1997, Experience Hendrix acquired an amateur open-reel tape recording of this concert. Captured by an audience member using a single microphone and a portable Sony tape deck, it remains the only known documentation of this performance.

This recording was used to create 1998's *The Jimi Hendrix Experience: Live In Oakland*. This double CD served as the debut release of Dagger Records, the official, mail-order-only "bootleg" label established by Experience Hendrix.

FRIDAY, MAY 2, 1969

COBO HALL, DETROIT, MICHIGAN. WITH FAT MATTRESS AND CAT MOTHER & THE ALL NIGHT NEWSBOYS. **PARTIAL SET LIST:** "FIRE" / "SPANISH CASTLE MAGIC" / "FOXEY LADY" / "I DON'T LIVE TODAY" / "SUNSHINE OF YOUR LOVE" / "VOODOO CHILD (SLIGHT RETURN)" / "RED HOUSE"

SATURDAY, MAY 3, 1969

MAPLE LEAF GARDENS, TORONTO, ONTARIO, CANADA. WITH CAT MOTHER & THE ALL NIGHT NEWSBOYS. **SET LIST:** "FIRE" / "HEAR MY TRAIN A COMIN'" / "SPANISH CASTLE MAGIC" / "RED HOUSE" / "FOXEY LADY" / "PURPLE HAZE" / "VOODOO CHILD (SLIGHT RETURN)"

The Experience flew from Detroit to Pearson International Airport in Toronto, Ontario and arrived at approximately nine-thirty a.m. As the group passed through Canadian customs, authorities searched one of Hendrix's travel bags and found what they believed to be an illicit substance. A laboratory examination later confirmed the substance as heroin. Hendrix was placed under arrest and transported to police headquarters in downtown Toronto. He was later released on a $10,000 cash bail and required to appear in court on May 5.

Despite the traumatic events earlier that day, Hendrix rallied at Maple Leaf Gardens and put forth a spirited performance. The concert included a superb version of "Spanish Castle Magic," complete with touches of both "Third Stone From The Sun" and "Little Miss Lover" interwoven within the song's extended instrumental break. Hendrix also performed a fascinating, early live version of "Room Full Of Mirrors."

SUNDAY, MAY 4, 1969

WAR MEMORIAL AUDITORIUM, SYRACUSE, NEW YORK. WITH CAT MOTHER & THE ALL NIGHT NEWSBOYS. **PARTIAL SET LIST:** "FIRE" / "I DON'T LIVE TODAY" / "STONE FREE" / "FOXEY LADY"

TUESDAY, MAY 6, 1969

RECORD PLANT, NEW YORK, NEW YORK. PLAYBACK:

6:30 P.M. TO 7:00 P.M. ROUGH MIX: 7:00 P.M. TO 12:30 A.M. RECORD PLANT, STUDIO B. MIXING: 1:00 A.M. TO 2:30 A.M. ENGINEERS: LEE BROWN AND TONY BONGIOVI.

After a trip to Toronto the day before to appear in court, Hendrix returned to New York and booked an evening session at the Record Plant dedicated to play-backs of previously recorded material and mixing. During a second session in Studio B, Hendrix prepared rough mixes of his October 1968 live performance at Winterland in San Francisco. What precipitated this unusual mixing session is not known, but after ninety minutes Hendrix left the studio at two thirty a.m. to go to the Scene Club.

WEDNESDAY, MAY 7, 1969

RECORD PLANT, NEW YORK, NEW YORK. ENGINEER: LEE BROWN.

After spending the early part of the evening at the nearby Scene Club, Hendrix invited Cox, Miles, and guitarists Stephen Stills and Johnny Winter to jam at the Record Plant.

The session began with a high-flying jam led by Stills, with Hendrix and Winter in close pursuit. As Stills's lead guitar soared above the music, Hendrix continued to build a furious foundation underneath. After "Jam #1" drew to a close, Hendrix initiated "Jam #2," a heavy-handed, three-guitar stab at "Earth Blues." As Hendrix had only provided the players with the song's main riff, the players struggled to maintain cohesion. Nonetheless, their enthusiasm continued to drive the jam, with Stills, Hendrix, and Winter all trading licks. Later, Hendrix yelled for them to bring the tempo down and make it more "bluesy." When they did so, Hendrix offered another rendition of "Ships Passing Through The Night," now including slide fills from Winter. When this effort came apart, Hendrix asked Brown whether he had been recording all of these various jams, and Brown replied in the affirmative. Hendrix then kicked the band off in the same tempo. A rendition of "Ships Passing Through The Night" broke down, but Hendrix changed gears and led the group through one of his favorite blues classics, Guitar Slim's "Things That I Used To Do." Unfortunately, technical difficulties—principally an excess of unwanted distortion on Hendrix's guitar and tape dropout on his

vocal track—somewhat marred the recording of this jam, titled "Jam Part II." Winter played well, with his slide fills an obvious highlight. No overdubs were attempted, as Hendrix correctly viewed the early morning's recorded efforts as little more than a welcome creative diversion.

THURSDAY, MAY 8, 1969

MEMORIAL COLISEUM, TUSCALOOSA, ALABAMA. WITH FAT MATTRESS AND CAT MOTHER & THE ALL NIGHT NEWSBOYS

After the all-night session wrapped up in the early hours of Thursday morning, Hendrix joined Mitchell, Redding, and his road crew to fly to Tuscaloosa, Alabama. The group checked into the Ramada Inn in Tuscaloosa prior to performing that evening at the Memorial Coliseum.

FRIDAY, MAY 9, 1969

CHARLOTTE COLISEUM, CHARLOTTE, NORTH CAROLINA. WITH CHICAGO TRANSIT AUTHORITY. **PARTIAL SET LIST:** "JOHNNY B. GOODE" / "FIRE" / "SPANISH CASTLE MAGIC" / "FOXEY LADY" / "RED HOUSE" / "PURPLE HAZE" / "VOODOO CHILD (SLIGHT RETURN)"

The next tour stop for the Experience was in Charlotte, North Carolina. Prior to the performance, Ronnie Parsons and Gary Rice, writers for the local underground publication *The Inquisition,* interviewed Hendrix at his hotel, the Red Carpet Inn at 615 East Morehead Street.

SATURDAY, MAY 10, 1969

CHARLESTON CIVIC CENTER, CHARLESTON, WEST VIRGINIA. WITH FAT MATTRESS AND CHICAGO TRANSIT AUTHORITY. **PARTIAL SET LIST:** "FIRE" / "COME ON (LET THE GOOD TIMES ROLL)" / "HEAR MY TRAIN A COMIN'" / "VOODOO CHILD (SLIGHT RETURN)" / "PURPLE HAZE" / "WILD THING"

The Experience traveled to Charleston, West Virginia, for their performance at the Civic Center. Ray Brack from the *Charleston Gazette* interviewed Hendrix in the dressing room afterwards for a feature that was published the following day.

SUNDAY, MAY 11, 1969

FAIRGROUNDS COLISEUM, INDIANAPOLIS, INDI-ANA. WITH CHICAGO TRANSIT AUTHORITY. **SET LIST:** "COME ON (LET THE GOOD TIMES ROLL)" / "HEY JOE" / "STONE FREE" / "HEAR MY TRAIN A COMIN'" / "FIRE" / "RED HOUSE" / "FOXEY LADY" / "VOODOO CHILD (SLIGHT RETURN)"

TUESDAY, MAY 13, 1969

RECORD PLANT, NEW YORK, NEW YORK. 4:30 A.M. TO 8:00 A.M. ENGINEER: BOB HUGHES.

This unusual session paired Hendrix with an unknown backing group consisting of a bass guitarist, a bongo player, and a second guitarist named Sean. The group struggled through a lengthy jam session based on Hendrix's "Keep On Groovin'." A second tape reel was filled with rather aimless jamming. Hendrix then attempted to record some solo demos, but this effort was marred by persistent amplifier distortion. The guitarist was unable to correct the problem, and the session came to an unceremonious close.

WEDNESDAY, MAY 14, 1969

RECORD PLANT, NEW YORK, NEW YORK. ENGINEER: BOB HUGHES.

Pianist Sharon Layne and an unnamed trumpet player joined Cox, Mitchell, and Hendrix in recording "Blues Jam," better known as "Jam 292." "Jimi wanted to try and take his music in a number of different directions," recalls Cox. "He asked if I knew of any organ players. I told him that I knew a pretty nice one in Nashville. He said, 'Get him up here.' I said, 'Hey, it's a girl.' He shot me a look, but told me to bring her up here anyway. She was playing at that time in a group called King James and The Scepters."

Under Hendrix's direction, the group's confidence grew over the course of their opening take, a free-wheeling jam. Energized by their shared grasp of his concept, Hendrix's enthusiasm transformed the mood of this session into clearly focused excitement. He signaled for a follow-up and made further refinements throughout take 2. A rousing third take came apart when Layne's playing went awry. Undeterred, Hendrix swiftly regrouped and launched into one last take.

The song's unusual designation derived from the markings on the original session tape box. Two highlights from this session have since been issued commercially. An edited portion of take 4 was issued as part of the posthumous 1973 compilation *Loose Ends*. Take 2 was mixed and included as part of the 1994 release *Jimi Hendrix: Blues*. *Hear My Music* presents a newly mixed, complete version of Hendrix's fourth and final effort.

THURSDAY, MAY 15, 1969

RECORD PLANT, NEW YORK, NEW YORK. 6:30 P.M. TO 9:30 A.M. ENGINEER BOB HUGHES.
Throughout May of 1969, Hendrix continued to pursue a series of intriguing creative alliances, experimenting with horns, electric sitar, keyboards, and additional percussion. Spurred by Cox's enthusiasm, another marathon jam session was recorded. "Jimi wanted to experiment with having three or four horns," remembers Cox. "The horn players from the Buddy Miles Express had said that they would help. I thought the move would have brought his music too far back to R&B—the style we had played long before the Experience. Jimi's success was beyond R&B. We both wanted to stay ahead of the rock movement and knew that horns could, eventually, be used in his music. He scratched his head, obviously thinking the plan over and decided to give it a shot."

"With The Power Of God," later known as "Power Of Soul," was recorded on this night, with Hendrix augmented by drums, horn, piano, and tambourine. Take 9 was marked as complete. Hendrix then overdubbed a second rhythm guitar part. "'Power Of Soul' came together when Jimi heard me playing a riff from 'Mary Ann,' an old song Ray Charles used to do," explains Cox. "I hadn't meant anything by playing it. I was just goofing around. But that was all he needed to get started."

Cox's inspiration would be indicative of the impact he would have on Hendrix's approach to composing. Because of their shared love for blues, rock, and R&B, a simple riff or rhythm pattern from Cox often ignited Hendrix's creativity. Inherently curious, Hendrix couldn't help but pick up on what he heard Cox play and add his own original twist. Cox explains: "With Jimi, the idea was always first. Then when he figured he had played the idea long enough, it went from there to a groove. Ninety-nine percent of the time he wouldn't have any lyrics. He would have to go home and write the words out. Jimi was a stickler for getting a reel-to-reel copy made, taking it home, and writing lyrics to that or making changes to what he had recorded."

A single, jazz-influenced take of the "Crash Landing/Freedom" hybrid was brimming with potential. "Ships Passing Through The Night" was also recorded, but like so many similar efforts from this period, Hendrix had not yet devised an appropriate ending, so the track fell apart. The final reel contained seven takes of "Jam w/piano." The seventh and final take was listed as complete. One false take of "Stone Free" was recorded before Hendrix chose to abandon the effort. One take of "Blues Shuffle" came apart fairly early, and Hendrix returned to "With The Power of God."

The May 14 and 15 sessions marked the beginning and end of Layne's brief tenure. "She did two nights in the studio, but it didn't work out too well," says Cox. "She was so taken with being in a recording studio with, as she put it, *the* Jimi Hendrix, that it made her uptight."

FRIDAY, MAY 16, 1969

CIVIC CENTER, BALTIMORE, MARYLAND. WITH CAT MOTHER & THE ALL NIGHT NEWSBOYS AND THE BUDDY MILES EXPRESS. **SET LIST:** "LOVER MAN" / "HEAR MY TRAIN A COMIN'" / "FIRE" / "RED HOUSE" / "I DON'T LIVE TODAY" / "FOXEY LADY" / "PURPLE HAZE" / "SPANISH CASTLE MAGIC" / "VOODOO CHILD (SLIGHT RETURN)"

SATURDAY, MAY 17, 1969

RECORD PLANT, NEW YORK, NEW YORK. 4:00 A.M. ENGINEER: EDDIE KRAMER.
After returning from a gig at the Baltimore Civic Center earlier that evening, Hendrix arranged for an early morning session at the Record Plant. The session paired Mitchell with Cox and seemed more a test of Cox's compatibility as a bassist than an effort to record new

material. The first reel sounded more like a rehearsal, with Hendrix guiding Cox through "Stone Free." Once Hendrix had established the groove, he retreated to the control room, where he and Kramer offered frequent instructions over the talkback microphone. Mitchell and Cox recorded a number of attempts before Hendrix deemed the exercise complete. Before the session concluded, it became apparent that Cox had confirmed his position, passing the audition easily as he and Mitchell meshed comfortably.

RHODE ISLAND ARENA, PROVIDENCE, RHODE ISLAND. WITH THE BUDDY MILES EXPRESS AND CAT MOTHER & THE ALL NIGHT NEWSBOYS. **SET LIST:** "LOVER MAN" / "SPANISH CASTLE MAGIC" / "RED HOUSE" / "HEAR MY TRAIN A COMIN'" / "SUNSHINE OF YOUR LOVE" / "FOXEY LADY" / "PURPLE HAZE" / "STAR SPANGLED BANNER" / "VOODOO CHILD (SLIGHT RETURN)"

Later on the same day, the Experience headed out to Providence for another performance.

SUNDAY, MAY 18, 1969

MADISON SQUARE GARDEN, NEW YORK, NEW YORK. WITH THE BUDDY MILES EXPRESS. **SET LIST:** "LOVE MAN" / "COME ON (LET THE GOOD TIMES ROLL)" / "RED HOUSE" / "FIRE" / "SPANISH CASTLE MAGIC" / "HEAR MY TRAIN A COMIN'" / "I DON'T LIVE TODAY" / "VOODOO CHILD (SLIGHT RETURN)" / "PURPLE HAZE"

The Experience sold out Madison Square Garden, a remarkable feat considering that just three years before Hendrix was struggling to earn seven dollars a night in Greenwich Village. As they had done at their Philadelphia concert in April, the group performed on a revolving stage. Hendrix delighted the packed house with inspired renditions of "Come On (Let The Good Times Roll" and "Fire" while his lengthened exploration of "Spanish Castle Magic" ranks among his finest ever performances of the song.

WEDNESDAY, MAY 21, 1969

RECORD PLANT, NEW YORK, NEW YORK. 3:30 A.M. TO 7:30 A.M. ENGINEER: DAVE RAGNO.

Hendrix engaged in another wild night of jamming

with few results to show for it at the end of the session. "The party atmosphere seemed to be a deterrent to what Jimi was trying to accomplish," says Ragno. "If Devon wasn't trying to drive him crazy, then someone else would come in to the control room chugging a bottle of tequila and portioning out cocaine to anybody who wanted it. The session was just a big party. Some of the things we laid down on tape were nice, but they weren't serious. They weren't the things he really wanted to do. I didn't care to be on the sessions, because I didn't approve of some of the attitudes that people around him had."

Joined by Cox and Miles and an unnamed conga player (who may have been Jerry Velez), Hendrix attempted loose renditions of "Earth Blues," incorrectly marked on the tape box as "Lullaby For The Summer," but none were cohesive. A particularly uninspired jam followed next, as Miles assumed lead guitar chores, supported by an occasional harmonica blast by an unnamed participant. Miles returned to his drum kit for the next jam Hendrix attempted, during which the group sounded as if they were simply having some spirited fun.

Following a tape change, the group again attempted, albeit unsuccessfully, to record the basic tracks for "Earth Blues." Their effort stalled due to tuning and

tempo problems. His interest in the track faltering, Hendrix only occasionally provided a lead vocal. The evening's highlight was "Bleeding Heart," labeled on the tape box as "Peoples, Peoples." Comfortable with the blues arrangement Hendrix desired, the group performed their most cohesive work of the evening. This take of "Bleeding Heart" was later edited and issued as part of 1994's *Jimi Hendrix: Blues.*

Before the session concluded, a ferocious rendition of "Hear My Train A Comin'" was also cut. In direct contrast to most of the evening's efforts, Hendrix's tone was superb and he sang and played with intense focus. He also attempted a disjointed "Villanova Junction Blues" and one final stab at "Earth Blues" before calling the session to a close.

THURSDAY, MAY 22, 1969

RECORD PLANT, NEW YORK, NEW YORK. 4:30 A.M. TO 7:30 A.M. ENGINEER: DAVE RAGNO. SECOND ENGINEER: LLYLLIANNE DAVIS.

Together again with Cox and Miles, Hendrix recorded "Message From Nine To The Universe," an engaging, early hybrid of what would later develop as two separate songs: "Message To Love" and "Earth Blues." Partway through this extended take, he coaxed his girlfriend Devon Wilson out on to the studio floor to contribute lead vocals. While hardly a polished vocalist, she accepted Hendrix's invitation and proceeded to trade portions of the song's lyrics with him. Soon after their impromptu call-and-response vocals had concluded, Hendrix brought the song to a close with a thunderous flourish.

A heavily edited version of this take was later issued as part of the 1980 *Nine to the Universe* compilation. For that album, all of Wilson's lively warblings were excised and left on the cutting-room floor.

FRIDAY, MAY 23, 1969

SEATTLE CENTER COLISEUM, SEATTLE, WASHINGTON. WITH FAT MATTRESS. **PARTIAL SET LIST:** "RED HOUSE" / "I DON'T LIVE TODAY" / "STAR SPANGLED BANNER" / "FOXEY LADY" / "PURPLE HAZE" / "VOODOO CHILD (SLIGHT RETURN)"

The Experience traveled to Hendrix's hometown of Seattle to perform. To the delight of his many family members in attendance, the guitarist thrilled the large

Seattle Center audience with memorable renditions of favorites such as "Red House" and "Purple Haze."

SATURDAY, MAY 24, 1969

SPORTS ARENA, SAN DIEGO, CALIFORNIA. ENGINEERS: WALLY HEIDER, ABE JACOB. **SET LIST:** "FIRE" / "HEY JOE" / "SPANISH CASTLE MAGIC" / "RED HOUSE" / "I DON'T LIVE TODAY" / "STAR SPANGLED BANNER" / "FOXEY LADY" / "PURPLE HAZE" / "VOODOO CHILD (SLIGHT RETURN)"

This San Diego concert was one of the group's more memorable performances, perhaps best known for the magnificent rendition of "Red House," which graced 1972's *Hendrix: In The West* and is now a part of the *Jimi Hendrix Experience* box set.

SUNDAY, MAY 25, 1969

SANTA CLARA POP FESTIVAL, COUNTY FAIRGROUNDS, SANTA CLARA, CALIFORNIA. **SET LIST:** "HEAR MY TRAIN A COMIN'" / "FIRE" / "SPANISH CASTLE MAGIC" / "RED HOUSE" / "I DON'T LIVE TODAY" / "FOXEY LADY" / "PURPLE HAZE" / "VOODOO CHILD (SLIGHT RETURN)"

FRIDAY, MAY 30, 1969

WAIKIKI SHELL, OAHU, HAWAII. WITH FAT MATTRESS. **PARTIAL SET LIST:** "FOXEY LADY" / "RED HOUSE" / "I DON'T LIVE TODAY"

Technical problems marred this concert. Amplifier hum and distortion caused Hendrix to cancel the performance shortly after it started. Promoters scrambled to placate the audience, offering refunds or admission to a show that would be organized for June 1.

SATURDAY, MAY 31, 1969

WAIKIKI SHELL, OAHU, HAWAII. WITH FAT MATTRESS. **PARTIAL SET LIST:** "FOXEY LADY" / "RED HOUSE" / "I DON'T LIVE TODAY" / "STONE FREE" / "STAR SPANGLED BANNER" / "PURPLE HAZE" / "VOODOO CHILD (SLIGHT RETURN)"

The Experience rebounded from the technical difficulties they had encountered the previous evening and put on a exciting performance much to the delight of the large audience.

SUNDAY, JUNE 1, 1969

WAIKIKI SHELL, OAHU, HAWAII. WITH FAT MATTRESS. **PARTIAL SET LIST:** "FOXEY LADY" / "RED HOUSE" / "PURPLE HAZE" / "VOODOO CHILD (SLIGHT RETURN)"

True to his word, Hendrix returned to perform for those patrons who had attended the aborted May 30 performance. Once again, he and the Experience rallied and delighted their audience with another fine performance.

SUNDAY, JUNE 8, 1969

STUDIO 3, WALLY HEIDER RECORDING, HOLLYWOOD, CALIFORNIA. PRODUCER: JIMI HENDRIX. ENGINEER: EDDIE KRAMER.

Kramer was dispatched to Los Angeles to review both of Heider's recent concert recordings, April 26, 1969, at the Los Angeles Forum and May 24, 1969, at the San Diego Sports Arena, as well as the magnificent February 24, 1969, concert at Royal Albert Hall. Manager Michael Jeffery hoped that a live album could be quickly prepared to serve as the album due to Capitol Records, to whom Hendrix still owed one album, per the court settlement order reached in his lengthy legal battle with Ed Chalpin and PPX Industries.

On this day, Kramer completed mixes and edits for "Star Spangled Banner" (from the San Diego show), "Purple Haze" (also from San Diego), and "Little Wing" (from the Royal Albert Hall show).

MONDAY, JUNE 9, 1969

STUDIO 3, WALLY HEIDER RECORDING, HOLLYWOOD, CALIFORNIA. PRODUCER: JIMI HENDRIX. ENGINEER: EDDIE KRAMER.

Kramer and Hendrix continued working on mixes for the proposed live album, preparing songs such as "I Don't Live Today" (from the Los Angeles Forum), but these would be replaced by efforts completed the following day. "Red House" (from the San Diego performance) was also reviewed and considered for the album.

TUESDAY, JUNE 10, 1969

STUDIO 3, WALLY HEIDER RECORDING, HOLLYWOOD, CALIFORNIA. PRODUCER: JIMI HENDRIX. ENGINEER: EDDIE KRAMER.

Kramer prepared final mixes of "I Don't Live Today" (from the Los Angeles Forum) and "Getting My Heart Back Together" (from Royal Albert Hall). After three days at Wally Heider Recording, Kramer and Hendrix had assembled a superb album of live performances. Tape copies were provided to Jeffery, but he appeared to take no action, as by June 15, 1969, the tape boxes containing the final mixes were marked "outtakes" and the project scrapped indefinitely. Reprise ultimately dismissed the concept of issuing a live album in early September 1969, but in the meantime, the decision was made to compile a U.S. version of Track Records' successful 1968 U.K. compilation *Smash Hits*. With permission from Jeffery, Reprise organized the details and scheduled a July release.

FRIDAY, JUNE 20, 1969

NEWPORT POP FESTIVAL. NORTHRIDGE, CALIFORNIA. **SET LIST:** "STONE FREE" / "ARE YOU EXPERIENCED?" / "STONE FREE" / "SUNSHINE OF YOUR LOVE" / "FIRE" / "HEAR MY TRAIN A COMIN'" / "RED HOUSE" / "FOXEY LADY" / "LIKE A ROLLING STONE" / "VOODOO CHILD (SLIGHT RETURN)" / "PURPLE HAZE"

The Experience were paid $100,000 to serve as the headline act for an ambitious three-day festival in Northridge that featured such popular groups as Creedence Clearwater Revival and Love.

Despite the fee—the highest paid to any act—and high expectations held by all, Hendrix's performance was beneath his usual standards. He seemed distracted by the unruly audience and expressed his disapproval of their response on more than one occasion, to little effect.

SUNDAY, JUNE 22, 1969

NEWPORT POP FESTIVAL. NORTHRIDGE, CALIFORNIA. Hendrix redeemed himself later on in the festival, delighting the audience by returning alone and unannounced for this Sunday-afternoon performance. Following the Experience's disappointing June 20 show, his guest appearance included an extended, free-wheeling jam session featuring Miles, Eric Burdon of the Animals, and Tracy Nelson of Mother Earth, among others. Hendrix's enthusiasm was visible throughout the segment and while the rhythm section was wobbly in parts, the crowd loved the interplay between the army of musicians who filled the stage. Passages of "Voodoo Child (Slight Return)," Guitar Slim's "Things That I Used To Do," and an early version of "We Gotta Live Together" were among the songs featured in this two-hour set.

SUNDAY, JUNE 29, 1969

DENVER POP FESTIVAL, MILE HIGH STADIUM, DENVER, COLORADO. **SET LIST:** "TAX FREE" / "HEAR MY TRAIN A COMIN'" / "FIRE" / "SPANISH CASTLE MAGIC" / "RED HOUSE" / "FOXEY LADY" / "STAR SPANGLED BANNER" / "PURPLE HAZE"

The Experience topped the bill at the 1969 Denver Pop Festival. The three-day festival, staged at Mile High Stadium, boasted a stellar lineup that also included Johnny Winter, Joe Cocker, Creedence Clearwater Revival, Poco, Frank Zappa and The Mothers of Invention, Iron Butterfly, Tim Buckley, and Big Mama Thornton.

An inspired set by the Experience was marred by a riot following the group's performance. Tensions between police and young audience members had been an issue since the previous day. On Saturday, Denver police had used tear gas in an effort to quell a large group of people who had been trying to crash the stadium's main gate. In the immediate aftermath of the Experience performance, police officers began firing tear gas at the audience while Eric Barrett, a roadie for the group, rushed the band off stage and into the back of their rented equipment truck. Fans climbed all over the vehicle, nearly buckling the roof before the Barrett and the road crew could whisk the group away.

The Denver Pop Festival proved to be the final performance by the original Jimi Hendrix Experience. Immediately afterwards, Redding left the group and returned to London to focus his energies on performing and recording with Fat Mattress, his solo vehicle.

JUNE 22, 1969: AT THE NEWPORT POP FESTIVA...

165

He cited Hendrix's stated desire to expand the group without consulting him as one of the factors influencing his decision.

JULY 1969

SHOKAN, NEW YORK.

With the Experience now disbanded, Hendrix, despite Jeffery's objections, was determined to try to realize a new concept he had in mind, namely a group whose extra percussion and second guitar would enhance and diversify his sound.

In this time of crisis, Hendrix reached back to those with whom his friendships were deepest. The recent arrival of Cox had helped provide a spark, so Hendrix now looked to reunite with another old comrade from his formative Nashville years, guitarist Larry Lee.

Hendrix had fallen out of touch with Lee—the two had not spoken in nearly five years and he had no idea as to Lee's present whereabouts. He gave the assignment of finding the guitarist to Cox. "Jimi had my mother's number and Billy called me," remembers Lee. "I had just come back from Vietnam. I think I had been home about maybe two weeks. I had just come from the unemployment office when the phone rang and it was Billy. I said, 'Wow! I haven't heard from any of the old guys.' I said, 'Billy, what's going on?' He said, 'Everything's fine.' I said, 'Where are you?' He said, 'I'm in New York.' I said, 'What you doing up there?' He said, 'I'm with Jimi.' I said, 'Where is Jimi?' I figured he was gonna say in England somewhere, because he was *hot* then, by the time I got out. He said that he was sitting right there. That kind of scared me, man! I spoke to Jimi and he was the same Jimi. I didn't know if he would even remember me, as much money as I heard he was making. He was the same Jimi, no change. He said, 'Hey, what you doing? We're gonna try out a few things up here. We'd like for you to come up here and join us.' He asked if I could come to New York. I said yes and we set a date three or four days from the telephone call."

That Hendrix chose the unsung Lee, rather than a more notable rock contemporary, surprised many in his camp—save for Cox, who understood Lee's unique link to Hendrix. "Jimi had played both the rhythm and the lead with the Experience," explains Cox. "He thought it might free him up to concentrate on his lead playing if he had someone else playing rhythm. Larry Lee was the first and only guy considered. In Nashville, Larry had been a sort of master to Jimi, teaching him some very important things that he would need on this journey. Larry had taken Jimi by the hand and taught him a lot of things about the blues that you couldn't find in a book. Jimi respected Larry and that instruction helped Jimi put everything in perspective. He said, 'If I get anybody in here to help, I want Larry, because he will know where to go.'"

Despite Cox's and Hendrix's unflinching admiration for Lee's ability, Lee had not quite grasped their new direction, a notion perhaps best exemplified by his decision to play the Gibson 335 guitar preferred by blues master Freddie King rather than the Fender Stratocaster, which Hendrix had long identified as his guitar of choice. "I preached to Larry about getting a different guitar, but he preferred to play that 335, which was not compatible with where we were at musically," says Cox.

With a second guitarist in tow, Hendrix next looked to bolster and diversify the role of percussion in his music. Percussionist Jerry Velez had met Hendrix prior to the breakup of the Experience. "I met Jimi at Steve Paul's Scene," remembers Velez. "I had just finished jamming with the McCoys, and when I walked over to my table, Jimi and his entourage were sitting behind me. A little later, I joined the band onstage again for a few more tunes. When I came back to sit down he leaned over and said, 'Listen, I'm recording this jam over at the studio tonight. We'll be starting around four, after this thing ends tonight. Do you want to come down and jam?' I said sure. I went over that night and jammed with Jimi and Buddy Miles and we seemed to hit it off."

Juma Sultan also joined Velez that night. Sultan was well known within the Woodstock artist community, a respected percussionist actively involved with the Aboriginal Music Society, which presented a broad mosaic of musical influences in semiconcert form on Sunday evenings at the Tinker Street Cinema. Sultan lived on a farm in Woodstock and accepted an invitation to jam with Hendrix during the country retreat Hendrix was planning.

"Jimi had broken up the Experience and wanted to do more ethnic music," explains Velez. "He wanted to try African and Afro-Cuban music with a bigger band." While Hendrix enjoyed jamming with Velez, Jeffery was suspicious of Velez's ability. "Jeffery said, 'Who the fuck is this kid Jerry Velez? I've never even heard of him.' Jimi explained that he liked playing with me and wanted me in the band. Then Jimi decided to have two percussionists, with Juma and I providing both an African and Latin flavor."

That decision, says Lee, came as Hendrix struggled to decide which of the two to part with. "Jimi met Juma Sultan and Jerry Velez on two different occasions and accidentally promised both of them the gig," explains Lee. "That is why we had two conga players. Having two conga players was unusual, but Jimi just took up with people, you know. That was his nature. Some people didn't think that was too good, but you have to be who you are out here. He was a person that had a lot of consideration for people. Phil Wilson, the drummer from the Paul Butterfield Blues Band, came by and we jammed at the house. Then Mitch showed up and that was the group."

Because Hendrix had not fully determined what his new musical direction would be, his struggled to verbalize his concept to each of the musicians he'd assembled. His ambiguity soon created friction among his supporting cast, as roles and responsibilities were never definitively outlined. The most pressing problem arose among the trio of percussionists, as Mitchell struggled to mesh with Velez and Sultan. "There was a *lot* of percussion," admits Velez. "I was a novice, and both Juma and I overplayed. Mitch's style involved a lot of playing as it was, with a lot of off-beat time signatures." The time issue frustrated Mitchell, who questioned the validity of Hendrix's concept, feeling that three percussionists hopelessly cluttered the group's sound. "There was a problem with keeping time," says Cox. "Mitch was a great player who always stayed right on the edge of keeping in time. There were many times when Jimi and I would sneak each other looks thinking, 'Oh, oh, Mitch ain't gonna make it,' but then *bang*, Mitch would be right there. Jimi's intentions were good, but it just didn't work when you had congas and tymbalis competing with what Mitch was trying to play."

A large house on Tavor Hollow Road in the Woodstock village of Shokan served as the base of operations for Hendrix and his crew of musicians. The concept behind the rental of this stately, eight-bedroom country home was to provide Hendrix with a comfortable base away from the pressures of Manhattan. Here, it was thought, Hendrix could rest, refocus, and work on new material. The reality, however, was that his troubles simply followed him upstate, as financial pressures, the ongoing studio project, the recent breakup of the Experience, and his impending trial for heroin possession in Toronto weighed heavily on his mind. The demands never diminished. "The telephone never stopped ringing," remembers Cox. "It was always, hurry up and do this, Get this done, get that going. They never let him have any peace."

Hendrix seemed to be a magnet for trouble and, as a result, was besieged by drug dealers hoping to win his favor. "Jimi wasn't a drug fiend by any means. He dabbled like all the rest of us, but on the coffee table downstairs, there would be every drug imaginable available," remembers Velez. "Every major drug dealer would come up to Jimi and say, 'Hey man, I just got this great stuff from Nepal,' or 'I just brought this from Marseilles.' These people all kept coming, wanting to get in with him."

Groupies and hustlers also streamed to the house hoping to win an audience with their idol. Most were turned away, but many succeeded, often disrupting whatever modicum of privacy Hendrix had been able to establish.

Most in Hendrix's management team never seriously considered the expanded band as a legitimate exercise, later pointing to Hendrix's uneven performance with the group at Woodstock on August 18 as conclusive proof. Cox thinks otherwise, citing the progress Hendrix made with his songwriting. "The time Jimi spent up at the house was very productive. He had broken away from the Experience and was able to place his focus on creating new ideas or tightening up 'Izabella' with small, intricate things that no one else would know except for those of us who had to play them. We weren't just jamming. Those patterns we created are what made the songs. Jimi would take Pattern 1, add parts of Pattern 9, and finish it off with a piece from Pattern 3. That's how the songs would come together."

Perhaps the finest example of this approach was "Dolly Dagger," which began as a simple bass riff. "Early one morning at the Woodstock house, I was sitting outside on the patio," says Cox. "Someone had set up the amplifiers the day before and we had let them stay outside all night. I don't know why, but I was thinking of Big Ben in England, so I grabbed my bass and started playing, *da do, da do da do da do*. Jimi came to the window in his shorts and started hollering, 'Hey man, keep playing that! Don't stop!' He came running down, grabbed his guitar, and said, 'How about this?' He had the first line almost together. Then I came up with some different notes to act as a close. 'Dolly Dagger' was born in that instant."

Writing sessions at the Shokan house were, as a rule, informal. "We would set up a circle in the round and play a lot," remembers Velez. "Upstairs, across from these two bedrooms was a large living room where we did a lot of acoustic jamming. Then downstairs, we had all of our heavy gear in a big room."

To maximize the creative potential of these spontaneous jam sessions, Hendrix and Cox began recording their free-form efforts. "Jimi knew I was a recording buff," explains Cox. "At first we set up a Scully two-track machine, but it was just too difficult to operate and haul around. So we went to the office and got enough money to buy a Sony, which had sound-on-sound recording capabilities. I mastered that machine!"

MONDAY, JULY 7, 1969

SHOKAN, NEW YORK. ENGINEER: EDDIE KRAMER.
Invited up to visit both Hendrix and Jeffery, Kramer and recently hired Electric Lady Studios maintenance engineer Shimon Ron installed a multitrack tape machine at Hendrix's rented house. While a number of tapes were no doubt recorded, only one remains in the Hendrix tape library. On this day, "Woodstock Jam" was recorded, featuring Hendrix, Cox, and Sultan. Incredibly, the contents were later erased in favor of three mediocre folk-rock takes recorded by an artist identified only as Dorothy. Hendrix did not take part in the new recording.

THE DICK CAVETT SHOW, ABC TELEVISION STUDIOS, NEW YORK, NEW YORK.

Later that day, Hendrix drove to Manhattan and made a rare television appearance on *The Dick Cavett Show*. In addition to giving an interview, he performed an abbreviated rendition of "Hear My Train A Comin'" backed by Cavett's studio band. This appearance was later released as part of the *Jimi Hendrix: The Dick Cavett Show* DVD.

THURSDAY, JULY 10, 1969

THE TONIGHT SHOW, NBC TELEVISION STUDIOS, NEW YORK, NEW YORK.

Hendrix made an appearance on *The Tonight Show* and was interviewed by guest host Flip Wilson before performing "Lover Man" with Cox on bass and famed *Tonight Show* drummer Ed Shaughnessy on drums. Partway though the song, Hendrix's amplifier blew, forcing Wilson to improvise until another amplifier could be connected. When this was done, Hendrix restarted the song and rushed through to its close.

Sadly, no footage of this appearance seems to have survived in either the official Carson/*Tonight Show* or Wilson archives. An amateur sound recording made from the original television broadcast stands as the only record of Hendrix's most prominent U.S. television appearance.

TUESDAY, JULY 22, 1969

SOUND RECORDERS STUDIOS, LOS ANGELES, CALIFORNIA. ENGINEER: ERIC WEINBANG.
When no album materialized from the June mixing sessions held by Hendrix and Kramer in Los Angeles, Warner Bros. made another attempt to cull a live album from existing vault tapes, titling this collection *The Jimi Hendrix Experience at Monterey*. Ultimately rejected by Jeffery, this single disc comprised the following performances: Side one: "Killing Floor" / "Like A Rolling Stone" / "Rock Me Baby" / "Foxey Lady" / "Can You See Me." Side Two: "Hey Joe" / "Purple Haze" / "The Wind Cries Mary" / "Wild Thing."

WEDNESDAY, JULY 30, 1969

SMASH HITS. REPRISE MS 2025. U.S. ALBUM RELEASE. PRODUCERS: CHAS CHANDLER, JIMI HENDRIX.

ENGINEERS: EDDIE KRAMER, DAVE SIDDLE. "PURPLE HAZE" / "FIRE" / "THE WIND CRIES MARY" / "CAN YOU SEE ME" / "HEY JOE" / "ALL ALONG THE WATCHTOWER" / "STONE FREE" / "CROSSTOWN TRAFFIC" / "MANIC DEPRESSION" / "REMEMBER" / "RED HOUSE" / "FOXEY LADY"

With the Experience's fans eagerly anticipating a sequel to *Electric Ladyland, Smash Hits*, an extremely popular and durable collection built around "Stone Free," "Remember," "Red House," and "Can You See Me"—the four tracks Reprise had withheld when it compiled its own version of *Are You Experienced* in 1967—filled the void nicely.

These four recordings, each new to the U.S. market, were presented along with standouts from *Are You Experienced* and *Electric Ladyland*, but the album strangely did not include any material from *Axis: Bold As Love*. Sales were significant, as *Smash Hits* rose to number 6 on the *Billboard* album chart. After Hendrix's death, the compilation became his top seller, outperforming all of his other Reprise albums. Though it has since been surpassed by sales of later CD compilations,

Smash Hits remains an important cornerstone of the Jimi Hendrix catalogue.

MONDAY, AUGUST 18, 1969

WOODSTOCK MUSIC AND ART FAIR, BETHEL, NEW YORK. ENGINEER: EDDIE KRAMER. SECOND ENGINEER: LEE OSBOURNE. **SET LIST:** "MESSAGE TO LOVE" / "HEAR MY TRAIN A COMIN'" / "SPANISH CASTLE MAGIC" / "RED HOUSE" / "MASTERMIND" / "LOVER MAN" / "FOXEY LADY" / "JAM BACK AT THE HOUSE" / "IZABELLA" / "GYPSY WOMAN" / "FIRE" / "VOODOO CHILD (SLIGHT RETURN)" / "STAR SPANGLED BANNER" / "PURPLE HAZE" / "WOODSTOCK IMPROVISATION" / "VILLANOVA JUNCTION" / "HEY JOE"

As the headline act for the festival, Hendrix's performance was originally scheduled to bring the three-day event to a dramatic close. A host of production and weather-related delays conspired to render the original festival schedule useless. With the festival originally set to close on Sunday evening, Woodstock co-promoter Michael Lang huddled with Hendrix and Jeffery that day

and offered them a spot at midnight—a position, Lang felt, that would fit Hendrix's unique status. For whatever reason, Hendrix and Jeffery stood firm in their desire to close the festival. As a result, Hendrix would not take the stage until Monday morning, by which time much of the audience had left the site.

After sets by the Paul Butterfield Blues Band and Sha Na Na, Hendrix took the stage, fronting his new rough-hewn ensemble: Cox, Mitchell, second guitarist Larry Lee, and percussionists Jerry Velez and Juma Sultan. From the stage he spoke of being tired of the Experience name for the time being and described his new group as Gypsy Sun & Rainbows, Band Of Gypsys, or simply anything the audience wanted to call them.

Prior to the gig, the group had regularly jammed at Hendrix's rented Shokan home, aiding the guitarist's effort to round out new songs such as "Izabella" and "Message To Love." Apart from Hendrix and Mitchell, veterans of the festival stage, none of the other musicians were prepared for such a massive reception.

There were many highlights scattered throughout Hendrix's unusually long, 140-minute performance with his new larger band, but none more significant than the

guitarist's unforgettable rendition of "The Star-Spangled Banner." "That was incredible," Cox remembers. "We had never practiced that. Jimi just did it. If you listen to it very carefully, you hear me start off with him. Then I said to myself, 'Sit a minute, he is going to another level. Let me just lay out and listen.' That's just what I did!"

Despite such brilliant moments, the group's uneven performance exposed the weaknesses of the big-band experiment that Hendrix announced from the Woodstock stage as Gypsy Sun & Rainbows. He struggled to integrate Lee's rhythm guitar fully, and Sultan's and Velez's percussion seemed extraneous, their contributions all but drowned out by the volume of the group's amplifiers. "I didn't feel that the band at Woodstock was as tight as it could have been," recalls Eddie Kramer. "I felt that Billy, Jimi, and Mitch were fairly tight together, but all the rest of the guys didn't really fit and it was excessive."

THURSDAY, AUGUST 28, 1969

HIT FACTORY, NEW YORK, NEW YORK. ENGINEER: EDDIE KRAMER. SECOND ENGINEER: JOEY ZAGARINO.

With new material ready to record, Hendrix bypassed the Record Plant, opting to record at the Hit Factory, a smaller studio owned by songwriter Jerry Ragavoy. These Hit Factory dates represented Hendrix's first formal return to the recording studio in some time. The full contingent of Gypsy Sun & Rainbows, the aggregation he had led just nine days before at the Woodstock festival in Bethel, joined him.

For these sessions, Hendrix asked Kramer to return, independently hiring the engineer to supervise the sessions. Kramer had some knowledge of the expanded group, having made infrequent trips to the Shokan house during Hendrix's stay, installing a tape machine on one occasion, and, later, recording their Woodstock performance. "Jerry Ragavoy was a great guy, but the Hit Factory was a dump of the first order with zero atmosphere," Kramer remembers. "The acoustics resembled those of an industrial cardboard box. Jimi asked me to make sure that his guitar tones were going to be correct and that all of these tape machines would work. Because he was planning to record with a bunch of new guys, he already had enough to deal with." While Kramer's name was not listed on each of the tape boxes used here, it was he, much more often than staff engineer Joe Zagarino, who can be heard offering instructions over the talkback microphone.

The evening began with an attempt at "Message To The Universe," an early, slower-paced rendition of what would become "Message To Love." "Jimi had the opening guitar riff on a little tape he had made at home," remembers Cox. "When he played it to me, I suggested some changes to the riff he was playing and that made one complete pattern. The next pattern was repeated twice before the melody came back to the top. That's all it was. It was nothing but two separate patterns linked together. The intro was really the same as the ending. We just went up the fretboard until we could go no further."

With Hendrix singing passionately along with the enthusiastic backing of his band, "Message To The Universe" had obvious promise. Thirty-six takes would be recorded and there were many fine moments throughout, most notably the infectious interplay between Cox and Hendrix. Takes 1 and 2 came apart but take 3 was a solid, complete effort. The group had performed the song as part of its Woodstock Festival set, but this arrangement differed substantially, most notably because of the Arabic figures Hendrix wove into his dramatic closing lead guitar work. Despite the rousing drum-and-guitar finish he and Mitchell had spontaneously created, by the very next take, Hendrix had returned to the ascending series of notes, which he and bassist Cox performed in unison to serve as the song's crescendo and finale.

Kramer mixed take 3 of "Message To The Universe" in 1997 so that it could be included as part of South Saturn Delta.

Interspersed between later takes of "Message To The Universe" was a sloppy, impromptu "Lover Man," offered without vocals. Some loose attempts at "Izabella" with vocals from Hendrix can also be heard, although they seem to represent more of a creative diversion rather than any kind of structured effort. Additional takes of "Message To The Universe" followed before Lee led the ensemble through an untitled blues original, of which his lengthy lead guitar work was the song's most prominent feature.

After a short break to accommodate a tape change, the group revisited "Message To The Universe" before Hendrix shifted once again, with only moderate success, to "Izabella." With their momentum stalled, a break was called so that the band could review what they had recorded. When recording resumed, Hendrix can be heard explaining the guitar parts of "Burning Desire," a promising new original, to Lee. To enhance his instructions, he performed the chord changes and made general comments on the song's construction. This led to a spontaneous jam based on the tune, but Lee's solo broke down, causing the effort to stall. Mitchell, who sat out the previous jam, rejoined the group as it began "Easy Blues," a marvelous, jazz-influenced instrumental jam. Years later, a heavily edited portion of this recording would be included as part of 1980's Nine To The Universe.

Recording continued with the group attempting six additional takes of "Izabella." An inspired workout of "Jam Back At The House" brought the session to a close. While none of these recordings would be designated as finished masters, "Izabella" and "Message To Love" were exceptional new originals.

After Hendrix's death, on May 21, 1975, Alan Douglas edited "Jam Back At The House" out of this session's master reel to include on *Midnight Lightning*. For that album, all original recordings—save for Hendrix's guitar parts—were scrapped in favor of new overdubs from guitarist Jeff Miranov, bassist Bob Babbit, drummer Allan Schwartzberg, and percussionist Jimmy Maeulen. The track was also retitled "Beginnings," a title used for a different recording of the same song issued on 1972's *War Heroes*.

FRIDAY, AUGUST 29, 1969

HIT FACTORY, NEW YORK, NEW YORK. ENGINEER: EDDIE KRAMER. SECOND ENGINEER: JOEY ZAGARINO. Hendrix and company struggled diligently to capture a suitable basic track of "Izabella." Despite this session's length—eight reels of tape were recorded, an unofficial record—Hendrix's lead vocal and guitar work were spirited throughout. The evening began with the band running through the song, making refinements outlined by Hendrix as he tried to establish the desired arrangement. The beginning of reel four, which featured three strong takes, represented significant progress. Take 3 from this reel was marked "hold."

Though Hendrix would ultimately select this take as his working master, a number of takes from reel five were equally worthy. A robust take 2 was listed as "good," but take 8, timed at 4:45, was especially noteworthy. This rendition, arguably tighter and more polished than any previous effort—including the live version performed at Woodstock—provided a tantalizing glimpse into Hendrix's new direction. While Hendrix did not specifically record a lead vocal for this track, he can occasionally be heard singing live, with his voice acting, in this instance, as his own metronome.

Satisfied with the group's hold on "Izabella," Hendrix revived "Message To The Universe." Three long, loose attempts filled reel six. These versions represented little more than extended jams, with the group experimenting with the song's main rhythm pattern.

By reel seven, the spotlight had once again revolved to "Izabella." A brief flurry of false starts prefaced a complete take of the song, which then evolved into a formative rendition of "Machine Gun." Despite this song's obvious promise, the effort gradually lost steam, quickly digressing into a frenetic jam that suffered from bad tuning and bad timing.

Additional takes of "Izabella" and "Message To The Universe," as well some ragged jamming, filled out the eighth and final reel of multitrack tape recorded on this evening. Before the session concluded, overdubs for "Izabella" were recorded, with Hendrix replacing his lead vocal and recording two separate, additional guitar tracks. A variety of percussion instruments were also overdubbed, including a shaker, a cowbell, and congas. Hendrix also tossed in some humor, starting his vocal overdub by licking his lips and making a huge chomping sound into the microphone. The evening ended with a mixing session, during which Hendrix and Kramer reviewed the evening's highlights and prepared a rough mix of "Izabella."

While none of the recordings made on this evening would be issued during Hendrix's lifetime, this skeletal rendition of "Machine Gun" was later overhauled by Douglas and Bongiovi with overdubs recorded in 1974 and added to the posthumous compilation *Midnight*

Lightning. Both the original demo and the overhauled master paled in comparison to the January 1, 1970, Fillmore East performance that formed the centerpiece of the *Band Of Gypsys* album issued in March of 1970.

SATURDAY, AUGUST 30, 1969

HIT FACTORY, NEW YORK, NEW YORK. ENGINEER: EDDIE KRAMER. SECOND ENGINEER: JOEY ZAGARINO.

This evening was largely dedicated to the recording of Hendrix's "Sky Blues Today" and Lee's "Mastermind." Nine takes of "Mastermind" were recorded, with Lee lending vocals to takes 1, 2, and 4. While the song's arrangement was nearly identical to the version performed at Woodstock, only take 4 was marked "good," and no finals were achieved.

"Sky Blues Today" was also recorded, although these versions were hardly polished. Marbled through the many takes were jams, but each sound cluttered, with Mitchell struggling to keep time amid the competing percussion accents provided by Velez and Sultan. An uneventful spontaneous effort entitled "Jimi's Jam" closed out the third and final reel.

WEDNESDAY, SEPTEMBER 3, 1969

"STONE FREE" / "IF 6 WAS 9." REPRISE 0853. U.S. SINGLE RELEASE.

Lifting "Stone Free" from the best-selling *Smash Hits* compilation, Reprise again tried, albeit unsuccessfully, to crack *Billboard*'s elusive Top 40 listing. For the first time since Reprise's May 1967 launch of "Hey Joe," a Jimi Hendrix Experience single missed the charts entirely.

THURSDAY, SEPTEMBER 4, 1969

HIT FACTORY, NEW YORK, NEW YORK. ENGINEER: JOEY ZAGARINO.

Perhaps eager to establish the proper mood, Hendrix kicked off this session with a robust workout of "Jam Back At The House." Punctuated by his blistering lead guitar work, this rendition jumped off to a rousing start before becoming unglued, as, unfortunately, an effective ending had yet to be devised. The take abruptly collapsed during Hendrix's final, frenetic climb up the fretboard of his guitar.

The balance of the session was dedicated to new takes of "Mastermind," with Lee again supplying lead vocals. Steeped in R&B, "Mastermind" provided Cox, Lee, and Hendrix with a welcome opportunity to pay homage to Curtis Mayfield, one of their primary influences. Lee's modest vocal effectively delivered the song's gentle plea, while Hendrix offered tasteful rhythm and lead guitar work in support. Eighteen takes in all were recorded, with take 4 the first to be highlighted, although that effort was only described as "fair." Take 9 was complete, as was 11, but neither could accurately be described as masters, lacking both cohesion and spirit. Recording continued until a complete take 18 ultimately yielded the finished master.

FRIDAY, SEPTEMBER 5, 1969

HIT FACTORY, NEW YORK, NEW YORK. ENGINEER: JOEY ZAGARINO.

Hours after the group's performance at the United Block Association Benefit show on 139th Street in Harlem, Hendrix and company returned to the studio to tackle "Burning Desire."

The session began with Hendrix recording a solo demo of the song. Working solely with Zagarino and the studio's eight-track tape machine, Hendrix recorded vocals, guitar, and a nimble bass line. He even climbed behind Mitchell's drum kit to establish the tempo he desired. Six takes were put down on tape, but Hendrix still seemed unsatisfied. While Zagarino was effusive in his praise, Hendrix remained unconvinced, instructing him to hold the tape aside for further consideration.

Hendrix had great faith in the song and was eager to begin making refinements with his band. The group worked their way through a full tape-reel's worth of unslated takes in an effort to refine their respective parts. Twenty-seven takes then followed, but while there were many splendid moments throughout, none truly came close to realizing a finished master. While Hendrix and Cox maintained a firm grasp on the song's melody, the multiple takes attempted were each hampered by a steady series of missed notes and timing problems. Hendrix added an additional guitar part, as well as a conga overdub from Sultan to take 27, but neither had a substantial impact. In its present form, "Burning Desire" required significant restructuring before additional recording would be warranted.

SATURDAY, SEPTEMBER 6, 1969

HIT FACTORY, NEW YORK, NEW YORK. ENGINEER: JOEY ZAGARINO.

Despite hints of promise from "Burning Desire" in the previous session, Hendrix chose instead to record "Valleys Of Neptune," another fine work in progress. Recording began with three meandering, incomplete takes, each without vocals. Hendrix's enthusiasm level seemed lukewarm, as the band struggled to master the song's arrangement. Unfortunately, "Valleys Of Neptune," despite its potential, was no more developed than either "Burning Desire" or "Sky Blues Today." The session's mood lightened when Hendrix and Lee kicked off "Blues For Me And You," a spontaneous, original, blues workout.

One of the more recognized and widely bootlegged of Hendrix's many unreleased jam sessions, "Blues For Me And You" was slated by Douglas to be featured as part of *Multicolored Blues*, an unreleased compilation of blues jams originally scheduled to have been released sometime in 1976. After that album was scrapped, "Blues For Me And You" was also left off of *Nine To The Universe*, a collection of edited studio jams aimed at showcasing Hendrix's jazz leanings. Ironically, this jam was even excluded by Douglas from the 1994 MCA compilation *Jimi Hendrix: Blues*.

Five additional attempts at "Valleys Of Neptune" followed, each with occasional vocals from Hendrix and disorganized support from his group. After take 5 collapsed, Hendrix, desperate to ignite his rhythm section, tore into "Lover Man," hoping to establish the groove he desired. As "Lover Man" came apart, Lee moved to the fore, stepping off an original blues jam during which he assumed lead guitar chores. A few shining moments ensued, but little more.

Undaunted, Hendrix returned to "Valleys Of Neptune," unsuccessfully directing the group through a host of unslated takes. Hendrix's passionate live vocals rose infrequently above the din created by the rhythm section. Sultan and Velez sounded hopelessly cluttered, struggling to stay in time with Mitchell. Long jams founded on the "Valleys Of Neptune" theme ensued, including one noteworthy effort during which an occasional snatch of "Angel" could be detected in Hendrix's playing. As with so many of Hendrix's sessions from this period, there were several shining moments captured on tape, but they were simply moments and nothing more.

After the session had ended, Hendrix remained behind at the studio, intent on creating another solo demo as he had done the previous evening. Working once more with the facility's eight-track tape machine, he recorded five takes of "Trying To Be," later titled "Stepping Stone." Two separate complete takes were also recorded and marked "Different."

TUESDAY, SEPTEMBER 9, 1969

THE DICK CAVETT SHOW, ABC TELEVISION STUDIOS, NEW YORK.

Hendrix had originally been booked to appear on Cavett's special post-Woodstock program on Monday, August 18, but his festival performance was pushed to that same morning and Hendrix management associate Bob Levine was forced to cancel on his behalf. Hendrix made good some three weeks later, though, returning to Cavett's program for an interview and a performance with Mitchell, Cox, and Sultan of a medley of "Izabella" and "Machine Gun." It is remarkable—particularly measured against contemporary record company practices—that Hendrix would premiere new, commercially unavailable songs such as these as opposed to promoting popular songs such as "Purple Haze."

Even though Hendrix had been provided Cavett's questions in advance—something his management demanded and received before this and the July 7 appearance—Hendrix was once again thoughtful and sincere if not altogether comfortable speaking about himself.

This appearance was later released in its entirety as part of the *Jimi Hendrix: The Dick Cavett Show* DVD.

WEDNESDAY, SEPTEMBER 10, 1969

SALVATION CLUB, NEW YORK, NEW YORK.

Hendrix had canceled a September U.S. tour at considerable expense because he felt that Gypsy Sun & Rainbows, as presently configured, was not ready for touring. If Hendrix would not tour, then Jeffery was determined that his artist complete the album owed to Capitol Records as per their settlement with Chalpin's PPX Industries. When the settlement album wasn't forthcoming, Jeffery demanded that Hendrix audition new musicians to back him. Much to Hendrix's frustration, such an audition was actually staged at the Salvation Club during the first week of September.

"Jimi called me to ask if I had received my ticket," explains former Buddy Miles Express bassist Roland Robinson. "I said, 'What?' He told me to come on up [and] try things with the band. When I got up there it was really screwed up, because I had quit the Express on bad terms. Billy Cox was there and he was really quiet. So I'm there feeling weird, and it occurred to me that Jimi hadn't told these guys that they weren't in the band anymore. We had two bands there. You had two bass players, two drummers, and a lot of real hostility in the air. Jimi's management was there, freaking out over all the people he was trying. Jimi started yelling, 'Just leave me the fuck alone! Let me play with the people I want to play with and I'll make you all the goddamn money you want!' We then got into this one jam and Billy Cox was sitting in front of me with his arms folded and Buddy was playing half-assed and scowling at me from behind the drums. Afterwards, Buddy started to get pissed off and he told Jimi that if I was in the band, I'd be trying to take it over. So that set me off and I'm shouting at Buddy that I'm going to kill him. It all got really funky and I just said forget it. It just wasn't going to fly. Jimi was embarrassed at what had happened. I got a week's pay and his apologies."

The audition didn't yield any changes to the band. Instead, they served only to widen the distance between Hendrix and his manager. "Jimi was wiped out," says Velvert Turner. "He grabbed me at the Salvation and whispered, 'Don't you ever fuck up your life like I have.' He seemed tortured."

On September 10, Hendrix performed one final, abbreviated concert at the Salvation with a scaled-back version of Gypsy Sun & Rainbows that included Cox, Mitchell, Lee, and Sultan. The group performed new material like "Izabella" before a confused nightclub audience expecting to hear standards such as "Purple Haze," and Hendrix was hampered by equipment problems throughout. "There had been a lot of technical problems that night at the gig," remembers Turner. "Jimi told me that there was some kind of sabotage going on with the amplifiers and there were cords that had been cut. He called the night a black Roman orgy. Jimi was very upset at what was going down."

MONDAY, SEPTEMBER 15, 1969

RECORD PLANT, NEW YORK, NEW YORK. 4:00 P.M. TO 6:00 P.M. ENGINEER: JACK ADAMS. SECOND ENGINEER: TOM FLYE.

Leaving the Hit Factory behind, Hendrix returned to the Record Plant for this bizarre session, during which the group's entire effort sounded oddly disjointed. Worse still, Hendrix's vocal microphone was incorrectly patched, rendering the tape's contents largely unusable. Recording began with a rehearsal of "Sky Blues Today," followed next by three formal takes. Take 1 was complete and, by a wide margin, the best of the lot. These initial takes were each recorded without bass. Hendrix and Lee, however, can be heard working out the song's structure between takes. Following a tape change, Cox joined the group for two lengthy, additional rehearsal takes during which sketches of "Villanova Junction" and "Burning Desire" can be heard. With rehearsals completed, six shambling takes of "Sky Blues Today" followed. The sixth and final take of the evening was complete and featured a vocal, but the tape box was marked "redo."

Nothing recorded on this evening came even remotely close to resembling a finished master. Hendrix's condition sounded dubious, and the session was entirely unproductive.

With the pressures mounting around him, Hendrix seemed increasingly incapable of reversing the tide. Unable to realize the sound and direction he'd envisioned for the expanded band, Hendrix's brief tenure with Gypsy Sun & Rainbows was fast unraveling. Shortly after the disastrous September 15 session, Lee threw in the towel and quietly returned to Memphis. "I don't know how much pressure the management put on Jimi, to be honest. I just know there was a conflict and that was the reason I told Jimi that I would leave. I was seeing that he was fighting a battle that maybe if I was gone it would be more like what they wanted. They wanted a three-piece [group] as far as I can gather. The Experience was a hit and a moneymaker for him so I just told him I was gonna leave. He said, 'Well, we'll get a drummer and we'll get back together.' I just came on back to Memphis. I was hoping that that would have taken some of the heat off Jimi."

Lee's selfless gesture spoke volumes about his friendship with Hendrix and the special value he placed on it as opposed to the celebrity or career opportunity he may have enjoyed had he impelled Hendrix to fight on his behalf. "Larry just said, 'I think I'm probably in the way,' and took it upon himself to leave on good terms," remembers Cox. "There was just too much bullshit around him to handle. He just decided that he had had enough."

TUESDAY, SEPTEMBER 23, 1969

RECORD PLANT, NEW YORK, NEW YORK. 3:00 A.M. EN-GINEER: JACK ADAMS. SECOND ENGINEER: TOM FLYE.
After Lee returned to Memphis, Velez also withdrew from the group to pursue other opportunities. In their absence, a scaled-down Gypsy Sun & Rainbows gamely attempted to finish "Valleys Of Neptune," "Message To Love," and "Jam Back At The House," arguably the most promising of Hendrix's most recent compositions.

Three takes of "Valleys Of Neptune" set the session in motion, but none of these efforts was cohesive. "Drinking Wine," a modest, impromptu blues original, came next and provided the evening's sole highlight. Hendrix then returned to "Valleys Of Neptune," recording seven instrumental takes. The take 7 version was complete, but it hardly resembled a finished master. Individual takes of both "Message To Love" and "Jam Back At The House" were equally dispirited and the session ground to a halt.

Hendrix then turned to upgrading the reel four, take 3 Hit Factory recording of "Izabella" from August 29. He recorded new vocal and lead guitar parts to this work in progress. For this session, he elected to use a Gibson SG model guitar as opposed to his normal instrument, the Fender Stratocaster. The Gibson SG provided Hendrix with the tight, biting sound texture he desired for the solo. Despite the song's promise, Hendrix was unable to complete the track to his satisfaction. In 1999, this recording of "Izabella" was mixed by Eddie Kramer and issued as part of the *Jimi Hendrix Experience* box set.

WEDNESDAY, SEPTEMBER 24, 1969

RECORD PLANT, NEW YORK, NEW YORK. ENGINEER: JACK ADAMS. SECOND ENGINEER: TOM FLYE.
Without a bassist, nineteen takes of "Jimi's Tune"—actually a roughly hewn attempt at "Power Of Soul"—were recorded, with the last marked "hold." Seven takes of "I'm A Man," later known as "Stepping Stone," were also recorded, as was a lengthy jam with Sultan.

FRIDAY, SEPTEMBER 25, 1969

RECORD PLANT, NEW YORK, NEW YORK. 12:00 A.M. ENGINEER: JACK ADAMS. SECOND ENGINEER: DAVE RAGNO.
Filling Mitchell's chair during this session was Buddy Miles. The session began with a raw stab at "Keep On Groovin'" punctuated at various intervals by a live vocal by Hendrix. Next, eight takes of "Sky Blues Today" were attempted, with Hendrix and Miles joined by Sultan. With seemingly little or no rehearsal prior to the session, Miles did his best to learn the song on the fly, making adjustments dictated by Hendrix. Despite Miles's enthusiasm, Hendrix was forced to devote crucial studio time to instructing him rather than focusing on improving his own performance. The eighth and final take would be held over, marked as the best effort of the evening. Hendrix then turned his attention to "Room Full Of Mirrors." No final master was achieved, as the arrangement too often sounded unrehearsed. The most promising effort, lasting nearly six minutes, would later be mixed by Kramer and added to the 2000 Dagger Records official "bootleg" release *Morning Symphony Ideas*.

SATURDAY, SEPTEMBER 26, 1969

RECORD PLANT, NEW YORK, NEW YORK. 12:00

A.M. ENGINEER: BOB HUGHES. SECOND ENGINEER: DAVE RAGNO.

This session took place in Studio C, the smaller studio located above the main rooms Hendrix normally used. Unlike Studios A and B, Studio C still featured the Scully twelve-track recording machine on which Hendrix had recorded much of *Electric Ladyland* the previous year.

Joined during this session by Mitchell, Hendrix worked through "Message To Love" informally, honing the arrangement but not completing any finished masters. Perhaps as a result of being in Studio C and only having access to the twelve-track machine, Hendrix seemed to view the session as an opportunity to develop the song as opposed to formally recording a finished master take. Short bursts of "Night Bird Flying," "Valleys Of Neptune," and "Stepping Stone" were marbled throughout the session but the focus remained on "Message To Love."

TUESDAY, SEPTEMBER 30, 1969

RECORD PLANT, NEW YORK, NEW YORK. 10:00 P.M. PRODUCERS: JIMI HENDRIX, ALAN DOUGLAS, STEFAN BRIGHT. ENGINEER: BOB HUGHES. SECOND ENGINEER: DAVE RAGNO.

During this, his first formal session to involve Alan Douglas and his associate Stefan Bright, Hendrix provided some inspired bass guitar work for much of the five reels recorded during this lengthy, impromptu workout. "We had set up a jam session with Buddy Miles, John Sebastian, Duane Hitchings, and Stephen Stills," explains Bright. "When we arrived at the studio, Hendrix was there. He wanted to know who was coming to the session. When he heard Steve Stills was expected, he didn't want to play lead guitar. We thought that was strange, but he did volunteer to play bass. There wasn't a left-handed bass in the studio, only a right-handed model, so he just turned it upside down and played some of the most fantastic bass guitar I've ever heard."

Of the invited guests, Stills was the last to arrive. He burst into the studio cresting upon a wave of inspiration. "Stephen Stills came in and said that he had come from Joni Mitchell's place," remembers Ragno. "She had just written 'Woodstock,' this great song that we

had to hear. It began as a jam, then those guys turned it into a really good piece of music by the time they were finished with it."

Led by Stills's energetic guitar, the assembled group wrestled with the "Woodstock" melody, with each player trying to establish their individual parts on the fly. A lengthy instrumental take began the session, followed by two takes voiced by Stills. For these takes, Stills also played organ, with Hendrix on bass and Miles on drums. The second of these efforts yielded a superb backing track.

More vocal takes of "Woodstock" by Stills filled a second reel of tape, and the group's enthusiastic efforts around this song would take up most of a third reel as well. "Woodstock" was set aside when John Sebastian joined the fray to lend harmonica to a rambling but well-played jam session.

Mitchell replaced Miles when reel four began. Stills led Hendrix and Mitchell through takes of another original song titled "One More Day/$20 Fine." Take 3 was particularly noteworthy and marked as the master. A final reel of jamming between Stills, Hendrix, and Mitchell alternated between the "Woodstock" theme and a promising country-styled rhythm pattern before the session ground to a close.

Neither Stills nor Hendrix returned to these tapes after this session. However, Douglas later excerpted an extended take 5 of "Woodstock" from reel three on February 18, 1970, and retitled it "Live And Let Live." It was released as part of the Timothy Leary album *You Can Be Anything This Time Around* issued by Douglas's own label, Douglas Records, that same year. "Alan Douglas had helped get Tim Leary out of jail in Texas, where he had been busted on a marijuana charge," Bright explains. "We held a press conference for Leary at our offices on 55th Street and decided to release his comments on an album called *You Can Be Anything This Time Around*. We used that 'Woodstock' jam for the first side of the album." Neither Douglas nor Bright had sought clearances from any of the artists featured prior to the recording session that yielded the jam, and elected to include the recording without identifying the players. "Nobody knew who was playing on the album because we weren't allowed to use their names on the sleeve," says Bright, "but we let the word slip out."

OCTOBER 1969

Exhausted and frustrated by the lack of progress made by Gypsy Sun & Rainbows, Mitchell returned to England. Unsure of Hendrix's immediate plans, he set no timetable for his return.

The mounting pressure and Hendrix's deteriorating condition had soured Cox's outlook as well. In late September, he, too, had decided to leave, checking out of the Penn-Garden Hotel and quietly returning to Nashville. "The whole problem started as soon as we got to the house in Woodstock," recalls Cox. "There were people who just did not want this band to succeed. It was one thing after another. There was the shoot-out down at the front gate of the Shokan house, the infiltration of people into the house, drugs being put into people's food—just a lot of unnecessary, underhanded things being done for no reason. I didn't have time to try and figure out who was behind all this and why were they doing so. When you get down to people fighting with guns out in front of the house, there is something

seriously wrong. All I knew was that I was going to do the Woodstock gig, help out my buddy, and carry my ass back to Nashville. That was my focus. After Woodstock, I hung around as long as I could, but there was just too much bullshit going down all around him."

Hendrix's nerves were equally frayed. "Jimi had gone down into this well," says Cox. "He said, 'Man, I just can't get it together. I've gotta rest my head.' He told me that if he could, he was thinking of going off to Africa with Colette [Mimram, his girlfriend at the time]. I wished him Godspeed and told him I was glad I had been able to help him. That was it. I didn't think I was ever going to be involved with him again."

Exhausted and deeply depressed, Hendrix shut everything down, retreating to his apartment and sinking beneath a wave of anxiety and self-doubt. As he had done once before, he appealed to Cox to return and help him regain his focus. Chief among his concerns was resolving his obligation to Capitol Records to deliver the album called for in the 1968 legal settlement with PPX. "When I agreed to come back, Jimi sat me down in his apartment and explained what was going on," recalls Cox. "My thought was to just give [PPX and Capitol Records] something. Over the next couple of days, he came up with the concept that we would try something outside of the Experience. I asked whether he had talked to Mitchell, but he only mumbled something I couldn't hear and wouldn't go any further with it. Buddy Miles called me, and I told him of the situation. He said, 'Well, I'll get help. Let's get him out and jam.'"

"The fall of 1969 was a real strange time for Jimi Hendrix," says Miles. "He wasn't doing anything. We were jamming constantly, but I wasn't getting paid for any of those sessions. I'm not the most subtle guy in the world, so I said, 'I have an idea. Let's put a band together.' We talked about different things, like having Stevie Winwood, who we both wanted, join the band, but in the end it came down to just the three of us."

Meanwhile, Hendrix's relationship with Jeffery had deteriorated, adding to the problems in his life. The breakup of the Experience had come at a bad time financially, as Hendrix and Jeffery, just months before, had agreed to construct a recording studio as equal partners. The funds to build the facility were to be generated by income created by touring. Jeffery had organized a short U.S. tour in September to raise some much-needed capital—the tour that Hendrix had vetoed at great financial cost, citing a lack of confidence in his new band.

With his relationship with his manager at a low point, Hendrix turned away, seeking and receiving advice from a host of friends and fellow travelers. One such advisor was Alan Douglas. Douglas had been introduced to Hendrix as the result of Devon Wilson's friendships with Douglas's wife, Stella, and Colette Mimram, who owned a popular Lower East Side clothing boutique and designed many of Hendrix's elaborate stage outfits. Hendrix and Mimram were also extremely close, and their relationship extended through Hendrix's death in September 1970.

Some fifteen years older than Hendrix, Douglas had little experience in rock and roll, but he had worked for such record companies as Barclay and United Artists. At UA, he'd compiled a handful of notable jazz releases, including John Coltrane and Cecil Taylor's *Stereo Drive*, and *Lady Love*, a collection of Billie Holiday recordings. Douglas was later promoted to the label's soundtrack division, overseeing, among other projects, the release of the Beatles' *Hard Day's Night* and the many James Bond albums.

In 1967, Douglas left UA and established his own company, Douglas Records. Beginning with an ambitious Lenny Bruce retrospective, the company later changed from a spoken-word label to Douglas Communications, which also encompassed music. Under this umbrella, Douglas, operating with a budget of just $25,000, signed Allen Ginsberg, spoken-word artists the Last Poets, and jazz guitarist John McLaughlin.

According to Douglas, Hendrix, a frequent guest at his wife's dinner parties, asked him to come down to the Record Plant to observe one of his recording sessions. That evening, Douglas claims, he witnessed a state of total disorganization. He returned the next night to take a more active role in the control room, organizing the session to lessen the burden on Hendrix. "I didn't even know where Hendrix was going," remembers Douglas. "He was talking about an album but I couldn't see it anywhere. I was just going to do some songs with him, 'Okay, you want to try this song? Let's

go do it,' type of thing. Hendrix himself didn't know where he was going."

"We basically put together the Band Of Gypsys group," says Bright. "This was going to be the first time that Jimi was going to play with Buddy [Miles] on a regular basis. The old group was gone, and Buddy was in because he gave Jimi a little more funk."

"The Band Of Gypsys were put together in Douglas's office," says Miles, "between Alan and [concert promoter] Bill Graham, who gave us the dates at the Fillmore East. Jimi and I had gone to him [Graham] to ask if we could do it, and he couldn't believe it."

Miles, Rich, Douglas, and Bright had worked together before, as Miles and bassist Billy Rich had joined organist Larry Young to serve as the backing unit for John McLaughlin's Douglas Records debut. Rich had been the consensus choice for the new group, but Hendrix opted instead for Cox, whose steady presence and trusted friendship he valued above all else.

"Not playing with the Band Of Gypsys and not being part of that live album [*Band Of Gypsys*] is one of my real regrets," admits Rich. "I had moved to Denver and begun working on a project in San Francisco for Columbia Records when Alan Douglas called asking if I wanted to do this album with Jimi Hendrix. At that time, I just couldn't get away to do it."

OCTOBER 1969

JUGGY SOUND, NEW YORK, NEW YORK. PRODUCERS: ALAN DOUGLAS, STEFAN BRIGHT. ENGINEER: STEVE KATZ. SECOND ENGINEER: RICHIE CICERO.
Juggy Sound was a small, predominantly R&B studio, which, ironically, had once been owned by legendary Sue Records chief Juggy Murray—to whom Hendrix had been under contract in July of 1965.

Douglas and Bright organized some sessions for the group here, but Cox and Bright clashed almost immediately. The root of their ill will came from Bright's preference for Rich over Cox. This issue caused considerable tension between the two men, leading to one control room incident that nearly resulted in a fistfight. "We were just goofing around during those sessions at Juggy," remembers Cox. "It was a lousy deal with a lot of bad vibes around. There was a spiritual side to the music we were creating, and the atmosphere at Juggy didn't allow Jimi to create. He sensed it and nothing we ever did there worked out. I had words with Alan's partner, Stefan Bright. I hated that guy with a passion. You couldn't create music under those circumstances. Those guys distracted my focus away from making music and I couldn't get it together. People forgot what the recording studio is all about. The studio was for creative ventures, not social gatherings. We weren't the type of musicians who had music on a music stand in front of us. We played by ear, feel, and spirit. If there is anything negative surrounding that effort, it stopped any creativity from occurring. There were times when Jimi would just shoot me a look and I would know what to do. I don't know if you would call that being telepathic, but those cues would come from him without words, and you had to be looking at him and concentrating on what you were playing—not on what was going on the control room."

Another point of contention: Cox placed little faith in the production skills of either Bright or Douglas. "Bright and Douglas knew that I didn't think they were necessary," remembers Cox. "I wasn't in their corner because I didn't think they were on Jimi's level. They weren't needed for the production of the music. Jimi was well equipped to do that. These songs were his creations and he was entitled to produce his own stuff. He didn't need any outside person to produce music for him. But because of that, Bright would do things like tell Jimi and Buddy that they didn't need me. But Jimi was determined to have me play with him. Regardless of whatever Alan or Stefan wanted, I played on most of those sessions anyway."

OCTOBER 1969

JUGGY SOUND, NEW YORK, NEW YORK. PRODUCERS: ALAN DOUGLAS, STEFAN BRIGHT. ENGINEER: STEVE KATZ. SECOND ENGINEER: RICHIE CICERO.

Working with an unnamed electric pianist, Hendrix, Miles, and Cox attempted multiple takes of "Nightbird Flying." The song had progressed considerably from its raw beginnings as "Ships Passing Through The Night," and the session began with eleven quickly

paced takes. Following a breakdown on take 11, work on the song stopped, so that Hendrix could offer instructions to the pianist and Miles regarding the song's tempo. Before work on the song resumed, Hendrix led the group through an impromptu, instrumental rendition of "Astro Man." Seven more attempts at "Nightbird Flying" were recorded, but no master was achieved.

NOVEMBER 1969

RECORD PLANT, NEW YORK, NEW YORK. PRODUCER: ALAN DOUGLAS.

One of Douglas Records' other artists sparked an impromptu session after a serendipitous meeting. "Jalal from the Last Poets was in my office just hanging out," says Douglas. "We walked down to the Record Plant, and Buddy Miles was there waiting for Hendrix. I said to Jalal, 'Why don't you do one of your poems for Buddy? Go ahead, he'll break up.' During the middle of it, Jimi arrived and got all excited about what was happening. When they finished, I went out into the studio and told Jalal to do 'Doriella Du Fontaine.' This piece was from a suite of things we were doing called *Jail Toasts*, like older black convicts would rap in prison. It started with 'Dear John' letters they would receive and in order for them to turn it around and have some fun, they would create poetry out of them. We did one take, thirteen minutes straight. When it was over, everybody was amazed that it came off nonstop. Jimi was on guitar and Buddy on drums. We overdubbed Jimi playing bass and Buddy on the organ."

While the Last Poets were the most successful act on Douglas's fledgling record label, "Doriella Du Fontaine" was never issued during Hendrix's lifetime. The track remained unreleased until 1984, when Douglas issued a 9:37 version as a twelve-inch single under license to Celluloid Records. It remains a pristine example of Hendrix's embrace of hip-hop during that music form's infancy.

FRIDAY, NOVEMBER 7, 1969

RECORD PLANT, NEW YORK, NEW YORK. ENGINEER: JACK ADAMS. SECOND ENGINEER: DAVE RAGNO.

Although Douglas's voice cannot be heard over the talkback microphone, he was most likely present at this session, as "Douglas Records," his recording label, was written on the tape box as the "client" on this evening. Cox did not take part in this session.

Without a bass player, Hendrix opened by launching directly into an up-tempo, untitled rhythm pattern that quickly took form as "Stepping Stone." Within this song he referenced "Ezy Ryder" before shifting effortlessly into a gorgeous reading of "Villanova Junction."

Recording then stopped and an unnamed pianist joined Hendrix and Miles when the tape began rolling again. "Izabella" came next, and the three tore into the song, with Hendrix confidently incorporating elements of "Freedom," another promising Hendrix original in development, before returning to the central "Izabella" rhythm structure. From "Izabella" Hendrix shifted into "Machine Gun." He viewed "Izabella" and "Machine Gun" as part of a larger musical suite, and the two had remained loosely connected during previous attempts at recording them as far back as the August Hit Factory sessions.

Hendrix's progress to date had been limited, as he had yet to devise an appropriate transition between the two songs. He tried playing them as a medley again in this recording, but Miles and the keyboardist lacked Hendrix's grasp on the still-unfinished piece, and it soon came apart.

Nonetheless, Hendrix was satisfied with the initial take of "Izabella" and requested a playback. After reviewing the group's work, he called for overdubs. The first was an inspired rhythm guitar overdub whose sound was fed through an octave-dividing tone-control pedal. Hendrix then moved the pianist to the organ, recording an overdub with that instrument before he added a driving lead guitar solo.

Shortly after reel two began, technical problems slowed the group's progress. Hendrix, in particular, was bothered by the volume and general quality of the levels being supplied to his headphones. Adams and Ragno feverishly attempted to remedy the situation, but, when recording resumed, Hendrix's amplifier started to malfunction, causing his guitar sound to drop out intermittently. This again caused a scramble in the control room. To help salvage the session, engineer

Tony Bongiovi was summoned, and though he was not listed on the tape box, his distinctive voice can be plainly heard from this point forward. When recording resumed, a series of unslated takes of "Room Full Of Mirrors" were attempted. Both Hendrix's and Miles's performances were inspired, with Hendrix singing live, straying from one take to an impromptu rendition of "Shame, Shame, Shame," a blues original whose lyrics seemingly detail Hendrix's tenuous relationship with his brother, Leon Hendrix. Another take included a raw, rough stab at "Ezy Ryder" before Hendrix returned to "Room Full Of Mirrors" with a flourish.

No masters were achieved during this session, and the tape box was marked "Outtakes." In 2006, "Stepping Stone/Villanova Junction" and "Izabella" were mixed and issued as part of Burning Desire, one of Dagger Records' official "bootlegs."

To the engineering staff at the Record Plant, the participation of Douglas and Bright had come as a surprise. "Douglas and Bright just sort of came in and took over," says Record Plant engineer Tom Erdelyi (later known as Tommy Ramone). "They were running the show. I was surprised, because I was a fan of the Jimi Hendrix Experience, and no one seemed to understand what Jimi was trying to accomplish. Jimi was such a perfectionist. It seemed as if he was just taking his time, because no tracks were being completed."

With respect to the relatively few multitrack tapes recorded under their supervision, Bright's and Douglas's specific roles were unclear. They did not seem to offer much musical guidance: of the two, Douglas was the more vocal in the studio, although only by a slight margin. "I don't know whether they had specific titles or not, but Stefan Bright was supposed to be the producer and Alan Douglas the executive producer," remembers Erdelyi. "There were times when just Stefan Bright was there, but Jimi just played what he wanted and those guys made comments from the control room."

MONDAY, NOVEMBER 10, 1969

RECORD PLANT, NEW YORK, NEW YORK. ENGINEER: BOB HUGHES. SECOND ENGINEER: DAVE RAGNO.
Hendrix, Miles, and an unknown percussionist premiered "Lonely Avenue," a new, up-tempo blues-based composition. Loosely structured on the "Blues For Me And You" demo recorded September 6, 1969, at the Hit Factory, "Lonely Avenue"'s most prominent characteristic was Hendrix's use of the Uni-Vibe tone-control pedal.

Eighteen takes were recorded on reel one, but Cox's absence had a marked effect on the proceedings. Miles struggled to establish the tempo Hendrix wanted, a problem further compounded by Hendrix's constant tinkering with the song's arrangement on the fly. A second reel of tape was loaded, and both Douglas and Hughes can be heard over the talkback microphone. "Take 1, reel two" was announced, followed by a single complete take. Hendrix then called the session to a close, seemingly distracted by a series of technical problems. No further recording was attempted.

One week later, during Hendrix's November 17 session at the studio, engineer Jack Adams returned to reel two, pulling the complete take so that additional recording, in the form of bass and guitar overdubs, could be attempted.

WEDNESDAY, NOVEMBER 12, 1969

RECORD PLANT, NEW YORK, NEW YORK. 2:00 A.M. TO 6:00 A.M. ENGINEER: BOB HUGHES.
For this session, Hendrix reached back to "Look Over Yonder," one of his oldest unfinished compositions. From the song's beginnings as "Mr. Bad Luck" during the 1967 sessions with the Experience at Olympic Studios, through its transformation as "Look Over Yonder" during the October 1968 TTG sessions, Hendrix never quite gave up on this up-tempo rocker.

Still lacking a bass player, Hendrix and Miles whipped through thirty-two largely instrumental takes during which Hendrix made an interesting alteration to the song's melody, fusing in elements of "Burning Desire," another of his unfinished pieces. While take 32 was designated as "complete," it is not known whether Hendrix ever did any further work on the song.

FRIDAY, NOVEMBER 14, 1969

RECORD PLANT, NEW YORK, NEW YORK. ENGINEER: BOB COTTO. SECOND ENGINEER: TOM ERDELYI.
Still hamstrung by the lack of a bassist, Hendrix and Miles continued their efforts to round Hendrix's new material into shape. Joined by an unnamed organist, the two kicked off this evening's session with a rambling nine-and-a-half-minute jam. Despite Miles's enthusiastic percussion, Hendrix seemed disinterested, allowing the organist to dictate the jam's direction shortly after starting.

At the jam's conclusion, the organist withdrew, leaving Hendrix and Miles to focus their energies on twenty-two takes of "Keep On Groovin'." Perhaps best described in this incarnation as an up-tempo adaptation of "Midnight Lightning," these renditions of "Keep On Groovin'" showed promise. Without Cox's rock-solid bass to maintain musical time and tempo, Miles struggled to establish the rhythm pattern Hendrix desired. Hendrix offered specific instructions to his drummer, but Miles's unfamiliarity with the song restricted his progress.

Perhaps recognizing the root of Miles's struggle, Hendrix shifted gears, kicking off reel two with a remarkable extended jam. To recapture the groove,

Hendrix and Miles locked in an extended medley that intertwined rhythm patterns from many of the promising songs the guitarist had been rounding into form including "Power Of Soul," "Burning Desire," and "Stepping Stone." Miles somehow managed to maintain musical time while Hendrix proceeded to incorporate rock, soul, funk, flamenco, and blues into this magnificent, twenty-eight-minute impromptu suite.

Reel three was dedicated to raw, driving attempts at "Stepping Stone," known at this stage as either "Trying To Be" or, as in this instance, "I'm A Man." Fifteen takes in all were recorded, with the fourteenth designated as the working master. The fourth and final reel recorded on this evening was dedicated to five takes of an instrumental effort entitled "Jungle." The exotic title seemed to have little significance, as Hendrix simply instructed the control room to label the song so that he would "know what to come back to later." "Jungle" owes much to the guitar stylings of Curtis Mayfield, one of Hendrix's favorite guitarists. Drawing heavily on his Uni-Vibe tone-control pedal, Hendrix sketched a gorgeous melody brimming with promise. Takes 1 and 4 were particularly noteworthy, each featuring strands of "Ezy Ryder" and "Villanova Junction." Sadly, Hendrix gave up on the song after five takes, calling the session to a close.

Take 1 of "Jungle" would later be mixed by Kramer and issued as part of the 2000 Dagger Records release *Morning Symphony Ideas*.

"FIRE" / "BURNING OF THE MIDNIGHT LAMP." TRACK RECORDS 604 033. U.K. SINGLE RELEASE.
With no new product forthcoming, Track Records tried the singles market again with "Fire," a favorite from *Are You Experienced*. Interest in the disc proved minimal, as "Fire" missed the U.K. charts entirely.

MONDAY, NOVEMBER 17, 1969

RECORD PLANT, NEW YORK, NEW YORK. ENGINEER: TONY BONGIOVI. SECOND ENGINEER: TOM ERDELYI.
With Cox back in the fold, convinced by Hendrix to return once more, the full contingent of Band Of Gypsys recorded "Room Full Of Mirrors," "Ezy Ryder," and "Stepping Stone." "Jimi had definitely come into the studio with a plan," says Bright. "Because 'Izabella' and 'Room Full Of Mirrors' were planned songs which took very little time to do. 'Machine Gun' was something he had been working on for quite some time. He jammed on songs like 'Dolly Dagger,' but the basic tracks for 'Izabella,' 'Stepping Stone,' 'Message To Love,' and 'Room Full Of Mirrors' were already arranged and were recorded in a very short time period."

The evening's primary focus centered on "Room Full Of Mirrors." "Jimi was a perfectionist," remembers Erdelyi. "He would record many different lead guitar solos, with each just as good as the other, but none to his satisfaction. It seemed to me that Jimi was looking for a sound that was in his head, and he was doing all kinds of things to try and capture that. He would do weird things like line a wall with stacks of Marshalls and crank them up to get this huge sustain. On 'Room Full Of Mirrors,' he was trying to get a particular slide sound. He tried all kinds of slides—glass slides, metal slides, steel-pedal slides—but none of them sounded like what he was hearing in his head."

According to Douglas, the solution to the problem came when Hendrix, still lacking the appropriate tool for his finger, slipped off his ring and used its stone to create the desired effect.

Hendrix did record a lead vocal track for "Room Full Of Mirrors," although not without incident. "Jimi hated his voice," says Bright. "I guess the other people who had worked with him knew this, but we didn't. When it came time to record his vocals, he instructed the engineer and the assistant engineer to set up baffles around him and turn all of the lights in the studio out. I said, 'What the fuck are you talking about your voice for? Your voice is unique and it's a part of your whole sound.' He said, 'I don't care what you say. This is the way I feel and this is what we are going to do.'"

In addition to recording a lead vocal, Hendrix recruited twin brothers Albert and Arthur Allen, his long-time friends from Harlem, to provide backing vocals. Hendrix escorted the pair, known professionally as the Ghetto Fighters, to the studio, where he instructed them on their parts. After running through the song, Hendrix and the twin brothers visited Studio B, where Mountain were mixing their album. "Leslie West was recording

'Mississippi Queen' in Studio B, and Hendrix was so knocked out by the riff that he invited him over for a jam," remembers Arthur Allen.

The chance meeting thrilled West. "I first saw Jimi play at Woodstock," recalls West. "I missed meeting him there, but when we were recording *Mountain Climbing* at the Record Plant, he heard the riff to 'Mississippi Queen' and just walked into the control room. He sat down next to [Mountain bassist and producer] Felix Pappalardi and I, and we played him the mix to 'Never In My Life.' He was the first guy outside of the band to ever hear it. When he heard the lick I was playing, he just turned and looked at me. For some reason, the riff sounded like a horn line and it got a rise out of him. Seeing him react like that made me think, 'Wow! He must think I have a little something in me!' In fact, he even came to see us play at the Fillmore East. He was sitting in one of those Opera seats next to [Mountain drummer] Corky Laing's mother. She didn't know who the hell he was, but when we saw him there watching *us* play, that was a big deal."

TUESDAY, NOVEMBER 18, 1969

RECORD PLANT, NEW YORK, NEW YORK. ENGINEER: DAVE RAGNO.

Take 14 of "I'm A Man," recorded on November 14, 1969, was pulled out and treated with multiple bass and guitar overdubs. Cox recorded new bass parts, while Hendrix added no fewer than four lead guitar parts. By the close of the session, Hendrix had come closer to recognizing a finished master, but additional work on the song would continue in the months to come.

THURSDAY, NOVEMBER 20, 1969

RECORD PLANT, NEW YORK, NEW YORK. 5:00 P.M. ENGINEER: BOB HUGHES. SECOND ENGINEER: DAVE RAGNO.

Hendrix, Cox, and Miles taped six solid but unspectacular takes of the Miles composition "Them Changes." Takes 5 and 6 were complete, though neither was considered a master. Twelve subpar instrumental takes of "Burning Desire" followed, presented with barely a trace of enthusiasm. None was complete, and few even remotely came close to the mark. Hendrix seemed

unsettled about his guitar tone, shifting, with little success, between takes.

Reel two began with two uninspired attempts at "Lover Man," described here as "Here Comes Your Lover Man." Three halfhearted takes of "Hear My Train A Comin'" followed, paced by a live vocal from Hendrix. "That was a song Jimi had done with the original Experience," remembers Cox. "It was a simple blues song in the key of B, but he felt comfortable doing it because it was Jimi's kind of blues. I think the lyrics he had for the song, about coming back to buy the town and put it all in his shoe, was his way of talking back to the establishment. That was Jimi's way of singing the blues. People weren't going to be able to push him out of the way because he was going to get rich and buy the town out from under them."

A return to "Burning Desire" met with similar disinterest, as did a brief reprise of "Them Changes." The session collapsed at this point. Though it's not clear what exactly soured Hendrix's mood on this occasion, this surely ranks among Hendrix's most unproductive experiences in the recording studio.

FRIDAY, NOVEMBER 21, 1969

RECORD PLANT, NEW YORK, NEW YORK. ENGINEER: TONY BONGIOVI. SECOND ENGINEER: TOM ERDELYI.

Bright and Douglas endeavored to try and redirect Hendrix's sagging spirits. "We specifically brought in Tony Bongiovi to engineer 'Izabella,'" explains Bright. "Jimi would say things about Tony like, 'What the fuck is this kid doing in the studio?' because Tony, at that time, looked very young. Tony gave Jimi's sound a groove, which, we felt, hadn't been done before. With 'Izabella,' the sound of the bass and drums was so funky. Tony had worked in Motown and he went for that element in his sound."

As intended, "Izabella" was reconstructed from the bottom up, beginning with a very loose initial take. Subsequent takes increasingly took shape. Via the talkback microphone, Douglas could be heard directing the session, providing comments along with Bright and Bongiovi. Of the nineteen attempts made on this reel, takes 1, 2, 4, 10, 12, 16, and 19 were complete.

Following a tape change, one last attempt at

"Izabella" was recorded, and this take, the twentieth of the evening, delivered the basic track.

The focus then turned to "Burning Desire." This effort, however, was not as successful. As "Izabella" had done, "Burning Desire" gradually improved over twenty-four takes, but none captured the intensity Hendrix was searching for. Not having a fully defined rhythm pattern caused some confusion for Miles, who struggled with some of the tempo changes. A version of "Machine Gun" was also attempted on this evening, but its arrangement had only slightly varied from that heard on the primitive demo Hendrix had recorded during the August 1969 sessions at the Hit Factory. Four takes were recorded, and only the fourth and final take was complete. There was nothing in this unrealized demo to even hint at Hendrix's evolving vision for this powerful song.

Unable to make progress at this stage with "Machine Gun," Hendrix turned to "Power Of Soul," described here as "Paper Airplanes." Twenty-four takes were attempted, with no live vocals from Hendrix. At this stage, the group was still honing the song's complex arrangement. In addition to the main riff, Hendrix liberally experimented with his rhythm and solo parts. Of the many takes recorded, only take 2 could be described as complete. That version was immediately cast aside as Hendrix, Cox, and Miles performed the song repeatedly in an attempt to learn their parts and establish the tempo Hendrix wanted.

Despite the hints of promise evident in these November sessions, neither Bright nor Douglas had been able to make any significant progress with Hendrix. Jeffery and his team took a dim view of Douglas, whom they viewed as little more than an opportunist. "They were a joke, not even in the same league as Hendrix," says Gerry Stickells. "That became evident in no time, as Hendrix's thinking was light-years ahead of those two. Nothing was ever used from those sessions with Douglas—he didn't do that many anyway. Tracks like 'Izabella'? Hendrix did those. As for Stefan Bright, that guy was supposed to be the producer and Douglas his supervisor or manager or something like that. He got heaved out and then Douglas tried to fill his shoes, but all he seemed to do was sit around the studio. Hendrix was too nice; he just couldn't turn these people away."

Douglas defends his short tenure with Hendrix, regretting that the guitarist's many previous months of undisciplined recording sessions had, in his opinion, compromised Hendrix's ability to work efficiently in the recording studio. "That was my frustration with him," explains Douglas. "That's why we got nowhere near what we should have gotten out of those sessions. Most of it was jamming because they couldn't get the tunes together."

FRIDAY, NOVEMBER 28, 1969

RECORD PLANT, NEW YORK, NEW YORK.

A two-track mix was made on this day of the May 22, 1969, "Message From Nine To The Universe." The only legend marked on the tape box was "Buddy Miles/Billy Cox." It is not known if further work was considered on this particular recording or if any other multitrack recording took place.

The November sessions mark the conclusion of Douglas's brief stint as a producer for Hendrix. In a December 4, 1969, letter to Hendrix, citing his own busy schedule, constant pressure from Jeffery, and Hendrix's own disinterest, Douglas parted company from the guitarist.

Save for the basic rhythm track for "Room Full Of Mirrors," which Hendrix would later overhaul at Electric Lady Studios in August 1970, not one of these November 1969 session tapes was recognized by Hendrix as candidates for his long-overdue fourth studio disc. Even Douglas could not make use of these tapes in his work after Hendrix's death, opting instead, when he began assembling the controversial *Crash Landing* album in 1974, to take creative license and overdub rhythm parts on to other unfinished Hendrix tapes—using session musicians to replace the original contributions made by Hendrix's sidemen.

In 1995, Hendrix's father, James "Al" Hendrix, won a protracted and bitterly contested legal victory against his former attorney, Leo J. Branton, and Douglas. As a result of the case, all of the Douglas-supervised albums, save for 1994's *Jimi Hendrix: Blues* (although Al Hendrix mandated that new liner notes and corrected track annotations be included in future editions of that album beginning in 1998) were

removed from the marketplace throughout the world. The conclusion of this case effectively ended the last chapter in Douglas's turbulent, twenty-year stewardship of the Hendrix catalog.

MONDAY, DECEMBER 15, 1969

RECORD PLANT, NEW YORK, NEW YORK. 3:00 A.M. ENGINEER: BOB COTTO. SECOND ENGINEER: R. BEEKMAN.
This upbeat session yielded some surprises, most notably the lengthy rendition of Albert King's "Born Under A Bad Sign," later released as part of the 1994 compilation *Jimi Hendrix: Blues*. Following "Born Under A Bad Sign," whose title, Hendrix quipped at the end of the song, was "Born Under A Bad Armpit," the session took on the appearance of a rehearsal. A spirited "Lover Man" came next, albeit without a vocal from Hendrix. Seemingly satisfied with the group's handle on that song, Hendrix suggested that they try "Izabella." What followed was a sped-up rendition with only occasional vocals from Hendrix. Hendrix then shifted to "Earth Blues," treating this single take in a similar fashion. Two promising takes of "Message To Love" followed, again with only casual vocal accompaniment from Hendrix. These two renditions sported a different arrangement from either of the versions issued as part of *Band Of Gypsys* or

Crash Landing. Miles assumed center stage for "Them Changes," enhanced by some strong rhythm and lead playing from Hendrix. The group managed to complete a single, effective take before abandoning the track.

Now locked in a groove, the group next recorded seven takes of "Lover Man." These versions, rather surprisingly, never quite gelled. Miles seemed to struggle with maintaining a consistent tempo. Switching to "Burning Desire," the musicians were beset by the same problems they encountered during "Lover Man." Moving on, the group recorded nine incomplete takes of "Power Of Soul," marked here as "With The Power." Hendrix offered no vocals, concentrating instead on developing the song's basic rhythm track.

THURSDAY, DECEMBER 18, 1969

RECORD PLANT, NEW YORK, NEW YORK. ENGINEER: JACK ADAMS. SECOND ENGINEER: TOM ERDELYI.
Significant progress was made on "Message To Love," "Ezy Ryder," and "Bleeding Heart." "Ezy Ryder" began this session on a high note, providing the basic track that, ultimately, would later be expanded and completed at Electric Lady Studios the following summer. Joining the group on this session was percussionist Billy Armstrong. "We started 'Ezy Ryder' here at the Record

Plant," explains Cox, "but it wasn't finished until the following summer at Electric Lady. Jimi had come up with the main pattern, but I had, '*da da da dum, da da did da da*,' and didn't know what to do with it. Jimi built on it from there and it became a living, breathing song, rather than just a combinations of patterns."

The group next turned its focus to "Message To Love." The early takes revealed problems the group was having establishing the desired tempo. "We toyed with the tempo on that song," admits Cox. "Buddy wanted to slow it down, but Jimi wanted it more upbeat. Jimi would say, 'If you can't see little kids skippin' on your fast songs, you got nothing.'" Eighteen takes in all were recorded, with the eighteenth denoted as the master.

Three takes of "Bleeding Heart" were also attempted, done up-tempo as opposed to a slower traditional twelve-bar blues arrangement. The third was complete but not identified as a master. Rough mixes were also prepared of "Ezy Ryder" and "Message To Love."

FRIDAY, DECEMBER 19, 1969

RECORD PLANT, NEW YORK, NEW YORK. 3:00 A.M. ENGINEER: BOB COTTO. SECOND ENGINEER: R. BEEKMAN.
Building on the momentum created the previous evening, the Band Of Gypsys completed basic tracks for both "Message To Love" and "Earth Blues." A single take of "Message To Love" captured the working master for that song, while "Earth Blues" required sixteen takes. Ultimately, Hendrix chose take 11 to serve as the basic track. At this stage, while the arrangement remained the same, Hendrix's lyrics for "Earth Blues" differed from later versions. Hendrix also superimposed both a lead vocal and lead guitar part on to this recording, but both of these efforts were later replaced by new overdubs. Backing vocals from Miles and the Ronettes were also recorded.

Also recorded on this evening was a short, untitled instrumental later named "Strato Strut." The group recorded only a single take of this infectious funk workout, nonetheless, "Strato Strut" offers telling insight into the influence the Band Of Gypsys, and Hendrix in particular, had on the funk movement of the 1970s and beyond. Many years later, in 1980, an edited section of this recording was slated to become part of the post-

humous compilation *Nine To The Universe*. It was, however, inexplicably removed from the album during its final production stages. The full-length recording was issued in 2000 as part of the Dagger Records "bootleg" album *Morning Symphony Ideas*.

DECEMBER 18–23, DECEMBER 27–29, 1969

BAGGY'S STUDIOS, NEW YORK, NEW YORK.
Under increasing pressure to deliver an album to Capitol Records to satisfy the outstanding Capitol/PPX legal settlement, Jeffery decided to record all four of the Fillmore East performances scheduled for December 31 and January 1. Hendrix redirected his energy away from additional studio recording and toward preparations for the live album. "With the Fillmore East shows coming up, the studio was laid aside and we rehearsed at a place called Baggy's in New York," explains Cox. "It was located down by Chinatown. We were there prior to Christmas and then a little after, practicing and rehearsing. We realized that we had to do four shows and were working up a set of the songs we were going to perform for the concerts."

Baggy's Studios was a nondescript Manhattan rehearsal facility opened by former Soft Machine road manager Tom Edmonston. It was not a recording studio designed to compete with the likes of the Record Plant; it offered no control room or sophisticated recording equipment. Its primary purpose was to provide a space for artists to rehearse without restriction. "Baggy's had two floors," remembers Cox. "It was essentially warehouse space. We worked in the large room downstairs. It was a pretty simple setup. There were rugs on the floor and the walls were padded and soundproofed." While commonplace now, the concept of a dedicated rehearsal room for rock acts—as opposed to vacant halls or theaters—had just begun to take hold in 1969. "The recording studio was exclusively used for creating and coming up with something new and different. This was something else," Cox explains. "Previous to that time, whenever Jimi wanted to rehearse something he would call me up and I would come over to his apartment and we would play through some small amps. Rehearsal space did not exist as we know it today." Perhaps most important, Baggy's rental rates were a fraction of the cost of similar time at the Record Plant. With Hendrix's finances hamstrung by the construction-cost overruns of his own Electric Lady Studios and the continuing PPX litigation in the U.K., this was an important consideration.

While Baggy's did not staff a recording engineer or technical staff, recordings could be made at 7 $\frac{1}{2}$ i.p.s. on a two-track reel-to-reel tape machine. Hendrix took full advantage of this and recorded several reels of the enthusiastic rehearsals. "It seemed like Jimi and I always had a recorder running there," recalls Cox. "It was like every move we were making there was being taped by somebody!" For Hendrix, these recordings served as a convenient tool to measure the group's progress throughout the rehearsals. Gene McFadden, a member of Hendrix's road crew, organized the group's equipment and installed a sound system from which a feed was patched into the tape recorder. Hendrix loaded a full spool of tape and essentially left the machine to run. Each song was recorded live with no overdubs.

The recordings made by Hendrix at Baggy's provide a fascinating insight into his unique approach to song development. Hendrix can be heard tinkering with both arrangements and lyrics, enthusiastically refining songs such as "Message To Love," "Ezy Ryder," "Power Of Soul," "Earth Blues," and "Burning Desire." By all accounts, Baggy's served its purpose well. Over the course of several marathon sessions at the facility, Band Of Gypsys made marked progress, rounding these budding prospects into form. "When we got together at Baggy's to prepare for the Fillmore East, from day one, it was really a trip," says Miles. He describes Hendrix as "a guy who could just play *anything* soulfully. I asked him where he came up with this stuff, and he said that he liked to listen and play a lot. He never knew how to write or read music."

Because these tapes were considered work tapes by Hendrix and therefore stored mostly at his home, they were among the many items looted from his apartment following his death. A few reels have survived, and they contain recordings made on December 18 and 19. These reels include, in order, six takes of "Message To Love," three takes of "Ezy Ryder," three additional takes of "Message To Love," one take each of "Ezy Ryder," "Power Of Soul," and "Earth Blues," two takes

of "Them Changes," two takes of "Lover Man," one take each of "Them Changes," "We Gotta Live Together," "Stop," "Burning Desire," "Baggy's Jam," "Earth Blues," "Ezy Ryder," and "Message To Love," six takes of "Who Knows," two takes of "Message To Love," one take of "Power Of Soul" and "Ezy Ryder," two takes of "Earth Blues," and one take each of "Burning Desire," "Izabella," "Machine Gun," "Power Of Soul," "Ezy Ryder," "Stepping Stone," and "Hoochie Coochie Man." In addition to these songs, Hendrix also recorded a superb medley of "Little Drummer Boy," "Silent Night," and "Auld Lang Syne."

Tapes of a Baggy's session loosely pegged as December 20 surfaced in recent years. These tapes include one take of "Come On (Let The Good Times Roll)," five takes of "Power Of Soul," one take of "Them Changes," three takes of "Burning Desire," and one take each of "Stone Free," "We Gotta Live Together," "Stop," "Take It Off Him And Put It on Me," and "Stepping Stone."

Despite the rough-hewn sonic quality of the Baggy's tapes, a few excerpts from Hendrix's rehearsals at Baggy's have been commercially issued. "Burning Desire" and "Hoochie Coochie Man" first appeared internationally in 1973 as part of the long since out-of-print *Loose Ends* compilation. In recent years, the Baggy's recording of Hendrix's yuletide medley of "Little Drummer Boy," "Silent Night," and "Auld Lang Syne" was issued on the CD single *Merry Christmas And A Happy New Year*. The 2002 Dagger Records compilation *Baggy's Rehearsals Sessions* provided a full picture of these interesting recordings. This album reintroduced "Burning Desire" and "Hoochie Coochie Man," as well as ten excerpts from the December 18 and 19 sessions.

TUESDAY, DECEMBER 23, 1969

RECORD PLANT, NEW YORK, NEW YORK. ENGINEER: BOB COTTO. SECOND ENGINEER: TOM ERDELYI.
Sadly, technical failures brought this spirited Band Of Gypsys session to an abrupt close, but not before "Honey Bed," a lively hybrid of "Bleeding Heart" and "Come Down Hard On Me," debuted. Hendrix was in fine spirits, remarking, in his best Pigmeat Markham voice, that the track was called, "Honey bed, sweet-

nins, and a yam!" which filled the control room with laughter. Three funky albeit incomplete takes were recorded, with Hendrix alternately singing and humming the lyrics. The majority of the lyrics Hendrix did sing—including such phrases as "Do I Live Or Do I Die?" and "You Got Me Sitting Up On Your Shelf"—were later grafted on to other Hendrix compositions.

As take 3 wound down, Hendrix guided Cox and Miles through a primitive, instrumental rendition of "Night Bird Flying." Just past the two-minute mark, a terrifying squelching sound caused Hendrix to shout, "Hey guys, what's that noise?" The sound rapidly grew louder before the recording cut out and the session came to a halt. No other recording was attempted.

WEDNESDAY, DECEMBER 31, 1969

FILLMORE EAST, NEW YORK, NEW YORK. TWO SHOWS. WITH THE VOICES OF EAST HARLEM. ENGINEER: WALLY HEIDER. SECOND ENGINEER: JIM ROBERTSON. **FIRST SET:** "POWER OF SOUL" / "LOVER MAN" / "HEAR MY TRAIN A COMIN'" / "CHANGES" / "IZABELLA" / "MACHINE GUN" / "STOP" / "EZY RIDER" / "BLEEDING HEART" / "EARTH BLUES" / "BURNING DESIRE." **SECOND SET:** "AULD LANG SYNE" / "WHO KNOWS" / "STEPPING STONE" / "BURNING DESIRE" / "FIRE" / "EZY RYDER" / "MACHINE GUN" / "POWER OF SOUL" / "STONE FREE" / "SUNSHINE OF YOUR LOVE" / "MESSAGE TO LOVE" / "STOP" / "FOXEY LADY" / "VOODOO CHILD (SLIGHT RETURN)" / "PURPLE HAZE"

While promoter Bill Graham had advertised the concerts as "Jimi Hendrix: A Band Of Gypsys," few could have possibly anticipated what Hendrix had prepared. There was no formal press announcement about the concerts from Hendrix's management team or Reprise. Because no one quite knew how well the concerts would go, no one at Capitol Records was informed that Hendrix hoped to form the new required settlement album from his Fillmore East performances. Nonetheless, the Band Of Gypsys were poised to surprise the sold-out Fillmore audiences. "We had two shows New Year's Eve and two shows New Year's Day," recalls Cox. "We didn't know what to expect from the audience, and the audience didn't know what to expect from us, but from the time we hit that first note, they were in awe."

"There was a lot of pressure," Cox adds, "because people were worried about the group because at one point in time you had Jimi Hendrix standing there with two white boys on his side. Then all of sudden he made a transition and there was two black guys. The executives were worried, but the fans didn't give a damn. The fans wanted good music and they had realized that this was about music, not color or gender. It was about good, get-down-to-earth music. That's what we were all about."

Both of the Band Of Gypsys' remarkable performances on this evening were preserved for posterity. The eleven-song first set was a tour-de-force, with Hendrix casting aside Experience favorites such as "Purple Haze" and "Foxey Lady" and instead presenting songs yet to grace a Hendrix album to an enthusiastic, packed house. "Our music was spread [across] a wide spectrum," recalls Miles. "You had rockers, you had R&B, soul, and most definitely blues. For instance, when we played 'Stop' by Howard Tate, the original version and the way that it was produced was most definitely uptown rhythm and blues, with a New York sound, but we kind of dissected it, which was cool. That's one of the things about the Band Of Gypsys that I loved, because we could kind of like make our own baby—blues baby, rock baby, pop baby—and put them all together, man, and come up with this formula. It was like a soulful fragment."

At midnight, Kip Cohen, the venue's master of ceremonies, rang in the new year—and decade—accompanied by Guy Lombardo's "Auld Lang Syne." Never one to be upstaged, Hendrix and company greeted the joyous house with their own inspired reading of the holiday staple. The balance of the group's performance was equally inspiring.

Hendrix was heartened by the warm response he received from the Fillmore audiences. "Jimi enjoyed doing those shows," remembers Cox. "He was enjoying himself because he had complete freedom, and freedom is a joyous thing when you've got it. We didn't have any worries about what we could or couldn't do. These were our first shows. We were pretty rebellious at that age. I guess that's why we played the music so loud. He didn't have any restrictions, and that is a lot of freedom. You can hear that on every song we played."

1970

"He would say, 'Man, we don't fish or go bowling like other people do. We make music and *this* is fun.'"
—BILLY COX, QUOTING JIMI HENDRIX

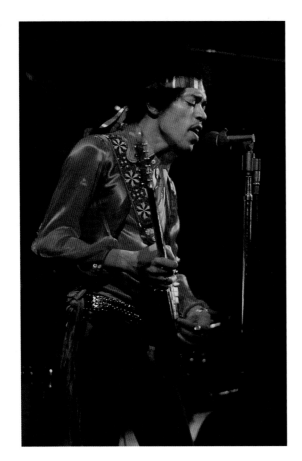

THURSDAY, JANUARY 1, 1970

FILLMORE EAST, NEW YORK, NEW YORK. ENGINEER: WALLY HEIDER. SECOND ENGINEER: JIM ROBERTSON. TWO SHOWS. WITH THE VOICES OF EAST HARLEM. **SET LIST, FIRST SHOW**: "WHO KNOWS" / "MACHINE GUN" / "CHANGES (THEM CHANGES)" / "POWER OF SOUL" / "STEPPING STONE" / "FOXEY LADY" / "STOP" / "EARTH BLUES" / "BURNING DESIRE." **SET LIST, SECOND SHOW**: "STONE FREE" / "POWER OF SOUL" / "CHANGES" / "MESSAGE TO LOVE" / "EARTH BLUES" / "MACHINE GUN" / "VOODOO CHILD (SLIGHT RETURN)" / "WE GOTTA LIVE TOGETHER" / "WILD THING" / "HEY JOE" / "PURPLE HAZE"

It is from these superb performances that the album *Band Of Gypsys* was drawn. "Who Knows" and "Machine Gun" hail from the first show; the four songs that formed the album's second side were selected from the evening's second performance. The unequivocal

highlight of this evening was Hendrix's definitive rendition of "Machine Gun." "That song was Jimi's personal condemnation of war in general," explains Kramer. "It was a revealing, dramatic statement that has always had tremendous emotional impact." "Jimi was aware of the political situation at the time," echoes Buddy Miles. "He purposely told me what 'Machine Gun' was all about. Beyond that, if you listen to the melody lines of 'Machine Gun,' it was really taken from a style of music which is called Delta blues. This is royal blues, like how they used to do it in the Deep South. Jimi had a deep fascination for Muddy Waters, but that particular song was definitely not Chicago blues style. I think it was most definitely from the Deep South that he came up with the time signature for that song."

On nights such as this, when called to give two performances, Hendrix had a tendency to treat the set list as one extended show, as opposed to playing the same songs twice in one evening. Some songs would invariably overlap, but the guitarist never worked with a prearranged script. On this evening, he once again eschewed most of his popular standards and instead concentrated on songs he had never before performed publicly, let alone issued on disc.

The evening's second set was as impressive as the first, beginning with an extraordinary, expanded performance of "Stone Free." During both sets, Hendrix generously extended center stage to Miles, who showcased two of his own compositions, "We Gotta Live Together," "Changes," and a cover of the Howard Tate R&B hit "Stop." Two of Miles's performances graced *Band Of Gypsys*, while "Stop," an alternate rendition of "Changes," and an expanded version of "We Gotta Live Together" later became part of *Live At The Fillmore East*. "We had rehearsed 'Changes' and a few others for Buddy," explains Billy Cox. "We didn't look at it as Buddy's part of the show. We were all there to give, we were all there to help, so it just happened. Material went on [the album] whether it was written by Jimi or not."

A spirited medley of "Voodoo Child (Slight Return)" and "We Gotta Live Together" brought the show to a close. The group then returned for a raucous, three-song encore that shook the venerable theater. "Hendrix made it a point of being modest during those Fillmore shows," remembers Miles. "But by [the end of the second January 1 performance], we had been jamming for almost four hours and I could see it building up in him. He wanted to cut loose and have some fun."

As the Fillmore audience roared with approval, the Band Of Gypsys left the stage confident that they had validated Hendrix's new music before his loyal followers. "We felt the concerts went well," explains Cox. "We felt good doing them, and Jimi did all of his powerful techniques he could think of. Then [during the first] show he just stayed there and got into it so heavy it was incredible. I might add that in previous gigs with the Experience he used a Fuzz Face and a wah-wah pedal, then at Woodstock he used a Fuzz Face, wah-wah pedal, and Uni-Vibe, but at the Fillmore East he used a Fuzz Face, wah-wah pedal, Uni-Vibe, and Octavia and it was incredible. In fact you could hear all of it kicking in on 'Machine Gun.' It was incredible. There were people in the audience with their mouths open. After the shows were finished, Jimi was quite relieved. He had fulfilled his obligation and was getting this whole [situation] off his back."

Despite the dizzying peaks of the Fillmore East performances, the four concerts seemed to confirm quiet reservations Hendrix and his management team had about Miles's undefined role in the group. Miles had a strong ego, and Hendrix did not view the Band Of Gypsys as a partnership. Moreover, he was aggravated by the drummer's presumptive behavior and abuse of privileges such as limousine services, dental work, and airline tickets for family members. "Jimi truly loved Buddy," explains Cox, "but *he* was the star. *He* was the boss. This was an unspoken issue, but all you have to do is listen to any Band Of Gypsys performance and you will hear it. We musicians have to be careful not to cross these boundary lines. You have to pay homage to Caesar. Render unto Caesar the things which are Caesar's. Sometimes that did not happen. That disturbed Jimi, and I think Buddy finally became aware of this by the end."

WEDNESDAY, JANUARY 7, 1970

RECORD PLANT, NEW YORK, NEW YORK. ENGINEER: BOB HUGHES. SECOND ENGINEER: TOM ERDELYI.
Following the success of the four Fillmore East

performances, much of the stress and discontent that had dogged Hendrix throughout 1969 began to subside. While he had not yet reviewed the Fillmore East live tapes, he was certain that there was sufficient material in hand to deliver the long-overdue PPX settlement album to Capitol Records.

January of 1970 was a productive time for Hendrix. As the month progressed, he split his time between mixing the *Band Of Gypsys* live album at Juggy Sound Studios with Kramer and staging enthusiastic sessions at the Record Plant with Cox and Miles.

This January 7 session was Hendrix's first since the triumphant Fillmore East performances the previous week. He returned to "Cherokee Mist," a song whose origins could be traced back more than two years prior. Interestingly, Hendrix sought to merge "Cherokee Mist" with "Astro Man," another exciting new composition. This spirited take, the only one attempted on this evening, once more reveals Hendrix's unique approach to song construction. His efforts to blend "Cherokee Mist" with "Astro Man" continued in the weeks that followed, but, over time, the latter emerged as a separate song. "Astro Man" was never released during Hendrix's lifetime, but Dagger Records later featured the version recorded on this evening as part of *Burning Desire*, an official "bootleg" compilation issued in 2006.

Hendrix followed "Cherokee Mist" with three complete takes of "I'm A Man." Take 3 provided the basic track on to which overdubs were recorded on January 20, 1970. This new master, retitled "Stepping Stone" and coupled with "Izabella," was later mixed and issued as a Reprise single in April of 1970.

Before the evening ended, a guitar overdub and new mix for "Roomful Of Mirrors" was completed before mixes were prepared for "Izabella" and "Ezy Ryder." Hendrix marked all three of these mixes "rough" on the tape box.

WEDNESDAY, JANUARY 14, 1970

JUGGY SOUND STUDIOS, NEW YORK, NEW YORK. ENGINEER: EDDIE KRAMER. SECOND ENGINEER: KIM KING.
Together with Kramer, Hendrix began to sift through the multitrack recordings made of the Band Of Gypsys' live performances at the Fillmore East. "I don't know

that Jimi felt that these concerts were his best performances, but there were parts of them that he was really happy with," says Kramer. "Certainly 'Machine Gun' and tracks like 'Message To Love' sounded pretty good. At the time, he didn't want to include new songs that he wanted to finish in Electric Lady. Jimi was kind of resigned to the fact that here we are, we have to mix this, we got to give it to Capitol, it wasn't a Warner's record, let's do the best we can with it. Let's cut it down and make it a decent album."

THURSDAY, JANUARY 15, 1970

JUGGY SOUND STUDIOS, NEW YORK, NEW YORK. ENGINEER: EDDIE KRAMER.

Hendrix and Kramer continued their review of the multi-track recordings made of the Band of Gypsys' live performances at the Fillmore East.

FRIDAY, JANUARY 16, 1970

JUGGY SOUND STUDIOS, NEW YORK, NEW YORK. ENGINEER: EDDIE KRAMER.

Hendrix began the evening with Kramer at Juggy Sound. The two continued to narrow their choices for the proposed Band Of Gypsys live album. "Mixing the *Band Of Gypsys* album was a challenge," remembers Kramer. "It was like Jimi was really almost pressured into doing it. Hearing Buddy's [vamping] seemed to bother him. We were sitting there and he was like, 'Oh man, I wish Buddy would shut the fuck up.' He would listen to him and say, 'Can we cut some of those parts out?' I ended up editing a lot of Buddy's quote unquote 'jamming', where he would go off and sing a lot."

RECORD PLANT, NEW YORK, NEW YORK. ENGINEER: BOB HUGHES. SECOND ENGINEER: DAVE RAGNO.
Following his work at Juggy Sound, Hendrix headed to the Record Plant to meet Cox and Miles. They began with a short, up-tempo instrumental jam, which, at this embryonic stage, was more a fertile rhythm pattern than a formal song.

Hendrix then presented a rough sketch of the medium-tempo ballad "Send My Love To Linda." With Hendrix's guitar and live vocal setting the pace, Cox and Miles established the tempo. Though Hendrix had only developed the song's rudiments, one take evolved into a lively, extended jam session. Encouraged by the group's progress, Hendrix began a second take. This effort was even stronger in parts than the first, but both takes lacked an ending. Five takes in all made it clear that, despite its promise, "Send My Love To Linda" was not yet fully developed.

Next came twelve takes of "Paper Airplanes," better known as "Power Of Soul." Take 6, which followed five incomplete efforts, held promise, but the song had not yet fully formed. Takes 11 and 12 were also complete, but, again, an acceptable basic track eluded Hendrix. He then turned his attention to "Burning Desire," and directed the group through five inspired instrumental takes, but the effort left him shy of a finished basic track.

SATURDAY, JANUARY 17, 1970

RECORD PLANT, NEW YORK, NEW YORK. ENGINEER: BOB HUGHES. SECOND ENGINEER: DAVE RAGNO.

This lengthy mixing and guitar-overdub session focused on "Izabella," "Roomful Of Mirrors," "Stepping Stone," "Message To Love," and "Ezy Ryder." No final masters, however, were achieved.

MONDAY, JANUARY 19, 1970

JUGGY SOUND STUDIOS, NEW YORK, NEW YORK. ENGINEER: EDDIE KRAMER.

A work pattern had begun to develop that saw Hendrix beginning his evening with Kramer at Juggy Sound before venturing to the Record Plant to meet up with Cox and Miles. Neither Cox nor Miles played any role in the mixing or song selection decisions for the *Band Of Gypsys* live album. As Hendrix was the producer, such decisions were reserved entirely for him.

NEW YORK, RECORD PLANT. ENGINEER: BOB HUGHES. SECOND ENGINEER: DAVE RAGNO.

At the Record Plant, Hendrix turned his attention once again to "Burning Desire." The group achieved several promising takes, but the master Hendrix sought still eluded him.

Hendrix then initiated an interesting recording that featured two backward guitars. No one knows the purpose behind this experiment, but it's clear that Hendrix was trying to achieve a particular sound and effect before work completed.

Prior the conclusion of the session, Hendrix created a mix of "Send My Love To Linda," drawing on the first take that had been recorded on January 16.

TUESDAY, JANUARY 20, 1970

RECORD PLANT, NEW YORK, NEW YORK. ENGINEER: BOB HUGHES. SECOND ENGINEER: DAVE RAGNO.
During this vibrant session, Hendrix made progress on "Message To Love," adding a new lead-guitar overdub to the song's December 19, 1969, working master.

Hendrix also added new guitar and lead-vocal parts to the eleventh take of "Earth Blues"— recorded during that same December 19 session as "Message To Love." These overdubs were replaced at Electric Lady Studios on June 26, 1970. Mixes of "Izabella" were also prepared during this January session, but Hendrix didn't deem any of them acceptable.

Take 3 of "I'm A Man," recorded on January 7, was rechristened "Sky Blues Today." Hendrix added overdubs to it, as well as to the December 18, 1969, recording of another promising albeit unfinished Band Of Gypsys rocker, "Ezy Ryder" (still known at that stage as "Easy Rider").

Hendrix's acquittal on drug charges in Canada, coupled with his recent progress with the Band Of Gypsys, had brightened his mood considerably. "You really could see that Jimi had turned the corner," says Ragno. "Jimi cut back on the party crowd and was trying to focus on his work. He came in alone on a lot of nights, just wanting to do guitar overdubs or experiment with some mix ideas that he had. His creativity was on the upswing because he didn't have all of these people around him. His own drug use, just by what we could see, had also diminished. It was a healthier situation. I got to see a different side of him as compared to when the Experience was falling apart during the spring. He was a sensitive, gentle person who was creative and enjoyed a genuine laugh. We would often go up to the roof of the Record Plant with [engineer] Jack Adams and make paper airplanes. We would have contests to see who could throw them farther across the street. [Record Plant co-owner] Chris Stone must have wondered where all the stationery was going!"

Mixes were prepared for all of the songs completed on this evening. "Earth Blues," "Sky Blues Today," and "Ezy Ryder" were reconstructed at Electric Lady Studios during the summer of 1970. "Message To Love," however, was not. While Hendrix had, for all intents and purposes, completed "Message To Love" at this point, he issued a superior live version first, as part of *Band Of Gypsys*. As the song's live version appeared on that album, this studio recording was never considered for *First Rays Of The New Rising Sun*, Hendrix's projected double album, which was to follow *Band Of Gypsys*.

In 1974, when Alan Douglas and engineer Les Kahn undertook a full review of the Hendrix tape library, this nearly finished studio version of "Message To Love" represented one of their strongest finds. Apart from some incidental percussion added by session musician Jimmy Maeulin in 1974, the track didn't require additional overdubs. Douglas did however edit the original multitrack master, removing a portion of the song's second verse during which Hendrix's vocal had wavered. This edited master was ultimately remixed and added to *Crash Landing*. Kramer prepared a mix in 1997 that eliminated the percussion overdubs made by Douglas; this mix was featured as part of the *Jimi Hendrix Experience* box set.

WEDNESDAY, JANUARY 21, 1970

JUGGY SOUND STUDIOS, NEW YORK, NEW YORK. ENGINEER: EDDIE KRAMER.
Progress continued on *Band Of Gypsys* as Hendrix and Kramer further narrowed the pool of songs considered for the album. "Message To Love" (January 1, second show) was an early contender, joining the ranks of "Hear My Train A Comin'" (December 31, first show) , "Power Of Soul" (January 1, both performances), "Hey Joe" (January 1, second show), "Izabella" (December 31, first show), "Wild Thing" (January 1, second show), and all four renditions of "Machine Gun" (December 31 and January 1, first and second shows).

Technical gremlins rendered the first two songs from the early show on December 31 unusable: Hendrix's vocals had not been recorded for either "Power Of Soul" or "Lover Man." Similar problems had intermittently dogged the opening medley of "Auld Lang Syne" and "Who Knows" from the second show. An edited version of the latter performance was later included as part of *Live At The Fillmore East*.

RECORD PLANT, NEW YORK, NEW YORK. ENGINEERS: BOB HUGHES, TONY BONJIOVI. SECOND ENGINEER: DAVE RAGNO.

Fourteen exuberant takes of "Power Of Soul," known at this stage as "Crash Landing," were recorded. Of these takes, 2, 4, and 6 were complete. Hendrix designated take 4 as the working master.

Hendrix then presented the evening's most pleasant surprise, seven intriguing attempts at "Astro Man." The song's inspiration was simple, with its lyrics drawing from Hendrix's love for animated cartoons. "That's what 'Astro Man' was all about," says Cox with a laugh. "We used to love watching cartoons at his apartment. He enjoyed *Mighty Mouse* and especially loved *Rocky and Bullwinkle*."

Though Hendrix had never before tackled a formal take of this song with Cox or Miles, these versions held surprisingly close to the finished master later recorded at Electric Lady Studios and released as part of *Cry Of Love*. While only takes 5 and 6 were complete, the playing throughout all attempts was upbeat and inspired. Between takes, Hendrix can be heard informing Cox that he's looking to inject more of a Spanish beat into the song's rhythm. While not listed on the tape box as among the staff employed for the session, engineer Tony Bongiovi can be heard offering take counts and occasional instructions. The complete fifth take displayed considerable promise, although no lead vocal was recorded. The sixth take started out strong, but it lacked cohesion and struggled to a close.

"This is gonna be fun!" laughed Hendrix before launching into an enthusiastic seventh and final take. "Was that fun?" he joked with Cox and Miles immediately afterwards. This exceptional take yielded the working master, on to which Hendrix overdubbed a lead vocal and a superb lead guitar part. While Hendrix bypassed this master in favor of the recording he made at Electric Lady in the summer of 1970, Kramer later mixed this alternate take and issued it as part of the 2000 *Jimi Hendrix Experience* box set.

The group ended the evening with an uneventful take of "Valleys Of Neptune." This version, while complete, lacked even a guide vocal from Hendrix. At its conclusion, Hendrix remarked, 'We'll just pack it up," which signaled the close of the session.

THURSDAY, JANUARY 22, 1970

RECORD PLANT, NEW YORK, NEW YORK. ENGINEER: BOB HUGHES.

Multiple attempts at preparing final mixes for "Izabella" and "Sky Blues Today" were made, yet Hendrix did not chose any of them. He was obviously searching for a specific sound—and not finding it. At this stage, "Sky Blues Today" was very close to the mix that Hendrix later designated as the final, but "Izabella" was still some distance away. Hendrix continued work on both songs into February, hoping to capture the exact sound balance he desired.

FRIDAY, JANUARY 23, 1970

RECORD PLANT, NEW YORK, NEW YORK. ENGINEER: BOB HUGHES. SECOND ENGINEER: DAVE RAGNO.

A wild evening of inspired jamming was recorded during this marathon session.

The twenty-minute "Ezy Ryder/MLK Jam" began on reel one and continued on to reel two as the tape operator scrambled to reload the tape machine with a fresh roll of tape. This extended passage is not a structured take but instead an exhilarating example of Hendrix's seemingly limitless imagination and uncanny command of his instrument. This is Hendrix at his improvisational best, soaring above a bedrock foundation set by Cox and Miles, shifting gears on the fly, alternatively modifying and shading his guitar tone to dramatically accentuate the moods, sounds, and textures he envisioned. Cox and Miles never wavered, their eyes and ears trained on Hendrix as they scanned the guitarist for his unspoken cues to their next pathway.

Nearly fourteen minutes into the recording, Hendrix shifted gears, dramatically transitioning into an exquisite collage of thunder, lightning, and other wondrous sounds, all created by way of his guitar and tremolo bar and buttressed by the insistent rhythm provided by Cox and Miles. He would finally close the jam with a quick, good-natured stab at "Tax Free," a favorite Experience improvisational device.

It is not known why the jam was titled "Ezy Ryder/MLK Jam." The original tape box from this session simply bears that title, written in pencil by one of the two engineers present.

An adventurous "Villanova Junction" evolved into a jam session on this evening, providing another session highlight. This version was a more detailed sketch than any previous recorded version. It is not known if Hendrix ever composed lyrics for this elusive beauty, but it seems clear that he was convinced of its prospects. At 3:30 into the recording, he called for Cox and Miles to "do some jungle sounds," and this continued for approximately two minutes.

The group meandered about for a few minutes before Hendrix kicked off what was noted on the tape box as "Record Plant 2X," likely given that name only because it was recorded on the second reel of recording tape used that evening. The engineers dared not interrupt Hendrix, Cox, and Miles for a song title or to slate a take number as the group barreled along. Hendrix, locked in step with Cox and Miles, glided spontaneously throughout this nearly twelve-minute passage, fluently drawing upon a wealth of ideas he wished to explore. The recording came to a close following the loping "Slow Time Blues," for which the group was now joined by an unnamed harmonica player.

A noteworthy stab at "Burning Desire" followed. This version incorporated the group's live arrangement of the song, principally its hypnotic opening pattern. Though this modification vastly improved their effort, the group still struggled to adapt the rhythm section to fit the song's intricate time signatures. Hendrix did not record a vocal track, indicating that he felt the song first required more work.

Following a break, Hendrix, Cox, Miles, and the harmonica player launched into a lengthy workout of Carl Perkins's rockabilly classic "Blue Suede Shoes," prefaced

by some clowning from Hendrix that foreshadowed his lack of serious effort on this tossed-off take. After Hendrix's death, "Blue Suede Shoes" was the first recording from this session to be issued commercially. Electric Lady Studios engineer John Jansen prepared an edited version of the song and added it to the 1973 Polydor compilation *Loose Ends*. In 1975, Douglas stripped the song of its original instrumentation—save for Hendrix's guitar—and redressed it with new overdubs and backing vocals (leaving Hendrix's lead vocal part in place) for *Midnight Lightning*. No amount of elaborate overdubs or posthumous tinkering, though, could rescue a second-rate Hendrix performance such as this. Like the *Midnight Lightning* album, the song disappeared from view and has not been commercially available for more than two decades.

Locked in a blues groove following "Blue Suede Shoes," Hendrix and Cox provided some tantalizing clues to the early development of "Freedom" while Hendrix sang a spontaneous blues original best described as "Highways Of Desire." Partway through, Cox and Miles slowed the tempo in half, much to Hendrix's approval. He then began "Seven Dollars In My Pocket," another impromptu blues original. As Hendrix sang of a lost love from Sugar Hill, the rhythm section struggled to maintain the tempo, causing him to react. "C'mon. C'mon, keep it," he ordered. Hendrix's concentration, however, was broken and the jam slowly came apart. Holding to the blues groove, the group transitioned into "Midnight Lightning," with Hendrix singing lyrics. They also put forth an embryonic rendition of "Freedom," which, though not fully developed, was energetically performed. Unfortunately, the unnamed harmonica player marred the recording of this song by droning on tunelessly throughout it. At one point during the session, Hendrix sarcastically remarked, "Find a key" to the hapless harmonica player.

The group recorded two other blues originals this evening, the instrumental titled "Country Blues," and "Once I Had A Woman," which featured a live vocal from Hendrix. Douglas overhauled "Once I Had A Woman" in 1974 with new overdubs, including a new harmonica part performed by session musician Buddy Lucas. An edited version was later added to 1975's *Midnight Lightning* compilation. A differently prepared version of the original recording, lasting an additional 2:05, was released as part of 1994's *Jimi Hendrix: Blues*.

Like "Once I Had A Woman," "Country Blues" was not a numbered take, but an inspired jam session loosely based on Howlin' Wolf's "44." "Blues was Jimi's background," explains Cox. "Jimi's record albums consisted of Howlin' Wolf, Lightnin' Hopkins, B. B. King, and Albert King. He had a lot of stuff by Wolf and Albert King. He really liked things of that nature. If you stop and really listen to Jimi's music, the basic element is blues."

Hendrix, Cox, and Miles relished musical interplay, and "Country Blues" is a joyous example of their shared musical vocabulary. "What made us different [from the Experience] was the communication between Jimi and Billy and myself," explains Miles. "I think our greatest attribute was that we could work together with little or no effort. It's one thing when you have to explain music to people, it's another thing to [follow] a musician, especially if they're paving the way. Jimi was the nucleus, he was the center of attention, which I had no problem with, because I just know that I wanted to be there with him. Billy must have felt the same way, because he had that bond with Jimi."

From "Country Blues," the group moved effortlessly into a single instrumental take of "Astro Man" before the session drew to a close. Electric Lady engineer John Jansen later considered an excerpt of this evening's opening exercise, "Ezy Ryder/MLK Jam"—beginning at approximately 13:50 and continuing through approximately 17:20—as a contender for the 1972 posthumous album *War Heroes*. In his effort to create a finished song, he transferred this recording to a new multitrack tape, then crafted an opening from the October 23, 1968, TTG Studios recording of "New Rising Sun," and an ending from two different Hendrix session tapes. However, when Kramer rejected the concept, the song was dropped from consideration. In 1974, Douglas found Jansen's work and replaced Miles's original drum parts with overdubs by session musicians Maeulen and Allan Schwartzberg. He renamed the song "Captain Coconut" and included it as part of the controversial 1975 album *Crash Landing*.

In 2006, the original, unedited recording of "Ezy Ryder/MLK Jam" was made available to fans as part of *Burning Desire*. That album featured much of the bounty from this remarkable session, including "Villanova Junction," "Record Plant 2X," "Burning Desire," and "Slow Time Blues."

WEDNESDAY, JANUARY 28, 1970

WINTER FESTIVAL FOR PEACE, MADISON SQUARE GARDEN, NEW YORK, NEW YORK. **SET LIST:** "WHO KNOWS" / "EARTH BLUES"

A disastrous performance by Hendrix at a Madison Square Garden antiwar benefit on this date brought the Band Of Gypsys' future to a sudden halt. Hendrix took the stage at three a.m. after appearances by several diverse performers, including Dave Brubeck, Harry Belafonte, and the cast of *Hair*. He lurched painfully through two numbers, "Who Knows" and "Earth Blues," before withdrawing from the stage. "What went down was very embarrassing, and it left Jimi angry and disillusioned," says Cox. "It was unfortunate. Buddy and I walked over to Madison Square Garden, went into the dressing room, and there was Jimi. He was not in the best shape. Jimi was sitting next to Jeffery and we *knew* it wasn't going to work. Jimi was in bad shape. We thought about not going out there, because someone was trying make assholes out of us, but we did. We thought Jimi might be able to make it, but we only got through that one song before it started coming apart."

The public debacle infuriated Hendrix's manager, Michael Jeffery, who promptly fired Miles backstage and brought the group's brief tenure to a close. "I was hurt when management told me that I was fired," remembers Miles. "It was for no obvious reason, as far as I could see. That rejection hurt me because I know that it didn't come from Jimi personally. Jimi never once said to me that I was fired or that he didn't want to use me anymore. I felt rejected. I was hurt because I broke up my band [the Buddy Miles Express]. Regardless of how fast I could have got back into it or not, that was neither here nor there. I was a part of somebody that I really wanted to be a part of. Of course I knew the man hadn't even reached his peak yet. I think he had reached the pinnacle with Mitch and Noel because he wasn't getting off anymore and I feel that me and Billy gave him that."

Though the relationship between Jeffery and Miles had always been strained, the notion that race may have played a role in their demise left Cox with a bitter taste. "Buddy and I thought that because they had successfully marketed the Jimi Hendrix Experience as being these two white guys, with Jimi in the middle, they didn't want to change horses midstream and go with three black guys up there," says Cox.

Members of Hendrix's management team strongly rejected the issue that race contributed to the dismissal of Miles. Jeffery's assistant Trixie Sullivan explains that he was operating on instructions from Hendrix. "The relationship Mike Jeffrey had as manager of the Hendrix Experience, had with Jimi, was very simple. Mike took care of all the business side of things, got money when he could, and he left Jimi *totally* in charge of the artistic side of it. Mike would arrange all his tours but he would not interfere with the music side of things. He didn't feel that he had that right. So when it came to Jimi not being happy, on any level with the music side of things, if he mentioned it to Mike, that he couldn't deal with it himself, or he wasn't happy, and he didn't know what to do . . . then Mike would have done it for him. But under no circumstances would Mike Jeffrey come in and sack people without Jimi's permission, approval, and in fact his instigation of the whole act. Because Jimi was very specific about his music, it was his, and that's where he really excelled. Mike was very good on the management side. So if you are talking specifically about Buddy Miles leaving the group and Mike sacking him, it would have been totally on Jimi's instigation, but he wouldn't have had the nerve to do it himself, because it was his friend, and he wouldn't know how to do it. So he would get Mike to do it for him. And that was normal in our organization."

With the Band Of Gypsys formally disbanded, Miles was left to reassemble the Express. Disheartened, Cox returned to Nashville. "I saw that I wasn't wanted," he explains, "so I came back to Nashville and decided to do something else." Miles extended an invitation to Cox to join his reformed group, but Cox declined. He did, however, fly to Chicago to lend fuzz bass to Miles's studio version of "Them Changes."

SATURDAY, JANUARY 31, 1970

RECORD PLANT, LOS ANGELES, CALIFORNIA. ENGINEERS: STAN AGOL, DAVE RAGNO.

Final production for *Woodstock*, the ambitious, Michael Wadleigh–directed documentary about the August 1969 festival, and its accompanying soundtrack album, had begun in Los Angeles. Hendrix was not present at these sessions, but portions from his performance were edited and later included as part of both the finished album and film released by Warner Bros. in May 1970. On this day, mixing of Hendrix's extended "Voodoo Child (Slight Return)" was completed.

FEBRUARY 1970

With the Electric Lady Studios project on the brink of bankruptcy, Jeffery was anxious to repair Hendrix's public image after the Madison Square Garden debacle, and pushed his artist in February of 1970 to reunite the original Experience. His vision was to reestablish the Jimi Hendrix Experience with a high-profile tour leading to the release of Hendrix's next studio album. Jeffery wanted to put as much distance as he could

between the Band Of Gypsys, a musical collaboration he considered a one-time creative diversion and the Experience, arguably the most popular rock-concert attraction in the world. Moreover, the lucrative tour would generate much-needed capital to shore up their finances, depleted due to the continuing construction of Electric Lady Studios. Electric Lady's original budget estimate of $500,000 had long since been surpassed, and work on the project had come to a halt due to lack of additional funding. Jeffery and his attorney, Steve Weiss, made a canny, eleventh-hour maneuver, securing a loan of $300,000 from Warner Bros. and agreeing to a repayment schedule that called for payments of $50,000 every six months. The loan would be guaranteed against Hendrix's music publishing royalties and Jeffery's share of the same.

An interview with *Rolling Stone* reporter John Burks was staged in Jeffery's East 37th Street office on February 4, 1970, during which Mitchell and Redding joined Hendrix. In the days following the interview, however, Hendrix got cold feet, and Cox, who reluctantly rejoined the musician after some heavy persuasion, again replaced Redding. "I got a phone call from Jimi and Michael Jeffery telling me, 'Billy, things are different. It's not what you think.' They got me to come

back to New York, but the scene still wasn't too good so I came back to Nashville again. I said, 'This is it. I'm through with this shit.'"

Mitchell was also unavailable, having committed to a short tour with Larry Coryell, Mike Mandel, and former Cream bassist Jack Bruce. That tour began with three performances in Coventry and London, England, followed by tour dates in the U.S. that began January 30 at the Fillmore East and continued through March 1 in San Francisco.

With his band in total disarray, Hendrix huddled with Kramer at Juggy Sound, where the engineer continued to review the remote recordings from the Band Of Gypsys' recent Fillmore East performances.

Juggy Sound staff engineer Kim King was very familiar with Jimi Hendrix. King, formerly the guitarist with Lothar and the Hand People, had jammed with the guitarist, known then as Jimmy James, on many occasions in the Village. "Juggy Sound had just installed a sixteen-track machine, but it was still a funky old R&B studio," says King. "Eddie and Jimi told me that they were tired of the Record Plant and wanted to work elsewhere. Eddie, in fact, was doing a few other things at Juggy, including a Buzzy Linhart album and some demos for a band from Queens called the Rosicrucians.

The first Hendrix sessions I did with Eddie was preparing rough mixes of the Band Of Gypsys live material. Kramer said, 'Let's see how good you are at editing. What I want is all of the guitar solos left in and all of the drum solos left out.' That was how we started. We also did a couple of oddball things with Jimi there. There was one session where Jimi was really into something good. Unfortunately, we ran out of tape, but I had found some hubs with bits of blank tape on them. After the session, one of them dropped out in the middle and I had to hand spool twenty-four hundred feet back on to the reel. Fortunately, this was out of the view of Eddie and Jimi!"

"On other occasions, Jimi would show up and we would do some bizarre guitar experiments or work on overdubs for things he had recorded at other studios, but the focus was on the live album, and the push was on to finish Electric Lady. I had developed a rapport with Eddie, and he offered me a job at the new studio during the sessions."

One such guitar overdub session at Juggy concentrated on "Stepping Stone." Kramer recorded a lead guitar part from Hendrix on to the Record Plant multitrack master, and it is his voice that can be heard informing the guitarist that he had "made it" at the end of the song.

MONDAY, FEBRUARY 2, 1970

JUGGY SOUND, NEW YORK, NEW YORK. ENGINEER: EDDIE KRAMER.

Hendrix engaged in two spirited jam sessions with the Rosicrucians. The first jam lasted approximately five minutes, while the second was considerably longer.

Afterwards, Hendrix and Kramer returned their focus to Band Of Gypsys. Mixes of "Machine Gun" (December 31, 1969, second show], as well as "Purple Haze," "Hey Joe," "Wild Thing," and "Earth Blues" (all from the January 1, 1970, second show), were among those contemplated for the album.

TUESDAY, FEBRUARY 3, 1970

RECORD PLANT, NEW YORK, NEW YORK. ENGINEER: BOB HUGHES.

Hendrix revisited take 4 from the January 21 master of "Paper Airplanes" (again, also known as "Power Of Soul," "Crash Landing," and "With The Power") on this evening, overdubbing guitar parts and completing a mix.

While this mix was never used during Hendrix's lifetime, it was later cut to a reference master by Electric Lady Studios engineer Andy Edlin on June 13, 1972, and was a contender for what would ultimately take form as Loose Ends.

"Power Of Soul" remained unavailable until Douglas prepared a truncated version in 1974 and included it as part of Crash Landing. The original master was edited and remixed to accommodate overdubs recorded in 1974 by session percussionist Jimmy Maeulen. Additionally, its elaborate introduction and two soaring lead guitar solos were scrapped. Lasting only 3:15 and renamed "With The Power," the song was stripped of its elaborate introduction and its two soaring lead guitar solos.

In 1997, Kramer restored the song, preparing a new mix without the posthumous additions and edits made by Douglas. Now lasting 5:20, this version was included as part of South Saturn Delta.

THURSDAY, FEBRUARY 5, 1970

JUGGY SOUND, NEW YORK, NEW YORK. ENGINEER: EDDIE KRAMER. SECOND ENGINEER: KIM KING.

In the early morning hours of February 5, Hendrix returned to Juggy Sound as mixing sessions for Band Of Gypsys continued. By this stage, final mixes for "Who Knows" and "Machine Gun"—the two songs that made up the album's first side—had been crafted and set aside. Hendrix now focused his energies on completing side two. Among the songs that he and Kramer mixed on this date, but did not select for the album, were "Stone Free" (January 1, second show) and "Stepping Stone" (January 1, first show).

SUNDAY, FEBRUARY 8, 1970

RECORD PLANT, LOS ANGELES, CALIFORNIA. ENGINEER: STAN AGOL. SECOND ENGINEER: DAN TURBEVILLE.

Although Hendrix was not present, a four-track mixing session of "Star Spangled Banner" was completed.

Take 7 was chosen as the master and included in the forthcoming *Woodstock* album and film.

WEDNESDAY, FEBRUARY 11, 1970

RECORD PLANT, NEW YORK, NEW YORK. ENGINEER: BOB HUGHES. SECOND ENGINEER: DAVE RAGNO.
Rough mixes of the Band Of Gypsys' studio version of "Izabella" were completed.

THURSDAY, FEBRUARY 12, 1970

RECORD PLANT, NEW YORK, NEW YORK. ENGINEER: BOB HUGHES.
Multiple rough mixes of "Izabella" and "Sky Blues Today" were prepared and a master of "Izabella" was achieved.

SATURDAY, FEBRUARY 14, 1970

JUGGY SOUND STUDIOS, NEW YORK, NEW YORK. ENGINEER: EDDIE KRAMER. SECOND ENGINEER: KIM KING.
During this session, Hendrix and Kramer focused on mixing and editing "Changes," "Power Of Soul," "Message To Love," and "We Gotta Live Together." For example, they trimmed a short burst of Hendrix's out-of-tune guitar from an early section of the "Power Of Soul" master. They also completed further editing of pre-song introductions and further fine cutting of "We Gotta Live Together."

SUNDAY, FEBRUARY 15, 1970

JUGGY SOUND STUDIOS, NEW YORK, NEW YORK. ENGINEER: EDDIE KRAMER. SECOND ENGINEER: KIM KING.
Hendrix and Kramer continued final editing and mixing of the *Band Of Gypsys* album.

RECORD PLANT, NEW YORK, NEW YORK. ENGINEER: BOB HUGHES.
Hendrix moved from Juggy Sound to the Record Plant to continue working. A master mix of "Sky Blues Today" was finally achieved during this session. This master, later renamed "Stepping Stone" by the guitarist, was later coupled with the February 12 master of "Izabella" and issued on April 13, 1970, as a Reprise Records single.

MONDAY, FEBRUARY 16, 1970

JUGGY SOUND STUDIOS, NEW YORK, NEW YORK. ENGINEER: EDDIE KRAMER. SECOND ENGINEER: KIM KING.
Hendrix and Kramer continued to refine the *Band Of Gypsys* live album at Juggy Sound.

RECORD PLANT, NEW YORK, NEW YORK. ENGINEER: BOB HUGHES. SECOND ENGINEER: TOM FLYE.
Hendrix traveled to the Record Plant later that evening, after mixing sessions at Juggy Sound had concluded. Upon his arrival, an informal jam session with Buddy Miles and an unnamed percussionist ensued. Hendrix recorded two muscular, instrumental attempts at "Blue Suede Shoes," both vastly different from the extended jam Hendrix had recorded on January 23. Hendrix then shifted into a loose "Hey Baby (Land Of The New Rising Sun)." Singing live, Hendrix evoked some gorgeous touches of Spanish flamenco stylings. When this jam broke down, Hendrix kicked off a true gem, an impish, instrumental rendition of "Summertime Blues." With Buddy locked in the groove, Hendrix rode the guitar's whammy bar with wonderful effect. A funky, impromptu original reminiscent of the Beatles' "Day Tripper" followed this bit of unrehearsed fun.

Another reel recorded on this evening was nowhere as inventive, as the trio—with the percussionist now on maracas—found themselves mired in a series of uneventful jams without direction. Soon thereafter, Cox and Mitchell, who was enjoying a day off from his tour schedule with Jack Bruce, arrived. Miles departed and work began on "Freedom." The musicians clearly rehearsed their parts before formal recording began, as each of them had a firm grasp on the song's tempo and arrangement. At this stage, "Freedom" had not yet fully evolved to the song that would later be included first as part of *Cry Of Love* and later, *First Rays Of The New Rising Sun*. For this session's recording, later issued as part of the 2000 *Jimi Hendrix Experience* box set, Hendrix devised an inventive, extended introduction and skillfully integrated the percussionist to accent Mitchell's distinctive cymbal and snare work. With Hendrix singing a live vocal, one strong take was committed to tape. At this stage, no formal ending had been devised, so the group continued until their effort came apart after close to five minutes. A short jam quickly followed, based on the main "Freedom" guitar line, but this effort lasted only a few minutes longer before Hendrix brought Cox and Mitchell to a halt.

Next, Hendrix directed the group without pause into a series of rhythm patterns reminiscent of "Bleeding Heart." He then shifted into an inspired attempt at "Bolero," and while a finished master was not achieved, it remains another sterling highlight from this evening.

TUESDAY, FEBRUARY 17, 1970

JUGGY SOUND STUDIOS, NEW YORK, NEW YORK. ENGINEER: EDDIE KRAMER. SECOND ENGINEER: KIM KING.

Hendrix and Kramer completed the final editing, mixing, and sequencing for the *Band Of Gypsys* album during this session. In doing so, the guitarist was finally free of his legal obligation and eager to refocus on *First Rays Of The New Rising Sun*, the ambitious double studio album he was planning.

WEDNESDAY, FEBRUARY 18, 1970

STERLING SOUND, NEW YORK, NEW YORK. ENGINEER: EDDIE KRAMER.

Hendrix and Kramer teamed up with mastering engineer Bob Ludwig to supervise the final mastering for *Band Of Gypsys*. Very few artists of Hendrix's era attended such sessions, but the guitarist had already been disappointed with the mastering of *Electric Ladyland* by Reprise Records. To ensure that the final sound quality of his music met his standards, Hendrix opted to work independently from his record companies and supervise the process with Kramer.

THURSDAY, FEBRUARY 19, 1970

STERLING SOUND, NEW YORK, NEW YORK. ENGINEER: EDDIE KRAMER.

After reviewing test pressings of the mastering efforts of the previous day, some minor sonic adjustments were made before *Band Of Gypsys* was officially completed. On February 25, Jeffery delivered the album to Capitol Records.

From the four Fillmore East performances, Hendrix chose six songs to make up the album. He excluded versions of such Experience favorites as "Fire" and "Voodoo Child (Slight Return)," as well as stirring performances of "Ezy Ryder," "Burning Desire," and "Earth Blues," perhaps because he wanted to perfect studio versions before releasing live cuts. Instead, Hendrix put forward four new songs: "Message To Love," "Machine Gun," "Power of Soul" (listed on the *Band Of Gypsys* album sleeve as "Power To Love"), and "Who Knows." "'Who Knows' was something Jimi started," says Cox. "Buddy thought up the stops, but it was really just a pattern that Jimi had that was great to play." Save for pre-concert rehearsals at Baggy's Studios, the group had never dedicated a great deal of studio time to the song. The resulting live performance suffered accordingly, and sounded underdeveloped despite the infectious interplay between Cox and Hendrix.

While the contagious "Message To Love" and "Power Of Soul" provided engaging examples of Hendrix's unique blending of rock, R&B, and blues, his live performance of "Machine Gun" was ultimately recognized as one of his greatest achievements. Seeking to be equitable, Hendrix included two songs composed by Buddy Miles on the final album: "Changes" and "We Got To Live Together." Both had to be considerably shortened, as Buddy's in-concert call-and-response vamping translated poorly to disc. The grand, final crescendo of "We Got To Live Together" had originally brought the second January 1 show to its pre-encore close, and was therefore positioned as the album's final track.

"When *Band Of Gypsys* came out, we both wished we had done it in the studio," remembers Cox. "We would have loved to have done some overdubs and correct some of the mistakes that we had made. These were mistakes that *we* were aware of, not the public. We had reached that point where we wanted everything to be perfect. Overall, the feeling was, 'What the heck, the album doesn't belong to us anyway. Let's just move on and forget it.'"

SUNDAY, MARCH 15, 1970

ISLAND STUDIOS, LONDON, ENGLAND. ENGINEER: BILL HALVERSON.

While Hendrix was in London for a brief visit, Stephen Stills recruited him to lend guitar to his upcoming solo debut, *Stephen Stills*. Hendrix added lead guitar to the track "Old Times, Good Times" and also recorded two additional tracks with Stills that remain unreleased.

TUESDAY, MARCH 17, 1970

OLYMPIC STUDIOS, LONDON, ENGLAND. ENGINEER: KEITH HARWOOD.

Invited by Love's Arthur Lee to contribute to his band's album, Hendrix returned to Olympic Studios, the recording facility where he had recorded *Are You Experienced* and *Axis: Bold As Love*. Hendrix and percussionist Remi Kabaka joined Love in recording "The Everlasting First," which came out in December of 1970 as part of Love's *False Start*. The three musicians recorded sixteen takes before a basic track met Lee's approval. Two clean, complete takes of Hendrix's own "Ezy Ryder" followed next. Hendrix then took part in an extended instrumental jam session before departing.

MONDAY, MARCH 23, 1970

STUDIO A, SOUND CENTER, NEW YORK, NEW YORK. 7:00 P.M. TO 12:00 A.M. PRODUCER: NOEL REDDING. ENGINEER: SKIP JURIED.

Now that he had delivered the *Band Of Gypsys* album to Capitol and resumed construction on his studio, two of Hendrix's most pressing concerns were lifted from his shoulders. He had signed a series of performance agreements set to commence in April, but Hendrix balked at reforming the Experience with Redding, with whom his relationship remained fragile. He wanted to bring Cox back into the fold. Cox, who had left Hendrix for Nashville twice in the previous ten months, was disillusioned. "After the business at Madison Square Garden, I was real suspect," recalls Cox. "I agreed to come back in February, but that fell apart as well. I didn't hear from Jimi for about a month. Then I got a phone call from him saying, 'C'mon, Bill. Let's get it on!' I said, 'Hey man, you ain't getting nothing on. I'm here in Nashville and I'm happy. I don't want to go through all that shit I went through again.' He promised and promised that I would have no hassles, so, like a fool, I came back for the third time."

While Hendrix had designated Cox as his bassist, he still felt some loyalty toward Redding, and so agreed to help Redding with his record. With his tenure in the Experience having come to a close, Redding had begun work on a solo album whose working title, appropriately enough, was *Nervous Breakdown*. For this session at Sound Center, Redding gathered vocalist Roger Chapman of Family and Paul Caruso, as well as drummer Steve Angel and organist Gerry Guida, formerly of the Big Three, a group managed by Jeffery associate Bob Levine.

Sessions for *Nervous Breakdown* began Friday, March 20, and continued through Monday, March 23, with Redding calling in favors from friends to contribute to the hastily organized project. Redding completed a remake of "Walking Through The Garden," which Fat Mattress had previously recorded. The group also recorded a cover of Eddie Cochran's "Nervous Breakdown," "Everything's Blue," "Highway" (with vocals by Fat Mattress's Neil Landon), and "Eric The Red," complete with bagpipes performed by the doorman at the Penn-Garden Hotel. Lee Michaels added piano and organ to "Wearing Yellow" and "Blues In 3/4," and Hendrix stopped by on March 23 to lend guitar to Redding's "My Friend."

Ever industrious, Redding quickly organized material for these sessions. "I started getting some demos together after Jimi and Mitch began rehearsing with Billy Cox," remembers Redding. "'My Friend' was a song I had written. It was a tune in the key of E. Jimi also had a song by that name, but I think he stole the title from me. Jimi came over to the studio and offered to play guitar. I think he was trying to make up with me, because he had never spoken to me or even called to say that he was going to be playing with another guy [Billy Cox]. Jimi played guitar on 'My Friend.' I got as far as putting a rough vocal on it." Unfortunately, Redding never completed the *Nervous Breakdown* album, and it remains unreleased.

RECORD PLANT, NEW YORK, NEW YORK. ENGINEER: JACK ADAMS. SECOND ENGINEER: DAVE RAGNO.

Following his work on Noel Redding's album earlier that evening, Hendrix arrived at the Record Plant intent on realizing a more traditional Delta blues arrangement of

"Midnight Lightning" than he had previously attempted. Working alone, Hendrix recorded three unfinished takes of the song during this short session. Singing and playing live as he sat on a chair, Hendrix utilized a finger-picking style he rarely incorporated on his own recordings. He accented the song's slow beat, in the tradition of such blues legends as Lightnin' Hopkins and John Lee Hooker, with the steady tapping of his foot on the floor. The beginning of the reel also captures some conversation between Hendrix and the control room. Hendrix remarked, "Instant Coma. Instant Coma, you know what I mean?" no doubt making a parody of John Lennon's recently issued single "Instant Karma." While none of the three takes which follow were complete, each—especially take 3—recalls the styling of the Delta blues masters Hendrix admired.

Initially, Hendrix had wanted to record the track live, and the tape captures a brief portion of Hendrix's disagreement with engineer Jack Adams regarding the recording of Hendrix's vocal. After take 2 broke down, Hendrix changed his mind. "I'll tell you what. I'm not going to do the words," Hendrix said. "I can't get no feeling with this thing only in my ear. I'm going to do the vocals over again anyway, so this vocal here won't be any good." Sensing his discomfort, Adams relented and offered to record the track as Hendrix had originally wished. "Could you get the feel of the vocal if we opened the door again?" asked Adams. "Because we can manage it if we've got to do it. Open the door. Open it wide." Hendrix attempted a third take, although it, too, fell incomplete. Sounding tired and depressed, Hendrix called the session to a close with a weary, 'Yeah, I'm going to give up on this one." No other recording was attempted.

Take 3 of this moody, evocative work in progress was mixed by Eddie Kramer and included as part of *South Saturn Delta* in 1997.

TUESDAY, MARCH 24, 1970

RECORD PLANT, NEW YORK, NEW YORK. ENGINEER: JACK ADAMS. SECOND ENGINEER: DAVE RAGNO.
This unusual session began with Hendrix accompanied by Steve Angel, a young drummer who Bob Levine, a member of Hendrix's management team, had taken

under his wing. Working without a bass player, a loose, energetic take of "Bleeding Heart" was recorded. "Call that right there "Bleeding Heart," Hendrix said directly after the take. This was followed by three takes of "Midnight Lightning," but none of these efforts was put forward with much spirit from Hendrix and no finals were achieved.

At this point, the session seemed to come to an end. When recording resumed, Cox had joined the proceedings. Some rehearsing may have taken place in the break from recording, as the group needed only four takes of "Bleeding Heart" before the fourth was marked as the master take. Hendrix's concentration and intensity level had improved considerably from the earlier takes.

Like many similar Record Plant efforts, this reel was later transferred to Electric Lady Studios, where Hendrix took steps toward completing the track to his satisfaction. Additional guitar parts were overdubbed at Electric Lady, and Mitchell replaced the existing percussion tracks with new drum parts. A rough mix by Hendrix and Kramer encompassing these improvements was made before the guitarist's death, but they did not achieve a final master. While Hendrix was unable to finish "Bleeding Heart" before his death, Eddie Kramer and John Jansen mixed take 4 on March 11, 1971, and set it aside for *Rainbow Bridge*. It did not make that album but was instead included as part of 1972's *War Heroes*. With *War Heroes* long out of print, "Bleeding Heart" is now available as part of *South Saturn Delta*.

Hendrix then turned his attention to "Earth Blues," returning to the working master from January 20. He overdubbed lead and rhythm guitar parts and completed a rough mix before ending the session. This alternate recording made its commercial debut as part of the *Jimi Hendrix Experience* box set.

WEDNESDAY, MARCH 25, 1970

BAND OF GYPSYS. CAPITOL RECORDS STAO-472. U.S. ALBUM RELEASE. PRODUCER: HEAVEN RESEARCH [JIMI HENDRIX]. ENGINEER: EDDIE KRAMER. "WHO KNOWS" / "MACHINE GUN" / "CHANGES" / "POWER OF SOUL" / "MESSAGE TO LOVE" / "WE GOTTA LIVE TOGETHER"

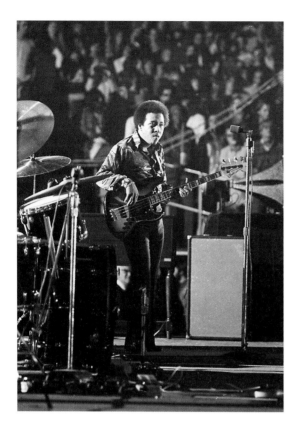

With *Band Of Gypsys* riding high on the *Billboard* album chart, Reprise Records issued the single "Stepping Stone," coupled with "Izabella." Capitol Records complained that Reprise was trying to distract consumers from *Band Of Gypsys*. As a result, a myth has developed, saying that Reprise was forced to remove the single from the marketplace for legal reasons, but that is not the case. Apart from "All Along The Watchtower," Hendrix had never had much success on U.S. Top 40 radio, and "Stepping Stone" and "Izabella" proved to be no exception. The single sold poorly and quickly faded from view—but it has since become a prized collector's item.

SATURDAY, APRIL 25, 1970

LOS ANGELES FORUM, INGLEWOOD, CALIFORNIA. WITH THE BUDDY MILES EXPRESS. **SET LIST:** "SPANISH CASTLE MAGIC"/ "FOXEY LADY" / "LOVER MAN" / "HEAR MY TRAIN A COMIN'" / "MESSAGE TO LOVE" / "EZY RYDER"/ "MACHINE GUN" / "ROOM FULL OF MIRRORS" / "HEY BABY (NEW RISING SUN)" / "VILLANOVA JUNCTION" / "DRUM SOLO" / "FREEDOM" / "STAR SPANGLED BANNER" / "PURPLE HAZE" / "VOODOO CHILD (SLIGHT RETURN)"

After the March sessions at the Record Plant and the two London sessions for Stephen Stills and Arthur Lee, no evidence exists to suggest that Hendrix attempted any further recording until May 14. In the interim, the new lineup of the Experience gathered to begin rehearsals for their upcoming U.S. tour, which began in Los Angeles on April 25.

Despite the tumultuous events of the past nine months, Cox remembers a warm camaraderie and no animosity between the three band members. "Mitch was cool," says Cox. "There were no problems at all. He didn't even talk about the Band Of Gypsys. He just went about his business and never mentioned it. There was a real respect between Mitch and Jimi. We just got down to playing, which is what it was all about."

While the Experience again headlined a mix of theaters, college auditoriums, and sports stadiums, this venture, loosely billed as the *Cry Of Love* tour, was unlike any previous Experience jaunt. With Electric Lady Studios nearly operational, Hendrix won a

Having waited so long for Hendrix to deliver this album, Capitol rushed the disc to stores as quickly as possible. Soon after postproduction was completed, Jeffery delivered the finished master to Capitol executives in Los Angeles, on February 25, 1970. Lacquers for vinyl manufacturing were made on March 4, 1970, and just three weeks later, Capitol had product in the shops. Despite the dramatic shift in Hendrix's sound and style, especially when compared to *Electric Ladyland*, *Band Of Gypsys* enjoyed wide approval from Hendrix's eager fans. The album debuted on *Billboard*'s Top 200 chart at 18 and climbed as high as number 5. The album remained on the chart for sixty-one weeks. At the time of his death, *Band Of Gypsys* was Hendrix's most commercially successful album since *Are You Experienced*, his 1967 debut.

WEDNESDAY, APRIL 8, 1970

"STEPPING STONE" / "IZABELLA." REPRISE 0905. U.S. SINGLE RELEASE.

bitterly contested compromise with Jeffery to limit the number of engagements to a series of three-day weekends throughout the summer. The cash generated by these dates kept the studio project solvent, affording Hendrix sufficient time to recuperate and record throughout the week at his new facility.

Hendrix's fortunes were further buoyed by the dramatic success of *Band Of Gypsys*, whose impressive sales showing would earn Hendrix his fifth consecutive U.S. *Billboard* Top 10 disc.

The tour kicked off with a superb, sold-out engagement at the Forum in Los Angeles. "Staying at the hotel in Los Angeles, we went up to the roof and looked out over the city," remembers Cox. "Jimi said, 'Man, we've come a long way.'"

Hendrix's Forum performance was well paced and enthusiastically received. The guitarist expanded the group's stage repertoire, blending favorites like "Spanish Castle Magic" and "Purple Haze" with developing songs such as "Hey Baby (Land Of The New Rising Sun)" and "Room Full Of Mirrors," as well as "Message To Love" and "Machine Gun" from the *Band Of Gypsys* album. "The older songs were new to me," remembers Cox. "They were old to Jimi and Mitch but I brought my flavor on the bass and then they enjoyed that."

Hendrix's Forum performance took on special significance after his death when an amateur audience recording was the source for a double-album bootleg pressed months after the concert. There have been countless bootlegs issued in the three decades since Hendrix's death, but perhaps none with the consistent appeal of this Los Angeles Forum recording.

SUNDAY, APRIL 26, 1970

CAL EXPO, SACRAMENTO, CALIFORNIA. WITH THE BUDDY MILES EXPRESS AND BLUE MOUNTAIN EAGLE. **SET LIST:** "LOVER MAN" / "SPANISH CASTLE MAGIC" / "FREEDOM" / "MACHINE GUN" / "FOXEY LADY" / "ROOM FULL OF MIRRORS" / "EZY RYDER" / "PURPLE HAZE" / "STAR SPANGLED BANNER" / "VOODOO CHILD (SLIGHT RETURN)"

The revelry after their successful opening night at the Los Angeles Forum resulted in the group missing their morning flight for this late-afternoon performance at the State Fairground in Sacramento. Tour manager Gerry Stickells hired a plane to ferry the band to Sacramento in time for the gig. Before an audience of some 17,000 people, Hendrix continued to showcase new material such as "Room Full Of Mirrors" alongside traditional Experience favorites.

FRIDAY, MAY 1, 1970

MILWAUKEE AUDITORIUM, MILWAUKEE, WISCONSIN. WITH OZ. "SPANISH CASTLE MAGIC" / "LOVER MAN" / "HEAR MY TRAIN A COMIN'" / "EZY RYDER" / "FREEDOM" / "MESSAGE TO LOVE" / "FOXEY LADY" / "STAR SPANGLED BANNER" / "PURPLE HAZE" / "VOODOO CHILD (SLIGHT RETURN)"

SATURDAY, MAY 2, 1970

DANE COUNTY COLISEUM, MADISON, WISCONSIN. WITH SAVAGE GRACE AND OZ. "FIRE" / "ROOM FULL OF MIRRORS" / "HEAR MY TRAIN A COMIN'" / "LOVER MAN" / "RED HOUSE" / "MESSAGE TO LOVE" / "EZY RYDER" / "MACHINE GUN" / "STAR SPANGLED BANNER" / "FOXEY LADY" / "VOODOO CHILD (SLIGHT RETURN)" / "PURPLE HAZE"

SUNDAY, MAY 3, 1970

ST. PAUL CIVIC CENTER, ST. PAUL, MINNESOTA. WITH SAVAGE GRACE AND OZ. "FIRE" / "ROOM FULL OF MIRRORS" / "LOVER MAN" / "HEAR MY TRAIN A COMIN'" / "EZY RYDER" / "MACHINE GUN" / "FREEDOM" / "FOXEY LADY" / "RED HOUSE" / "STAR SPANGLED BANNER" / "PURPLE HAZE" / "VOODOO CHILD (SLIGHT RETURN)"

These three weekend performances showcased the continuing evolution of this new edition of the Experience. With each performance, the group grew tighter, and the rhythmic connection between Cox and Mitchell more assured. "I enjoyed the creative songs that were done, especially like 'Machine Gun,'" says Cox. "When Mitch did it, he came in with a different flavor than what Buddy Miles had done, yet his flavor was good. People ask me time and time again, 'Who's the best drummer, Buddy or Mitch?' I say that both of them are dynamic and they have two different styles. A good musician is a good musician and Mitch just brought his own personal flavor to the song."

MONDAY, MAY 4, 1970

HOLDING TOGETHER, THE VILLAGE GATE, NEW YORK, NEW YORK. **SET LIST:** "HEAR MY TRAIN A COMIN'" / "FREEDOM" / "RED HOUSE"

Hendrix, Mitchell, and Billy performed three songs as part of "Holding Together," a benefit for Timothy Leary and his family at the noted New York nightspot The Village Gate. The event followed a similar benefit that had been staged at San Francisco's Family Dog in April. Leary had been recently sentenced for a 1968 drug possession charge, and friends such as Alan Douglas organized this New York event on his behalf.

In addition to readings and speeches, the other artists performing that evening included Johnny Winter and former Experience bassist Noel Redding.

FRIDAY, MAY 8, 1970

UNIVERSITY OF OKLAHOMA FIELDHOUSE, NORMAN, OKLAHOMA. TWO SHOWS. WITH BLOODROCK. **SET LIST, SECOND SHOW:** "FIRE" / "SPANISH CASTLE MAGIC" / "MACHINE GUN" / "LOVER MAN" / "FOXEY LADY" / "HEAR MY TRAIN A COMIN'" / "MESSAGE TO LOVE" / "RED HOUSE" / "STAR SPANGLED BANNER" / "PURPLE HAZE" / "VOODOO CHILD (SLIGHT RETURN)"

SATURDAY, MAY 9, 1970

WILL ROGERS COLISEUM, FORT WORTH, TEXAS. **SET LIST:** "FIRE" / "LOVER MAN" / "HEAR MY TRAIN A COMIN'" / "FOXEY LADY" / "ROOM FULL OF MIRRORS" / "RED HOUSE" / "FREEDOM" / "EZY RYDER" / "MACHINE GUN" / "STAR SPANGLED BANNER" / "PURPLE HAZE" / "VOODOO CHILD (SLIGHT RETURN)"

SUNDAY, MAY 10, 1970

HEMISPHERE ARENA, SAN ANTONIO, TEXAS. **SET LIST:** "FIRE" / "FOXEY LADY" / "MACHINE GUN" / "FREEDOM" / "RED HOUSE" / "MESSAGE TO LOVE" / "HEAR

MY TRAIN A COMIN'" / "EZY RYDER" / "ROOM FULL OF MIRRORS" / " STAR SPANGLED BANNER" / "PURPLE HAZE" / "VOODOO CHILD (SLIGHT RETURN)"

The tragic killings on the campus of Kent State University earlier in the week heightened tensions in cities and college campuses across the nation. The outrage over these senseless deaths stoked campus demonstrations, marches, and protests and provided the emotionally charged backdrop for these three inspired performances in Oklahoma and Texas.

An amateur audience recording made at Hendrix's concert at the University of Oklahoma reveals an extraordinary "Machine Gun" that Hendrix dedicated to "the soldiers fighting in Chicago, Berkeley, Kent State, and Oklahoma." Hendrix's emotional rendition of this song stands as one of the finest of all of the 1970 U.S. tour performances.

SATURDAY, MAY 16, 1970

TEMPLE STADIUM, PHILADELPHIA, PENNSYLVANIA. WITH THE GRATEFUL DEAD, STEVE MILLER BAND, AND CACTUS. **PARTIAL SET LIST:** "SGT. PEPPER'S LONELY HEARTS CLUB BAND" / "JOHNNY B. GOODE" / "MACHINE GUN" / "LOVER MAN" / "FOXEY LADY" / "RED HOUSE" / "FREEDOM" / "FIRE" / "HEAR MY TRAIN A COMIN'" / "PURPLE HAZE" / "VOODOO CHILD (SLIGHT RETURN)"

Hendrix was set to headline an impressive bill that featured Cactus, Steve Miller, and the Grateful Dead, but he almost missed this performance when one of the limousines taking the Experience and several friends broke down en route from Greenwich Village. Hendrix and the band, plus roadies Gerry Stickells and Eric Barrett, jumped into one of the other cars and rushed on to Temple Stadium.

The group tore through the evening's performance, thrilling an audience estimated at 10,000 people with a high-velocity medley of "Sgt. Pepper's Lonely Hearts Club Band" and "Johnny B. Goode" and a confident blend of old favorites and new fare such as "Freedom."

THURSDAY, MAY 14, 1970

RECORD PLANT, NEW YORK, NEW YORK. ENGINEER: EDDIE KRAMER. SECOND ENGINEER: THOM FLYE.

Throughout the spring of 1970, Kramer and Electric Lady Studios president Jim Marron built a staff for the new studio. Maintenance engineer Shimon Ron, a hard-nosed former Israeli paratrooper, was recruited from A&R Studios in New York, where his work during Kramer's sessions with Led Zeppelin made a distinct impression. Rather than hire veteran engineers from established studios, Kramer opted for a pair of former musicians just breaking into the engineering field. During the spring of 1970, Amboy Dukes drummer Dave Palmer joined ex-Lothar and the Hand People guitarist Kim King as Kramer's assistant engineers. "The whole idea was to create a top-notch creative *and* technical support staff for the studio," explains Kramer. "I wanted to recruit and train people that were sensitive to the needs of the artist. I focused on young, intelligent people whose background was musical rather than strictly technical. The training was *very* strict and based on the old school. I was a bastard, a complete dictator, but if you had talent, you moved up. If you did drugs, you were fired. Fortunately, my first recruits were very good."

While the $300,000 loan secured from Warner Bros. Records had infused Electric Lady Studios with much-needed cash for equipment orders and day-to-day operations, a seemingly endless string of technical complications tested Hendrix's patience and kept him from recording until mid-May. "Jimi was pissed off that the studio wasn't ready," admits Kramer. "He was terribly impatient, wanting to know why it wasn't ready when he had been assured that it would be. There was a tremendous amount of pressure on us to get Electric Lady open. We had promised Jimi the moon and he had waited thirteen months to get in and start recording."

With the completion of Electric Lady tantalizingly close at hand, Hendrix opted to wait rather than return to other facilities such as the Hit Factory and Record Plant during his spring tour.

Simple test recordings with Kramer on piano were made in early May. These revealed that more was required before Hendrix could come in. Originally, Hendrix intended to begin recording at Electric Lady on May 14, but technical issues forced Kramer and the group to move to the Record Plant, where two days of recording were booked for Thursday and Friday, May 14 and 15. "It was a bit of an embarrassment to have to

book time at the Record Plant," recalls Kramer. "While I had full confidence in Shimon Ron to get everything working right, Studio A at Electric Lady still had problems with hum and distortion. We just were not ready to start recording."

Despite the setbacks at Electric Lady, the mood inside the Record Plant's Studio C, the third and most recent addition to the storied facility, was spirited and upbeat. While Kramer's name was not listed on the tape boxes, the session tapes reveal that he is clearly directing the session.

The session began with three takes of "Come Down Hard On Me," followed by rough, instrumental attempts at "Straight Ahead." At this stage, the song had a noticeably slower tempo and a much different arrangement from the version later released as part of *Cry Of Love*. Take 4 evolved into a jam of "Night Bird Flying." When this broke down, a short discussion between Hendrix, Mitchell, and Cox was briefly audible. Hendrix then announced, "L.A." Over the talkback, Kramer asked, "What in L.A.?" "L.A.—without the bullshit or the words," was Hendrix's sly reply, which set off laughter in both the control room and studio. A false start caused Kramer to remark, "Get it together," over the talkback microphone. Hendrix briefly mimicked the tone of Kramer's request on the guitar, composed himself, and kicked off a unique hybrid of "Midnight Lightning" and "Keep On Groovin'." The track began with an instrumental introduction, before Hendrix signaled an unusual tempo change midway through, which seemed to momentarily confuse Mitchell and Cox. Though the group carried the song to a finish, it lacked a strong ending and remained, at this early juncture, another inspired demo teeming with potential. "That [untitled front part] was a pattern we had worked out in Los Angeles," says Cox. "That was all we had, was that first part. We weren't playing by notes. We were playing by patterns. It was kind of weird, but that's how we thought. We were always trying to hook these patterns together to make songs. Jimi would just give you a look, and Mitch and I would know where he was going."

After strumming the distinctive introductory notes to "Power Of Soul," Hendrix started an infectious instrumental workout of "Straight Ahead." In direct contrast to the versions that began the evening, this rendition was much more compact, with a faster tempo and an arrangement nearly identical to the finished master. Hendrix's exuberant playing provided several highlights throughout.

"Freedom" followed next, with Hendrix supplying a charged live lead vocal as the three recorded the basic track. "Freedom" was one of the stronger songs to emerge from the March and April rehearsals for the Cry Of Love tour. Impressed with its progress, Hendrix had inserted the song into the group's stage repertoire, where it debuted at the April 25 Los Angeles Forum performance. In this early incarnation, his girlfriend Devon Wilson's voracious appetite for heroin was the primary focus of Hendrix's lyrics. His intent was obvious, as Hendrix, with great conviction, sang of his desire to "take the junk out of her hand." While uneven in spots, this particular attempt at "Freedom" was still first-rate, fueled by Hendrix's powerful emotion. Perhaps to counter the intensity of "Freedom," Hendrix then lurched into a high-pitched, woefully off-key rendition of Frankie Laine's "Catastrophe." At its conclusion, Kramer deadpanned, "At $150 an hour, that's pretty good." As the laughter subsided, recording continued with an inspired single take of "Hey Baby (Land Of The New Rising Sun)."

FRIDAY, MAY 15, 1970

RECORD PLANT, NEW YORK, NEW YORK. ENGINEER: EDDIE KRAMER. SECOND ENGINEER: THOM FLYE.

"Freedom" again dominated the focus, as Hendrix was keen to develop this exceptional track to its full potential. He attempted nineteen new takes, with take 15 particularly strong thanks to his tremendous enthusiasm. Despite an exceptional effort, no masters were achieved, as Hendrix would continue to make a series of minor refinements over the coming weeks before finally succeeding at Electric Lady in late June.

A promising instrumental version of "Valleys Of Neptune" was also attempted, but it fell incomplete, causing Hendrix to admit that he hadn't actually devised an appropriate ending yet. "Peter Gunn" and a short reprise of "Catastrophe"—both of which were later issued as part of 1972's *War Heroes*—kept spirits loose before Hendrix directed the group through a muscular stab at

"Freedom." Not quite satisfied, Hendrix again shifted gears, kicking off a slower-paced "Hey Baby (Land Of The New Rising Sun)." Similarly styled to the arrangement preserved on *Rainbow Bridge*, Hendrix's extended solo was marvelous. An energetic "Lover Man" followed.

FRIDAY, MAY 22, 1970

CINCINNATI, OHIO.

SATURDAY, MAY 23, 1970

KEIL AUDITORIUM, ST. LOUIS, MISSOURI.

SUNDAY, MAY 24, 1970

ROBERTS STADIUM, EVANSVILLE, INDIANA.

This weekend of performances was canceled due to illness and not rescheduled. Hendrix, reportedly suffering from influenza and swollen glands, remained at home in Greenwich Village.

LATE MAY 1970

ELECTRIC LADY STUDIOS, NEW YORK, NEW YORK. ENGINEER: EDDIE KRAMER.

Even without a number of essential conveniences, such as a freight elevator, Hendrix was eager to make use of his new studio. Though its lengthy construction had exacted an emotional and financial toll, Electric Lady represented an impressive achievement for him. While his only design stipulation had been round windows, Electric Lady Studios was crafted with great care. "We were committed to creating an artist's environment at the studio," says Electric Lady Studios president Jim Marron. "This would not be a facility dominated by technical types who had wires and cables all over the place. This was to be Hendrix's creative home." Kramer echoes Marron, saying, "We built that studio for Jimi to work and feel comfortable in, contrary to the antiseptic boxes then in vogue."

To foster such an environment, architect John Storyk incorporated a host of ideas, with direct input from Hendrix, including the soundproofed, curved walls that shaped the exterior of Studio A's control room and studio.

There were white-carpeted walls and colored lights, complete with a control panel for Hendrix that allowed him to match his mood with the colors he desired. These were small touches, yet they drove home the point that this facility had been tailored for him exclusively. "He just loved being in the studio," remembers Kramer. "He would say, 'Give me red lights or yellow lights tonight,' and wash the walls in a rainbow of different colors. It had always been his intent to have the studio loose and casual, yet at the same time we worked hard to maintain a high standard of professionalism. We were trying to create a womblike environment for Jimi, which the sophisticated theater lighting system complemented."

With Studio A inching closer to becoming operational, Kramer and the engineering staff tested the facility by making a number of experimental recordings throughout May of 1970. Rather than raise Hendrix's hopes prematurely, these practice efforts were done without him present. "We did a lot of testing," recalls Kim King. "I brought in a band I would later produce, and Michael Jeffery brought in a couple of bands that he was considering for his management company."

WEDNESDAY, MAY 27, 1970

WOODSTOCK SD3 500. U.S. ALBUM RELEASE. PRODUCER: ERIC BLACKSTEAD. ENGINEERS: EDDIE KRAMER, LEE OSBOURNE. "STAR SPANGLED BANNER" / "PURPLE HAZE" / "INSTRUMENTAL SOLO"

Timed to coincide with *Woodstock*'s massive Memorial Day weekend opening in cinemas throughout the country, the film's triple-disc soundtrack enjoyed widespread popularity, entering the *Billboard* album chart at number 4 before claiming the magazine's coveted top position for four weeks.

While the album overflowed with highlights from the likes of Sly and the Family Stone and the Jefferson Airplane, Hendrix's stunning rendition of the "Star Spangled Banner" provided one of the film's defining moments.

SATURDAY, MAY 30, 1970

BERKELEY PERFORMANCE CENTER, BERKELEY, CALIFORNIA. TWO SHOWS. ENGINEER: ABE JACOB. **SET LIST,**

FIRST SET: "FIRE" / "JOHNNY B. GOODE" / "HEAR MY TRAIN A COMIN'" / "FOXEY LADY" / "MACHINE GUN" / "FREEDOM" / "RED HOUSE" / "MESSAGE TO LOVE" / "EZY RYDER" / "STAR SPANGLED BANNER" / "PURPLE HAZE" / "VOODOO CHILD (SLIGHT RETURN)." **SET LIST, SECOND SET:** "PASS IT ON [STRAIGHT AHEAD]" / "HEY BABY (NEW RISING SUN)" / "LOVER MAN" / "STONE FREE" / "HEY JOE" / "I DON'T LIVE TODAY" / "MACHINE GUN" / "FOXEY LADY" / "STAR SPANGLED BANNER" / "PURPLE HAZE" / "VOODOO CHILD (SLIGHT RETURN)"

Both of Hendrix's superb performances at this 3,000-seat venue were professionally recorded. Hendrix hired noted remote engineer Wally Heider's mobile recording truck and designated Abe Jacobs, who handled sound for the guitarist on tour, to engineer the location recording. A film crew dispatched by Jeffery was also present. Led by Peter Pilafian, the crew covered portions of both concerts and also filmed street scenes throughout Berkeley, a tinderbox of unrest in the aftermath of the killings at Kent State and regular demonstrations against the Vietnam War.

Hendrix could have easily filled the nearby Oakland Coliseum, the location of the last Experience concert the previous year, but Jeffery elected to have local promoter Bill Graham schedule two shows on one night at the venerable Berkeley Performance Center. More than a thousand empty-handed fans were turned away from the venue, and when the doors opened for the first concert, a mass of unruly gate-crashers stormed the building. Local police and Graham's security staff were overrun as angry fans scaled the building's walls and roof while others lobbed rocks at ticket holders trying to gain legitimate entrance. After the concert began, in an effort to pacify the hostile crowd outside the building, engineer Abe Jacob swung open the rear doors of the remote sound truck, filling the street with the sounds of the Experience.

Nearly all of the high points from these two concerts were later released in one form or another. Many were issued as part of the film *Jimi Plays Berkeley*. The album *Live At Berkeley: The Second Set* presented the complete second performance while other songs, such as "Johnny B. Goode" from the first concert, formed the backbone of such posthumous compilations as *Hendrix: In The West*. Reworking cover material for his live performances was a time-honored Hendrix tradition. "Two weeks earlier," Cox says, "we were playing at Temple University and just before we went onstage, Jimi said we were going to start the show with 'Sgt. Pepper's Lonely Hearts Club Band' and 'Johnny B. Goode.' I just looked at him. 'Sgt. Pepper' and 'Johnny B. Goode'? He laughed and said, 'C'mon man, you know all that old shit!'"

The group's late-afternoon sound check was also recorded and partially filmed, yielding the spontaneous "Blue Suede Shoes," which was later issued as part of *Hendrix: In The West* and subsequently the *Jimi Hendrix Experience* box set.

FRIDAY, JUNE 5, 1970

MEMORIAL AUDITORIUM, DALLAS, TEXAS. WITH BALLIN' JACK. **PARTIAL SET LIST:** "SPANISH CASTLE MAGIC" / "FOXEY LADY" / "MACHINE GUN" / "FREEDOM" / "EZY RYDER" / "STAR SPANGLED BANNER" / "PURPLE HAZE" / "VOODOO CHILD (SLIGHT RETURN)"

While this show was not professionally recorded, someone did make a sixty-five minute open-reel video recording of Hendrix's appearance. Pat Pope, a journalist who covered the performance for a local Dallas underground publication, reported that a closed-circuit color television camera projected Hendrix's image live on a screen at the front of the stage. Such coverage, commonplace at concerts today, was unheard of at Jimi Hendrix events.

On October 8, 1970, just two weeks after Hendrix's death, a videotape of this performance was offered to Reprise. The label did not acquire the recording, presumably certain that it had no immediate commercial value, as a market for home video releases did not yet exist. Unfortunately, all traces of the video recording have since vanished, making it one of the most highly sought-after Hendrix treasures.

SATURDAY, JUNE 6, 1970

SAM HOUSTON COLISEUM, HOUSTON, TEXAS. WITH BALLIN' JACK. **SET LIST:** "JOHNNY B. GOODE" / "HEAR MY TRAIN A COMIN'" / "FIRE" / "FOXEY LADY" / "I DON'T LIVE TODAY" / "PURPLE HAZE" / "RED HOUSE" / "EZY

RYDER" / "MACHINE GUN" / "STAR SPANGLED BANNER" / "HEY JOE" / "VOODOO CHILD (SLIGHT RETURN)"

The *Houston Chronicle* in a review hailed Hendrix's nearly ninety-minute performance as "one of the finest rock concerts that Houston's hip audiences ever experienced."

SUNDAY, JUNE 7, 1970

ASSEMBLY CENTER ARENA, TULSA, OKLAHOMA. WITH BALLIN' JACK. **SET LIST:** "FIRE" / "SPANISH CASTLE MAGIC" / "STONE FREE" / "HEY BABY (NEW RISING SUN)" / "HEY JOE" / "FREEDOM" / "I DON'T LIVE TODAY" / "FOXEY LADY" / "RED HOUSE" / "MESSAGE TO LOVE" / "ROOM FULL OF MIRRORS" / "STAR SPANGLED BANNER" / "PURPLE HAZE" / "EZY RYDER" / "VOODOO CHILD (SLIGHT RETURN)"

MONDAY, JUNE 8, 1970

ELECTRIC LADY STUDIOS, NEW YORK, NEW YORK. ENGINEER: EDDIE KRAMER.

Prior to this session, only the control room in Studio A had been semioperational, essentially allowing Hendrix and Kramer to work on existing multitrack tapes the guitarist had created at other studios in 1969 and 1970. With Hendrix away on tour, another critical step forward was achieved when successful test recordings were made of Kramer playing the new piano in Studio A. Though further refinements would continue to be made throughout the summer, Electric Lady Studios was now ready for new recordings.

TUESDAY, JUNE 9, 1970

MID SOUTH COLISEUM, MEMPHIS, TENNESSEE.
In Memphis, Hendrix had the opportunity to greet Larry Lee backstage before the performance. The bond of friendship between the two remained, despite Lee's departure in the aftermath of the Woodstock performance. "Jimi was sincere about his music," says Lee. "I guess he felt he had a right to do what kind of music he wanted to. Sometimes, though, you can't get away from yourself if you have a couple of big hits. You can

do what you want, but if you play for a crowd of people you're going to come back to those hits. When he came to Memphis we met backstage. He had a Gibson Flying V and was playing some blues with it. He was playing me a few of his things on it and asking if I liked it. I asked him to play that guitar that night. He told me he was going to get up and play it for me. So he started to make his show with the Flying V but it didn't seem to move the crowd all that much. He put that guitar down and grabbed the Fender and played "Foxey Lady." It was a whole new deal after that. The crowd went wild. I would have never asked him to grab that Gibson no more, you know, because that Fender and "Foxey Lady" was what they wanted and he gave it to them. You got to please the people."

WEDNESDAY, JUNE 10, 1970

ROBERTS STADIUM, EVANSVILLE, INDIANA. **SET LIST:** "SPANISH CASTLE MAGIC" / "FIRE" / "LOVER MAN" / "RED HOUSE" / "FOXEY LADY" / " MACHINE GUN" / "MESSAGE TO LOVE" / "FREEDOM" / "HEAR MY TRAIN

A COMIN'" / "STAR SPANGLED BANNER" / "PURPLE HAZE" / "VOODOO CHILD (SLIGHT RETURN)"

Following their Evansville performance, the Experience flew back to New York. These "fly-out" gigs became increasingly common for Hendrix in 1970 and were far less taxing than the grinding pace set by previous Experience tours. "Jimi seemed quite happy," remembered Stickells. "When we weren't on the road we didn't see as much of him. Jimi had a life in New York. He had an apartment—much to the frustration of his neighbors. We used to get the occasional call from the police saying that he was playing guitar in his apartment at four o'clock in the morning and everybody was on the street complaining. But he was happy to be able to play the new songs and get ready for the new studio."

SATURDAY, JUNE 13, 1970

CIVIC CENTER, BALTIMORE, MARYLAND. WITH BALLIN' JACK AND CACTUS. **SET LIST:** "STRAIGHT AHEAD [PASS IT ON]" / "LOVER MAN" / " MACHINE GUN" / "EZY RYDER" / "RED HOUSE" / "MESSAGE TO LOVE" / "HEY JOE" / "FREEDOM" / "HEAR MY TRAIN A COMIN'" / "ROOM FULL OF MIRRORS" / "FOXEY LADY" / "PURPLE HAZE" / "STAR SPANGLED BANNER" / " VOODOO CHILD (SLIGHT RETURN)"

For their performance in Baltimore, the group traveled from New York in two limousines with their crew and gear in a separate truck. An exuberant "Pass It On" opened the performance at the sold-out Civic Center and set the tone for the evening. A powerful "Machine Gun," complete with a superb solo from Hendrix, confirmed this concert as one of the best of the entire 1970 tour.

EARLY JUNE 1970

ELECTRIC LADY STUDIOS, NEW YORK, NEW YORK. Electric Lady Studios offered Hendrix tangible proof that his talent had not only paid off but created a facility that would allow him to do what he loved best: write and record his music. Hendrix's closest friends were equally impressed. "I was awed," says Cox. "I had never seen a studio like that in my life. It was both unique and very personal."

The first order of business at the new studio was to evaluate the piles of multitrack tapes Hendrix had recorded over the previous nine months. Hendrix and Kramer dedicated a considerable amount of time to selecting the masters that warranted overdubs, those that would need to be recut, and those that would be scrapped entirely. Kramer explains. "When [the control room for] Studio A had been completed and Jimi wanted to start working, all of the tapes from the previous year when he had been jamming and writing stuff at places like Record Plant and Hit Factory were dumped in our laps. We started to listen to them, trying to make some sense out of this huge backlog of stuff. Jimi knew exactly what was on those tapes and he knew which tapes he wanted to work on first. We would listen to them, define whether the song was worth recutting—which we did on many occasions—editing, or overdubbing, which we also did." One of the first songs Hendrix tackled at Electric Lady was the Band Of Gypsys funk masterpiece "Ezy Ryder." "That had begun at the Record Plant," says Cox, "but Eddie pulled out the tapes and Jimi spent a lot of time doctoring up and trying to improve those tracks we had already recorded. We spent a bunch of time doing this before we started creating new material."

Enhancing previously recorded tracks only served to whet Hendrix's appetite to begin recording new material. "Jimi was so enthused about recording again he would arrive at sessions right on time—even early on occasion—something he rarely did," says Kramer. "We would spend up to ten or twelve hours at a time recording take after take. Unlike in the past, where, through jamming, he would try to develop the germ of an idea into a song, Hendrix came into Electric Lady with a distinctive idea as to how he wanted each track to sound."

It was during this evaluation process, says Kramer, that Hendrix began to realize just how considerable an upgrade in overall recording quality Electric Lady offered him. "Having come from working on all of his old tapes—where people at other studios clearly were intimidated by him or just didn't give a shit—Jimi could hear that *his* studio offered him a better bass sound, better drum sound, better everything," says Kramer. "Once the trust between us had been reestablished, I think Jimi relished the challenge that the studio represented."

"Once things at Electric Lady got rolling, Jimi generally booked open-ended nights," remembers King. "Normally, the start time was eight p.m., so Kramer would want us set up by seven. Then we would sit around and wait . . . and wait . . . and wait. There were times when Jimi wouldn't show up, but other times when he would come in at midnight raring to go. You never knew what the situation was going to be. We had to be at the height of readiness. Eddie would say, 'He's here, let's go.' We had to keep this edge and be on standby, ready to record at the drop of a hat."

While Hendrix's enthusiasm had been renewed by the possibilities that Electric Lady offered him, his vacillating moods were still the driving force behind his creativity. "There were times when he would say, 'I'm not into this,' and bail and go home," says King. "Then there were the nights when he was *on*. Even if Jimi was like that for only one night during the week, it made up for everything."

Hendrix's mood swings, acknowledges Cox, played a primary role in the outcome of each session. "Jimi's spirit had to be flowing in order for him to be creative," Cox says. "If there were things on his mind—and there was plenty—dampening his spirit, then we were in for an unproductive evening. If there was nothing bothering him, then we were in for a helluva night. Man, we'd get in there and just go on and on."

Hendrix's stormy relationship with his girlfriend, Devon Wilson, directly affected his concentration. Their volatile arguments tended to darken his mood considerably. "If his old lady had pissed him off, things weren't going to be too good," says Cox. Hendrix, however, internalized these disputes, as he was not prone to airing his personal problems, even to close friends like Cox and Mitchell. Instead, they respected Hendrix's unspoken language, recognizing when to push and when to lie back without addressing the issue or verbally confronting him. "If you were around Jimi, you could tell when something was bothering him," says Cox. "We would try to do something to take his mind off of his situation. Mitch or I would crack a joke or do something silly, while Eddie would try to divert Jimi's attention into the music. He'd say, 'Let's mix that track we did last night.' Pretty soon, Jimi's head would be back into it and he'd want to do an overdub or go

out in the studio to try something new. Mitch, Eddie, and I would look at each other like, 'Phew, worked that one out.'"

Over the summer, Electric Lady often served as a safe haven for Hendrix. He would leave the apartment he shared with Wilson at 59 West 12th Street, and walk the few blocks to the studio. "Jimi enjoyed recording at Electric Lady, but there were also times when he just wanted to cool out there," recalls Jim Marron. "Devon was giving him a bitch of a time, so he would stay at the studio and listen to playbacks. He used to let Kramer go home to catch a few hours sleep while he would just cool out. Eddie would offer to stay and keep working, but Jimi just wanted some playtime. It was part of the reason we built the place for him. He would just sit in the control room and have one of Kramer's assistants thread up the tapes he wanted to hear."

While Hendrix's closest associates knew that Devon's relationship with Hendrix was a double-edged sword, no one dared pry into the intimate details of his private life. "*Hell* no," says Cox. "You just accepted that that was part of the whole experience. Jimi had to work that out alone. Advice wasn't offered because it was not asked for."

The escalating tide of this political and emotional intrigue was something the newly hired staff at Electric Lady was utterly unprepared for. "We were kept in the dark about a lot of stuff," admits King. "Rumor was rampant in the studio, much of it was unconfirmed. What was going on upstairs in the office, which did not necessarily have anything to do with what was going on downstairs—and yet it did—had an impact."

And what of the Experience? Were they still a viable group or simply Hendrix's backing musicians? "Initially it was strange," says King, "because Mitch was back in the band and when we weren't cutting new tracks, we would be working with tapes which had Buddy Miles on drums."

Understandably, Mitchell's enthusiasm had been tempered by his ongoing financial battles with Jeffery. "At that time, we didn't get paid as session players," explains Cox. "There was really no reward other than finishing these songs and trying to get the album together. My obligation was to myself first, and to Jimi, so I was always there and always punctual. If Jimi called me and said we were all going to meet at the studio at seven thirty, I would be there at seven waiting on him. I would sit around in the control room with Eddie until he came in. He knew he could count on me. But there were a lot of times early on when Mitch would show up late, or not show up at all. That got Jimi very frustrated. He would want to cancel the session and I would say, 'Don't worry about it. That will give us a chance to tighten up our shit.' There were times when we would try to do some things without Mitch and overdub his part later, but that never worked, as our time would either fluctuate up or down without Mitch acting as our timekeeper. After a while, though, Mitch got into what we were doing. It was something different for him, because it was more of a creative process. When he got into the spirit of things, his attitude changed."

Another crucial change was the increased privacy afforded by the studio's locked front door and twenty-four-hour security. No longer could uninvited guests simply walk into the studio and disrupt the control room, as had become the norm at the Record Plant. Kramer seized the opportunity to enforce a new set of rules, aimed at stopping the hordes of hangers-on who jammed the control room and lobbied for Hendrix's attention. "The control room was the inner sanctum, and Eddie, especially, was very strict," says King. "On any given night, there were instructions from Jimi as to who to let in and who was to be excluded."

These changes had to be enforced, in Kramer's opinion, if Hendrix was going to maximize the opportunities the new studio presented. "It had been impossible trying to get work done during those sessions at the Hit Factory and the Record Plant," says Kramer. "At one point, I remember there were thirty people in the control room. That would never happen at Electric Lady. I wouldn't allow it. I knew he enjoyed this carnival atmosphere at times, because he still occasionally would bring in a bunch of people, but if I felt they were imposing, I would turn to him and say, 'Jimi, we can't get any work done.'"

Kramer was not alone in his call for heightened security. Cox had also endured far too many frustrating sessions disrupted by Hendrix's guests. "When I first came on board, Jimi's sessions were nothing but a big party," says Cox. "He saw that I would get up-

tight when a lot of those strangers would come in and disrupt our sessions. It just wasn't productive. I wasn't a party person, so I didn't want to waste all that time standing around doing nothing. I would let off some bad vibes when all those people would crowd our sessions. The studio was the place where you could experiment and make mistakes while you were getting songs together. The studio was not our stage. Jimi knew what was happening. He would privately say, 'If I was a janitor, do you think all of these people would want to watch me mop the floor?' But then he wouldn't throw anybody out because he didn't want to create a scene. All that changed at Electric Lady. We were finally able to get our work done without being disturbed. As a result, Jimi's spirits were higher and the recordings sounded better. We accomplished so much that summer."

Since Electric Lady did belong to him, Hendrix loosened the rules on some occasions. "There definitely was a different atmosphere in the studio when Kramer wasn't around," says King. "Jimi was like a schoolboy playing hooky. On one of these nights, I was engineering a session he was producing for the Patterson Singers. There were people all over the control room and Jimi was bouncing around between the studio and the console. It was almost more than I could handle."

FRIDAY, JUNE 12, 1970

BAND OF GYPSYS. TRACK RECORDS 2406 001. U.K. ALBUM RELEASE. PRODUCER: JIMI HENDRIX. ENGINEER: EDDIE KRAMER. "WHO KNOWS" / "MACHINE GUN" / "CHANGES" / "POWER OF SOUL" / "MESSAGE TO LOVE" / "WE GOTTA LIVE TOGETHER"

Because Track Records and Polydor Records had not yet reached a settlement in their longstanding legal battle with Ed Chalpin and PPX Industries over ownership rights to Hendrix's master recordings, the British release of *Band Of Gypsys* was delayed nearly three months. The wait served to whet the appetite of Hendrix's legion of fans, and the album jumped to number 6 during a lengthy thirty-week stay on the album chart.

Once again, Track's choice of cover artwork was the subject of controversy, as their version featured an unflattering puppet of Hendrix flanked by similar dolls made to resemble Bob Dylan and Brian Jones. Whatever their original intent, Track eventually succumbed to public pressure and months later substituted a new cover: a photo of Hendrix performing at the massive August 1970 Isle of Wight festival.

EARLY JUNE 1970

ELECTRIC LADY STUDIOS, NEW YORK, NEW YORK. ENGINEER: EDDIE KRAMER. SECOND ENGINEER: DAVE PALMER.

Two reels of free-form jamming with blues guitarist Richie Havens were recorded on this undated early June session. Cox and an unnamed drummer and piano player joined Havens and Hendrix. No formal takes were attempted: instead, the group created a long, rambling, mid- to fast-tempo blues jam.

MONDAY, JUNE 15, 1970

ELECTRIC LADY STUDIOS, NEW YORK, NEW YORK. ENGINEER: EDDIE KRAMER. SECOND ENGINEER: DAVE PALMER.

In the first known session to feature Hendrix, Cox, and Mitchell at the new studio, the trio recorded "All God's Children," a promising, up-tempo instrumental. Unlike "Beginnings" or "Bolero," two predetermined instrumental efforts Hendrix frequently attempted throughout the summer of 1970, the structure of "All God's Children" more resembles a backing track on to which Hendrix would have added a lead vocal performance. However, he did not record any vocals on this evening or any other: there is no record of Hendrix ever returning to the song. Nonetheless, it stands among the few tantalizing clues to the new music Hendrix planned for his future.

A revamping of "Ezy Ryder" came next. This song was one of the select Record Plant multitracks from 1969 and early 1970 that Hendrix had set aside for additional work. A rough mix from this session was issued in 2000 as part of the *Jimi Hendrix Experience* box set, and it reveals how Hendrix began to extensively retool the original recording through multiple overdubs. Hendrix saved only the original drum parts by Miles before rebuilding the song front to back. On this evening, Hendrix attempted a number of different lead guitar overdubs.

Sometime thereafter, Traffic's Chris Wood and Steve Winwood paid a visit to the studio and the two were so impressed with the facility that they decided to jam. With Mitchell no longer available, having departed some time earlier, the group needed a drummer on short notice. Kramer volunteered Dave Palmer, a one-time member of Ted Nugent's Amboy Dukes turned Electric Lady engineer. Palmer, who lived across the street from the studio, was rousted out of bed by a telephone call from Kramer. Palmer explains, "Kramer called me at two a.m. saying, 'Hendrix is down at the studio and we need a drummer. Get your ass over here and bang on those tubs.' When I got there, Hendrix and Kramer were showing Steve Winwood the place. Nothing was really set up, but Jimi and Stevie had the itch to play, so Eddie set up a couple of microphones and I got behind the drums and jammed with the two of them."

Before Palmer's arrival, Hendrix previewed some of his recent recordings for Winwood and Wood, coaxing the two of them into providing backing vocals for "Ezy Ryder."

The first jam—a spirited workout loosely founded on Traffic's "Pearly Queen"—featured Hendrix on bass, Winwood on electric piano, and Palmer on drums. Palmer then returned to the control room and Hendrix took over on guitar. After some discussion, Hendrix and Winwood began a slow, soulful rendition of "Valleys Of Neptune." In addition to his electric piano, Winwood's Rhythm Ace, an electronic metronome device, provided a steady backbeat for the two to play against. The pairing of these two special talents clicked instantly, as Winwood quickly grasped Hendrix's arrangement and began to provide not just simple accompaniment, but his own accents as well. While the quality of this recording is raw—just room microphones set up in a rush—several brilliant moments were captured on tape. Kramer, who enjoyed the privilege of recording both Hendrix and Traffic, especially appreciated the limitless possibilities of any such collaborative effort. "Steve was the perfect foil for Jimi and one of the very few musicians who could have kept up with him," says Kramer.

Chris Wood had not participated in Winwood's jam

with Hendrix, and Winwood did not take part in Wood's wild, free-form jazz jam with Hendrix, which filled an entire reel of tape. There were no takes of any kind, just exuberant, unstructured jamming, much to the pleasure of all involved. Later jams intermittently involved Winwood, as well as Jenny Dean, a mutual friend who lent vocals to a similar free-form effort entitled "Slow Blues." In all, it was a wild night to remember.

TUESDAY, JUNE 16, 1970

ELECTRIC LADY STUDIOS, NEW YORK, NEW YORK. ENGINEER: EDDIE KRAMER. SECOND ENGINEER: KIM KING.
Hendrix enjoyed an extremely productive evening, arguably his strongest studio performance since the closing days of the *Electric Ladyland* album. Joined by percussionist Juma Sultan, the group began the evening by debuting "Night Bird Flying," a superb new Hendrix original.

"Night Bird Flying" had been in development for some time. Small elements of the song's rhythm pattern can be traced to jams staged at TTG Studios in October 1968. In early 1969, the song began to take form as "Ships Passing Through The Night." Hendrix revisited the song on a number of occasions throughout 1969, weaving selected portions into various jam sessions. A series of demos were also recorded, with the first known recording made on April 14, 1969, at the Record Plant, but none could be described as definitive. On this evening, Hendrix began anew, recording thirty-two takes before the final master was achieved. While take 7 held together until just prior to the close, a complete take 12 provided the first real glimpse of the song's vast promise. Take 17 was appropriately listed as "good," but Hendrix was not satisfied. Take 23 narrowed the margin even further, but it, too, was rejected. A marvelous take 24 was listed as "good" and timed at 3:45. Following a playback, however, the engineers put in a new reel of tape, and work resumed. Takes 29 and take 30 were marked "good," but, still unsatisfied, Hendrix pressed on. Finally, a superb take 32 confirmed his vision. Following a playback, the group attempted three edits, with the second ultimately inserted into the final master. At the close of the master take, after the song fades out, Hendrix and Kramer can be heard

discussing how and where to fade out the song to create a proper ending.

While much time over the following weeks was dedicated to recording overdubs and preparing a final mix for "Night Bird Flying," everyone involved in this special evening knew that Hendrix had created a masterwork indicative of his growth as a musician and composer: certainly a worthy representation of his new musical direction. "'Night Bird Flying' was truly a superlative effort," says Kramer. "Mitch was great on that track, really on the mark." As complex as the basic rhythm track had been, recording Hendrix's overdubs proved equally challenging. "That song was a bastard to mix because we had so many guitar parts," remembers Kramer. "There's one bit in there [beginning at 2:22 and lasting until 2:30] where Jimi displayed his country influence. He did it as a piss-take and was laughing when he played it. I loved when Jimi would throw bits like that in."

With a basic track for "Night Bird Flying" completed to his satisfaction, Hendrix initiated work on "Straight Ahead." The versions recorded here showed the group tightening their grasp on the song's arrangement, honing the various rhythm patterns in preparation for more formal takes.

After "Straight Ahead," Hendrix debuted a brand new instrumental. "Messing Around," as the recording was described on the tape box, was a funky, mid- to fast-tempo instrumental with an arrangement that evolved gradually over multiple takes. Before take 17, Hendrix made some specific refinements, instructing Cox to try playing his bass line with simpler notes. While Cox responded accordingly, Hendrix was unable to bring the song to an effective close. Despite such structural problems, the last three takes each brimmed with promise. Hendrix, however, seemed to recognize that it would take more work to achieve a proper master. After take 20, he abandoned the track entirely.

Next came "Beginnings," the instrumental originally conceived as "Jam Back At The House" at Hendrix's Shokan retreat in July 1969. While some takes were highly charged, the four appeared to be working the parts out as they went, with Hendrix intermittently addressing each musician with thoughts and instructions. None of these versions was complete or formally slated as a take. They did, however, serve to rally the group, as an extremely potent, instrumental rendition of "Freedom" followed. While the song's structure was immediately recognizable, it had a noticeably slower pace. The gritty texture of Hendrix's guitar tone was also dissimilar, as Hendrix adopted a higher-pitched, jangling tone not featured anywhere on the finished master. Hendrix's exceptional chord styling, like the demo itself, was earthy and raw. While no match for the finished master, which was recorded nine days later on June 25, this sparkling demo provided a fascinating window into the song's evolution. At its conclusion, a tired Hendrix remarked, "That's good enough for tonight. We'll come back and do that tomorrow."

WEDNESDAY, JUNE 17, 1970

ELECTRIC LADY STUDIOS, NEW YORK, NEW YORK. ENGINEER: EDDIE KRAMER. SECOND ENGINEER: KIM KING. This exceptional evening session began with an enthusiastic reprise of "Straight Ahead." Following some twenty-five rehearsal takes, take 1, the first formal take,

was complete and timed at 4:20. After a playback, Hendrix asked Kramer, "What guitar tone was I using, this one or the one with more bass?" He demonstrated the first tone with a quick burst of treble notes, and Kramer replied, "The one with more bass." All three musicians sounded confident and in obvious good spirits as work steadily progressed. Take 7 was listed as having a "nice feel," while take 11 was cited as complete. Following take 18, an edit of the song's front part was attempted. Two takes were done and the second was kept. After a playback and evaluation of their efforts, Hendrix added a lead guitar overdub.

Next, Hendrix, Cox, and Mitchell concentrated on creating a section of "Straight Ahead" to edit into the new master take. Various sections were recorded, showcasing superb performances from all three. "Thank you, everyone!" Kramer said over the talkback microphone when they had finished. Hendrix's enthusiasm was on full display throughout, creating a momentum that had been conspicuously absent from far too many of Hendrix's 1969 sessions.

Similar edit sections were then recorded for "Astro Man." This effort featured Hendrix and Cox playing the same part simultaneously, a driving, distorted rhythm pattern. While this, too, was extremely well performed, there is no evidence that this overdub—unlike the edit sections created for "Straight Ahead"—made the final master.

With "Straight Ahead" deemed finished for the time being, Hendrix's interpretation of Bob Dylan's "Drifter's Escape" came next. Hendrix had originally decided to begin the song alone, but he suggested that Cox initiate the track on bass. As Cox pumped the song's distinctive opening notes, Hendrix countered with quick, sparse strokes on the guitar. This won his immediate approval, as his excited, "Yeah!" was also captured on tape. Having seized the idea, Hendrix abruptly brought the group to a halt. "Run the tape! Run the tape!" he demanded. "We are, we are, we are," Kramer reassured him. Hendrix then began to sing, "Help me in my weakness" in a high-pitched voice, then "Help me in my . . . aah" in an even higher octave, with his voice on the verge of cracking. Straining, Hendrix's voice finally does give in on the third, and highest, "Aah!" which brings a laugh from Kramer.

"Oh fuck!" laughs Hendrix. "The devil made me sing like that!" When Hendrix announced the song, Kramer asked him to sing along live. "You want me to sing it?" asked Hendrix with a laugh. A promising albeit incomplete take of "Drifter's Escape" then followed. Take 2, also incomplete, was even stronger, with Hendrix supplying a charged live vocal throughout the song's first half. At the conclusion of this take, Hendrix teased roadies Eric Barrett and Gene McFadden, who wanted to make some equipment changes. "Don't worry, Eric Barrett and Gene McFadden," said Kramer, adding in a mock cockney accent, "Eric says he's dying a death out here." "Well, listen," Hendrix joked, "I'm going to save him right this very instant . . . if we can just get it right this time." "Just play!" bellowed Mitchell. "You have three minutes," says Kramer. "Oh three minutes, no wonder we have so much time," Hendrix added with a laugh. His misfiring of the song's introduction caused him to remark, "Oh fuck! Two and a half minutes," which brought a laugh from everyone. Eric Barrett continued the horseplay with a remark about Mitchell's earphones falling off his head. "We'll have to get you a special pair of cans [headphones], Mitch," deadpanned Kramer. "Ones weighted with lead." "No, the kind with the gum on the insides," suggested Hendrix instead, which cracked everyone up. As Barrett and McFadden changed amplifiers, installing a new Ampeg for Cox, the group took a break in the control room. After the work was completed, they returned to the studio to record the third take, an exceptional effort that yielded the working master. On July 19 and 20, Hendrix returned to the master to overdub additional lead and rhythm guitar parts, as well as a lead vocal.

Beginning with the two May dates at the Record Plant, Kramer's role had evolved, and now encompassed dual responsibilities as engineer and co-producer. Hendrix was still in charge of each session, deciding which songs to record and what arrangements to utilize, but the working relationship between the two had matured, allowing Kramer to maximize his contributions without clashing with Hendrix's eager attitude and desire to try to do everything. "Except for Gary Kellgren, the other engineers we had worked with at the Record Plant gave us very little input," says Cox. "They just figured that Jimi knew what he was doing, so they left him alone.

They would make suggestions like changing the batteries in the wah-wah pedal or replacing a Fuzz Face unit if it was causing problems, but none of them would get into a song like Eddie would do. Kramer got totally absorbed into what we were doing. Jimi appreciated that. Eddie wasn't the type of guy who would come over the talkback and say, 'Guys, you were playing an F sharp there instead of an F.' He never got into that. He stayed on top of Jimi's tuning and every now and then would say, 'What's that I hear?' and Jimi would say, 'Yeah, I hear that, too. Let's change or fix that.'"

For Kramer, the key to maximizing their working relationship was simply maintaining a clear understanding of each other's strengths and responsibilities. "At this point, now that we had started working together again, his sense of involvement behind the console was not as heavy as it had been before," recalls Kramer. "He left it more or less up to me, and was showing more interest in what was happening out in the studio rather than the control room. However, we still mixed songs together and the old team feel came back immediately."

"Kramer was like a director," says King. "There was no telling Jimi *what* to play, but if he was on, Kramer would channel him into something productive, because if he hadn't, Hendrix would have gone on all night long recording some marvelous jam that was simply unusable."

Kramer's complete commitment to Hendrix's music endeared him to Hendrix. "We felt that a lot of the engineers we had worked with at the Record Plant had been nice guys, but Eddie had his head into what we were all about," says Cox. "We were all comfortable with Eddie and knew that he could help us make magic out of what we put down on tape. Eddie was into our music and would add direction to our creativity. He would hear something we'd play and want to try something backward or make adjustments to Jimi's guitar sound. Here was an engineer who was really concerned—heretofore, the other engineers we had used would ask us whether or not to use EQ or which tracks the drums should be recorded on. We didn't want the engineer to ask *us*, we wanted him to feel it and get involved. Kramer got involved. You needed that with Jimi Hendrix because he was such a perfectionist. There were many times when I would say, 'Damn, that's

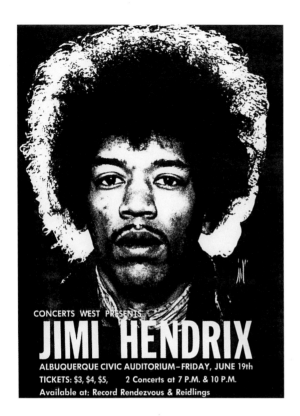

JUNE 19, 1970: POSTER FOR A SHOW AT CIVIC AUDITORIUM, ALBUQUERQUE, NEW MEXICO.

CONCERTS WEST PRESENTS
JIMI HENDRIX
ALBUQUERQUE CIVIC AUDITORIUM—FRIDAY, JUNE 19th
TICKETS: $3, $4, $5,   2 Concerts at 7 P.M. & 10 P.M.
Available at: Record Rendezvous & Reidlings

good! You can't improve that,' but he would try-ing. He would record a great guitar overdub and Eddie would tell him that it was great. He'd think we were all putting him on and that he could do it better. There were times—even at Electric Lady—when he would take two hours to come to the conclusion that what he was playing now was great, but not better than the take we had thought was great."

THURSDAY, JUNE 18, 1970

ELECTRIC LADY STUDIOS, NEW YORK, NEW YORK. ENGINEER: EDDIE KRAMER.
Hendrix dedicated this long evening session to guitar overdubs for "Ezy Ryder." At this stage, the song's ending still comprised a long, slow fade-out rather than the panning effect featured on the finished master.

FRIDAY, JUNE 19, 1970

CIVIC AUDITORIUM, ALBUQUERQUE, NEW MEXICO. TWO SHOWS.

SATURDAY, JUNE 20, 1970

SWING AUDITORIUM, SAN BERNADINO, CALIFORNIA. **SET LIST:** "ALL ALONG THE WATCHTOWER" / "ROOM FULL OF MIRRORS" / "MACHINE GUN" / "MESSAGE TO LOVE" / "HEAR MY TRAIN A COMIN'" / "FOXEY LADY" / "HEY JOE" / "PURPLE HAZE" / "VOODOO CHILD (SLIGHT RETURN)"

SUNDAY, JUNE 21, 1970

VENTURA COUNTY FAIRGROUNDS, VENTURA, CALIFOR-NIA. WITH BALLIN' JACK AND GRIN. **PARTIAL SET LIST:** "MACHINE GUN" / "FOXEY LADY" / "PURPLE HAZE"
Hendrix left Electric Lady for a three-day run of West Coast tour dates that began with two performances in Albuquerque, New Mexico.

In San Bernadino, Hendrix broke the attendance record at the Swing Auditorium when 7,300 fans witnessed Hendrix open this exciting performance with "All Along The Watchtower," the first known rendition of the song by this lineup. Despite the song's popularity, Hendrix regularly spurned audience requests in 1968 and 1969 for the song. In 1970, Hendrix began to incor-porate the song into his stage repertoire more often. "I wanted to play those songs," says Cox. "I wanted him to play 'Crosstown Traffic,' but we never got around to rehearsing it."

A crowd in excess of 4,000 came to see the group perform outdoors at the Ventura County Fairgrounds while police battled with some 400 people fighting outside the main gate to get inside and catch sight of the show.

WEDNESDAY, JUNE 24, 1970

ELECTRIC LADY STUDIOS, NEW YORK, NEW YORK. ENGINEER: EDDIE KRAMER. SECOND ENGINEER: DAVE PALMER.
Hendrix stuck to his hard-won bargain that left touring for weekends and recording for weekdays. He can-celed two scheduled concert dates—June 23 in Denver and June 25 in Pittsburgh—and remained at Electric Lady, eager to build upon the encouraging progress he had made in recent weeks. The group's efforts on

this evening did not disappoint, as Hendrix centered his focus squarely on "Astro Man." Hendrix had frequently incorporated portions of the rhythm pattern of "Astro Man"—or "Asshole Man," as he would occasionally label the song—in a number of his Record Plant jams during 1969. Previously, the most developed attempt at recording the track had been made by the Band Of Gypsys in January 1970. That version, however, was never completed.

Capturing the song's infectious groove was Hendrix's primary task on this evening, and the group filled two reels of tape with instrumental takes. Each new effort inched closer to the arrangement eventually featured on the finished master. "'We were in a groove that night," remembers Cox. "'Astro Man' was such a fun song to play. By that time, we knew those patterns extremely well. We enjoyed building on them." Reel three began with a loose run-through of Muddy Waters's "Rolling Stone," marked incorrectly on the tape box as "I Just Want To Make Love to You." Six incomplete takes of "Astro Man" followed. An extended take 7 was spectacular, with Cox and Mitchell firmly interlocked and teaming up with Hendrix to expand the boundaries of the arrangement.

Hendrix changed direction after this, guiding Cox and Mitchell into "Cherokee Mist." What started as a diversion from "Astro Man" quickly took hold as the three locked into the song's rhythm patterns. As their momentum swelled, Hendrix shifted gears, incorporating elements of what would ultimately develop as "In From The Storm" one month later. This recording was later mixed and released as part of the *Jimi Hendrix Experience* box set.

At the conclusion of "Cherokee Mist," Cox led Hendrix through a short burst of Cream's "Politician." Four additional takes of "Astro Man," numbering 11 through 14, came next. Though none yielded a finished master, Hendrix's playing was nevertheless especially noteworthy. With the band in full flight, lost within another electrifying take, the reel of tape abruptly ended, forcing assistant engineer Dave Palmer to hurriedly change reels. As soon as the new reel was installed, Palmer snapped on the record button, capturing the final forty seconds of the jam. Hendrix then tore into a stunning medley that lasted—without pause—nearly

twenty-six minutes. He began with a slow, blistering, seven-minute rendition of "Beginnings," with Mitchell and Cox swinging tightly behind him. This evolved into an up-tempo "Hey Baby (Land Of The New Rising Sun)," which boasted several thrilling moments. Hendrix then downshifted, cruising into a spirited jam that evolved as "Keep On Movin'," a spontaneous hybrid of "Straight Ahead" and "Midnight Lightning." A furious instrumental take of "Freedom" followed next, carried to a close with a rousing flourish. Kramer's enthusiasm came immediately over the talkback, and applause from guests seated in the control room was audible. Hendrix seemed genuinely surprised by the reaction, and called for the band to come in and listen to what remains today, more than thirty-five years later, a fascinating document of his magnificent talent.

Sessions such as these emphatically underscored Hendrix's creative rejuvenation. Electric Lady had sparked his imagination, challenging him to maximize his immeasurable gifts as both a musician and composer. Within the private confines of his new studio, Hendrix had successfully refocused his energy and concentration on his music "Inside the studio, we were never bothered by outside influences," says Cox. "Even Michael Jeffery stayed away. I only saw him come down once, and that was just to see what was going on. He didn't have any input whatsoever. We were left to create music and that's what we loved to do. That made Jimi so happy. He would say, 'Man, we don't fish or go bowling like other people do. We make music and *this* is fun.' I said, 'It sure is. I feel sorry for a whole lot of musicians who can't do this.' Electric Lady was home to us. Even when we would be out on the road we'd be thinking up little patterns, showing them to each other and saying, 'We'll have to try that at the studio when we get back.'"

THURSDAY, JUNE 25, 1970

ELECTRIC LADY STUDIOS, NEW YORK, NEW YORK. ENGINEER: EDDIE KRAMER. SECOND ENGINEER: DAVE PALMER.

Work continued on "Astro Man," with the group, joined by Juma Sultan, applying finishing touches to the new basic track. More overdubs as well as a number of rough mixes would follow later, but the version recorded on this day served as the final master.

Hendrix then focused on new takes of "Valleys Of Neptune," continuing his effort to realize this promising song. A final master for the song, however, continued to elude him.

"Drifting," a superlative new ballad, made its recorded debut. The group recorded a backing track, with Hendrix playing through a Leslie organ speaker while simultaneously contributing a guide vocal track. Following that successful take, they also recorded the song's introduction. Both of these efforts were marked "master."

Putting "Drifting" aside, Hendrix turned to "Freedom." After an incomplete initial take, take 2 was especially lively. A brief conference between Hendrix and Kramer ensued, as Kramer felt the entry position of the bass guitar required repositioning. The group came back into the control room for a listen, and the meeting was clearly beneficial, as, following a false start marked as take 3, take 4 was especially confident. Having missed an occasional note, Hendrix knew he could improve upon his own performance so after a false start on take 5, an exceptional sixth take captured the master.

"Originally, all Jimi had was just that opening riff," recalls Cox. "I remember him playing it to me at his apartment during the time of the Band Of Gypsys. We spent a lot of time working that song out before we finally recorded it at Electric Lady. Back then, what we did was to always record a work track. A work track was simply a basic track: just the basic guitar, bass, and drum parts down on tape. With that work track, the possibilities were unlimited. You could go over that guitar, you could erase that bass part because you already had the basic ingredients of a dynamic song recorded. We did not work with paper and pen or bars and time signatures. We had all this in our head. With a work track down, we could build something and that's how 'Freedom' finally came about."

Hendrix's plan was to prepare a double album of new material called *First Rays Of The New Rising Sun*. At some point during this day, Hendrix took stock of his progress, composing a memo to himself that listed the following tracks as having backing tracks completed:

"Ezy Ryder," "Room Full of Mirrors," "Earth Blues Today," "Have You Heard" (also known as "Straight Ahead"), "Freedom," "Stepping Stone," "Izabella" ("complete, needs new mix"), "Astro Man," and "Night Bird Flying." He listed "Drifter's Escape" and "Burning Desire" as well, but put questions marks beside them. He also made a note to get the Olympic Studios April 1967 master tape of "Highway Chile."

FRIDAY, JUNE 26, 1970

ELECTRIC LADY STUDIOS, NEW YORK, NEW YORK. ENGINEER: EDDIE KRAMER. SECOND ENGINEER: KIM KING.
On this busy evening, the group revisited and overdubbed previously recorded masters. The December 19, 1969/January 20, 1970, Record Plant recording of "Message To Love" was reviewed, but no overdubbing was attempted. This decision, says Kramer, was made because Hendrix felt that songs such as "Message To Love," "Machine Gun," and "Power Of Soul" had been given over to *Band Of Gypsys*. Issuing studio versions—however different in their style or arrangement—seemed like a step backward and didn't fit with his plans for the projected double album.

The December 19, 1969/January 20, 1970, Record Plant recording of "Earth Blues," however, received an extensive overhaul. Rather than simply recut the track, Hendrix chose to reconstruct the song from within, replacing the bulk of the original recording with new overdubs. A decision was made to replace Miles's original drum parts with a new overdub by Mitchell. Cox improved upon his original bass line, and Hendrix kept busy as well, overdubbing a new rhythm guitar line as well as two new lead tracks. The backing vocals from Miles and the Ronettes stayed in, but Hendrix also added a new background vocal to complement their original effort.

Though the group had invested considerable time and effort in revamping "Earth Blues," Hendrix stopped short of designating this track as finished, believing that he might still be able to improve on his performance. "While 'Earth Blues' very much fit musically into the framework of his new direction, we were never certain that it was ever going to make the final record," says Kramer. Of all of Hendrix's new material, "Earth Blues," with its overt R&B influence, seemed to best clarify the deepening creative divide between Hendrix and Jeffery. "'Earth Blues' was a good track," says engineer John Jansen. "But nobody upstairs wanted to hear those 'Everybody!' chants on a record by Jimi. When Jimi wasn't around and Jeffery heard us working on it, he would wave his hands in the air and roll his eyes."

"Stepping Stone" was another Band Of Gypsys staple retooled at Electric Lady. On this evening, Hendrix overdubbed additional rhythm and lead guitar parts. Later, undocumented sessions would result in more guitar overdubbing from Hendrix, a vocal overdub, and new drum parts from Mitchell, replacing those originally recorded by Miles. Nevertheless, Kramer feels that Hendrix would have continued to tinker with "Stepping Stone," had he lived. "The tempo was always the problem with this song," explains Kramer. "Both Buddy and Mitch had trouble staying with Jimi on that one."

"Stepping Stone" became the subject of considerable controversy when Alan Douglas had former Knack drummer Bruce Gary record new drum parts for the song in January 1995. This bastardized version was included as part of the ill-fated *Voodoo Soup* compilation Douglas issued in April 1995. "Room Full Of Mirrors" suffered a similar fate, as Gary recorded new drum parts for that song as well.

Critics and Hendrix fans alike savaged *Voodoo Soup* upon its release. When confronted by journalists, Douglas and Gary offered a variety of explanations for the overdubs, including claims that the work was necessary because the original multitrack master for "Stepping Stone" was damaged, or lost, or the original drum parts by Miles were mysteriously missing. Nothing could be farther from the truth. The irony is that the original multitrack master for both songs featured drum parts by both of Hendrix's drummers. Miles cut the original tracks for both songs, and Mitchell overdubbed drum parts at Electric Lady in 1970. Mitchell's playing on "Stepping Stone" can be heard on *First Rays Of The New Rising Sun,* while his version of "Room Full Of Mirrors" remains unreleased. For *Voodoo Soup*, engineer Mark Linett transferred the original sixteen-track multitrack masters to forty-eight-track digital (thus ensuring that none of the original performances would be lost), recorded Gary's overdubs, and remixed

both tracks for the album. Deleting *Voodoo Soup* from the official Hendrix catalog and removing it from retail stores was the first order of business for Experience Hendrix. *Voodoo Soup* stands as the bookend to *Crash Landing* and Douglas's tenure as the supervisor of the Jimi Hendrix catalog.

Later on the night of June 26, the group completed additional bass and guitar work on "Valleys Of Neptune," another promising track that was making encouraging strides at the studio. The origins of "Valleys Of Neptune" took shape during Hendrix's summer retreat at the Shokan house near Woodstock during the summer of 1969. Beginning at the Hit Factory in September 1969 and continuing for nine more months, Hendrix recorded a number of unrealized versions, clearly aware of the song's potential. Despite this extraordinary effort, he never completed a master take to his satisfaction. "I loved that song," says Cox. "Jimi spent a lot of time at his apartment trying to tighten it up. He kept adding to his original idea. We almost completed that song at Electric Lady, and if we had, it would have been a monster."

Also on this evening, sandwiched between overdub attempts by Hendrix and Cox for "Valleys Of Neptune," strains of another intriguing Hendrix original debuted, a sparse, solo demo entitled "Heaven Has No Sorrow." Building on this skeletal take, Hendrix labored closely with Cox in an attempt to establish an appropriate bass line and further develop the song's existing rhythm pattern. "'Heaven Has No Sorrow' was an idea of Jimi's that we never really got to do," says Cox. "The demo we cut was nothing of any real significance, but it probably could have evolved into a pretty dynamic song, something along the lines of 'Angel.'"

With the studio becoming more functional each day, Hendrix's enthusiasm grew. "That studio was like our laboratory," says Cox. "We would go out on the road and work, so that he could *create* back at Electric Lady."

While Kramer's presence may have served to sharpen Hendrix's focus, the studio's policy of minimizing the many distractions he suffered elsewhere played a critical role in his creative rejuvenation. Kramer and studio president Jim Marron lectured both the employees and engineering staff to allow Hendrix whatever distance he desired. "Beyond the front door to the studio, Jimi did not exist for any of the assistant engineers," explains King. "His private life was absolutely separate from the studio. That was one of the things about Electric Lady. Jimi would be able to walk through the door and be someplace else—the real world would stop once he came in the front door."

While the majority of his previous sessions at the Record Plant began after midnight, Hendrix's sessions at Electric Lady usually started at seven p.m. "We would know when Jimi had arrived, because he would have to be buzzed in at the front door," says King. "Jimi rarely came down the stairs and walked straight into the control room. He generally would head to the office upstairs. Eddie usually had a rough mix of something set up and ready to go, but often it would turn out that Jimi would want to work on something else. When Jimi would come into the control room, he would have a private meeting with Eddie, and assistant engineers were not party to that. When they were finished, Jimi would head out to the studio and Eddie would tell us what we would be doing that night. But even then, Jimi's sessions were almost entirely directed by his mood and whims. Some nights we would stick to the game plan, other nights he would want to change midstream and get into something else."

While the elimination of the hordes of hangers-on had improved the creative climate within the studio, it did little to stabilize the delicate condition of Hendrix's private life. The volatility of his relationship with Devon Wilson, coupled with his many battles with Jeffery, took a heavy toll. "There were also some nights where Jimi would arrive, head upstairs, and not come down at all," remembers King. "We would wait and sometimes Eddie would get a phone call from upstairs saying that Jimi was not going to work that night. There were some serious politics going on up there, but Eddie forbade us from getting involved with it in any way. We were *not* to put our two cents in."

Devon Wilson cast a large shadow at Electric Lady. Her standing as Hendrix's girlfriend lent considerable weight to her criticisms and observations. "Devon was just as cunning as Michael Jeffery," remembers Jim Marron. "She was intensely into anything that she perceived as being good for Jimi. Jeffery would not take any shit

from her, but at the same time, she used to try and see just how far she could push him."

Wilson's reach extended right through to the control room, where she was a frequent spectator throughout the long summer. "She wanted to be there all the time, saying once, 'If you're going to be making music or mixing music with Jimi, I've got to be there,'" recalls engineer Dave Palmer. "That was weird, a necessary evil for Hendrix, I guess. Kramer got along well with her, but I always sensed he would have just preferred she not be there."

The depth of Wilson's influence at Electric Lady fluctuated wildly, bound to the present status of her relationship with Hendrix. Their relationship was so volatile that Hendrix would occasionally bar her from the studio. "Devon was more often part of the scene than not, but there were times when she was not allowed in," says King. "On some evenings, as per Jimi's instructions, we were not to answer the door to Devon."

SATURDAY, JUNE 27, 1970

BOSTON GARDEN, BOSTON, MASSACHUSETTS. WITH CACTUS AND THE ILLUSION. **SET LIST:** "STONE FREE" / "LOVER MAN" / "RED HOUSE" / "FREEDOM" / "FOXEY LADY" / "PURPLE HAZE" / "STAR SPANGLED BANNER" / "ALL ALONG THE WATCHTOWER" / "MESSAGE TO LOVE" / "FIRE" / "SPANISH CASTLE MAGIC" / "HEY BABY (NEW RISING SUN)" / "VOODOO CHILD (SLIGHT RETURN)"

As they had done for their other East Coast stops on this tour, the Experience drove from New York to Boston by limousine, with their crew and equipment traveling by truck.

Hendrix once again tinkered with his set list for this lively performance. The group had been working on "Freedom" at Electric Lady in recent days and decided to feature it here. "Machine Gun" was discarded in favor of "Stone Free" and a rare "All Along The Watchtower." A rousing "Voodoo Child (Slight Return)" closed the show, thrilling the sold-out sports arena.

MONDAY, JUNE 29, 1970

ELECTRIC LADY STUDIOS, NEW YORK, NEW YORK. ENGINEER: EDDIE KRAMER. SECOND ENGINEER: KIM KING.

Hendrix devoted this session to recording overdubs, concentrating mostly on "Drifting." He overdubbed a lead vocal and experimented with a number of interesting ideas, including a recording of his breathing superimposed backward as an effect. A number of electronic sound effects were also tested, including an attempt to recapture the "seagull" sound originally featured as part of *Electric Ladyland*'s "1983... (A Merman I Should Turn To Be)." Hendrix moved his headphones into the vocal microphone to create feedback and other sounds that could be incorporated during mixing.

Save for the lead vocal part, none of the ideas presented on this evening was ultimately included on the master prepared for *Cry Of Love*.

TUESDAY, JUNE 30, 1970

ELECTRIC LADY STUDIOS, NEW YORK, NEW YORK. ENGINEER: EDDIE KRAMER. SECOND ENGINEER: DAVE PALMER.

Overdubs and mixes for a number of songs were attempted, including "Freedom." The June 17 recording of "Drifter's Escape" was revisited, but overdubs attempted on this date were later scrapped in favor of new parts added on July 19.

WEDNESDAY, JULY 1, 1970

ELECTRIC LADY STUDIOS, NEW YORK, NEW YORK. ENGINEER: EDDIE KRAMER. SECOND ENGINEER: DAVE PALMER.

For many years, this date has been inaccurately referred to as Electric Lady's unofficial opening date. While that claim is untrue, this lengthy session was, arguably, Hendrix's most productive there. On this evening, "Dolly Dagger," one of Hendrix's most promising new songs, came to life. Unlike the majority of Hendrix's other compositions from this period, "Dolly Dagger" did not evolve through repeated jam sessions at the Record Plant during 1969. "Jimi cut 'Dolly Dagger' twice," recalls Kramer. "He had recorded a rough demo at the Record Plant [in November 1969], but that was scrapped entirely. We cut the new basic track [during this session], but spent three or four days overdubbing guitars and finishing the background vocals."

Where Cox's bass line had originally inspired Hendrix to develop the song's rhythm pattern, "Dolly Dagger"'s colorful lyrics, says Love guitarist Arthur Lee, were inspired by Devon Wilson. Wilson told Lee that the lyric "She drinks her blood from a jagged edge," drew its origins from Hendrix's November 27, 1969, birthday party, when Mick Jagger accidentally pricked his finger. When he asked for a bandage, Devon rushed to him and told him that wouldn't be necessary. Then, in front of Hendrix, she sucked the blood from his finger.

The Experience, joined again by percussionist Juma Sultan, began recording with six rehearsal takes of "Dolly Dagger," each performed without Mitchell on drums. These six takes revealed Hendrix and Cox, supported by Sultan's insistent conga work, developing the song's distinctive groove. After the sixth rehearsal, Hendrix and company retreated to the control room to assess their progress. When recording resumed, Mitchell was now seated behind his Gretsch double drum kit, contributing to a charming interpretation of "Bolero." "Bolero" was actually marked take 1, followed by an ineffective complete take of "Dolly Dagger." With the group not entirely in sync, Hendrix shifted gears, guiding them through the more familiar "Hey Baby (Land Of The New Rising Sun)." Hendrix sang the first line off-key, which caused him to unceremoniously remark, "Flat," before continuing the song as an instrumental. Their next attempt was considerably upgraded, creating the version later issued as part of *Rainbow Bridge*. An instrumental stab at "Drifting" followed and closed out the reel.

With fresh tape ready to go, a hearty "Dolly Dagger" opened reel two, ignited by Hendrix's energy and enthusiasm. Singing and playing live, Hendrix can be heard improvising the song's lyrics as he shapes the infectious rhythm track.

Their focus sharpened, and work on "Dolly Dagger" began in earnest. A series of takes, numbered 3 through 17, followed, but each was incomplete. Though it did not yield the master, an encouraging eighteenth take finally turned the corner. Primed for success, take 19 provided the master, as well as "Slow Part," an unexpected delight. "As 'Dolly Dagger' began to come apart," explains Kramer, "Billy Cox started playing the bass line to 'Gimme Some Lovin',' the Spencer Davis Group song, and that developed into a jam lasting nearly ten minutes."

"'Dolly Dagger' had broken down," says John Jansen, "but the band continued to play. After three minutes or so, Hendrix began playing this beautiful melody and the rest of the guys fell in behind him."

"When the jam started, Jimi was just fucking around," says Kramer. "The tone he was using was just his quiet jam tone, with the amplifier turned down some and not the full-bore Marshall sound he had used to cut the basic track. Afterwards, when he realized that there might be something in this after all, he overdubbed a second guitar and a new solo with the Marshall back at full volume. He did these with the Uni-Vibe, as well as a Leslie at the end."

Marked on the tape box as "Slow Part" by second engineer Dave Palmer, an edited version of this instrumental would be posthumously renamed "Pali Gap," and join "Dolly Dagger" as part of the *Rainbow Bridge* film and its accompanying soundtrack album. Jeffery gave it the title "Pali Gap" in an attempt to

further associate the song with the film's Hawaiian setting. While Hendrix had taken the additional step of adding overdubs to "Slow Part," Kramer recalls that there was no plan ever to include the instrumental as part of *First Rays Of The New Rising Sun*.

Next came two attempts at the blues-based "Midnight Lightning," neither of which was complete. Considering his many attempts throughout 1969 and 1970 to record this song, it was obvious that Hendrix was keen to develop the definitive rendition and include it as part of the projected double album. At this stage, however, a suitable arrangement still eluded him. "There was a point in time where 'Midnight Lightning' got kind of repetitious," admits Cox. "It was a good song, but we were just bogged down with it. When we started touring, we got some new, refreshed ideas as to how to try and do it, but the process still wasn't complete."

A jam based on an entirely new pattern followed, but Hendrix soon directed this into "Beginnings." The group recorded five exceptional takes, with the fifth later edited and released as part of 1972's *War Heroes* and subsequently *First Rays Of The New Rising Sun*.

At the session's conclusion, it was obvious to all that in "Dolly Dagger" Hendrix had created a special work, wholly indicative of both his impressive abilities and new musical direction. While additional work on "Dolly Dagger" would be completed over the following weeks, the music made on that evening reinforced Hendrix's confidence and reaffirmed the promise that Electric Lady Studios would foster more such achievements.

SUNDAY, JULY 2, 1970

ELECTRIC LADY STUDIOS, NEW YORK, NEW YORK. ENGINEER: EDDIE KRAMER. SECOND ENGINEER: KIM KING. Important work on "Ezy Rider" was completed on this evening. "Ezy Ryder," says King, was one of a number of older recordings from the Record Plant that were reserved for nights when Hendrix would come in alone and just want to replace lead vocal or guitar parts. On this night, Hendrix prefaced his lead vocal overdub with his own risqué variation of Chick Willis's "Stoop Down Baby": "Old Mother Hubbard went to the cupboard to find her poor dog a bone. But when she bent over,

Rover took over, because Rover had a bone of his own. Shakespeare! Page 35!" "I thought it was hilarious," remembers Kramer, "but Jimi thought it too vulgar and instructed me to keep it out of the mix."

Hendrix had invested heavily in "Ezy Ryder," dedicating hours to searching for the exact guitar sounds he wanted. "Jimi would come up with a riff, and we would dub it down to two-track," remembers King. "That idea would lead to something else, as he would come back and want to change one of the guitar tracks, or replace a specific measure on one of the lead guitar tracks. The fight for open tracks had been a bear on some of the songs we had added overdubs to, but this was a guitar song, a *symphonic* guitar song. It was handled like string quartet parts, although nothing was written on paper, it was all improvised. We overdubbed eight tracks of guitars. Everything in pairs—four tracks of lead and four tracks of rhythm—all at Electric Lady. This work took weeks and involved a number of intricate punch-ins. There were no tape counters or auto locators or anything like that, so I was tape jockey. We settled into a unit and we didn't have to talk about what to punch in or keep."

Preparing the song's final mix proved equally eventful. "During the song's final mixing session," King explains, "we were using two tape machines, and Eddie and Jimi were doing a four-handed mix on the console while I was doing the flanging—actually holding my thumb on the tape reel and varying the pressure on the flange of the tape reel. You're controlling the speed, which is controlling the pitch. By varying the pitch by microcycles, you're varying the angle of phase between those two notes. The actual sound you are hearing is the two notes beating against each other. I was playing the flange, and Jimi and Eddie were doing these very elaborate pans, where sounds were changing sides and coming out of the middle. I had terrible blisters on my thumb, but the sound was fantastic, in fact, the entire mix was magical. Eddie, Jimi, and I were rocking and leaning back in our chairs throughout. Right near the end of the song, we leaned back too far and all fell over. We were scrambling around the floor before Eddie got to the board, grabbed the master fader, and brought it up full to make sure we had hit the end of the tune correctly. Actually we hadn't,

there was some garbage there at the end, but the mix worked and Jimi thought the whole thing was hilarious, so we left it in!"

Also recorded on this day were two four-track demos of "Belly Button Window" that featured Hendrix alone on guitar and vocals. "When Jimi got his apartment on West 12th Street," explains Velvert Turner, "he used to use his Stratocaster and a small Princeton amp to write songs. He would play the melody and then hum or occasionally sings words that came to him. 'Belly Button Window' and 'Ezy Ryder' were two songs that took shape like that."

Among the invited guests in the Studio A control room on this evening was flautist Kenyatta Arrington, a friend of Juma Sultan. Once work on "Belly Button Window" concluded, Hendrix invited Arrington to record what was noted on the tape box as "Flute Piece." This recording featured Arrington on flute, Sultan on percussion, an unknown tabla player, and Hendrix on bass. After the session was recorded, Hendrix noted on the tape box that Kenyatta Harrington—which he crossed out and corrected as Arrington—had written the song.

SATURDAY, JULY 4, 1970

ATLANTA POP FESTIVAL, BYRON, GEORGIA. **SET LIST:** "FIRE" / "LOVER MAN" / "SPANISH CASTLE MAGIC" / "RED HOUSE" / "ROOM FULL OF MIRRORS" / "HEAR MY TRAIN A COMIN' " / "MESSAGE TO LOVE" / "ALL ALONG THE WATCHTOWER" / "FREEDOM" / "FOXEY LADY" / "PURPLE HAZE" / "HEY JOE" / "VOODOO CHILD (SLIGHT RETURN)" / "STONE FREE" / "STAR SPANGLED BANNER" / " STRAIGHT AHEAD" / "HEY BABY (LAND OF THE RISING SUN)"

After the July 2 session for "Ezy Ryder," the Experience resumed their touring schedule, with Hendrix's next engagement a headline appearance at the massive Atlanta Pop Festival. His fine set showcased a number of songs currently in development at Electric Lady, including "Room Full Of Mirrors," "Freedom," and "Straight Ahead."

Though Hendrix's touring commitments may have pulled him from the recording studio, he continued to write on the road, exchanging and recording ideas with Cox within the confines of his hotel suites. Serious work on new material was never accomplished during preconcert sound checks—a formality that Hendrix loathed. "Sound checks were the worst time in the world to work on songs," says Cox. "Jimi especially hated them. We both felt that they were intimidating and unnecessary. People would be there looking for him to put on a show and it wasn't time for that. It was time to check our monitors and amplifiers, which we could do by running through one or two songs. Even then, I would basically strum my E- and G-strings back and forth just make sure we had a good sound. Once we did, we'd call it a day."

Rather than tinker with such songs as "Straight Ahead" during sound checks, Hendrix instead preferred to perform them in front of his audiences. "We'd get in the dressing room and Jimi would say, 'Hey, let's try this song or that song tonight,'" remembers Cox. "And the people loved it. Now he always had to do 'Fire,' 'Foxey Lady,' and 'Purple Haze,' if he didn't do anything else. Sometimes, if the crowd pushed, he'd do 'All Along The Watchtower.' On the whole, he got tired of playing every one of those songs except 'Foxey Lady.' He loved playing that song because it wasn't too cluttered and it allowed him to do his splits and all of his stage things. But after the show, he'd talk about how the new songs went down."

SUNDAY, JULY 5, 1970

MIAMI JAI ALAI FRONTON, MIAMI, FLORIDA.

The Experience had been originally scheduled to perform two sets, but faced a series of logistical hurdles trying to depart Byron, Georgia, in the early hours of July 5 to get to Atlanta and their flight to Miami. As a result, the group arrived late in Miami and was only able to perform a single show as opposed to two separate sets.

After his performance, Hendrix extended his time in Miami to accommodate some additional rest and relaxation. During his short stay, Hendrix was introduced to the jazz bassist Jaco Pastorius, although the two did not attempt any recording.

From Miami, Hendrix returned to New York and Electric Lady. The studio commanded his attention, replacing the nights of late-night jam sessions at the Scene and other nightspots that he had enjoyed in years past. "Jimi was really a loner," says Cox. "He liked his women and his privacy, and I respected that. His big thing was *ladies,* and New York was his harem. I never made an unannounced visit to his apartment, except maybe once or twice. A lot of times, Devon was not around and he would spend time alone with his choice of women."

"Jimi was not a whiner," says Cox. "He had a lot of things worrying him, but I knew that and I didn't want him to have to repeat it all to me. I could tell how he was doing by the look on his face. It was my job to keep his spirits up. I'd pull out an Albert King or Albert Collins tape for us to listen to, just something to take his mind off of all that bullshit. I would say, 'Hey man, we're here making music, we enjoy some semblance of stardom, let's get down!' and he would always laugh. I was the entertainment director. I'd pull out my pocket color television and we would watch that. I'd tell jokes—anything to try and keep his spirits up. Mitch was great at that, too, he'd have more shit going on while we were on the road. We never had any problems when just the three of us were together and that spirit can be heard in the music we made."

Cox continues, "One time that summer I said, 'C'mon, man, let's go to Palisades [Amusement] Park. I've always wanted to go. I've seen pictures and read about it in brochures.' Jimi said, 'Oh man, if I go up there they'll recognize me.' I told him, 'Look, put your ass in a pair of blue jeans, put on a funky hat, call the limousine driver, and let's go to fucking Palisades Park!' So we got these two chicks and went to the park. Jimi and I rode the roller coaster, we rode the bumper cars, we ate cotton candy and had the time of our lives. No one even recognized him. After a while he said, 'Bill, I ain't had no fun like this in a *long* time!' Even in the limo on the way back to Manhattan, he said, 'Man, that was great. I got to get out more often!'"

JULY 1970

Despite the considerable role Electric Lady—even in its unfinished state—had in renewing Hendrix's creative spirit, new problems emerged, raising questions hidden beneath the recent euphoria. Despite having given over

Band Of Gypsys to Capitol Records as per the negotiated settlement of his bitter lawsuit with Ed Chalpin's PPX Industries, the demands Jeffery placed on Hendrix never diminished. Jeffery was determined to get a Jimi Hendrix Experience album into the marketplace quickly so as to make clear the "side project" nature of the *Band Of Gypsys* album. To keep both the studio and his entire company solvent, there was the hard-fought compromise on the issue of touring. While Jeffery had, so far, honored his concession to limit Hendrix's schedule of engagements to a series of three-day weekends, Hendrix sometimes had to alter his recording schedule to facilitate sessions by paying clients, an issue that rankled with him. The philosophical divide between the two men could not have been more distinct. Electric Lady Studios, or at the very least Studio A, was supposed to have been Hendrix's creative space. With only one functional room available, Hendrix felt Jeffery had breached their unspoken agreement, namely that the profit generated by the rental of Studio B would cover

the facility's operating costs, service the outstanding loan to Warner Bros., and allow Hendrix to maintain a private, creative space available twenty-four hours a day. Jeffery, however, soon succumbed to financial pressures and was eager to market the studio's state-of-the-art equipment and artist-friendly environment. Prospective clients peppered Jeffery and Marron with requests for studio time. The locked doors, security cameras, and closed sessions that had vastly improved the creative atmosphere for Hendrix's sessions directly contributed to Electric Lady's mystique. Jeffery began accepting bookings during the profitable daytime hours and during weekends when Hendrix was on the road.

While Hendrix had established his own schedule at the studio, preferring to begin in the early evening, the entire facility had been his to use. While he worked with Kramer in Studio A, Shimon Ron worked feverishly to complete Studio B. A great number of minor technical issues still remained unresolved, leaving Kramer, Ron, Palmer, and King with innumerable tasks. By July, with

Studio B still unfinished, there were occasions when Hendrix was denied time or forced to curtail his session so the studio could be reset for outside clients. Such interruptions left Hendrix infuriated. "While it didn't happen that often, there were times when Jimi had to leave the studio because there would be a morning session booked," recalls King. "That pissed him off. There was one big flap in particular where I recall him complaining, 'This is my studio. Why do I have to leave?'"

King was not the only Electric Lady employee who witnessed such incidents. "Jimi would complain that he could never get in to record," says Electric Lady staff member Linda Sharlin. "There were times when he would have to wait until the daytime sessions were finished so that he could get in. He wanted to know if *his* studio was for him or if it was to make money. Other times, he'd come in unannounced, and if the studio was booked, he'd leave. He just wanted to plug in his guitar and play, that's all he ever wanted to do."

"Deep down in his heart, Jimi knew that the studio was not his to claim solely," says Cox. "But he accepted that. He wasn't naive enough to think that he could own a recording studio in Greenwich Village all by himself. He knew that he had to have powerful people behind him."

In addition to early clients like Jeremy Steig, studio president Jim Marron actively recruited work from Madison Avenue, creating a lucrative cash flow stream that required relatively short sessions and few technical demands. Weekend sessions were frequently staged, usually while the Experience were on the road, so that Jeffery could audition new talent or have staff engineers record demos for groups he was considering. "That's how I got to sit in the big chair," adds Dave Palmer with a laugh. "Michael Jeffery would arrange these sessions for his management company. He would bring in bands to cut demos and tracks with the hope of landing them a record deal."

While Hendrix and Jeffery may have been equal partners in the venture, their goals for the studio couldn't have been more different. To Hendrix, Electric Lady represented one the few tangible measures of his success and hard work. The studio was his creative haven, a home built with the proceeds of his music and forever supported by it. For Jeffery, the rental of the studio was necessary to keep the facility solvent. Despite their standing as equal partners, Hendrix and Jeffery simply did not share the same operating philosophy.

In just two short months, as many of the final touches were completed, Electric Lady had reached heights Hendrix may never have imagined. The studio, in its entire celebrated splendor, was nothing like the simple, creative workspace he had originally requested. And while the release of *Band Of Gypsys* had helped to ease the oppressive grasp of the PPX lawsuit, the pressure to produce had not subsided. The stakes, in fact, had grown even higher. In addition to owing Reprise a long-overdue sequel to *Electric Ladyland*, Hendrix was beholden to Warner Bros. for their $300,000 loan, guaranteed against any future royalties he might earn. Electric Lady was more than just a workspace for Hendrix; Jeffery's headquarters controlled the entire second floor, a not-so-subtle reminder that the studio accommodated both work and play. "Michael Jeffery had removed all of whatever existed in a sleazy old nightclub and built this plastic spaceship," recalls King. "And now, Jimi had to deliver. There was a real push/pull dynamic at work there. Hendrix had to show up to go to work, and he didn't want to go to work. On any given day, he'd play hooky, he'd show up begrudgingly, or he'd show up and things would click and we would record some magical, high-quality music. Jimi wanted a place to record where he could leave everything set up and walk in and walk out. He wanted it to be *his* studio. Suddenly, the whole thing had snowballed so far away from whatever his original idea had been that there was a certain resentment at Michael. Then there was the dynamic between Michael and Eddie. Electric Lady was not Jimi's studio, it was Eddie's studio. Eddie wanted Jimi to have the best damn studio in the world with everything state-of-the-art. Jimi appreciated the studio's complexity, and the lengths that people went to so that he would be able to deliver product. But, much to the consternation of everyone upstairs, Jimi obviously didn't give a shit about product. Eddie was in a very tough position. It was his responsibility to see that product was delivered, and there was resentment in general on Jimi's part in that he had to deliver it all. That was a constant undercurrent."

"I had many masters to please," admits Kramer. "My first priority was Jimi. He was the guy I wanted to please more than anybody. Jeffery and Bob Levine were the power brokers upstairs and I was well aware that the studio had taken that loan from Warner Bros. When Jimi was away touring, they made it known—in a conversational as opposed to a confrontational manner—that we needed money. I was so proud of that studio. I ran myself ragged that summer, often working double shifts because we did not have the staff fully trained for outside clients. I busted my balls to help build that studio and I wanted it to succeed for Jimi. I knew how proud he was of it."

Kramer's relationship with Jeffery started poorly and never improved. Jeffery openly mistrusted Kramer, and remained wary of his relationship with Hendrix. "Jeffery always wanted to limit Kramer's role at Electric Lady," explains Jim Marron. "The right way of doing it, had Eddie not been in such an adversarial position with Michael, would have been to bring him into the family and make a mutually beneficial deal. That's not how things were handled. Jeffery was leery of Kramer's relationship with Hendrix. He always wanted to be kept abreast of what Eddie was up to downstairs."

TUESDAY, JULY 14, 1970

ELECTRIC LADY STUDIOS, NEW YORK, NEW YORK. ENGINEER: EDDIE KRAMER. SECOND ENGINEER: DAVE PALMER.

Eighteen takes of "Jam," later titled "Comin' Down Hard on Me Baby," and finally "Come Down Hard On Me," were recorded. While no takes were complete, takes 11 and 18 were marked as having "good front sections." These renditions featured a slightly altered arrangement and a more intricate rhythm-guitar pattern from Hendrix. Timing problems, however, repeatedly hampered the group's progress. Hendrix can be heard offering instructions to Mitchell, Cox, and Sultan throughout, leading what clearly resembled a rehearsal at this stage.

"Jam" followed, but this was actually a rough sketch of "Bolero," with Hendrix guiding Cox and Sultan through the song's chord changes. Mitchell did not participate, and no masters or even formal takes were achieved. When recording resumed once more,

Mitchell had returned, and the group attempted "Midnight Lightning." Despite its promising start, Hendrix had still not fully developed the song, and this effort came apart shortly after the four-minute mark. At this stage, "Midnight Lightning," despite its engaging rhythm pattern and novel adaptation of Chick Willis's risqué classic "Stoop Down Baby," was abandoned. After making a series of technical adjustments, Hendrix shifted to "Bolero." These takes represent a vast improvement over their earlier effort, showcasing several highlights from Hendrix.

From "Bolero," Hendrix returned to "Come Down Hard On Me." These, too, were vastly improved. Incredibly, earlier discarded takes can be heard in between these newly recorded takes: engineer Dave Palmer simply wound the tape back to the start of the reel when formal takes were initiated, erasing these early rehearsals and takes. Hendrix obviously thought little of the entire night's work—both erased and recorded—as the tape box was marked "Do Not Use." These versions were replaced by new takes and overdubs recorded the following evening.

WEDNESDAY, JULY 15, 1970

ELECTRIC LADY STUDIOS, NEW YORK, NEW YORK. ENGINEER: EDDIE KRAMER. SECOND ENGINEER: DAVE PALMER.

Hendrix successfully reprised "Come Down Hard On Me" here, recording several new basic tracks, followed by overdubs and a rough mix. He then turned his attention to "Dolly Dagger," making numerous attempts to capture a definitive lead vocal performance. In addition, he recorded several lead guitar overdubs.

The version later issued as part of 1973's *Loose Ends* compilation was drawn from these takes, edited after Hendrix's death by Electric Lady engineer John Jansen. Jansen did not use a single, complete take; rather, he combined two separate takes with the guitar overdubs and lead vocal Hendrix recorded on this evening. Ironically, when Alan Douglas and Tony Bongiovi were preparing *Crash Landing* in 1974, they were unaware of Jansen's work, and when they could not locate the actual multitrack tape master, Bongiovi and Douglas simply overdubbed on to Jansen's composite master, adding a rhythm guitar line from session guitarist Jeff Mironov, while replacing Cox's and Mitchell's original contributions with new overdubs from bassist Bob Babbitt and drummer Allan Schwartzberg. The 2000 box set *Jimi Hendrix Experience* featured a complete track from this session that Hendrix and Kramer mixed on August 22, 1970.

FRIDAY, JULY 17, 1970

NEW YORK POP FESTIVAL, DOWNING STADIUM, RANDALL'S ISLAND, NEW YORK. **SET LIST:** "STONE FREE" / "FIRE" / "RED HOUSE" / "MESSAGE TO LOVE" / "LOVER MAN" / "ALL ALONG THE WATCHTOWER" / "FOXEY LADY" / "EZY RYDER" / "STAR SPANGLED BANNER" / "PURPLE HAZE" / "VOODOO CHILD (SLIGHT RETURN)" The New York Pop Festival was a three-day event staged across the East River from Manhattan at Downing Stadium on Randall's Island. Haphazardly organized and plagued by radical infighting among the Young Lords, Black Panthers, and other local community groups, who had threatened to publicize the event as a "free" concert if they weren't dealt in for a cut of the proceeds, many of the acts advertised never materialized. Nearly 8,000 of the nearly 25,000 in attendance did not pay to see the likes of Steppenwolf and Jethro Tull.

The Experience's uneven performance at this chaotic outdoor event was both filmed and recorded. Eddie Kramer had been asked by Hendrix to record the performance but he declined, due to illness. Hendrix struggled to maintain his focus amid an unruly crowd and general chaos. "It was a complete mess," says Stickells.

There were highlights in this set, most notably Hendrix's version of "Red House," now available as part of *Voodoo Child: The Jimi Hendrix Collection*. Save for the sections of "Foxey Lady" and "Star Spangled Banner" included in *Free* or *Freedom*, the rarely seen documentary of this event, no other selections from this performance have ever been released.

SUNDAY, JULY 19, 1970

ELECTRIC LADY STUDIOS, NEW YORK, NEW YORK. ENGINEER: EDDIE KRAMER. SECOND ENGINEER: KIM KING. Overdubs and mixes of "Night Bird Flying," "Straight Ahead," "Astro Man," "Freedom," and "Dolly Dagger" were completed on this evening.

Hendrix overdubbed a new lead vocal for "Freedom" first. A second lead vocal overdub gave the guitarist the opportunity to double the lead vocal part beginning at 1:39 into the song and to punctuate the phrase "Set me free!" at 1:55. Throughout the parts of the song where there were no lead vocals, Hendrix returned to the technique of moving the headphones back and forth around the microphone as he first did for "Purple Haze" in 1967 at Olympic. This swirling effect can be faintly heard throughout the song.

Hendrix then called for a lead guitar overdub. Using a small Fender amplifier, Hendrix's first attempt was quite scratchy and not in keeping with the feel he had established for the song. He then rolled off all of the bass tone, and it is this sound that appears during his guitar solo. According to Kramer, Hendrix intended to replace this part with a later overdub, but because none was ever attempted, it remained in the song.

Cox then replaced his bass part with an entirely new effort. Mitchell doubled his drums in parts, playing the same patterns but recorded twice. Kramer then suggested a piano overdub, demonstrating his idea to Hendrix, who then recorded a terrific part that became an integral part of the song's rhythmic structure.

A lead vocal for "Night Bird Flying" was also completed. Hendrix again utilized the technique of moving the headphones around the vocal microphone, this time to create a wah-wah-like effect. He also provided a superb lead guitar overdub that Kramer recorded in stereo, with Hendrix's amplifier close-miked and his vocal microphone left open for effect.

Mixes of "Straight Ahead" and "Dolly Dagger" were prepared, and much work was also completed for "Drifter's Escape." Hendrix returned to the basic track he had achieved during his enthusiastic June 17, 1970, session on to which he recorded rhythm and lead guitar overdubs as well as lead vocals.

MONDAY, JULY 20, 1970

ELECTRIC LADY STUDIOS, NEW YORK, NEW YORK. ENGINEER: EDDIE KRAMER. SECOND ENGINEER: DAVE PALMER.

Hendrix sought to record the definitive studio rendition of "Lover Man" on this evening. Fifteen takes were recorded, with the Experience electing to feature the arrangement used during their recent performances, such as the version recorded May 30, 1970, in Berkeley, California. The group's initial takes were curiously devoid of the energy and enthusiasm that had made it a staple of the Experience's stage repertoire. Take 10, recorded without a vocal from Hendrix, was briefly considered as a master. Timed at 3:00, two guitar overdubs were attempted, with the first deemed "no good," while the second was apparently successful. After reviewing this new master, Hendrix chose to scrap it and try again. The group finished four more takes, with take 14 now deemed best. It was only marginally better than take 10, however, both surprisingly uninspired by recent Electric Lady standards.

After a break to review their work in the control room, Hendrix reverted to form with a superb fifteenth take. As the basic track drew to a close, Mitchell finished with a drumroll and loud cymbal crash that Hendrix cleverly answered by making the sound of laughter with his guitar. Kramer joined in over the talkback microphone and his laughter caused Hendrix to joke, "That's a perfect ending. Good thing you laughed!"

With a strong basic track in hand, Hendrix went to work in earnest. He added a new lead vocal track as well as rhythm and lead guitar parts, including passages of both "Flight of the Bumblebee" and the *Batman* theme within the song. Once this work was completed, a rough mix was made to measure their progress. Satisfied for the time being, Hendrix led Cox and Mitchell back into the studio to focus on "Midnight Lightning."

A cohesive basic rhythm track seemed to elude Hendrix once again, and the group's efforts evolved into a mere jam. One particularly humorous moment came when Hendrix launched into a falsetto as he performed Tommy Roe's "Dizzy," a pop hit from the previous year. "That's going to be the next single," teased Kramer over the talkback. "No," Hendrix replied, mimicking a rasping Howlin' Wolf, "that's going to be the B-side. The single is going to be 'Evil.' 'Your Evil Underwear!'"

This cracked everyone up. Hendrix then retreated to the control room while Mitchell recorded a drum overdub for "Dolly Dagger."

Additional overdubbing for "Angel" was also attempted, with Hendrix, Mitchell, and Cox all completing a series of subtle refinements. At Electric Lady, guitar and bass overdubs like these were often undertaken in the control room, with Cox and Hendrix sitting close to the console, rather than out in the studio. This practice, while common today, was not the custom in 1970. The primary benefit, according to Cox, was that the artist could hear the full recording played through the control speakers, rather than through headphones. Moreover, Hendrix and Cox could receive immediate, face-to-face feedback from Kramer, who was seated at the console. "Jimi and I were most comfortable doing our overdubs at the board," says Cox. "You didn't have the obstruction presented by those earphones. You could get right into it when you heard the music through those speakers. That was another benefit of working at Electric Lady. Eddie understood that this was our way of doing overdubs. We didn't have to fight or explain *why* we were doing things. We just did them."

As Hendrix's music had evolved, so had Mitchell's style. Mitchell's playing now reflected a more subtle and intricate approach rather than his previous display of power, speed, and dexterity. New songs, such as "Freedom," "Straight Ahead," and "Hey Baby (Land Of The New Rising Sun)," steeped in rhythm and blues, dictated such a shift. "Mitch certainly did contribute a lot to Jimi's music," says Cox. "Even though we all played different instruments, we were united in making this work as a three-piece. Jimi and I were thinking about the patterns we were playing, but Mitch came at the music from a different perspective. He would hear something and say, 'That's good, but when you come to the end of the bar, let me try *this*.' He did that on all the stuff we recorded there."

"Jimi and Mitch were always throwing each other curveball riffs," says King. "Mitch's role was to play lead drums, not to supply rhythm. On bass, Billy Cox kept everything moving straight ahead while Jimi and Mitch would battle it out."

While Hendrix accepted suggestions from Cox, Mitchell, and Kramer, the one area closed to scrutiny was his lyrics. "That was an area we all left alone," says Cox. "Jimi's lyrics were sacrosanct. If there was something that obviously didn't fit, he knew and we knew. We would never say anything, but he would remark, 'Well, this is all I have written down right now. I'll put the rest on tomorrow.' I would ask him who he was singing about in some of those songs, but he would just fall out laughing and never tell me."

TUESDAY, JULY 21, 1970

ELECTRIC LADY STUDIOS, NEW YORK, NEW YORK. ENGINEER: EDDIE KRAMER. SECOND ENGINEER: DAVE PALMER.

"Tune X—Just Came In," better known as "In From The Storm," was the focus of this evening. "That song was put together in one session in Jimi's hotel room when we were on the road," says Cox. "We had a little amplifier with us and we worked out the whole song. Room service came up with some steaks and trays of food and I said, 'Jimi, do remember the times when we used to share chili in Indianapolis?' He grabbed one of the dishes and said, 'Yeah, man. Look at us now, eating *horsie doors*!' I couldn't help but to break out laughing." After dinner and a few hours of concentrated effort, Cox and Hendrix had polished off a strong new original destined to become one of the highlights of both the fateful September 1970 European tour and *Cry Of Love*.

While the group did not achieve a master over the course of this session, Hendrix, Cox, and Mitchell ran through thirty takes, honing the arrangement and making subtle changes to their individual parts. There was much discussion between Hendrix and Mitchell regarding the guitar and drum interplay. Hendrix's enthusiasm was evident throughout the evening. He prefaced one take by shouting, "Record *this* motherfucker!" which cracked everyone up. Following take 30, Hendrix led the band through a single, spirited workout of "Hear My Train A Comin'" before calling the evening to a close.

WEDNESDAY, JULY 22, 1970

ELECTRIC LADY STUDIOS, NEW YORK, NEW YORK. ENGINEER: EDDIE KRAMER. SECOND ENGINEER: DAVE PALMER.

Work on "Tune X—Just Came In" resumed, beginning with a series of advanced rehearsals cited as "trial takes" that sounded substantially stronger than those from the previous day. Hendrix asked Mitchell to begin the song with a drum break not dissimilar to the part Mitchell would play during later 1970 live performances.

The first eight takes gradually improved, with the complete eighth take the most promising so far. The mood among the musicians and Kramer was very upbeat. Hendrix seemed to sense he was onto something special and live vocals were quite spirited. "She even eats chitlins on the side!" was one lyric line and "There was a rainbow bridge" another. One take developed into a lively hybrid of the lyrics to "Midnight Lightning" atop the same "In From The Storm" rhythmic structure. At the end of the second take, Hendrix had devised an ending for the song. Prior to take 6, Hendrix cut the drum introduction to the song by half.

A break was called so that the group could return to the control room and review their progress. Eleven new takes followed, with numbers 5, 6, 10, and 11 complete. The song's arrangement was clearly in place, as each of the complete takes sounded nearly identical. Hendrix, however, seemed particularly intent upon upgrading his own performance before designating any of these takes as finished. After one particularly strong take, Hendrix exclaimed, "And your mama, too!" which made everyone laugh. Take 10 was originally considered the master, and the group successfully inserted an edit section. Following a playback, however, Hendrix opted to scrap this take and begin again. An inspired take 11 provided the new master, requiring no edits.

While the song's basic track had been achieved, later overdub sessions were scheduled to accommodate additional rhythm and lead guitar parts. Hendrix and Emmaretta Marks recorded backing vocals, after an experiment with Cox and Mitchell joining their effort was rejected. Hendrix would also replace his lead vocal, and the comment that prefaced his effort, "Regardless of whether you can use it or not," was preserved for posterity at the beginning of the finished master.

Rough mixes were also completed for both "Just Came In" and "Come Down Hard On Me." While Hendrix would supervise additional rough mixes of "Just Come In" over the next month, an approved, final mix was never completed before his death. So that "Just Came In" could become part of Cry Of Love, Kramer and Mitch Mitchell mixed the finished master on November 29, 1970. Renamed "In From The Storm," the song was added to that album's master reel on December 3, 1970.

THURSDAY, JULY 23, 1970

ELECTRIC LADY STUDIOS, NEW YORK, NEW YORK. ENGINEER: EDDIE KRAMER. SECOND ENGINEER: DAVE PALMER.

With two major engagements looming—in San Diego on July 25 and Seattle's Sicks' Stadium on the 26th—Hendrix rallied, making significant advances on two of Cry Of Love's most evocative ballads, "Drifting" and "Angel."

The evening began with a magnificent take of "Drifting," followed by two incomplete but equally inspired takes. "We didn't do much rehearsing of that song before we recorded the basic tracks," remembers Cox. "That one just flowed from Jimi. It was very spiritual and didn't require many takes at all."

In addition to reprising the Leslie organ speaker he had prominently featured during the June 25 recording of "Drifting," Hendrix was eager to realize a "watery" tone from his guitar. Kramer, intrigued by Hendrix's fascination with water, sent Shimon Ron off to purchase a plastic speaker. When Ron returned, Kramer placed the device in a large pail of water, fed Hendrix's guitar to it, and set up a microphone to record the results. "It sounded like shit," laughs Kramer. Hendrix enjoyed far more success with another innovative yet far more familiar technique, the backward insertion of various guitar parts. These session tapes definitively document Hendrix's relative ease with this complicated technique.

"Drifting" directly merged into another Leslie guitar effort, "Angel." Hendrix had had "Angel" under wraps for quite some time, as evidenced by the version of "Sweet Angel" he had recorded at Olympic Studios in November 1967. Long before putting the song forward at Electric Lady, he took pains to see that it would be recorded exactly as he desired. "Before we had gone in to cut 'Angel,' we had gone over and over it because Jimi wanted to make it a nice, sweet song," explains Cox. "We made some adjustments here and there, just

AUGUST 1970: MAUI, HAWAII.

practicing in our hotel rooms on the road, but Jimi had it completed. The bass line for that was inspired by an old record we loved called 'Cherry Pie' [recorded originally by Skip & Flip in 1960]," remembers Cox. "That gave the record the feel of those great 1950s R&B ballads." The group recorded seven takes, with numbers 2 and 6 complete, and 7 considered the working master. A lead vocal for the song was then completed.

A series of rehearsals prefaced the recording of a single, complete take of "Belly Button Window." Using just six of the available sixteen tracks, this version, quite unlike the finished master, was performed as a slow-to-medium-tempo blues shuffle.

Though a basic track for both songs had been completed to Hendrix's satisfaction, neither "Angel" nor "Drifting" were ever finished during his lifetime. So that "Angel" could be included as part of *Cry Of Love*, the first album to be issued after Hendrix's death, Mitchell overdubbed a series of percussion elements, each treated with VFO manipulation to create various effects. He also replaced his drum parts, vastly upgrading his original performance.

FRIDAY, JULY 25, 1970

SPORTS ARENA, SAN DIEGO, CALIFORNIA. WITH CAT MOTHER & THE ALL NIGHT NEWSBOYS. **PARTIAL SET LIST:** "FIRE" / "HEY JOE" / "FOXEY LADY" / "RED HOUSE" / "HEY BABY (NEW RISING SUN)" / "STAR SPANGLED BANNER" / "PURPLE HAZE" / "VOODOO CHILD (SLIGHT RETURN)"

The Experience gave an inspired performance before a packed house at the Sports Arena. Paul Omundson, writing for the *San Diego Evening Tribune*, noted in his review that "[t]he applause was so enthusiastic that the group returned to do a song from their upcoming album as an encore."

SATURDAY, JULY 26, 1970

SICKS' STADIUM, SEATTLE, WASHINGTON. WITH CACTUS, RUBE TUBEN, AND THE RHONDONNAS. **SET LIST:** "FIRE" / "MESSAGE TO LOVE" / "LOVER MAN" / "MACHINE GUN" / "STAR SPANGLED BANNER" / "PURPLE HAZE" / "HEAR MY TRAIN A COMIN'" / "VOODOO CHILD (SLIGHT RETURN)" / "HEY BABY (NEW RISING SUN)" / "FREEDOM" / "RED HOUSE" / "FOXEY LADY"

A homecoming for Hendrix was scheduled at Sicks' Stadium, which had briefly been the home for the Seattle Pilots major league baseball franchise during the previous year. Hendrix and the Experience performed in a driving rainstorm before a large, patient audience that included his family and friends.

Following the Seattle concert, Mitchell, Cox, and the group's small road crew traveled to Hawaii. Hendrix elected to postpone his flight so that he could spend the next few days relaxing at his father's Seattle home. This brief respite provided the guitarist with an opportunity to reconnect with his family before leaving for Maui to join the others for a three-week retreat.

THURSDAY, JULY 30, 1970

MAUI, HAWAII. TWO SHOWS. **SET LIST, FIRST SHOW:** "SPANISH CASTLE MAGIC" / "LOVER MAN" / "HEY BABY" / "IN FROM THE STORM [MEDLEY]" / "MESSAGE TO LOVE" / "FOXEY LADY" / "HEAR MY TRAIN A COMIN'" / "VOODOO CHILD (SLIGHT RETURN)" / "FIRE" / "PURPLE HAZE." **SET LIST, SECOND SHOW:** "DOLLY DAGGER" / "VILLANOVA JUNCTION" / "EZY RYDER" / "RED HOUSE" / "FREEDOM" / "JAM BACK AT THE HOUSE" / "STRAIGHT AHEAD" / "HEY BABY (NEW RISING SUN)" / "MIDNIGHT LIGHTNING" / "DRUM SOLO" / "STONE FREE"

Hendrix's afternoon concert on a Maui pasture remains one of his best known and least understood performances, memorialized by the disjointed 1971 hippie "docudrama" *Rainbow Bridge*.

Michael Jeffery was making *Rainbow Bridge,* originally titled *Wave,* with producer Barry De Prendergast and independent film maverick Chuck Wein. Hendrix's association with the project originated in February of 1970, when Jeffery secured funding for the film from Warner Bros. in exchange for a soundtrack album featuring Hendrix. Soon thereafter, Jeffery began to push for his artist to make some kind of an onscreen cameo. By July, this request manifested as the filming of a concert in Maui. "We were there to relax for a few weeks," explains Mitchell. "We then got involved in *Rainbow Bridge*, this crazy film that Mike Jeffery was working on in Maui. At any rate, Mike and a few other people from the film came up with this idea of literally going through the streets with a truck and a few placards saying, 'Anyone that wants to come, come up to the crater of the sun, to the volcano. We are going to have a concert.' If my memory serves me right, it was like a four-mile hike. Even if you had a car to drive on where it was, you still had one hell of a walk."

The film's concert scene was filmed on July 30 atop a makeshift stage on a hillside. The hastily arranged concert proved to be a logistical disaster. The wind howled so fiercely that Hendrix's crew were forced to cut foam from the group's instrument cases to serve as microphone windscreens. With no hardwired power available, the group had to share a generator run by the film crew. The concert was recorded on an eight-track tape machine installed in a rented panel truck. Technical gremlins plagued the recording, preventing Mitchell's drums from being properly picked up. To salvage the material, Mitchell later overdubbed his drum parts at Electric Lady, listening to the performance on headphones while Kramer watched the film footage on a makeshift Moviola.

Despite the chaos of their surroundings, the group relished the opportunity to play in such a relaxed, informal outdoor setting. While Hendrix had headlined the recent Atlanta Pop Festival before more than 200,000 people, the group turned in an inspired set before a sparse audience of a few hundred people. "The main thing was that the band just enjoyed playing," remembers Mitchell. "All of these people turned up and we were having some fun."

Hendrix's performance was poorly served by the *Rainbow Bridge* filmmakers. Seventeen minutes of his lengthy performance was haphazardly edited together and stuck in the middle of the movie after his death. The 1971 soundtrack album was also confusing in that it did not feature any of the Maui live performances seen in the film. In their place were studio recordings such as "Dolly Dagger" and a live version of "Hear My Train A Comin'" from the May 30, 1970, Berkeley Community Theater concert. Marketing and promotion for the film and subsequent home-video release have routinely overemphasized the Hendrix content and his actual association with the project.

Two fine examples from the Maui concert have been issued in recent years. The first, the unique hybrid of "Hey Baby (New Rising Sun)" and "In From The Storm," was one of the strongest efforts recorded that afternoon. Hendrix had recently recorded studio versions of both songs at Electric Lady but had never combined them in such a dramatic fashion, either before or after this recording. The concert piece was issued as part of the *Jimi Hendrix Experience* box set. A potent rendition of "Foxey Lady" was later issued as part of *Voodoo Child: The Jimi Hendrix Collection*.

SATURDAY, AUGUST 1, 1970

INTERNATIONAL CENTER, HONOLULU, HAWAII. **PARTIAL SET LIST:** "STRAIGHT AHEAD" / "EZY RYDER" / "HEY BABY (NEW RISING SUN)" / "SPANISH CASTLE MAGIC" / "RED HOUSE"

The Experience flew from Maui to Oahu to perform at the Honolulu International Center on August 1. In contrast with the shambling, hastily arranged affair filmed for *Rainbow Bridge*, this evening saw the Experience in top form. Unfortunately, this concert was neither professionally filmed nor recorded. Hendrix spent another ten days vacationing in Maui before returning to New York during the second week of August.

FRIDAY, AUGUST 14, 1970

ELECTRIC LADY STUDIOS, NEW YORK, NEW YORK. ENGINEER: EDDIE KRAMER.

Once back at Electric Lady, Hendrix took stock of his progress in the studio, creating yet another list of songs he wanted to include on his next album. He titled the memo "Songs for the LP *Straight Ahead*" before proceeding to list the following: "'Ezy Ryder,' 'Room Full Of Mirrors,' 'Earth Blues Today,'' 'Valley Of Neptune,' 'Cherokee Mist'—that's going to be an instrumental, 'Freedom,' 'Stepping Stone,' 'Izabella,' 'Astro Man,' 'Drifter's Escape,' 'Angel,' 'Bleeding Heart,' 'Burning Desire,' 'Nightbird Flying,' 'Electric Lady'—slow, 'Getting My Heart Back Together Again,' 'Lover Man,' 'Midnight Lightning,' 'Heaven Has No Tomorrow'—slow, 'Sending My Love'—slow to medium, 'This Little Boy,' 'Locomotion,' 'Dolly Dagger,' and 'The New Rising Sun' ['Hey Baby']."

Dating as far back as January of 1969, Hendrix had stated a preference for the title *First Rays Of The New Rising Sun*. At Electric Lady, *Straight Ahead* had emerged as a working title, although *First Rays Of The New Rising Sun* had not been dismissed. So much progress had been made at Electric Lady on the project by August that Hendrix even considered releasing, instead of a two-disc set, a three-record set entitled *People, Hell And Angels*. While the three-disc concept may have been overly ambitious, he fully intended on delivering a two-disc set to Warner Bros. to meet their request for a Hendrix album in time for the lucrative Christmas season. "The record was coming together," recalls Kramer. "The record had momentum and we could see that there was a shape to it. I remember Jimi writing up some of the song titles, saying 'That will make a good Side A. That will make a good Side B. We have enough

for a Side D and C.' That was pretty cool, to see all of the effort of the last two years just coming together. You could see the end in sight."

Upon his return from Hawaii, with a framework now in mind for the shape of the album, Hendrix's August 1970 sessions were principally reserved for mixing. 'We spent a great deal of time overdubbing and mixing, and trying to finish tracks," recalls Kramer. "Some of the material, such as 'Room Full Of Mirrors,' required a great deal of work. I was never happy with the drum sound on the original master, as it sounded squashed; therefore, that track required a considerable amount of time. In a continuing series of overdubs and remixes, we added guitars and created some intricate panning effects before finishing."

The evening of August 14 marked Hendrix's first known session since his return from Hawaii. Among the work completed were overdubs and mixes for "Dolly Dagger" and "Freedom."

All three members of the Experience routinely attended mixing sessions. Kramer would begin these sessions by organizing a rough mix and presenting his ideas. Hendrix would follow in kind, remaining open to suggestions from Cox and Mitchell. "Jimi wanted Eddie to set mixes up because he knew he had that ear," says Cox. "Eddie could hear things we couldn't. Mitch would occasionally want his drums to sound a certain way or I might suggest an idea, but once Eddie got things started for him, Jimi could really do some things behind that board. Eddie would push Jimi, creating effects and always asking, 'What about this? How about that?' and Jimi liked that. He knew exactly how he wanted the music to sound. Jimi would say that he wanted his guitar to sound like *that* and Eddie could do that. They had worked together for so long that Jimi knew Eddie would get him what he wanted."

TUESDAY, AUGUST 18, 1970

ELECTRIC LADY STUDIOS. NEW YORK, NEW YORK. ENGINEER: EDDIE KRAMER: SECOND ENGINEER: DAVE PALMER.

Hendrix recorded a series of lead guitar and vocal parts for "Dolly Dagger" on this evening. Albert and Arthur Allen, known professionally as the Ghetto Fighters, recorded background vocals for the song.

Despite the privacy that Electric Lady now accorded him, Hendrix remained steadfast in his demand that he always record his lead vocal part from behind barricades, out of view from everyone in the studio. Ironically, while Kramer would routinely construct the barricades Hendrix desired, Hendrix regularly sang during the recording of basic tracks without barricades. To Hendrix, whose self-conscious qualms about the quality of his voice had never fully diminished, recording a lead vocal track required specific concentration. "When Jimi would sing while he was cutting basic tracks, he was *performing*," says Kramer. "He would *sing* when he was putting [lead] vocals on."

"Jimi was self-conscious about his voice," explains Cox. "He had to have that wall up. I told him, 'Man, you don't need to have that.' But he wouldn't record his vocals unless it was. Mitch, Eddie, and I would crack up sometimes because the irony was that even though he was hiding from us, we could still hear him. But that was his thing and we didn't knock it. If he had to have that wall to make him comfortable, that's what would be done."

In addition to recording lead vocals and replacing guitar parts with new overdubs, Hendrix was also trying to catch up on his lyrics. "Because of all of the pressure he was under, Jimi had been a little behind getting his lyrics together," says Cox. "Musically, he could count on support from Mitch and I, but lyrically, he had to rely on himself. If he didn't do it, it didn't get done. That's simply because we had no input regarding his lyrics. We let him handle that."

THURSDAY, AUGUST 20, 1970

ELECTRIC LADY STUDIOS, NEW YORK, NEW YORK. ENGINEERS: EDDIE KRAMER. SECOND ENGINEER: DAVE PALMER.

The sole remaining reel of multitrack tape from this session captured a jam already in progress. Hendrix had been focusing on recording overdubs for "In From The Storm" when this jam session with Cox and Mitchell began. Sensing the guitarist's sudden inspiration, Kramer and assistant engineer Palmer quickly pulled the previous tape off the machine, threw on a fresh reel, and snapped the record button to capture what they could of the gorgeous, slow blues jam. Hendrix effortlessly guided his bandmates, utilizing a warm, stinging guitar tone he rarely featured. Sadly, the recording inexplicably cut out and ended. Unbeknownst to anyone that evening, this was the last multitrack studio-session tape that Hendrix ever recorded. Titled "Slow Blues," it was later mixed by Kramer and issued as part of the 2000 *Jimi Hendrix Experience* box set.

In recent years, a quarter-inch tape that had been running simultaneously in the Electric Lady control room surfaced, and it reveals that almost immediately after the multitrack tape stopped, the jam came apart. The trio then returned to "In From The Storm" as Mitchell focused on his drum sound. The group made one incomplete pass at the song without vocals from Hendrix before work stopped. Some conversation ensued when Kramer and road manager Barrett came into the studio from the control room. Barrett brought smiles and laughter to the group when he began to tinker at the piano. Shortly thereafter, the group returned to the control room to begin an extensive mixing session.

With Hendrix's focus for the proposed double album beginning to narrow, no fewer than nine different songs were mixed. Additional work was completed for "Room Full Of Mirrors," while tape box notes suggest that a final mix of "Straight Ahead" was achieved. Like "Ezy Ryder," "Room Full Of Mirrors" had been virtually transformed by the number of overdubs recorded at Electric Lady throughout the summer. The complete song list of mixes prepared this evening included "Straight Ahead," "Room Full Of Mirrors," "Lonely Avenue (Ezy Ryder)," "In From The Storm," "Drifting," "Angel," "Belly Button Window," "Dolly Dagger," and "Freedom."

SATURDAY, AUGUST 22, 1970

ELECTRIC LADY STUDIOS, NEW YORK, NEW YORK. ENGINEER: EDDIE KRAMER.

With no appearances scheduled, Hendrix enjoyed a rare weekend session. Working alone with Kramer, he initiated yet another marathon mixing and overdub session that stretched well into the following day. Hendrix had developed a wealth of strong material over the summer, and he now began to taper his final choices for the double album he planned.

Mixes of multiple songs were prepared, with the August 20 "final" mix of "Straight Ahead" replaced by another mix. Mixes were also made of "Ezy Ryder," "Night Bird Flying," "Drifter's Escape," "Astro Man," "Power Of Soul," "Bolero," "Come Down Hard On Me," "In From The Storm," "Bleeding Heart," "Hey Baby," "Message to Love," "Midnight Lightning," "Beginnings," "Drifting," and "Cherokee Mist (Valleys Of Neptune)."

Two of the mixes prepared by Hendrix and Kramer during this session have been made available in recent years. The mix of "Come Down Hard On Me" created during this lengthy session was included as part of the 2000 *Jimi Hendrix Experience* box set. The version of "Drifter's Escape" prepared here made its debut as part of the 1997 album *South Saturn Delta*.

"Night Bird Flying" had emerged as one of the brightest examples of Hendrix's summer tenure at Electric Lady. Not only had the guitarist reserved a space for the song on the forthcoming double album he now planned to title *First Rays Of The New Rising Sun*, he had also designated the song to be issued alongside "Dolly Dagger" as a single. On this evening, he and Kramer created a number of interesting mixing ideas that suggested the flight of a bird or a spacecraft. These would be abandoned before the finished master was completed later that same evening. Hendrix would also layer additional lead guitar parts on to the song's dramatic closing. By this stage, multiple overdubs had been recorded, so, to accommodate yet another guitar part that Hendrix wished to include, Kramer added it on to a track that featured an incomplete vocal performance. Kramer had not erased the alternate vocal track and wanted to use portions of it in the final mix. When the alternate vocal dropped out before the solo, he simply filled the space with the new guitar part.

One version of "Dolly Dagger" from this session has since been issued as part of the *Jimi Hendrix Experience* box set. It provides a window into the construction of this complex track. Hendrix and Kramer can be heard at the end of that recording discussing the exact location of the song's fade ending.

Hendrix also recorded on this evening a charming four-track demo of "Belly Button Window." Three takes were attempted with the final effort designated as the master. "'Belly Button Window' was cut as a demo," remembers Kramer. "We both liked it so much." The song's simple beauty caused Kramer to enthusiastically remark that the track reminded him of Mose Allison's work. Intrigued, Hendrix added a second guitar. "I'm sure Jimi would have done something different had he lived," says Kramer. "But even in demo form, it was such a cool song."

While some have suggested that the inspiration for "Belly Button Window" was drawn from Hendrix's own childhood experiences, or worse, a foreboding hint of his forthcoming demise, Cox heartily disagrees. "Jimi told me that 'Belly Button Window' had been written about the baby Mitch and his wife, Lynn, were expecting. He used to say that the baby was looking out Lynn's belly button window at us."

As so much of Hendrix's time at Electric Lady had been dedicated to completing works already in progress, demos such as "Belly Button Window" were the exception rather than the norm. Yet, when the inspiration hit him, Hendrix would put these ideas down on tape for future reference. "On a lot of sessions, Hendrix would come to the studio without Mitch Mitchell or Billy Cox," explains engineer Dave Palmer. "He would just use the time to write. It wasn't, 'Okay, this is *the* tune for *the* record, let's *go*.' It was mainly, 'Okay, let's do some things and see what we have.'"

"We kept a half-inch four-track machine loaded with tape in case Jimi was inspired to just do some writing," explains Kim King. "Rather than do it straight to sixteen-track or quarter-inch two-track, he would record demos on the four-track machine. His first two albums had been entirely recorded on four-track, so having this was a luxury for him."

Sadly, however, nearly all of Hendrix's four-track recordings from Electric Lady—save for the aforementioned "Belly Button Window"—have vanished, leaving no clues to such unrealized Hendrix ideas as "Locomotion," "Electric Lady—slow," and "This Little Boy."

MONDAY, AUGUST 24, 1970

ELECTRIC LADY STUDIOS, NEW YORK, NEW YORK. ENGINEER: EDDIE KRAMER. SECOND ENGINEER: KIM KING.
This evening was dedicated to enhancing the "Dolly Dagger" master and mixing "Dolly Dagger," "Night Bird Flying," "Ezy Ryder," "Belly Button Window," "In From The Storm," and "Freedom." Final mixes of "Night Bird Flying," "Ezy Ryder," and "Dolly Dagger" were achieved, with an experimental edit considered for "In From The Storm," and "Dolly Dagger" the subject of some last-minute tinkering. Cox completed a fuzz bass overdub, another of "Dolly Dagger"'s distinctive accents, while Hendrix attempted some final guitar overdubs, some of which were keyed in and out of the final mix by Kramer. "Jimi and Eddie gave me a lot of freedom to try different ideas," says Cox. "I did the fuzz bass overdub in one take, punching in an occasional note to make sure it was just right."

In addition to his fuzz bass overdub, Cox was also asked to handle some faders on the console while Hendrix and Kramer began the intricate mixing of "Dolly Dagger." "I was in hog heaven," laughs Cox. "Eddie and Jimi put me in between them and I got to do some fading while they were flying around the board doing the mix. It was great."

The final mix of "Dolly Dagger" was completed on this evening, creating the master first issued on *Rainbow Bridge* and now part of *First Rays Of The New Rising Sun*. "'Dolly Dagger' was a finished performance," says Kramer. "It was well planned and thought out. Jimi eliminated everything he didn't like. The mix was complete. All of the perspectives were there. The sound of the lead guitar was exactly as he had wanted it. The bass had the right relationship to the guitar, which had the right relationship with the drums. And his voice was complete."

As his sessions at Electric Lady Studios had served to refocus Hendrix's energies, "Dolly Dagger" represented the sweeping return of his artistic powers. To many, the song provided a shining example of just what Hendrix could and would continue to achieve at the new facility. With the finest tools now at Hendrix's disposal, impressive results had already began to flow. Sadly, following Hendrix's untimely death less than a month later, "Dolly Dagger" became the symbol of unfulfilled promise, a bittersweet reminder of what might have been. "After Jimi had died, we used to play 'Dolly Dagger' a lot," recalls engineer John Jansen, "especially during other mixing sessions—just to see if whatever we were doing was up to that." The difference, explains Kramer, was entirely due to the unique perspective Hendrix provided. "When Jimi Hendrix was there, something extra always got done," says Kramer. "It was a mental thing. You would always push the faders differently with Jimi present than you would have if you were by yourself. He was so inspirational."

TUESDAY, AUGUST 25, 1970

ELECTRIC LADY STUDIOS, NEW YORK, NEW YORK. ENGINEER: EDDIE KRAMER. SECOND ENGINEER: KIM KING.
Hendrix and Kramer worked well into this day, scrambling to finish as many mixes as possible before departing for a short European tour. A mix of "Straight Ahead" was deemed final and added to the growing

pile of songs Hendrix had set aside for the proposed *First Rays Of The New Rising Sun*. "Jimi really wanted to finish this album," says Kramer. "That was a big question mark in his mind. To finish it and then to figure out its direction. I felt pretty confident that we had an album, a single album. I wasn't sure about the double album, which was the direction he wanted to go in. I felt very strongly that we had the *material* for a double album but we still had a lot of work to do to finish it off."

WEDNESDAY, AUGUST 26, 1970

STERLING SOUND, NEW YORK, NEW YORK. MASTER-ING ENGINEER: BOB LUDWIG.

Hendrix and Kramer booked a mastering session at Sterling Sound, the New York facility where they had mastered the *Band Of Gypsys* album. Hendrix wanted to master and cut a lacquer for "Dolly Dagger" and "Night Bird Flying," two songs he wanted to deliver to Reprise as a single. Test pressings were cut and taken away by both Hendrix and Kramer for review.

August 26 was also the date for the public unveiling of Electric Lady Studios. No recording was scheduled on this evening, as the studio staff frantically prepared for their gala opening party. Though Studio B was still unfinished, Shimon Ron plugged in the console to make the room appear fully operational. After much prodding from Jim Marron, Hendrix made an appearance, but he maintained a low profile, content to remain with his own small band of friends. "I remember Jimi sitting in this little lounge area where we had put this barber's chair," says Kramer. "Jimi was sitting in this thing, sort of lying back talking about how he had to go to Europe. I got the impression that he did not want to be there for the party and he really didn't want to get on a plane and go to Europe. There was this sort of general reluctance and feeling that here we go again, we are going to interrupt the flow of what we were doing. We had just mixed four songs and they sounded really great. *That* he had been extremely happy about."

The studio party was a smash success. Recordings recently made at the studio entertained the guests. In addition to recordings by such Michael Jeffery–man-

aged clients as the Patterson Singers and Jimmy & Vela, some of Hendrix's new music was debuted. "We made a tape of four finished mixes ["Dolly Dagger," "Night Bird Flying," "Ezy Ryder," and "Straight Ahead"] to play at the party," remembers Kim King. "It was played over and over that night."

After leaving the party to fly to London, Hendrix never returned to Electric Lady.

HISTORIC PERFORMANCES RECORDED AT THE MONTEREY INTERNATIONAL POP FESTIVAL. REPRISE MS 2029. U.S. ALBUM RELEASE. "LIKE A ROLLING STONE" / "ROCK ME BABY" / "CAN YOU SEE ME" / "WILD THING"

More than three years after this milestone festival took place, Reprise issued this collection of performances by Hendrix and Otis Redding.

Save for "Wild Thing," which had been included in the documentary film made at the festival and later broadcast by ABC, none of these songs had been previously released. Despite the fine performances throughout, the album's sub-par final mix did the collection little justice. Neither Hendrix nor Kramer had any role in the production of this album.

Backed by a modest promotional effort by Reprise, sales of the album only began to escalate after Hendrix's death on September 18, 1970. Later that month, the album peaked on the *Billboard* album chart at number 16, eventually spending twenty weeks on the magazine's Top 200 chart.

SUNDAY, AUGUST 30, 1970

ISLE OF WIGHT FESTIVAL. EAST AFTON, ISLE OF WIGHT, ENGLAND. **SET LIST:** "GOD SAVE THE QUEEN" / "SGT. PEPPER'S LONELY HEARTS CLUB BAND" / "SPAN-ISH CASTLE MAGIC" / "ALL ALONG THE WATCHTOW-ER" / "MACHINE GUN" / "LOVER MAN" / "FREEDOM" / "RED HOUSE" / "DOLLY DAGGER" / "MIDNIGHT LIGHT-NING" / "FOXEY LADY" / "MESSAGE TO LOVE" / "HEY BABY (NEW RISING SUN)" / "EZY RYDER" / "HEY JOE" / "PURPLE HAZE" / "VOODOO CHILD (SLIGHT RETURN)" / "IN FROM THE STORM"

Hendrix appeared before 600,000 people at this massive outdoor music and arts festival hailed as Europe's

ISLE OF WIGHT FESTIVAL
AUGUST 26-30 1970 Weekend £3
Friday 20/-   Saturday 35/-   Sunday 40/-

FRIDAY	SATURDAY	SUNDAY
CHICAGO	DOORS	JIMI HENDRIX EXPERIENCE
FAMILY	JONI MITCHELL	JOAN BAEZ
TASTE	WHO	LEONARD COHEN
JAMES TAYLOR	SLY AND THE FAMILY STONE	RICHIE HAVENS
ARRIVAL	CAT MOTHER	MOODY BLUES
LIGHTHOUSE	FREE	PENTANGLE
	JOHN SEBASTIAN	GOOD NEWS
	EMERSON, LAKE AND PALMER	
	MUNGO JERRY	
	SPIRIT	

anticipated that it was going to be a job like Sicks' Stadium [in Seattle] or something of that nature. But it was a phenomenon like Woodstock. At that point in time, these things were happening all over the world but I hadn't anticipated anything that large in stature."

Originally scheduled to go on the evening of August 30, Hendrix took the stage well into the early morning hours of August 31 due to a series of logistical delays endured throughout the festival. His two-hour performance was highlighted by his rendition of "All Along The Watchtower," as well as searing, extended takes of "Machine Gun" and his blues masterwork "Red House." Hendrix appeared tired and was dogged throughout the set by technical setbacks that hampered his amplifiers, stage monitors, and spirit. New songs such as "Freedom" and "In From The Storm" were enthusiastically performed but favorites such as "Hey Joe" and "Purple Haze" seemed perfunctory. "I can't say if Jimi's heart was in it," says Mitchell. "One thing, looking back in retrospect, was that we should have definitely had a rehearsal. That's strange because the band was working so well, it was like clockwork. At that point in time, we were relaxed with each other's playing. There is no real reason why it should have been, you know, just grim. But the feeling just wasn't there.

"You know, Jimi had so much on his mind with the opening of Electric Lady. Maybe in his heart he just wanted to be there, quite honestly.

"It was just one of those situations. No gig can be 100 percent perfect all of the time. You can come off some nights and people will pat you on the back, 'Great show, great show,' and you know it was a bunch of . . . I don't think there was a particularly morbid feeling about it. We had some other gigs directly after [the Isle of Wight], but I do remember that we all spoke and said, 'Well, what was the reason for the lack of feeling at the gig?' Maybe it was because it was one of those large festival situations."

MONDAY, AUGUST 31, 1970

TIVOLI GARDENS, STOCKHOLM, SWEDEN. **SET LIST:** "LOVER MAN" / "CATFISH BLUES" / "EZY RYDER" / "RED HOUSE" / "COME ON (LET THE GOOD TIMES ROLL)" / "ROOM FULL OF MIRRORS" / "HEY BABY

Woodstock. He headlined an impressive bill at the Isle of Wight, whose three-day roster also included The Who; The Doors; Emerson, Lake & Palmer; and Miles Davis. Hendrix's performance represented his first British concert in eighteen months. The guitarist had last appeared in Britain fronting the original Experience for two sold-out February 1969 appearances at London's Royal Albert Hall. "When we got to the Isle of Wight, Jimi said, 'I don't even know if I can do this,' remembers Cox. "He was quite apprehensive. You know, 'I've been gone so long they've forgotten about me.' I was apprehensive because I didn't know if they were going to accept *me*. Here I am black and I'm replacing Noel Redding. Hendrix had anticipated disaster, but when we hit the stage, we hadn't even played a note before the crowd started cheering."

The 1969 Isle of Wight festival, which featured Bob Dylan as its headline act, drew an audience of 150,000 people. The festival promoters hoped for the same in 1970, but were greeted instead by more than a half million people. "Before I arrived on the island I had no idea what it was going to be like," says Cox. "I had

(NEW RISING SUN)" / "MESSAGE TO LOVE" / "MACHINE GUN" / "VOODOO CHILD (SLIGHT RETURN)" / "IN FROM THE STORM" / "PURPLE HAZE" / "FOXEY LADY"

Later that morning, the band flew to Stockholm, Sweden, for a concert at Tivoli Gardens. With little time to recuperate from their Isle of Wight performance, they performed their second concert in less than twenty-four hours.

TUESDAY, SEPTEMBER 1, 1970

STORA SCENEN, LISEBURG, SWEDEN. **SET LIST:** "SPANISH CASTLE MAGIC" / "KILLING FLOOR" / "HEAR MY TRAIN A COMIN'" / " MESSAGE TO LOVE" / "HEY BABY (NEW RISING SUN)" / "IN FROM THE STORM" / "HEY JOE" / "FOXEY LADY" / "RED HOUSE" / "ROOM FULL OF MIRRORS" / " PURPLE HAZE" / "VOODOO CHILD (SLIGHT RETURN)"

The Experience traveled to Gothenburg to perform at Stora Scenen, an outdoor facility familiar to Hendrix and Mitchell from previous Experience concerts held there. The group had an opportunity to rest, and Hendrix's mood and energy level seemed brighter. "Hear My Train A Comin'" and a rare version of "Killing Floor"—which had not performed by Hendrix in nearly eighteen months—stood as the memorable high points.

WEDNESDAY, SEPTEMBER 2, 1970

VEJLBY-RISSKOV HALLEN, AARHUS, DENMARK. WITH BLUE SUN. **SET LIST:** "FREEDOM" / "MESSAGE TO LOVE" / "HEY BABY (NEW RISING SUN)"

Hendrix suffered a complete reversal on this night, ending his set after just three songs. Explanations for Hendrix's dark mood and behavior ranged from illness to exhaustion to drugs. The true reason may well have been a combination of the three. Patrons received refunds, and Hendrix left the venue to return to his hotel suite.

THURSDAY, SEPTEMBER 3, 1970

K.B. HALLEN, COPENHAGEN, DENMARK. WITH BLUE SUN. **SET LIST:** "STONE FREE" / "FOXEY LADY" / "MESSAGE TO LOVE" / "HEY BABY (NEW RISING SUN)" / "ALL ALONG THE WATCHTOWER" / "MACHINE GUN" / "SPANISH CASTLE MAGIC" / "EZY RYDER" / "FREEDOM" / "RED HOUSE"

/ "IN FROM THE STORM" / "PURPLE HAZE" / "VOODOO CHILD (SLIGHT RETURN)" / "HEY JOE" / "FIRE"

Hendrix rebounded from the Aarhus debacle with a vigorous performance. His strong connection with the audience was underscored by a rare two-song encore of "Hey Joe" and "Fire."

FRIDAY, SEPTEMBER 4, 1970

BERLIN SUPER CONCERT '70, DEUTSCHLANDHALLE, BERLIN, GERMANY. WITH TEN YEARS AFTER, PROCOL HARUM, COLD BLOOD, AND CAT MOTHER. **SET LIST:** "STRAIGHT AHEAD" / "SPANISH CASTLE MAGIC" / "SUNSHINE OF YOUR LOVE" / " HEY BABY (NEW RISING SUN)" / "MESSAGE TO LOVE" / "MACHINE GUN" / " PURPLE HAZE" / "RED HOUSE" / "FOXEY LADY" / "EZY RYDER" / "HEY JOE" / "LOVER MAN"

The Experience headlined this impressive bill, and, while their performance was not as strong as it had been on the previous evening, their set list was again peppered with some pleasant surprises including "Sunshine Of Your Love" and a unique hybrid of "Power Of Soul" and "Lover Man."

SUNDAY, SEPTEMBER 6, 1970

OPEN AIR LOVE AND PEACE FESTIVAL, ISLE OF FEHMARN, GERMANY. **SET LIST:** "KILLING FLOOR" / "SPANISH CASTLE MAGIC" / "ALL ALONG THE WATCHTOWER" / "HEY JOE" / "HEY BABY (NEW RISING SUN)" / "MESSAGE TO LOVE" / "FOXEY LADY" / "RED HOUSE" / "EZY RYDER" / "FREEDOM" / "ROOM FULL OF MIRRORS" / "PURPLE HAZE" / "VOODOO CHILD (SLIGHT RETURN)"

This festival appearance on Germany's Isle of Fehmarn proved to be the final performance of Hendrix's extraordinary career.

Hendrix and his entourage had traveled from Berlin to Fehmarn on Saturday, September 5. The Experience had been scheduled to perform that evening but, due to steady rain and gale-force winds, tour manager Gerry Stickells had argued that the performance would have to be moved to Sunday or not take place at all.

The skies had cleared temporarily by the time the Experience finally took the stage on Sunday afternoon.

Some in the audience heckled the guitarist, booing and offering chants of "Go home." Hendrix took it all in stride, though, apologizing for not performing the night before and asking only that the audience boo in key. The crowd's frustration subsided as soon as the band began to play and each of the thirteen songs to follow was greeted warmly.

While the quality of the Experience's performances on this short European tour could best be described as uneven, their effort at Fehmarn was focused and enthusiastic. Hendrix kicked off the set with a pleasant surprise, an up-tempo reading of Howlin' Wolf's "Killing Floor." The group then shifted easily between favorites such as "Hey Joe" and samples from their new material such as "Freedom" and "Ezy Ryder." The rain resumed during "Red House" and continued until the end of Hendrix's performance. At the close of a spirited "Voodoo Child (Slight Return)," Hendrix thanked the audience, and the group scurried offstage and away from the festival grounds.

Following the Fehrman festival, the Experience returned to London. Cox had become ill during the European tour, and a decision was made to cancel the remaining dates and allow him to return to the U.S. to recuperate. On September 9, he traveled to his family's home in Pennsylvania to rest and recover.

THURSDAY, SEPTEMBER 10, 1970

ELECTRIC LADY STUDIOS, NEW YORK, NEW YORK. ENGINEER: EDDIE KRAMER.

With Hendrix still in London, Kramer prepared rough mixes of "Spanish Castle Magic," "Lover Man," "Hey Baby (New Rising Sun)," "In From The Storm," "Message To Love," "Foxey Lady," and "Hear My Train A Comin'" from the July 30 Maui concert.

SEPTEMBER 1970

After leaving Germany, Hendrix remained in London while considering whether to continue touring or return to New York to continue recording. While waiting for a decision, he sat for an interview with journalist Keith Altham on September 11 and engaged in a jam session with Eric Burdon & War at Ronnie Scott's on

September 16. He also reconnected with Chas Chandler, opening a dialogue about Chandler becoming involved again in his music.

Hendrix contacted Kramer at Electric Lady and asked the engineer to bring the tapes they were working on to London. Kramer convinced the guitarist to wait until he returned so that they could take advantage of the new studio. Hendrix agreed and promised to return on Monday, September 21.

He was never able to keep this promise: Hendrix was found dead in the London flat of a girlfriend, Monika Dannemann, on Friday, September 18, 1970. An official inquest held on September 28 ruled that Hendrix asphyxiated in his own vomit as a result of barbiturate intoxication. Dannemann later claimed that Hendrix had taken nine of her Vesperax sleeping pills, unaware of its high potency.

As word of Hendrix's death filtered back to Electric Lady, the shock was nearly overwhelming. A pall hung over the studio and its grief-stricken employees. Local reporters came by, seeking an explanation as to how such a tragedy could have taken place. In Studio A, an engineer recorded the news reports for historical purposes. "We were a recording studio—Jimi's recording studio—and it made sense to record it," explains Electric Lady engineer John Jansen. A quarter-inch tape of a feature aired by Channel 7, New York's ABC affiliate, on September 18 and 19, was among the area reports that were documented.

FRIDAY, OCTOBER 23, 1970

"VOODOO CHILD (SLIGHT RETURN)/HEY JOE/ALL ALONG THE WATCHTOWER." TRACK RECORDS 2095 001 U.K. EXTENDED-PLAY SINGLE.

This posthumously issued extended-play disc coupled *Electric Ladyland*'s "Voodoo Child (Slight Return)" and "All Along The Watchtower" with the original single "Hey Joe." "That single was a tribute to Jimi," says Track executive Daniel Secunda. "We priced that record as close to actual cost as possible." The love and sympathy held by British record buyers for Hendrix was clearly expressed when the single reached the top position on the U.K. chart, posthumously providing Hendrix with his first British number 1 disc.

WEDNESDAY, MARCH 5, 1971

CRY OF LOVE, REPRISE MS 2034. U.S. ALBUM RELEASE.
PRODUCERS: JIMI HENDRIX, EDDIE KRAMER, MITCH
MITCHELL. ENGINEER: EDDIE KRAMER. SECOND EN-
GINEERS: KIM KING, DAVE PALMER. "FREEDOM" /
"DRIFTING" / "EZY RYDER" / "NIGHT BIRD FLYING" /
"MY FRIEND" / " STRAIGHT AHEAD" / "ASTRO MAN" /
"ANGEL" / "IN FROM THE STORM"

Despite the encouraging progress made throughout
the previous summer at Electric Lady, at the time of
Hendrix's death all of the material he'd recorded, overdubbed, and mixed for the proposed double album
was in various stages of completion. "Had Jimi not

left for that European tour we would have finished
the entire album in a month," says Kramer. "Look at
how much we had accomplished over the summer.
We had been on a roll. There was momentum and no
question in my mind that we would have been able to
complete the album."

Beginning in late October 1970, Kramer and
Mitchell had begun the painful process of compiling an
album from the tapes available. Though Hendrix had
been committed to the double-album concept, Jeffery
ordered Kramer and Mitchell to construct two albums,
including one that would serve as the soundtrack for
his still-unfinished feature film *Rainbow Bridge*. Save
for "My Friend" and "Ezy Ryder," all the tracks featured

on *Cry Of Love* had been recorded at Electric Lady, with "Ezy Ryder" having been virtually transformed at the studio by the recording of new overdubs. While "Dolly Dagger" and "Room Full Of Mirrors" were held back at the last minute for the forthcoming *Rainbow Bridge* album, the best of Hendrix's new material was mixed and put forward for the album. Some songs were more polished than others, ranging from "Night Bird Flying" and "Freedom," which lacked only minor finishing touches, to "Angel" and "Drifting," which required considerable attention.

During what all involved recall as a tense, emotional session, Mitchell returned to Electric Lady's Studio A and replaced all of his original drum parts for "Angel." "Mitch was around the control room listening to playbacks and I was wondering if he was up to it," remembers John Jansen, assistant engineer on the session. "Then he got behind his kit and doubled his original drum line in one take. It was amazing."

"I remember that we applauded him for doing so," adds Kramer.

Mitchell's heartfelt effort, says Kramer, added a special significance to the track. "Mitch had always intended to overdub tom-tom [drums] with mallets, because that was a sound we were particularly good at getting. This was an idea that had been discussed originally, something we all—Jimi included—felt would embellish the track. Therefore, I had no problem with Mitch adding the overdub at all."

Where Mitchell's drum overdub for "Angel" solidified an existing rhythm pattern, "Drifting" posed a more intricate challenge, requiring considerable reconstruction. While the song's basic track featured the combined efforts of Hendrix, Mitchell, and Cox, the song's delicate melody was framed by just two guitar lines and buttressed by generous insertions of Hendrix's backward guitar. Kramer fused portions from the June 25 recording to the July 23 master in order to further develop the song's basic track. To match the guitar sound, he was forced to improvise. "I was working on 'Drifting' late one night in Studio A when I realized that I only had a DI [direct-injection] guitar track for this very important lead-rhythm part. Originally, wanting a very clean guitar sound, Jimi had put this part on tape to act as a guide. There was no amplifier track, so in order to create the amplifier sound, I ran the DI out of the console, through the cue system into the studio, fed it through a transformer into Jimi's Marshall stack, and miked it up. All of the lights were out in the studio, save for the glow of the Marshall headstack, and it sounded just as if Jimi were playing through the amplifier. The back door to the studio had been open and in the midst of transforming the sound to tape, an assistant engineer was startled to hear Jimi's screaming guitar in Studio A. He came running into the control room, flustered, his face white as a sheet, sure that he had heard Jimi playing again, before he realized what I had been doing."

With Hendrix's guitar tracks in place, Mitchell replaced his drum parts, "Mitch just shined at this type of playing," says Kramer. "It was perfectly within his scope, with gentle playing, a lot of cymbal work, double stops, and smashes on the downbeats. A superb performance." To add a final touch, vibraphonist Buzzy Linhart was recruited to contribute a charming, tastefully muted overdub. "It was a difficult session," remembers Kramer. "Buzzy Linhart was deadly serious about what he was to play."

"Eddie Kramer and Mitch Mitchell called me up," recalls Linhart, "and told me they had one track where Jimi hadn't been sure if he wanted vibes playing the song's chords or an additional rhythm guitar, and would I play on this song for them? It was just so touching to be in the studio he built, playing back this tape and hearing Jimi's beautiful voice."

Hendrix's untimely death also robbed Cox of his due, as no publishing credit was given to him on *Cry Of Love.* "Those songs were a part of my soul. I enjoyed the camaraderie and I enjoyed helping Jimi create those songs, but my name is nowhere in sight. Had Jimi lived, I know my name would have appeared on some of them, but who do I complain to? Mitch and Buddy can verify to what I contributed, but we also did a lot in private. I also felt slighted when I wasn't asked to help put the *Cry Of Love* together. I might have been quiet in the studio, but that didn't diminish the contributions that Jimi himself acknowledged."

Critics and fans warmly received *Cry Of Love,* and the album peaked at number 3, spending a total of thirty-nine weeks on the *Billboard* chart.

ACKNOWLEDGMENTS

Without the kind assistance and contributions from the following people, neither this book nor *Hendrix: Setting The Record Straight*, its companion, could have been written. Leslie Aday, Tunde and Taharqa Aleem (Albert and Arthur Allen), Carmine Appice, Dan Armstrong, Bob Babbitt, Angel Balestier, Frank Barselona, Jeff Baxter, Danny Blumenauer, Tony Bongiovi, Joe Boyd, Stefan Bright, Al Brown, Terry Brown, Baird Bryant, Randy California, Jim Capaldi, Paul Caruso, Jack Casady, Ed Chalpin, Chas Chandler, Neville Chesters, George Chkiantz, Larry Coryell, David Crosby, Monika Dannemann, Lillian Davis, Spencer Davis, Leon Dicker, Alan Douglas, Andy Edlin, Tom Edmonston, Tom Erdelyi, Kathy Etchingham, Mike Finnigan, Robert Fitzpatrick, Tom Flye, John Gardiner, Jeff Gold, Jerry Goldstein, Michael Goldstein, Keith Grant, Gerry Guida, John Head, Michael Hecht, John Hillman, Duane Hitchings, Elliot Hoffman, Tom Hulett, Abe Jacob, John Jansen, Andy Johns, Glyn Johns, Les Kahn, Henry Kalow, Steve Katz, Linda Keith, Marta Kellgren, Kim King, Al Kooper, Howard Krantz, Bob Krasnow, Bob Kulick, Kevin Laffey, Steve Lang, Joe LaNostra, Arthur Lee, Bill Levenson, Bob and Kathy Levine, Mark Linett, Al Marks, Emmeretta Marks, Jim Marron, John Marshall, Paul Marshall, Dave Mason, Roger Mayer, Paul and Linda McCartney, Jim McCarty, Eugene McFadden, Terry McVey, Buddy Miles, Jeff Miranov, Mitch Mitchell, Tom Moffat, Nigel Morgan, Juggy Murray, Graham Nash, Mike Neal, Stevie Nicks, Dave Palmer, Peter Pilafian, Ken Pine, Faye Pridgeon, Dave Ragno, Noel Redding, Bill Rich, Barry Reiss, Jim Robinson, Roland Robinson, Shimon Ron, Mike Ross, Tony Ruffino, Ron Saint Germain, Don Schmitzerle, Abby Schroeder, Alan Schwartzberg, Daniel Secunda, Mickey Shapiro, Linda Sloman, Joe Smith, Chris Stamp, Jeremy Steig, Mark Stein, Gerry Stickells, Stephen Stills, Bill Stoddard, Chris Stone, John Storyk, Ron Terry, Ed Thrasher, Velvert Turner, Willie Vacarr, Larry Vaughan, Jerry Velez, John Veneble, Johanan Vigoda, Chuck Wein, Steve Weiss, Judy Wong and Herbie Worthington.

I am especially grateful to Janie Hendrix for her friendship and support.

It has been a privilege for me to serve Experience Hendrix, the family company started by Jimi's late father Al. Sincere thanks go out to Bob Hendrix, Amanda Howell, Reed Wasson, Marsha Lake, Donna Jinka, Linda Anderson, Willie Jinka, Tamera Kearney, Steve Pesant, Bruce Kuhlman, Kathy Brunson and all of the EH staff past and present.

Very special thanks to Kjersti Egerdahl for her patience and support. Thanks as well to Peter Shukat, Amy Pickard, who helped transcribe interviews, and becker&mayer!'s Chris Campbell, Jenna Free, and Andy Mayer.

I am grateful for the friendship and support of many Hendrix archivists who were always eager to answer questions and volunteer information to help improve this project. Barry Gruber deserves special mention. For nearly three decades he has uncovered a host of previously unknown Hendrix ephemera. Bill Nitopi has uncovered many unique Hendrix photographers over the years. Steve Rodham and Gary Geldeart at Jimpress keep us all on our toes and are always willing to share research. Steve and Gary helped connect me with Niko Bauer, who has done fine work unraveling Jimi's pre-Experience sessions with Lonnie Youngblood and others.

Thanks to all, including the McDermott family and those whose names we may have missed. Enjoy!

For Laura, Jeff & Alison
J. McD. Newton 2008

INDEX OF SONG AND ALBUM TITLES

IMAGE CREDITS

Cover: Courtesy of Jim Marshall

Page 2: Chuck Boyd/Authentic Hendrix LLC

Page 5: K&K Ulf Kruger OHG/Redferns

Page 7: Courtesy of David Sygall/e-shot.com

Pages 8-9: Ulrich Handl/Authentic Hendrix LLC

Page 11: Experience Music Project permanent collection, © EMP

Page 13: Experience Music Project permanent collection, © EMP

Page 16: Photo by William "PoPsie" Randolph. © 2008 Michael Randolph. www.PoPsiePhotos.com. PoPsie-photos@att.net

Page 19: Robert A. Johnson/Authentic Hendrix LLC

Page 25: Courtesy of KRAMER ARCHIVES INC.

Pages 30-31: Authentic Hendrix LLC

Page 37: Courtesy of KRAMER ARCHIVES INC.

Page 42: Courtesy of KRAMER ARCHIVES INC.

Page 47: Authentic Hendrix LLC

Page 51: Authentic Hendrix LLC

Page 53: Sandra Shepherd/Authentic Hendrix LLC

Page 57: Wilson Lindsey/Authentic Hendrix LLC

Page 60: Authentic Hendrix collection

Page 62: Courtesy of Mojo Magazine

Page 65: Ray Stevenson/Rex USA

Page 67: Courtesy of KRAMER ARCHIVES INC.

Page 72: Authentic Hendrix LLC

Page 77: Authentic Hendrix LLC

Page 78: Mick Gold/Redferns

Page 83: Bentley Archive/Popperfoto/Getty Images

Pages 84-85: Courtesy of the Estate of Linda McCartney

Page 89: Chuck Boyd/Authentic Hendrix LLC

Page 91: Experience Music Project permanent collection, © EMP

Page 92: Authentic Hendrix LLC

Page 96: Courtesy of KRAMER ARCHIVES INC.

Page 104: Bob Davidoff/Rick Kohl/Authentic Hendrix LLC

Page 107: Courtesy of KRAMER ARCHIVES INC.

Page 109: Experience Music Project permanent collection, © EMP

Page 113: Authentic Hendrix LLC

Page 114: Experience Music Project permanent collection, © EMP

Page 116: Chuck Boyd/Authentic Hendrix LLC

Page 118: Chuck Boyd/Authentic Hendrix LLC

Page 122: Chuck Boyd/Authentic Hendrix LLC

Page 125: Chuck Boyd/Authentic Hendrix LLC

Page 129: Jeremy Ross/Authentic Hendrix LLC

Page 131: Courtesy of David Sygall/e-shot.com

Page 132-133: Walter looss Jr./Getty Images

Page 136: Authentic Hendrix LLC, © EMP

Page 138: © John Gardiner

Page 143: David Redfern/Redferns

Page 145: Experience Music Project Permanent Collection, © EMP. Photographer Willis Hogans Jr.

Page 153: Experience Music Project Permanent Collection, © EMP. Photographer Willis Hogans Jr.

Page 154: Willis Hogans Jr./Authentic Hendrix LLC

Page 159: Experience Music Project Permanent Collection, © EMP. Photographer Willis Hogans Jr.

Page 162: Experience Music Project Permanent Collection, © EMP. Photographer Peter Riches

Page 165: Authentic Hendrix LLC

Page 169: Jonathan Stathakis/Authentic Hendrix LLC

Page 170: Jonathan Stathakis/Authentic Hendrix LLC

Page 172: Jonathan Stathakis/Authentic Hendrix LLC

Page 177: Experience Music Project Permanent Collection, © EMP. Photographer Willis Hogans Jr.

Page 181: Authentic Hendrix LLC

Page 186: Courtesy of David Sygall/e-shot.com

Page 190-191: Torben Dragsby/Authentic Hendrix LLC

Page 192: Experience Music Project Permanent Collection, © EMP

Page 197: Experience Music Project Permanent Collection, © EMP

Page 200: © Doug Collup

Page 206: Chuck Boyd/Authentic Hendrix LLC

Page 209: © Doug Collup

Page 213: Don Nix/Authentic Hendrix LLC

Page 214: Frank Sherack/Authentic Hendrix LLC

Page 219: Courtesy of Bill Henke; www.henkephotography.com

Page 222: Authentic Hendrix collection

Page 227: Joe Cestaro/Authentic Hendrix LLC

Page 231: Courtesy of KRAMER ARCHIVES INC.

Page 235: Daniel Tehaney/Authentic Hendrix LLC

Page 238: Daniel Tehaney/Authentic Hendrix LLC

Page 241: Hulton-Deutsch Collection/Corbis

Page 246: Authentic Hendrix LLC

Page 249: Torben Dragsby/Authentic Hendrix LLC

Page 251: Michael Ochs Archives/Getty Images